5 STEPS TO A 5

AP World History

2012-2013

Get ready for your AP exam with McGraw-Hill's **5 Steps to a 5!**

AP Exam Guides
AP Biology *(book and book/CD set)*
AP Calculus AB/BC
AP Chemistry
AP English Language *(book and book/CD set)*
AP English Literature *(book and book/CD set)*
AP Environmental Science
AP European History
AP Human Geography
AP Microeconomics/Macroeconomics *(book and book/CD set)*
AP Physics
AP Psychology *(book and book/CD set)*
AP Spanish Language *with MP3 disk*
AP Statistics
AP U.S. Government and Politics *(book and book/CD set)*
AP U.S. History *(book and book/CD set)*
AP World History
Writing the AP English Essay

***500 Must-Know Questions* Series**
500 AP Biology Questions to Know by Test Day
500 AP English Language Questions to Know by Test Day
500 AP English Literature Questions to Know by Test Day
500 AP Psychology Questions to Know by Test Day
500 AP U.S. History Questions to Know by Test Day
500 AP World History Questions to Know by Test Day

Flashcards
AP Biology Flashcards
AP U.S. Government and Politics Flashcards
AP U.S. History Flashcards

Apps
AP U.S. History
AP World History
AP Psychology
AP U.S. Government and Politics
AP European History
AP Biology Flashcards
AP Microeconomics/Macroeconomics

5 STEPS TO A 5™

AP World History

2012-2013

Peggy J. Martin

New York   Chicago   San Francisco   Lisbon   London   Madrid   Mexico City
Milan   New Delhi   San Juan   Seoul   Singapore   Sydney   Toronto

Copyright © 2011, 2010, 2008 by The McGraw-Hill Companies, Inc. All rights reserved.
Printed in the United States of America. Except as permitted under the United States
Copyright Act of 1976, no part of this publication may be reproduced or distributed in
any form or by any means, or stored in a database or retrieval system, without the prior
written permission of the publisher.

4 5 6 7 8 9 10 11 12 13 14 15   QDB/QDB   1 9 8 7 6 5 4 3 2

ISBN 978-0-07-175097-4 (print book)
MHID   0-07-175097-5

ISSN 2150-6337

ISBN 978-0-07-175098-1 (e-book)
MHID   0-07-175098-3

Trademarks: McGraw-Hill, the McGraw-Hill Publishing logo, 5 Steps to a 5 and related
trade dress are trademarks or registered trademarks of The McGraw-Hill Companies
and/or its affiliates in the United States and other countries and may not be used
without written permission. All other trademarks are the property of their respective
owners. The McGraw-Hill Companies is not associated with any product or vendor
mentioned in this book.

The series editor was Grace Freedson, and the project editor was Del Franz.
Series design by Jane Tenenbaum.

AP, *Advanced Placement Program*, and *College Board* are registered trademarks of the
College Entrance Examination Board, which was not involved in the production of, and
does not endorse, this product.

McGraw-Hill books are available at special quantity discounts to use as premiums and
sales promotions or for use in corporate training programs. To contact a representative,
please e-mail us at bulksales@mcgraw-hill.com.

ABOUT THE AUTHOR

PEGGY J. MARTIN teaches Advanced Placement World History, Economics-Free Enterprise, and U.S. Government at Del Rio High School in Del Rio, Texas. She is the author of *Kaplan's SAT Subject Test: World History* and *5 Steps to a 5: AP World History Flashcards for Your iPod with MP3 Disk.* As a consultant in Advanced Placement World History, she has presented workshops in the southwestern region of the United States and served as an essay reader for the Advanced Placement World History Exam since the inaugural reading in 2002. The mother of four grown children, she and her husband make their home in Del Rio, Texas.

CONTENTS

STEP 5 Build Your Test-Taking Confidence

PREFACE

Welcome to the adventure of Advanced Placement (AP) World History! Enjoy the challenges of your studies. During the course of the year, you should be prepared to read widely in both your text and readers. Expect to analyze all sorts of primary documents, from text to political cartoons, photographs, paintings, maps, and charts; analytical skills are essential to success on both the multiple-choice questions and the essay questions. You will write essay after essay as you not only analyze primary documents but also compare issues and analyze continuity and change over periods of time. Along the way, enjoy the fascinating story of humankind and find a little of yourself among the peoples of other societies.

This study guide will ease your passage through the challenges of AP World History to success on the AP examination. At first sight, the amount of material in the AP World History course can appear a bit overwhelming. The goal of this manual is to present the content material and test-taking skills so that you can approach the AP exam with confidence. As a first step, turn now to the Introduction to learn about the 5-step study program and how it can help you to organize your preparation.

ACKNOWLEDGMENTS

I would like to thank my husband, Gary, and our children Sarah, Keren, Abigail, and Jonathan and their families for their loving encouragement throughout the course of this project. Also, I would like to express my appreciation to my editors, Grace Freedson and Del Franz, for their guidance during the preparation of the manuscript.

Special thanks go to the following family members for their contributions:

Carmen Rebekah Ramos   Crescent and star drawing
Keren M. Martin   Panama Canal photograph
                                  Altar photograph
Willy and Irmgard Marick   Translation of "The German Fatherland"
Credits for illustrations
Paresh Nath, http://www.internationalcartoons.com   China 2008
                                                               West Asia
                                                               Road Map
                                                               AIDS Cartoon

CIA Factbook 2003   Map of Bosnia

INTRODUCTION: THE 5-STEP PROGRAM

Introducing the 5-Step Preparation Program

This book is organized as a 5-step program to prepare you for success on the exam. These steps are designed to provide you with vital skills and strategies and the practice that can lead you to that perfect 5. Here are the 5 steps.

Step 1: Set Up Your Study Program

In this step you'll read a brief overview of the AP World History exam, including an outline of topics and the approximate percentage of the exam that will test knowledge of each topic. You'll learn:

- Background information about the AP exam
- Reasons for taking the exam
- What to bring to the exam
- Other tips to prepare you for the exam
- How to choose the preparation plan that's right for you
- Calendars for three suggested plans

Step 2: Determine Your Test Readiness

In this step you'll take a diagnostic exam in AP World History. This pre-test should give you an idea of how prepared you are before beginning your study program.

- Go through the diagnostic exam step-by-step and question-by-question to build your confidence level.
- Review the correct answers and explanations so that you see what you do and do not yet fully understand.

Step 3: Develop Strategies for Success

In this step you'll learn strategies that will help you do your best on the exam. These strategies cover all four question types: multiple choice, document-based, continuity and change over time, and comparative. This part of your preparation program will help you to learn:

- How to read multiple-choice questions
- How to answer multiple-choice questions, including whether or not to guess
- How to analyze primary documents, including texts, photographs, political cartoons, maps, and charts
- How to write free-response essays for the document-based, continuity and change over time, and comparative questions

Included are some commonly asked questions as well as advice taken from my experience as a reader of the AP World History exam.

Step 4: Review the Knowledge You Need to Score High

In this step you'll learn or review the material you need to know for the test. This review section takes up the bulk of this book. It contains not only summaries of key events and concepts, but also vocabulary lists and review questions. The material is organized according to the time periods in the AP World History course. Each unit in this review section is followed by a timeline, a list of key comparisons, and a change/continuity chart. The chart will show you at a glance key events and issues in the major world regions. It will also refresh your memory of changes and continuities within each region during the time period covered by the unit.

As you review this material, it may be helpful to work with others. Find a study pal or form a small study group, and set a time when you can get together to review.

Step 5: Build Your Test-Taking Confidence

In this step you'll complete your preparation by testing yourself on two full-length practice exams modeled after the actual examination. Each test is followed by a discussion of the answers. Be aware that these practice exams are *not* reproduced questions from actual AP exams, but they mirror both the material tested and the way in which it is tested.

- Try the strategies provided in Chapter 4 of this book for each type of question on the test.
- For the document-based, comparative, and continuity and change over time essays, have another student read and critique your essays.
- Take the time not only to check whether or not your answers are correct, but also to read the explanation for the correct answers. By doing this, you will review a broad body of concepts in a shorter period of time.

Finally, at the back of this book you'll find additional resources to aid your preparation. These include:

- Glossary of terms
- Bibliography for further reading
- List of Web sites related to the AP World History exam

The Graphics Used in This Book

To emphasize particular concepts and strategies, we use several icons throughout this book. An icon in the margin will alert you that you should pay particular attention to the accompanying text. We use these three icons:

 The first icon points out a very important concept or fact that you should not pass over.

 The second icon calls your attention to a strategy that you may want to try.

 The third icon indicates a tip that you might find useful.

5 STEPS TO A 5

AP World History

2012-2013

Set Up Your Study Program

CHAPTER 1

What You Need to Know About the AP World History Exam

IN THIS CHAPTER

Summary: Learn background information on the AP program and exam, how exams are graded, what types of questions are asked, what topics are tested, and basic test-taking information.

Key Ideas

✪ Many colleges and universities will give you credit for exam scores of 3 or above.

✪ Multiple-choice questions reflect the amount of course time spent on each of the five AP World History periods.

✪ The three types of essay questions are based on the broad course themes.

Background Information

What Is the Advanced Placement Program?

The Advanced Placement (AP) program was begun by the College Board in 1955 to construct standard achievement exams that would allow highly motivated high school students the opportunity to be awarded advanced placement as freshmen in colleges and universities in the United States. Today, there are more than 30 courses and exams with well over a million students taking the annual exams in May.

There are numerous AP courses in the social studies besides World History, including U.S. History, European History, U.S. Government, Comparative Government, Macroeconomics, Microeconomics, and Psychology. The majority of students who take AP tests are juniors and seniors; however, some schools offer AP courses to freshmen and sophomores, especially in World History.

Who Writes the AP World History Exam? Who Corrects the Exams?

Like all AP exams, the World History exam is written by college and high school instructors of world history. This group is called the AP World History Test Development Committee. The Committee constantly evaluates the test, analyzing the test as a whole and on an item-by-item basis. All questions on the World History exam are field-tested before they actually appear on an AP exam.

A much larger group of college and secondary teachers meets at a central location in early June to correct the exams that were completed by students the previous month. The scoring procedure of each grader (or "reader") during this session is carefully analyzed to ensure that exams are being evaluated on a fair and consistent basis.

How Are Exams Graded?

Sometime in July the grade you receive on your AP exam is reported. You, your high school, and the colleges you listed on your initial application will receive scores.

There are five possible scores that you may receive on your exam:

- 5 indicates that you are extremely well qualified. This is the highest possible grade.
- 4 indicates that you are well qualified.
- 3 indicates that you are qualified.
- 2 indicates that you are possibly qualified.
- 1 indicates that you are not qualified to receive college credit.

Individual colleges and universities differ in their acceptance of AP exam scores. Most will not consider a score below a 3 on any AP exam. Many highly competitive colleges and universities honor only scores of 5 on AP exams.

Reasons for Taking the Advanced Placement Examination

There are several very practical reasons for enrolling in an AP World History course and taking the AP World History exam in May. In the first place, during the application process colleges look very favorably on students who have challenged themselves by taking Advanced Placement courses. Although few would recommend this, it is possible to take any AP exam without taking a preparatory course for that exam.

Most important, most colleges will reward you for doing well on your AP exams. Although the goal of this manual is to help you achieve a 5, if you get a 3 or better on your AP World History exam, many colleges will either give you actual credit for a required introductory world history course or allow you to receive elective credit. You should definitely check beforehand with the colleges you are interested in to find out their policy on AP scores and credit; they will vary.

Taking a year of AP World History (or any AP) course will be a very exacting and challenging experience. If you have the capabilities, allow yourself to be challenged! Many students feel a great personal satisfaction after completing an AP course, regardless of the score they eventually receive on the actual exam.

The higher order thinking skills that characterize the AP World History course provide an excellent preparation for college and university studies.—College professor

What You Need to Know About the AP World History Examination

The AP World History exam consists of both multiple-choice and essay questions. The multiple-choice portion is worth 50 percent of the total exam grade, whereas the three essays together count equally for the other 50 percent. Your score on the multiple-choice section is based on the number of questions you answer correctly. There is no "guessing penalty." No points will be deducted for incorrect answers; unanswered questions will be graded as incorrect answers.

Format of the Exam

The following table summarizes the format of the AP World History exam.

SECTION	NUMBER OF QUESTIONS	TIME LIMIT
I. Multiple-Choice Questions (50% of total grade)	70	55 minutes
II. Free-Response (Essay) Questions (50% of total grade)	1 Document-Based Essay Question (DBQ)	Suggested Reading Time: 10 Minutes
		Suggested Writing Time: 40 Minutes
	1 Continuity and Change over Time Essay	Suggested Writing Time: 40 Minutes
	1 Comparative Essay	Suggested Writing Time: 40 minutes

The Multiple-Choice Questions

This section consists of 70 questions. Each question has four possible answers. You will have 55 minutes to complete this section.

The College Board annually publishes material on the breakdown of questions on the multiple-choice test. According to their most recently published information, the multiple-choice section is broken down as follows:

Periodization:
- 5 percent of the questions deal with the period to c. 600 B.C.E.
- 15 percent of the questions deal with the period c. 600 B.C.E. to c. 600 C.E.
- 20 percent of the questions deal with the period c. 600 C.E. to c. 1450.
- 20 percent of the questions deal with the period c. 1450 to c. 1750.
- 20 percent of the questions deal with the period c. 1750 to c. 1900.
- 20 percent of the questions deal with the period c. 1900 to the present.

The information provided above is extremely valuable as you prepare for the multiple-choice section of the test. As you study, you should obviously concentrate your efforts on the periods since 600 C.E.

For DBQs, group your information and then analyze all the details. Find what will actually be useful for your essay. Be clear, concise, and to the point. —AP student

The Essay Questions

During the remaining 2 hours and 10 minutes of the test you will be asked to write three essays: a document-based essay question (DBQ), a continuity and change over time essay, and a comparative essay. The essays will be based on the broad themes that form the background of the AP World History course. According to the College Board description of the AP World History course, these themes include:

- Human-environmental interaction
  - Disease and its effects on population
  - Migration
  - Settlement patterns
  - Technology
- Cultural development and interaction
  - Religions, belief systems, and philosophies
  - Science and technology
  - The arts and architecture
- State-building, expansion, and conflict
  - Political structures and forms of government
  - Empires
  - Nations and nationalism
  - Revolts and revolutions
  - Regional, transregional, and global organizations and structures
- Creation, growth, and interaction of economic systems
  - Agriculture and pastoralism
  - Trade and commerce
  - Labor systems
  - Industrialization
  - Capitalism and socialism
- Development and change of social structures
  - Gender roles
  - Family and kinship relations
  - Race and ethnicity
  - Social and economic class structures

Also essential to success on the essays is the ability to visualize global patterns and the reactions of societies to global processes. The ability to interpret the context of a document, as well as to analyze point of view, is necessary to compose a satisfactory response to the DBQ.

For further information on the multiple-choice and essay questions, refer to Step 3 of this manual.

Taking the Exam

When you arrive at the exam site, you should have brought the following:

- Several pencils for the multiple-choice questions.
- Several black or blue pens for the essays.
- A watch. Silence any alarms that would go off during the exam period.
- Tissues.
- Your school code.
- Your driver's license and Social Security Number.

Leave the following items at home:

- A cell phone, beeper, PDA, walkie-talkie, or calculator.
- Books, a dictionary, study notes, flash cards, highlighters, correction fluid, a ruler, or any other office supplies.
- Portable music of any kind; no MP3 players, iPods, or CD players are allowed.

Other recommendations:

- Don't study the night before. Arrive at the exam rested.
- Wear comfortable clothing. It's a good idea to layer your clothing so that you are prepared for a variety of temperatures in the exam room.
- Eat a light breakfast and a light lunch on the day of the exam.

CHAPTER 2

How to Plan Your Time

IN THIS CHAPTER:

Summary: The right preparation plan for you depends on your study habits and the amount of time you have before the test.

Key Idea

✪ Choose the study plan that's right for you.

Three Approaches to Preparing for the AP World History Exam

What kind of preparation program for the AP exam should you follow? Should you carefully follow every step, or are there perhaps some steps you can bypass? That depends not only on how much time you have, but also on what kind of student you are. No one knows your study habits, likes, and dislikes better than you do. So you are the only one who can decide which approach you want and/or need to adapt. This chapter presents three possible study plans, labeled A, B, and C. Look at the brief profiles below. These may help you determine which of these three plans is right for you.

You're a full-school-year prep student if:

1. You have a definite love of world history.
2. You are certain that history will be your major in college.
3. You are not a procrastinator; you like to get things done.
4. You like detailed planning and everything in its place.

5. You feel you must be thoroughly prepared.
6. You have been successful with this approach in the past.

If you fit this profile, consider **Plan A**.

You're a one-semester prep student if:

1. You are pretty interested in world history.
2. You usually plan ahead but sometimes skip some of the little details.
3. You feel more comfortable when you know what to expect, but a surprise or two does not floor you.
4. You're always on time for appointments.
5. You have been successful with this approach in the past.

If you fit this profile, consider **Plan B**.

You're a 6-week prep student if:

1. World history is somewhat interesting to you.
2. You work best under pressure and close deadlines.
3. You think the work you have done in your world history class has prepared you fairly well for the AP test.
4 You decided late in the year to take the exam.
5. You like surprises.
6. You have been successful with this approach in the past.

If you fit this profile, consider **Plan C**.

Look now at the following calendars for plans A, B, and C. Choose the plan that will best suit your particular learning style and timeline. For best results, choose a plan and stick with it.

> To review for the World History AP test, I went over the major concepts and periods in my notes. I also found it helpful to read outside world history books and sources. Also, practice, practice, practice on multiple-choice world history questions, because they are half of the AP test. As far as the AP essay section, DBQ practice all year was great preparation.
> —AP student

Calendar for Each Plan

Plan A: You Have a Full School Year to Prepare

September–October
(Check off the activities as you complete them.)

— Determine into which student mode you would place yourself.
— Read Step 1 of this manual.
— Take a look at the Diagnostic Test in Step 2 to get an idea of the expectations of the AP exam.
— Become acquainted with the College Board AP Web site.
— Read and study the sections for Periods 1 and 2 in this manual.
— Begin to do outside reading on world history topics.
— Begin to use this book as a resource.

November

— Read the section of Chapter 4 on strategies for the continuity and change over time essay.
— Take the continuity and change over time section of the Diagnostic Test.
— Read and study the world history review sections that correspond with the period(s) you are studying in class.

December

— Study the world history review sections in the manual for the areas you have already studied in class. Note the connections of trade, exchange, and migration among world societies.
— Read additional sources to supplement the material in your textbook. Consult the bibliography of this manual for suggested titles.

January

— Form a study group to prepare for the AP exam.
— Continue critical reading of material to supplement your textbook.
— Study the world history review sections for material you are currently covering in class.

February–March

— Read the section of Chapter 4 of this manual on the comparative essay.
— Write the comparative essay from the Diagnostic Test.
— Read the section of Chapter 4 of the manual on the document-based essay question.
— Write the DBQ (document-based essay question) from the Diagnostic Test.
— Continue reviewing content from the world history review chapters.
— Read the section of Chapter 4 on the multiple-choice section.
— Take the multiple-choice section in the Diagnostic Test.

April

— Take Practice Test One in the first week of April.
— Evaluate your strengths and weaknesses.
— Study appropriate chapters to correct weaknesses.
— Study the Period Summary for each period in this manual to review key comparisons and changes and continuities.
— Within your study group, construct your own comparative and continuity and change over time charts for each unit.

May—First Two Weeks (You're almost there!)

— Make a list of materials that you are unsure of, and ask your teacher or study group to explain them.
— Take Practice Test Two.
— Evaluate your performance.
— On the day before the test, put away your books, do something fun, and get a good night's rest.
— Walk into the examination room with confidence. You're ready!

Get more in-depth with your readings. If you can spark a stronger interest in the subject, it is much less difficult to retain the information.—AP student

Plan B: You Have One Semester to Prepare

January–February

— Carefully read Chapters 1, 2, and 4 of this manual.
— Take the Diagnostic Test.
— Read and study the world history review sections that pertain to material that you have covered in class.
— Read at least one source outside of class on a topic you are studying.

March

— Review the world history content sections that cover the material you have studied in class.
— Form a study group.
— In your study group, practice writing and answering comparative and continuity and change over time questions.

April

— Take Practice Test One in the first week of April.
— Evaluate your strengths and weaknesses.
— Study appropriate chapters to correct weaknesses.
— Review the Period Summary after each period in this manual to review key comparisons and changes and continuities.
— In your study group, create your own comparative and continuity and change over time charts.

May—First Two Weeks (You're almost there!)

— Ask your teacher to clarify things in your textbook or in this manual of which you are unsure.
— Review the historical material for as much of the year as you can.
— Take Practice Test Two.
— Score your answers and analyze what you did wrong.
— On the day before the test, put away the books, do something fun, and get a good night's rest.
— Walk into the testing room with confidence; you're ready!

Commitment and discipline in studying are the most important factors in preparing well for the test. —AP student

Plan C: You Have 4 to 6 Weeks to Prepare

April

— Read Chapters 1, 2, and 4 of this manual.
— Take the Diagnostic Test.
— Review your strengths and weaknesses.
— Read the world history review chapters in this manual.
— Take Practice Test One.
— Score your exam and analyze your errors.
— Develop a weekly study group.
— Skim the glossary.

May—First Two Weeks (You're almost there!)

— Complete Practice Test Two.
— Score your exam and analyze your errors.
— Review the world history review section of this manual.
— Review Chapter 4 on strategies for each question type if necessary.
— On the day before the test, put away the books, do something fun, and get a good night's rest.
— Take the AP exam with confidence; you're ready!

STEP 2

Determine Your Test Readiness

CHAPTER 3

Take a Diagnostic Exam

IN THIS CHAPTER

Summary: In the following pages you will find a diagnostic exam that is modeled after the actual AP exam. It is intended to give you an idea of your level of preparation in world history. After you have completed both the multiple-choice and the essay questions, check your multiple-choice answers against the given answers and read over the comments to the possible solutions to the free-response questions.

Key Ideas

✪ Practice the kind of multiple-choice and free-response questions you will be asked on the real exam.
✪ Answer questions that approximate the coverage of periods and themes on the real exam.
✪ Check your work against the given answers and the possible solutions to the free-response questions.
✪ Determine your areas of strength and weakness.
✪ Earmark the concepts that you must give special attention.

WORLD HISTORY DIAGNOSTIC TEST

Answer Sheet

1 Ⓐ Ⓑ Ⓒ Ⓓ	26 Ⓐ Ⓑ Ⓒ Ⓓ	51 Ⓐ Ⓑ Ⓒ Ⓓ
2 Ⓐ Ⓑ Ⓒ Ⓓ	27 Ⓐ Ⓑ Ⓒ Ⓓ	52 Ⓐ Ⓑ Ⓒ Ⓓ
3 Ⓐ Ⓑ Ⓒ Ⓓ	28 Ⓐ Ⓑ Ⓒ Ⓓ	53 Ⓐ Ⓑ Ⓒ Ⓓ
4 Ⓐ Ⓑ Ⓒ Ⓓ	29 Ⓐ Ⓑ Ⓒ Ⓓ	54 Ⓐ Ⓑ Ⓒ Ⓓ
5 Ⓐ Ⓑ Ⓒ Ⓓ	30 Ⓐ Ⓑ Ⓒ Ⓓ	55 Ⓐ Ⓑ Ⓒ Ⓓ
6 Ⓐ Ⓑ Ⓒ Ⓓ	31 Ⓐ Ⓑ Ⓒ Ⓓ	56 Ⓐ Ⓑ Ⓒ Ⓓ
7 Ⓐ Ⓑ Ⓒ Ⓓ	32 Ⓐ Ⓑ Ⓒ Ⓓ	57 Ⓐ Ⓑ Ⓒ Ⓓ
8 Ⓐ Ⓑ Ⓒ Ⓓ	33 Ⓐ Ⓑ Ⓒ Ⓓ	58 Ⓐ Ⓑ Ⓒ Ⓓ
9 Ⓐ Ⓑ Ⓒ Ⓓ	34 Ⓐ Ⓑ Ⓒ Ⓓ	59 Ⓐ Ⓑ Ⓒ Ⓓ
10 Ⓐ Ⓑ Ⓒ Ⓓ	35 Ⓐ Ⓑ Ⓒ Ⓓ	60 Ⓐ Ⓑ Ⓒ Ⓓ
11 Ⓐ Ⓑ Ⓒ Ⓓ	36 Ⓐ Ⓑ Ⓒ Ⓓ	61 Ⓐ Ⓑ Ⓒ Ⓓ
12 Ⓐ Ⓑ Ⓒ Ⓓ	37 Ⓐ Ⓑ Ⓒ Ⓓ	62 Ⓐ Ⓑ Ⓒ Ⓓ
13 Ⓐ Ⓑ Ⓒ Ⓓ	38 Ⓐ Ⓑ Ⓒ Ⓓ	63 Ⓐ Ⓑ Ⓒ Ⓓ
14 Ⓐ Ⓑ Ⓒ Ⓓ	39 Ⓐ Ⓑ Ⓒ Ⓓ	64 Ⓐ Ⓑ Ⓒ Ⓓ
15 Ⓐ Ⓑ Ⓒ Ⓓ	40 Ⓐ Ⓑ Ⓒ Ⓓ	65 Ⓐ Ⓑ Ⓒ Ⓓ
16 Ⓐ Ⓑ Ⓒ Ⓓ	41 Ⓐ Ⓑ Ⓒ Ⓓ	66 Ⓐ Ⓑ Ⓒ Ⓓ
17 Ⓐ Ⓑ Ⓒ Ⓓ	42 Ⓐ Ⓑ Ⓒ Ⓓ	67 Ⓐ Ⓑ Ⓒ Ⓓ
18 Ⓐ Ⓑ Ⓒ Ⓓ	43 Ⓐ Ⓑ Ⓒ Ⓓ	68 Ⓐ Ⓑ Ⓒ Ⓓ
19 Ⓐ Ⓑ Ⓒ Ⓓ	44 Ⓐ Ⓑ Ⓒ Ⓓ	69 Ⓐ Ⓑ Ⓒ Ⓓ
20 Ⓐ Ⓑ Ⓒ Ⓓ	45 Ⓐ Ⓑ Ⓒ Ⓓ	70 Ⓐ Ⓑ Ⓒ Ⓓ
21 Ⓐ Ⓑ Ⓒ Ⓓ	46 Ⓐ Ⓑ Ⓒ Ⓓ	
22 Ⓐ Ⓑ Ⓒ Ⓓ	47 Ⓐ Ⓑ Ⓒ Ⓓ	
23 Ⓐ Ⓑ Ⓒ Ⓓ	48 Ⓐ Ⓑ Ⓒ Ⓓ	
24 Ⓐ Ⓑ Ⓒ Ⓓ	49 Ⓐ Ⓑ Ⓒ Ⓓ	
25 Ⓐ Ⓑ Ⓒ Ⓓ	50 Ⓐ Ⓑ Ⓒ Ⓓ	

WORLD HISTORY DIAGNOSTIC TEST

Section I

MULITPLE-CHOICE QUESTIONS

Time—55 minutes
70 questions

Directions: Each of the incomplete statements or questions below is followed by four answer choices. Choose the answer that is best and mark the letter of your choice on the answer sheet supplied.

1. Which of the following belief systems were characterized by a belief in prophets and were spread through missionary effort?
   (A) Christianity and Judaism
   (B) Christianity and Islam
   (C) Buddhism and Islam
   (D) Buddhism and Christianity

2. Which of the following is true of both the Han Empire and the Gupta Empire?
   (A) Both empires had long-established traditions of dynastic rule.
   (B) Both were overrun by Germanic tribes in their declining years.
   (C) Both empires were characterized by religious unity.
   (D) Both saw a number of technological advances.

3. The Buddhist social order included
   (A) strict adherence to patriarchal authority
   (B) opposition to caste systems
   (C) well-defined gender-role distinctions
   (D) emphasis on well-educated rulers

4. Which of the following was most characteristic of the Neolithic Revolution?
   (A) Widespread epidemic disease
   (B) An increase in the nomadic way of life
   (C) Greater numbers of settled communities
   (D) Global population decline

5. Which of the following describes a difference between Arab expansion of the seventh century and Viking expansion of the ninth century?
   (A) Viking expansion required greater maritime technology than Arab expansion.
   (B) Arab expansion included Western Europe, whereas Viking expansion did not.

   (C) Arab expansion took place over longer distances than Viking expansion.
   (D) The Vikings attempted to change the culture of conquered peoples, whereas the Arabs did not.

6. In the period between 600 and 1450, Indian Ocean trade differed from that of the Pacific Ocean in that it
   (A) involved contacts with the islands of Southeast Asia
   (B) involved only spices
   (C) involved competition among a more diverse group of traders
   (D) involved commerce across large stretches of water

7. During the fourteenth century, Ibn Battuta traveled to all the following regions EXCEPT
   (A) East Africa
   (B) West Africa
   (C) East Asia
   (D) Central Asia

8. Which of the following was the most urbanized during the period 1750 to 1914?
   (A) China
   (B) India
   (C) Russia
   (D) England

9. The responsibilities of the *samurai* to the *shogun*
   (A) were based on individual, rather than group, loyalties
   (B) involved a contractual relationship similar to that of feudal Europe
   (C) provided an honorable alternative to retreat or defeat
   (D) promoted centralized government in Japan

10. In the period between 600 and 1450,
  (A) European women gained an increasingly greater role in political life
  (B) African women were confined to domestic roles
  (C) the Chinese custom of footbinding began
  (D) there were few role distinctions between women of elite and peasant classes globally

11. Traders spread both Christianity and Islam to present-day
  (A) South Africa
  (B) Indonesia
  (C) Japan
  (D) North Africa

12. All of the following were true of the Renaissance EXCEPT
  (A) it was influenced by the Muslim occupation of Spain.
  (B) it resulted from Mediterranean trade during the Crusades.
  (C) it began after the development of regional states in Europe.
  (D) it began in England in the fourteenth century.

13. Which was true of the Mongol Empire?
  (A) It was characterized by efficient administrators.
  (B) It did not interfere with Islamic societies.
  (C) It caused Eurasian trade routes to move farther north.
  (D) It opened up trade relations between Russia and the West.

14. Compared to European exploration in the Indian Ocean, that of the Chinese
  (A) used fewer and smaller ships
  (B) covered shorter distances
  (C) was designed to establish a military presence
  (D) gained strength after the mid-1430s

15. The key location of Malucca placed it in a position to trade in porcelain and silk from China, and other luxury goods from the Maluccas and the Philippines. The statement above describes what region about the year 1500?
  (A) The southern tip of Africa
  (B) The Malay Peninsula

  (C) Sri Lanka (Ceylon)
  (D) The Horn of Africa

16. The plantations of Sicily and the Madeira and Canary Islands were most like those of
  (A) British North America
  (B) the Congo
  (C) Brazil and the Caribbean
  (D) India

17. Between 1450 and 1750, European voyages of exploration
  (A) were designed to break Italian and Muslim trade monopolies
  (B) were carried out without knowledge of oceanic conditions
  (C) were confined to the Atlantic Ocean
  (D) opened up trade relations with Polynesian islanders

18. The statue below combines modern sculpture with that of ancient cultures of
  (A) Japan
  (B) West Africa
  (C) India
  (D) Mexico

19. The statue below best represents which of the following historical processes?
  (A) Migration
  (B) Syncretism
  (C) Cultural diffusion
  (D) Global exchange

Statue of Tlaloc

20. Which of the following was NOT true of trade patterns between 1450 and 1750?
(A) African kingdoms became dependent on European technology.
(B) China engaged only in regional trade.
(C) Triangular trade patterns crossed the Atlantic.
(D) The Ottoman Empire depended on Western technology.

21. Which of the following was true of the cultures of Ming and Qing China?
(A) The concept of filial piety was abandoned.
(B) The custom of footbinding became less frequent.
(C) The Chinese were introduced to American food crops.
(D) China developed an egalitarian society.

22. Between 1500 and 1800, the Islamic empires
(A) abandoned the tradition of steppe diplomacy
(B) failed to urbanize the lands they conquered
(C) steadily strengthened in power
(D) were ethnically diverse

23. Compared to British colonial administration in the Americas, Spanish colonial administration
(A) attempted to set up democratic rule for its colonies
(B) preferred to be based on rural rather than urban areas
(C) was more tightly controlled by its European government
(D) imported African slaves later than did the British

24. "It being obviously necessary and desirable that British subjects should have some port whereat they may [maintain] and refit their ships when required, and keep stores for that purpose, His Majesty the Emperor of China cedes to her Majesty the Queen of Great Britain, &c., the Island of Hong Kong, to be possessed in perpetuity by Her Britannic Majesty, her heirs and successors, and to be governed by such laws and regulations as Her Majesty the Queen of Great Britain, &c., shall see fit to direct." The above quotation is an excerpt from the treaty ending which war?

(A) The Seven Years' War
(B) World War I
(C) The Opium War
(D) The Sino-Japanese War

25. The underlying cause of the above war was
(A) a trade imbalance between Great Britain and China
(B) Chinese and British competition over the establishment of trading posts in northern India
(C) competition among the holders of the spheres of influence in China
(D) British attempts to colonize China

26. Which of the following was true regarding Latin American women in the nineteenth century?
(A) They enjoyed the right to vote.
(B) They were subjected to the values of *machismo*.
(C) They could not work outside the house without supervision.
(D) They could hold political office.

27. Which of the following did NOT facilitate European imperialist efforts in Africa?
(A) The end of slavery in Africa
(B) The invention of the steamship
(C) The discovery of quinine
(D) Ethnic divisions in Africa

28. Which of the following was true of the new imperialism?
(A) The Berlin Conference accommodated Africa's ethnic diversity.
(B) The United States favored economic imperialism rather than direct political control in South America.
(C) France favored economic imperialism over settler colonies.
(D) British settlers integrated easily with Australian aboriginal peoples.

29. In the nineteenth and early twentieth centuries, indentured servants
(A) had the same status as slaves
(B) went mostly to Europe
(C) received free passage to their destinations
(D) usually came from Europe

30. Within colonial empires
(A) Hawaii's ethnic diversity produced continuing tensions
(B) the Japanese were tolerant of ethnic diversity
(C) Social Darwinism was implemented to combat racism
(D) Most subject people welcomed the introduction of European schools

31. Which of the following best describes the cartoon below?
(A) China is actively preparing to host the 2008 Olympics.
(B) China's track record includes human rights violations.
(C) China's effort to host the Olympics meets with worldwide approval.
(D) China's traditions have prevented modernization.

China in 2008 Cartoon

(Used by permission of www.InternationalCartoons.com.)

32. In the latter part of the twentieth century, China was accused of all of the following EXCEPT
(A) human rights violations in Tibet
(B) a one-child policy
(C) suppression in Tiananmen Square
(D) preventing women from entering the professions

33. Which of the following was true concerning decolonization in Africa?
(A) Imperialist powers planned for rapid decolonization after World War II.
(B) African participation in global trade markets increased.
(C) The Negritude movement was similar to black pride movements in the United States.
(D) Boundaries of independen nations accommodated ethnic diversity.

34. Which of the following countries experienced the greatest economic growth during World War I?
(A) Japan
(B) The United States
(C) Russia
(D) France

35. Twentieth-century population studies show that
(A) fertility rates in poor societies increased rapidly
(B) the use of insecticides plus increased agricultural productivity have caused a decline in death rates
(C) AIDS has caused overall population decline in Africa
(D) regions with high fertility rates continue to show high mortality rates

36. The Maya and Gupta empires had in common
(A) the construction of ceremonial pyramids
(B) the independent discovery of the value of zero as a place holder
(C) persistent pressure from invaders in frontier areas
(D) the knowledge that the earth is round

Bosnia Map

(Source: www.cia.gov/publications/factbook.)

37. Incidents in the region included in the map above gave rise to the terms
    (A) Green Revolution and commercial agriculture
    (B) ethnic cleansing and balkanization
    (C) globalization and multinational corporations
    (D) imperialism and colonization

38. Which of the following pairs of religions uses images to represent their respective deities?
    (A) Hinduism and Christianity
    (B) Judaism and Christianity
    (C) Confucianism and Buddhism
    (D) Islam and Hinduism

39. The best reason for the division of early world history at 600 B.C.E. is that the period between 600 B.C.E. and 600 C.E. is characterized by
    (A) the development of agricultural societies
    (B) the rise of classical civilizations
    (C) the beginnings of global exchange
    (D) the beginnings of interaction between pastoral and agricultural societies

40. Compared to Daoism, Confucianism
    (A) places greater emphasis on the balance of nature
    (B) is less concerned about authoritative government
    (C) also arose in response to turmoil at the end of the Zhou dynasty
    (D) places less emphasis on education

Panama Canal

41. Which of the following is NOT true of the canal pictured above?
    (A) Its construction involved the imposition of the Monroe Doctrine.
    (B) It facilitated the establishment of empires.
    (C) It lowered trade costs between imperialist powers and subject regions.
    (D) Its construction involved U.S. intervention in South American politics.

42. Which of the following best describes a reason for the construction of the canal?
    (A) Economic imperialism
    (B) Environmentalism
    (C) *Laissez-faire* economics
    (D) Alignment

43. Which of the following did NOT trade with the Roman Empire?
    (A) the Kingdom of Axum
    (B) India
    (C) Southern Africa
    (D) Malaysia

44. Before the European Renaissance, most philosophies in Europe and Asia
    (A) were spread through the printing press
    (B) were spread through conquest
    (C) relied on religious faith
    (D) involved the social contract

45. By 1500, Islam had extended to all of the following areas of Africa EXCEPT
    (A) East Africa along the Indian Ocean
    (B) West Africa
    (C) Central Africa along the Atlantic Ocean
    (D) North Africa along the Mediterranean Sea

46. Which of the following is true of the bubonic plague?
    (A) It followed established trade routes.
    (B) It affected West Africa.
    (C) It began in Europe and spread to China.
    (D) It died out completely after the fourteenth century.

47. Which major language family arose as a result of migrations beginning in central Asia and spreading westward?
    (A) Indo-European
    (B) Romance
    (C) Sino-Tibetan
    (D) Semitic

48. The Mongols
    (A) were capable administrators
    (B) persecuted Christians and Muslims within territories they conquered
    (C) were interested only in Asian territories
    (D) moved main trade routes farther north

49. Migration forged contacts between all of the following peoples EXCEPT
    (A) Bantu peoples and cattle herders of sub-Saharan Africa
    (B) Aryans and Mongols
    (C) Germanic peoples and Romans
    (D) Hittites and Assyrians

50. A thirteenth-century traveler described the city he was visiting as one with numerous craft guilds and wealthy merchants. Its people used paper money and the city showed signs of highly efficient administration. The traveler was describing a city in
    (A) India
    (B) Persia
    (C) England
    (D) China

51. As a result of African long-distance trade patterns in the period 1450 to 1750,
    (A) Islam and Christianity increased their influence over sub-Saharan Africa
    (B) eastern African city-states came under Spanish domination
    (C) central Africa remained under the rule of stateless societies
    (D) indigenous African religions declined in popularity

52. In the period between 1500 and 1800, European exploration accomplished all of the following EXCEPT
    (A) charting of eastern Australia
    (B) study of the geography of the Pacific Ocean
    (C) discovery of the northwest passage through North America
    (D) study of Pacific societies

53. Which of the following is true regarding a comparison of trade between Spain and the Netherlands between 1450 and 1750?
    (A) The Dutch concentrated on the Indonesian spice trade.
    (B) The Dutch were more concerned than the Spanish with spreading Christianity.
    (C) Trade made Spain the wealthiest state in Europe in the seventeenth century.
    (D) The Dutch were more interested in changing native societies than the Spanish were.

54. By the eighteenth century, the basis of European diplomacy was
    (A) the establishment of empire
    (B) absolutism
    (C) the balance of power
    (D) the limitation of standing armies

55. In the thirteenth century, the most urbanized region in the world was
(A) Europe
(B) Russia
(C) Latin America
(D) China

56. The millet system in the Islamic empires
(A) was especially effective in India
(B) created cooperation among the ethnic groups of the Ottoman Empire
(C) interfered with religious freedom
(D) promoted nationalist sentiment within the Ottoman Empire

57. Under the Tokugawa Shogunate, Japan
(A) became increasingly accepting of foreigners
(B) entered an extended period of peace
(C) encouraged expeditions to show the glory of Japan
(D) followed China's example of acceptance of Neo-Confucianism

58. British intervention in the Indian cotton industry
(A) resulted in Indian refusal to purchase British textiles
(B) enhanced Indian domestic industries
(C) produced more cotton for Indian consumption than for export
(D) transformed India from a producer of manufactured goods to a supplier of raw cotton

59. Which of the following is true concerning the Ottoman Empire in the period from 1750 to 1900?
(A) Reform movements brought long-term political and economic stability.
(B) It welcomed the influx of European technology.
(C) Foreigners were driven from the empire.
(D) The fate of the Ottoman Empire was tied to the concept of balance of power in Europe.

60. From the mid-nineteenth century to the period before World War I, Japan
(A) became a world power
(B) developed an industry run on its vast natural resources
(C) rejected Western intervention
(D) adopted a constitution modeled on that of the United States

61. During the nineteenth century, Asian and African rulers were most interested in
(A) Western medical treatments
(B) Western agricultural techniques
(C) Christianity
(D) Western technology

62. In the nineteenth century, both Austria-Hungary and the Ottoman Empire
(A) were culturally diverse
(B) ruled over a kingdom within their borders
(C) gained political strength
(D) disrupted the balance of power in Europe

63. The Industrial Revolution in Europe
(A) decreased demands for African raw materials
(B) initially improved the quality of life in European cities
(C) contributed to the end of the trans-Atlantic slave trade
(D) caused European powers to construct textile factories in their colonies

64. Which of the following nations was most similar to Brazil in gaining its independence?
(A) Haiti
(B) Argentina
(C) Mexico
(D) Canada

65. "The participating States will respect human rights and fundamental freedoms, including the freedom of thought, conscience, religion or belief, for all without distinction as to race, sex, language or religion. They will promote and encourage the effective exercise of civil, political, economic, social, cultural and other rights and freedoms all of which derive from the inherent dignity of the human person and are essential for his free and full development."

    The quotation above is taken from the
    (A) Helsinki Accords
    (B) Camp David Accords
    (C) Truman Doctrine
    (D) Treaty of Versailles

66. Which of the following describes a change in religious history in the twentieth and twenty-first centuries?
    (A) Declining popularity of traditional religions worldwide
    (B) Declining popularity of Liberation Theology in Latin America and Africa
    (C) Declining prominence of Pentecostalism in Latin America
    (D) Native Africans serving as Christian missionaries in Europe

67. Which of the following describes the Great Depression in Latin America?
    (A) It resulted in part from agricultural underproduction in the United States and Western Europe.
    (B) It was unaffected by diminished global trade.
    (C) It resulted in increased government involvement in national economies.
    (D) It resulted in a decrease in national social welfare programs.

68. Globalization has produced all of the following EXCEPT
    (A) modification of American products to suit international cultures
    (B) a return to traditional and fundamental religions
    (C) the end of patriarchal societies
    (D) charges of environmental destruction

69. Post–World War II Japan and India were alike in that
    (A) neither adopted autocratic government
    (B) they enjoyed economic prosperity
    (C) they successfully implemented the Green Revolution
    (D) they were faced with secessionist movements

70. After the end of colonization, both Latin America and sub-Saharan Africa
    (A) developed egalitarian societies
    (B) experienced intense ethnic rivalries
    (C) enjoyed political stability
    (D) failed to achieve the prosperity they had anticipated

End of Section I

› Answers and Explanations for the Multiple-Choice Questions

1. **B** Christianity and Islam are both missionary religions; both hold a belief in prophets. Judaism (A) believes in prophets, but is not a missionary religion. Buddhism (C) was spread to some extent by missionaries, but does not believe in prophets.

2. **D** Both made advances in scientific technology. The Gupta Empire did not involve the rule of numerous dynasties, as did the Han Empire (A). Both were overrun by tribes from central Asia (B). Although Han China was characterized by religious unity, Gupta India ruled over Buddhists and Hindus (C).

3. **B** The Buddhist emphasis on equality placed the religion in opposition to the caste system. The remaining choices refer to Confucianism.

4. **C** As agriculture spread throughout the eastern, and later the western, hemispheres, a larger portion of the population settled in villages near agricultural plots. Epidemic disease (A) did not become widespread until global contacts increased. As more sedentary villages arose, the nomadic way of life decreased (B). Stable communities with abundant crops resulted in an increase in global population (D).

5. **A** Arab expansion in the seventh century occurred over land routes. In the ninth century, Viking expansion included the rivers of Western Europe, whereas that of the Arabs did not (B). Viking expansion took place over longer distances (C). Arabs attempted to change the religious and social culture of the people they conquered, whereas the Vikings were interested primarily in trade (D).

6. **C** Although Pacific Ocean trade involved primarily Polynesians and East Asians, that of the Indian Ocean involved Muslims and non-Muslims from Southeast Asia, South Asia, East Asia, East Africa, and Europe. Indian Ocean trade involved spices, food crops, slaves, textiles, and European technology (B). Indian Ocean trade was both regional and long distance (D), while Pacific Ocean trade was mostly regional.

7. **D** Ibn Battuta's travels bypassed central Asia. The other choices involve regions he visited.

8. **D** England, the home of the European Industrial Revolution, counted over half of its people living in urban areas during the period, making it the most urbanized country in the period 1750 to 1914.

9. **C** The custom of *seppuku* provided an honorable alternative to defeat or retreat. The *samurai* relationship was based on group loyalties (A). It was a one-sided relationship, rather than the reciprocal relationship of European feudalism (B). It continued to a degree through the nineteenth century and promoted decentralized government in Japan, especially before the rise of the Tokugawa Shogunate (D).

10. **C** Footbinding began under the Song dynasty. European women did not have a role in political life during the period (A), whereas some African women did (B). Class distinctions often defined the role of women (D).

11. **D** North Africa, although dominated by Islam, also saw the beginnings of a Christian community at Axum, where traders spread Christianity during the time of the Roman Empire. Axum, in present-day Ethiopia and Eritrea, was responsible for spreading Christianity to Egypt. South Africa is an area associated more with Christianity (A), Indonesia with Islam (B), and Japan with Buddhism and Shinto (C).

12. **D** The Renaissance began in the Italian city-states as a result of Mediterranean trade during the Crusades (B) and spread later to northern Europe. The Muslim culture in Spain preserved the learning of the Greeks and Romans, which was the nucleus of Renaissance knowledge (A). There were regional states in France and Germany and other portions of Europe prior to the Renaissance (C).

13. **C** The Mongols moved trade routes farther north to their home territory. The Empire was characterized by a relative lack of attention to administration (A). The Mongols conquered the Islamic society of Persia (B). They discouraged the Russians from contact with the West (D).

14. C Chinese trade in the Indian Ocean also was designed to establish respect with regard to the military might of the Chinese. The Chinese ships were larger and covered larger distances, and their expeditions included more ships than those of Europe (A, B). Chinese expeditions stopped suddenly in the 1430s (D).

15. B The reference to Malucca and its trade position refers to the Malay Peninsula.

16. C Sugar plantations were established in Sicily, the Canaries, the Madeiras, and the Caribbean and Brazil. British North America featured cotton, rice, and tobacco plantations (A); the Congo, rubber plantations (B); and India, cotton cultivation (D).

17. A European explorers attempted to find alternate routes to the east that would interfere with Muslim and Italian monopolies. New technology promoted knowledge of oceanic waters (B). Explorers sailed the Indian and Pacific Oceans as well as the Atlantic (C). The Polynesian islands were largely bypassed in this time period (D).

18. D The statue is of Tlaloc, the Aztec god of rain. The large facial features were typical of Mesoamerican statuary.

19. B The statue of Tlaloc, the Aztec god of rain, best illustrates syncretism, or a blend of two processes or cultures, in this case a blend of Mesoamerican and modern statuary.

20. B China carried on trade with Mexico and the Philippines via the Manila galleons. The other answer choices are reflective of trade in the period.

21. C The Manila galleons introduced American food crops to the Chinese. Filial piety remained an integral part of Confucian culture (A), and footbinding extended to more girls in lower classes as well as elite classes (B). China was still a stratified society (D).

22. D People of various ethnic backgrounds as well as diverse religions lived within the Islamic empires. Islamic Turks continued to engage in steppe diplomacy (A), and Islamic cities grew in conquered lands (B). Islamic empires were in decline (C) by the mid-seventeenth century.

23. C Spain's Council of Indies maintained closer ties with its colonies than did the British, who largely left its colonies in North America to govern themselves. Spain did not prepare its colonies for self-rule (A). The Spaniards preferred to dwell in urban areas (B), and imported African slaves in the sixteenth century, about 100 years earlier than the British (D). They had administrative precedents in the *encomiendas* in the Canaries and Madeiras that they followed (E).

24. C The reference to British takeover of Hong Kong indicates the excerpt is from the Treaty of Nanking, which ended the Opium War between Britain and China.

25. A The immediate cause of the Opium War, the introduction of the opium trade between British-held India and China, was the result of a trade imbalance between Britain and China. This imbalance occurred when China sold tea to Britain but was largely uninterested in purchasing British trade products.

26. B *Machismo*, or the celebration of male strength, often was manifested in abusive treatment of women. Latin American women in the nineteenth century were not allowed to vote (A) or hold political office (D). After the middle of the century, they could work as teachers or as laborers with the permission of their father or husband (C).

27. A Although the trans-Atlantic slave trade had ended, slavery had not ended within Africa during the age of the new imperialism. The steamship allowed Europeans to navigate the treacherous African rivers (B), whereas the discovery of quinine lessened the threat of malaria for Europeans (C). Ethnic divisions within Africa made the continent more vulnerable to imperialist advances (D).

28. B In general, the United States was more interested in acquiring South America's raw materials than in establishing direct political control over the region. The Berlin Conference divided Africa without consideration for Africa's ethnic groups (A). France established settler colonies in Africa and Indochina (C). British settlers inflicted their diseases on aborigines and drove them off their land (D).

29. C Indentured servants received free passage to their destination. They were free people, and, therefore, had a status different from that of slaves (A). Indentured servants usually migrated to subtropical and tropical regions in the Americas, Oceania, and Africa (B). They usually came from Asia, Africa, and the Pacific (D).

30. **A** Hawaiian sugar plantations employed workers from China, Japan, the Philippines, Korea, Portugal, and the Pacific islands; this situation produced ethnic divisions and tensions. Japanese intolerance was displayed in violence toward the people of Nanking (B). Social Darwinism was used to support racism (C). Most subject peoples preferred to be educated in their native language rather than in a European language (D).

31. **B** The "track" being laid out covers up the bodies of victims of its policies. Although China was preparing to host the 2008 Olympics, choice (A) is neither the best answer nor the subject of the cartoon. The newspaper headline does not indicate worldwide approval (C). The traditional Great Wall is shown with the modern city of Beijing, indicating China's efforts at modernization (D).

32. **D** Chinese women are allowed to enter the professions. China has been criticized for imposing its one-child policy in Tibet and driving Tibetans from their country (A). The one-child policy has led to forced abortions and sterilizations as well as increased female infanticide (B). In 1989, government forces put down student protests in favor of greater political rights in Tiananmen Square (C).

33. **C** The Negritude movement attempted to foster pride in being African and to encourage the fight for independence. Imperialists planned for a slow transition to independence (A). After colonialism, Africa's trade advantage decreased or remained constant (B). Boundaries of independent nations tended to coincide with colonial boundaries, perpetuating divisions between ethnic groups (D).

34. **B** By the end of World War I, the U.S. economy soared, increasing its status as a key world power. Whereas Japan prospered to a lesser extent (A), Russia and France suffered economically because the war was carried out within their borders (C, D).

35. **B** The nutrients generated by improved agricultural methods have contributed to lower mortality rates. Fertility rates have tended to decrease even in poor societies (A). In spite of the AIDS crisis, the population of Africa is increasing (C). Regions with high fertility rates also show lower mortality rates (D).

36. **B** Both independently discovered the value of the zero as a place holder, allowing them to engage in complex mathematical calculations. The Mayans alone were known for the construction of large ceremonial pyramids (A). The Gupta experienced constant threats from frontier peoples (C), and they knew that the earth is round (D).

37. **B** The map is of Bosnia, which gave the term "ethnic cleansing" to the genocide carried out in its conflict with Serbia in the 1990s. Located in the Balkans, the region also contributed the word "balkanization" to describe the nationalist sentiment emerging from the various nations located within the country of Yugoslavia. The other responses do not pertain to Bosnia.

38. **A** Christianity uses pictures and statues of Jesus, whereas Hinduism uses images to represent the various forms of its deity. Judaism does not represent its deity through images (B). Confucianism does not worship a deity, and the Buddha is considered a deity only in Mahayana Buddhism (C). Islam does not represent Allah or any human form through images (D).

39. **B** The period from 600 B.C.E. to 600 C.E. marks the rise of classical civilizations and empires such as those of Persia, Han China, Rome, and Gupta India. Agricultural societies had developed throughout most of the world before 600 B.C.E. (A). Although trade had begun to develop more widely in this period, it was not global (C). Pastoral and agricultural societies had interacted in the period before 600 B.C.E. (D)

40. **C** Both philosophies emerged as a response to the political unrest at the end of the Zhou dynasty. Daoism places greater emphasis on the balance of nature (A). Confucianism is more focused than Daoism on authoritative government (B), and good education (D).

41. **A** The construction of the Panama Canal was realized by U.S. intervention, but not through imposition of the Monroe Doctrine. The canal offered steamships a route through the

Americas that facilitated transportation between imperialists and their holdings, furthering the establishment of empires (B, C). Its construction involved U.S. intervention in the politics of Colombia, from which the province of Panama revolted (D).

42. **A** Economic imperialism, or the control of a country's economy by the businesses of another nation, played a major role in the construction of the Panama Canal because of the desire of the United States and other nations to facilitate both travel and commerce by cutting a canal through Central America. Conservation of Central American territories was not a motive (B), nor was *laissez-faire* economics, or the belief in only minimal government intervention in the economy. (C). Alignment (D) involves the Cold War relationship of developing nations with one of the two superpowers.

43. **C** The southern portion of Africa was not part of Rome's trade pattern. The Kingdom of Axum in North Africa (A), India (B), and Malaysia (D) were all located along trade routes that connected to the Roman routes.

44. **C** Most philosophies of this period were traditional and relied on religious faith. Movable type was invented in China around 1000, but had just been invented in Europe (A). Only Islamic philosophies were largely spread by conquest in the period (B). The social contract was a concept of seventeenth-century philosophy (D).

45. **C** By 1500, Islam had extended to all of the regions listed except for Central Africa.

46. **A** The bubonic plague was spread over trade patterns. It did not spread to West Africa (B). It began in central Asia, spread to China, then Europe (C), and caused at least one major outbreak in Great Britain in the seventeenth century (D).

47. **A** Indo-European, the largest language family, originated in central Asia, then spread throughout India and Europe beginning about 2000 B.C.E. Romance languages are branches of Indo-European (B). Sino-Tibetan spread from central Asia to East Asia (C). Semitic languages are related to the language of ancient Sumer (D).

48. **D** The Mongols moved trade routes north into their territories. The Mongols were skilled conquerors but not capable administrators (A).

They allowed religious freedom within territories they conquered (B). They were interested in Europe but were defeated at the outskirts of Vienna (C).

49. **B** The Aryans invaded the Indus valley, not Mongol territory. The migrating Bantu encountered cattle herders in sub-Saharan Africa (A). Germanic peoples migrated into the Roman Empire (C). Hittites migrated from central Asia to Southeast Asia, transmitting the knowledge of ironworking to the Assyrians (D).

50. **D** The traveler, Marco Polo, was describing his journey to the principal cities of China. Thirteenth-century China was known for its craft guilds, numerous merchants, use of paper money, and efficiently administered urban areas.

51. **A** Both Islam and Christianity introduced by traders increased their influence in Africa, even as indigenous African religions retained their popularity and blended with Islamic and Christian beliefs (D). Eastern African city-states came under Portuguese domination (B). In central Africa, stateless societies gave way to centralized kingdoms such as Kongo (C).

52. **C** The northwest passage through North America was not discovered until the twentieth century. Captain Cook charted eastern Australia in the eighteenth century (A) and studied Pacific societies (D). English explorers began studying the geography of the Pacific Ocean in the sixteenth century (B).

53. **A** The spice trade was the main preoccupation of the Dutch. The Spanish were more concerned with spreading Christianity (B) and changing native societies through education (D). Trade made the Netherlands the wealthiest European state in the seventeenth century (C).

54. **C** The maintenance of the balance of power to prevent the dominance of one nation was the hallmark of early modern European politics. The establishment of empire went contrary to the concept of a balance of power (A). Absolutism was a characteristic of most European states (B). Standing armies emerged as a means of achieving a balance of power (D).

55. **D** Song China had the greatest number of large cities in the world. At the same time, Europe (A), Russia (B), and Latin America (C) were more rural.

56. D Millets allowed ethnic and religious groups within Islamic empires to be responsible only to the sultan, decreasing ethnic cooperation (B) and strengthening ethnic identities. The large number of communities in India made the millet system impractical (A). The millets allowed religious freedom (C).

57. D Neo-Confucianism, which emphasized obedience to authority, was popular in both China and Japan. As the Tokugawa family continued in power, it became increasingly suspicious of foreigners (A). The sixteenth and seventeenth centuries saw civil war in Japan (B). Japanese were forbidden to journey outside Japan (C).

58. D India purchased British manufactured goods rather than manufacturing its own textiles. British sale of inexpensive manufactured goods to the Indians (A) destroyed much of India's domestic textile production (B). The British made sure that more cotton was produced for export than for Indian consumption (C).

59. D The Ottomans survived into the early twentieth century because the European powers could not decide what to do about the Ottomans without disrupting the European balance of power. Tanzimet reforms and those of the Young Turks failed to bring long-term changes (A). Ottoman artisans rioted against the influx of foreign goods (B). European powers were granted the right of extraterritoriality (C).

60. A Its victory in the Russo-Japanese War in 1904–5 made Japan a world power. Japan developed industrially, but its natural resources were scarce (B). It accepted Western intervention to further industrialization (C), and adopted a parliamentary government (D).

61. D Asian and African rulers were most interested in Western technology, especially weaponry. They already had their own form of medical treatments (A) and agricultural techniques (B). Although some African rulers embraced Christianity, the religion was generally unpopular in Asia in the nineteenth century (C).

62. A Both Austria-Hungary and the Ottoman Empire were composed of diverse national cultures. Austria-Hungary included the Kingdom of Hungary (B). Austria lost some of its power to Germany, while the Ottoman Empire continued a steady decline (C). Neither was sufficiently powerful to disrupt the balance of power; the Ottoman Empire was not disbanded by European nations because the breakup might destroy the balance of power (D).

63. C The efficiency of machinery decreased the need for human labor. The need for African palm oil increased because of its use as a lubricant for machinery (A). Initially, European industrial cities were crowded, unsanitary, and dangerous (B). European imperialist powers tended not to construct factories in their colonies (D).

64. D Brazil gained its independence relatively peacefully; similarly, Canada received its independence peacefully from the British in 1867. Haiti became independent from France after a revolution in 1804 (A); Argentina (B) and Mexico (C) also underwent revolutions to win their independence from Spain.

65. A The subject of the passage, human rights, is an indication that it is excerpted from the Helsinki Accords, which deals with human rights. The Camp David Accords dealt with peace in the Middle East (B). The Truman Doctrine pledged the assistance of the free world to nations threatened with Communist aggression (C). The Treaty of Versailles dealt harsh terms to Germany after World War I (D).

66. D During the twentieth century, native Africans began serving as Christian missionaries to Europe because of Europe's declining participation in Christian worship. Worldwide, young people especially are reacting to globalization by returning to the traditional religions of their respective cultures (A). Liberation Theology has gained popularity in both Latin America and Africa (B), while Pentecostalism is increasingly practiced in Latin America (C).

67. C During the Great Depression, Latin American governments became more involved in national economies through the creation of new social programs (D). Overproduction of U.S. and Western European farm crops resulted in lower prices on Latin American plantation-grown crops (A). Diminished global trade (B) created massive unemployment.

68. C In spite of international conferences on women's issues and other efforts to produce gender equality, patriarchal societies persist in many world cultures. Some products, such as U.S. toys and popular restaurant selections, have been modified to become more attractive to other cultures (A). Traditional religions such as Shinto and Islamic fundamentalism are becoming more attractive, especially to young people (B). Critics of globalization assert that its rapid economic development has destroyed the environment (D).

69. **A** Japan adopted a constitution modeled on that of the United States; India is a parliamentary democracy. Only India was divided by secessionist movements (D). Only Japan enjoyed economic prosperity (B). Only India was affected by the Green Revolution (C).

70. **D** Both Latin America and sub-Saharan Africa had expected to prosper economically after independence; the expected prosperity did not materialize. Latin America especially continued to observe a social hierarchy with a vast gap between rich and poor (A). Sub-Saharan Africa experienced intense ethnic rivalries within its new states (B). Both regions experienced numerous political coups and changes in government (C).

WORLD HISTORY DIAGNOSTIC TEST

Section II

DOCUMENT-BASED QUESTION (DBQ)

Suggested reading time—10 minutes

Suggested writing time—40 minutes

1. Using the documents and your knowledge of world history, analyze the unifying and divisive forces of nationalism in the ninteenth and twentieth centuries.

Document 1

Source: Giuseppe Mazzini, the founder of Young Italy, from an essay entitled "Europe: Its Conditions and Prospects," 1852.

Europe no longer possesses unity of faith, of mission, or of aim. Such unity is a necessity to the world. . . . There are in Europe two great questions; or rather, the question of the transformation of authority, that is to say, of the Revolution, has assumed two forms; the question which all have agreed to call social, and the question of nationalities. The first is more exclusively agitated in France, the second in the heart of the other peoples of Europe . . .

The question of nationality can only be resolved by destroying the treaties of 1815, and changing the map of Europe and its public Law. The question of nationalities, rightly understood, is the alliance of the peoples; the balance of powers based upon new foundations; the organization of the work that Europe has to accomplish . . .

They speak the same language, they bear about them the impress of consanguinity, they kneel beside the same tombs, they glory in the same tradition; and they demand to associate freely . . . in order to elaborate and express their idea . . .

The map of Europe has to be remade.

Document 2

Source: Theodor Herzl, Zionist leader, from a pamphlet entitled The Jewish State, *1896.*

In countries where we have lived for centuries we are still regarded as strangers, and often by those whose ancestors were not yet dwelling in the land where the Jews had already experienced suffering . . .

Let us be granted sovereignty over a part of the globe large enough to satisfy the rightful requirements of a nation; the rest we shall handle ourselves.

Document 3

Source: Ho Chi Minh, president of the Democratic Republic of Vietnam, from his Declaration of Independence of the Democratic Republic of Viet Nam, 1945.

"All men are created equal. They are endowed by their Creator with certain unalienable Rights; among these are Life, Liberty, and the pursuit of Happiness."

This immortal statement appeared in the Declaration of Independence of the United States of America in 1776. In a broader sense, it means: All the peoples on the earth are equal from birth, all the peoples have a right to live and to be happy and free . . .

Nevertheless, for more than eighty years, the French imperialists . . . have enforced inhuman laws; they have set up three different political regimes in the North, the Center, and the South of Viet Nam in order to wreck our country's oneness and prevent our people from being united.

Viet Nam has the right to enjoy freedom and independence and in fact has become a free and independent country. The entire Vietnamese people are determined to mobilize all their physical and mental strength, to sacrifice their lives and property in order to safeguard their freedom and independence.

Document 4

Source: Declaration of the Rights of Man and the Citizen, issued by the French National Assembly, 1789.

The source of all sovereignty resides essentially in the nation; no group, no individual may exercise authority not emanating expressly therefrom.

Document 5

Source: Simón Bolívar, "The Angostura Address," delivered before a congress convened to organize a republic for Venezuela, 1819.

Americans by birth and Europeans by law, we find ourselves engaged in a dual conflict: we are disputing with the natives for titles of ownership, and at the same time struggling to maintain ourselves in the country that gave us birth against the opposition of the invaders.

Document 6

Source: Ziya Gokalp, Turkish nationalist, from an essay entitled "On Turkism," 1923.

The Tanzimatists said to them: "You are Ottoman subjects. Do not claim a national existence that is distinct from that of other nations. If you do, you will cause the destruction of the Ottoman Empire."

Document 7

Source: Ernst Moritz Arndt, nineteenth-century German poet and nationalist.

What is the German's fatherland?
So name me that big land!
Wherever the German language is spoken
And God sings hymns in heaven,
That's what it shall be! That's what it shall be!
Brave German, call that your own!

Document 8

Source: Louis Kossuth, Hungarian nationalist leader, in a speech at a Congressional banquet given in his honor in Washington, D.C., 1852.

We Hungarians are very fond of the principle of municipal self government, and we have a natural horror against the principle of centralization. That fond attachment to municipal self-government without which there is no provincial freedom possible, is a fundamental feature of our national character . . .

Where the cradle of our Savior stood, and where his divine doctrine was founded, there now another faith rules, and the whole of Europe's armed pilgrimage could not avert this fate from that sacred spot, nor stop the rushing waves of Islamism absorbing the Christian empire of Constantine. We stopped these rushing waves. The breast of my nation proved a breakwater to them. We guarded Christendom, that Luthers and Calvins might reform it.

CONTINUITY AND CHANGE OVER TIME ESSAY

Suggested writing time—40 minutes

Directions: Write an essay on the following topic:

2. Analyze the changes brought about by migration in ONE of the following regions between 1500 B.C.E. and 1000 C.E. Be sure to include a discussion of continuities during the same period.

South Asia   sub-Saharan Africa

COMPARATIVE ESSAY

Suggested writing time—40 minutes

Directions: Write an essay on the following topic.

3. Compare trade patterns in TWO of the following oceans during the period 1450 to 1750.

Indian Ocean   Pacific Ocean   Atlantic Ocean

❯ Comments on Possible Solutions to the Free Response Questions

Document-Based Question

A good response may begin by considering the divisive forces of nationalism, such as the need to redraw boundaries and alter laws in order to accommodate nationalist goals (Document 1). Those who attempt to assert their nationalist sentiments within the borders of another larger political unit often must endure suffering and conflicts (Document 3). Struggles against imperialism present another divisive effect of nationalism (Document 3).

The majority of the documents deal with the positive aspects of nationalism, such as freedom (Document 3) and sovereignty (Document 4). Nationalism provides a solidarity that empowers the nation to work for the welfare of the larger political unit (Documents 1, 8). Nationalists are asking for nothing more than the opportunity to be self-sufficient (Documents 2, 3, 5, 8). Linked to the empowerment of the nation-states is the sheer joy of sharing a common culture expressed through language, music, religion, and common traditions (Documents 1, 7, 8). Students may also mention the diversity of world areas addressed in the documents and the wide range of chronology to point out the commonality of nationalist sentiment.

The backgrounds of the authors of the documents provide ample opportunity to illustrate point of view. One example of point of view is Mazzini's address. As the leader of the nationalist Young Italy, his views would reflect a pro-nationalist sentiment. Ho Chi Minh, as the leader of a country subject to French imperialism, also speaks from that point of view. More information on the nature of nationalism might be obtained through the examination of sources that reflect the opinions of members of the lower classes who live in multinational states such as the Ottoman Empire or Austria-Hungary, or by reading documents from the leaders of the Austrians.

Continuity and Change over Time Essay

A good response concerning migration in South Asia would begin with discussion of the major wave of Aryan migrations (a branch of the Indo-European migrations) moving through the Khyber Pass into South Asia about 1500 B.C.E. After conquering the agricultural peoples of the Indus valley, the nomadic Aryans imposed their class system based on skin color. This class system would develop into the Hindu caste system. Aryan literature, the *Vedas,* became the basis for Hindu belief. Following Aryan tradition, cattle became the symbol of wealth.

Early Aryans settled in the Punjab region between present-day India and Pakistan. By 1000 B.C.E., they had settled throughout much of the Indian subcontinent and learned to use iron tools. Regional kingdoms were established throughout most of India. Around 1000 B.C.E., the caste system was further broken down into subcastes known as *jati*. The Aryans developed a patriarchal society that included the custom of *sati.*

About 800–400 B.C.E., the beliefs of indigenous Dravidians, who were animists, combined with Aryan beliefs to produce a series of works known as the *Upanishads.* These works added the concepts of reincarnation and *karma* to Hindu belief. About 600 B.C.E., the *Vedas* had been written down in the Aryan sacred language of Sanskrit, which became a major Indian tongue. By 1000 C.E., the *Upanishads* had become a code of ethics that valued respect for all living things. Animals might hold the reincarnations of those with poor *karma*. Vegetarian diets had become commonplace. Also by 1000 C.E., the *jati* had been further defined.

A good response regarding migration in sub-Saharan Africa may begin by stating that around 1500 B.C.E., small numbers of Bantu-speaking peoples had already begun to migrate from present-day Nigeria, possibly because of population pressures. They carried with them the knowledge of agriculture and ironworking.

Subsequent massive migrations of Bantu-speaking peoples moved out of the Bantu homeland beginning about 700–500 B.C.E. Moving southward and eastward throughout sub-Saharan Africa, they farmed along the riverbanks, especially along the Congo River. There they transmitted their knowledge of agriculture and ironworking to cattle herders and, in turn, learned cattle-herding techniques. The Bantu peoples also contributed their language to the cultures of sub-Saharan Africa. The Bantu were organized into stateless societies based on age grades.

About 300 to 500 C.E., sailors from Malaysia brought to Madagascar and Africa the knowledge of banana cultivation. The Bantu learned to cultivate the banana, whose nutrients contributed to population growth among them. As they continued their migrations, they spread the knowledge of this new crop as well. By 1000 C.E., the major wave of Bantu migrations had ceased. By this time, the Bantu had reached the eastern coast of Africa, where contact between the Bantu languages and the Arabic of traders in East Africa combined to form the new language of Swahili. From stateless societies emerged regional kingdoms of Bantu peoples.

Comparative Essay

A good response concerning the Indian Ocean would begin by mentioning that in 1450, the Chinese had recently withdrawn from exploration in the Indian Ocean to attend to the defense of their own borders. Meanwhile, Europeans were becoming extremely active in that same body of water. Portugal, the Netherlands, and later the English became interested in the spices and luxury goods of Indonesia and other islands and mainland territories in the Indian Ocean. European entrance into the waters of the Indian Ocean caused an intense competition with Muslim traders already active in the region; Muslim dominance in the Indian Ocean declined as that of Europeans took hold.

The Atlantic world also saw European dominance during the period 1450 to 1750. Students should discuss the impact of the Columbian Exchange between the Eastern and Western hemispheres. Like the Indian Ocean, Atlantic traffic also dealt with trade in African slaves; Atlantic slave trade, however, dealt with a much higher volume of trade in human beings. During this period, Atlantic trade also involved the transfer of huge amounts of gold and silver from Spain's American colonies to Europe.

Trade in the Pacific Ocean involved several interactions. Polynesian peoples continued to trade regionally among fellow islanders. The Manila galleons sailed from the Philippines to follow a route that took them to Mexico to acquire loads of silver to trade through Philippine ports for luxury goods and tea from China. Europeans largely bypassed the Polynesian islands until the eighteenth century. Thus, Pacific Ocean trade did not see the dominance of Europeans in its waters as the Atlantic and Indian oceans did.

STEP 3

Develop Your Study Program

CHAPTER **4** Tips for Taking the Exam

CHAPTER 4

Tips for Taking the Exam

IN THIS CHAPTER

Summary: Use these question-answering strategies to raise your AP score.

Key Ideas

✪ On the multiple-choice questions, try to eliminate one or more answer choices.

✪ Write a solid thesis statement on all essays.

✪ On the DBQ, use document grouping to analyze the question.

✪ On the DBQ, analyze point of view and the need for an additional document.

✪ On the continuity and change over time essay, analyze the causes and effects of continuity and change.

✪ On the comparative essay, make and analyze direct comparisons.

The Multiple-Choice Question

The multiple-choice section of the Advanced Placement World History examination consists of 70 multiple-choice questions. You will have 55 minutes to complete the multiple-choice section. Each multiple-choice question has four answer choices.

The multiple-choice questions require you to analyze the material you have covered in the course. Many of the questions require you to compare among societies, events, or processes, or to indicate how they have changed over a period of time. Some of the questions require you to interpret a written passage, photograph, political cartoon, map, chart, or graph. The following question is an example of one that compares two colonial societies during the new imperialism.

Compared to most African colonies, the British colony in India

(A) was allowed more practice in self-government.
(B) was a model of technology transfer.
(C) did not receive the benefits of improved transportation.
(D) did not rebel against its European imperialist power.

Answer (A) is correct; the British allowed Indians to engage in some local rule. Answer (B) is incorrect; neither African colonies nor India were recipients of much technology transfer. Answer (C) is incorrect because both benefited from the transportation systems initially established for the colonizing nations. Answer (D) is incorrect; the Sepoy Rebellion was a revolt against British rule in India.

The following are some frequently asked questions concerning the multiple-choice section.

1. **If I don't know an answer, should I guess or leave the question unanswered?** There is no guessing penalty on the multiple-choice section. If you do not know an answer, you should select the answer choice that you think is correct. Unanswered questions will be scored as incorrect answers.

2. **What strategy should I use to narrow the possible answer choices?** Of the four answer choices found in each question, one is often obviously incorrect. In addition to the correct choice, there is often another answer which is almost correct. Another possibility is that two of the answer choices are correct, but one is a better answer than the other. The best advice is to read the question very carefully to determine exactly what the question is asking, then eliminate the weaker answers until you arrive at the best answer.

3. **Will I be required to know a lot of dates and people to answer the multiple-choice questions?** Some knowledge of specific dates and people will be necessary to answer the multiple-choice questions. For the most part, however, the multiple-choice questions on the Advanced Placement World History examination ask you to compare societies, issues, or trends within one or more of the Advanced Placement World History time periods or to analyze how societies, issues, or trends have changed and remained the same over one or more time periods.

The Document-Based Question

After completing the multiple-choice section, you will have the remaining 2 hours and 10 minutes of the exam to complete the three essays, or free response, questions. You will receive a booklet that contains the prompts for all three free-response questions, and a second booklet with lined paper for your responses. You may answer the free response questions in any order. During this portion of the test, you will have to budget your own time; you will not be told at which point you are to move on to the next question.

The suggested time for answering the document-based question is 50 minutes. You should spend approximately 10 minutes reading the documents, 5 minutes in prewriting, and 35 minutes writing your essay. The document-based question usually contain between 4 and 10 documents. Although some of the documents will be text, others may be photographs, drawings, political cartoons, maps, graphs, or charts. In order to successfully answer the document-based question (DBQ), you need to meet the following requirements:

1. **Write a solid thesis statement.** Do not simply restate the question. Be sure that you take a stand on one side of the topic addressed by the essay prompt.

2. **Show by your analysis of the documents that you understand their meaning.** You may misinterpret one document and still receive the point for this task.

3. **Use evidence from all or all but one of the documents to support your thesis.** Give specific supporting details from the documents.

4. **Analyze the documents by grouping them in two or three ways, depending on the question.** Do not merely list your documents or summarize them individually in the order in which they appear in the text.

5. **Analyze point of view in at least two documents.** Begin this task by looking at the author, the author's background, the date on which the document was written, and any other information provided in the attribution, or the introductory information given before the document. In your essay, discuss how the author's background formed his or her point of view.

6. **Identify one type of additional document or source that would be useful in analyzing the essay prompt.** Ask yourself, "Whose voice or opinion is missing?" Explain why the document or source is needed.

If you perform all the above tasks satisfactorily, you will receive a total of seven points on the document-based question. You are then eligible to earn one or two additional points by writing an essay that displays one or more quality points such as:

- An exceptionally clear, analytical thesis.
- Exceptionally strong analysis of the documents.
- Analysis of point of view in most of the documents.
- The addition of appropriate additional historical evidence or more than one additional document.

The following are some frequently asked questions regarding the document-based question:

1. **How do I begin answering the question?** Read the question carefully so that you know what the question is asking you to do. A good idea is to underline the task word (such as analyze, compare, evaluate), the topic, and the time parameters (dates, centuries, or periods) contained in the essay prompt.

2. **What is the next step?** Group your documents in several useful categories.

3. **How do I cite the documents?** A manner of citation that is especially useful for the reader who scores your essay is to include the number of the document in parentheses after making a reference to it, for example: (Document 2). You also may choose to mention the name of the author or quote or paraphrase from the document to identify it.

4. **Where do I place the analysis of bias or point of view?** This analysis may be placed anywhere in the essay. It is most effective, however, if discussed in the same paragraph in which the document is analyzed.

5. **Where do I mention the need for an additional document?** The discussion of the additional document may be included anywhere in the essay.

6. **Will I lose points for incorrect spelling or grammar?** No. Each essay begins with a score of "0." As each task required by the question is accomplished, the reader adds a point to the score. Points are never deducted. Because spelling and grammar are not included in the tasks required to complete the essay, incorrect usage will not result in denial of a point.

7. **Will I lose points for errors such as incorrect dates?** Refer to the description of scoring in Question 6. If a date or other information is incorrect, the incorrect information will not be scored. If you have included an abundance of correct evidence in your essay, the incorrect material will not result in loss of opportunity to receive the points for historical evidence.

8. **What are some of the most common errors students make in answering the question?** The most common errors on the DBQ are forgetting to include a discussion of bias or point of view and omitting a discussion of the additional document. Another common error is not answering the question asked in the essay prompt.

9. **Should I underline my thesis statement?** No, the reader is capable of determining whether or not you have included an appropriate thesis statement in your essay.

10. **May I use a highlighter?** Highlighters are not permitted.

The Continuity and Change over Time Essay

The continuity and change over time essay tests your ability to analyze how societies, trends, or issues have changed and remained the same over long periods of time. The suggested writing time for this essay is 40 minutes, including 5 minutes devoted to prewriting. You will be given a choice of several geographical or cultural regions and will be asked to choose either one or two of those regions on which to base your essay. The continuity and change over time questions will involve change and continuity over one or more of the Advanced Placement World History time periods.

Begin by writing a thesis statement that addresses the topic. Be sure to mention the dates or time periods from the essay prompt in your thesis statement.

Depending on the wording of the essay prompt, you may choose to divide your essay into three sections. Begin by describing the region(s) that you chose at the beginning date mentioned in the essay prompt. In the second part of your essay, describe the region(s) during the middle portion of the time period. In the third section of your essay, discuss the region(s) at the end of the time period addressed in the essay prompt.

In order to address continuity in your essay, consider how the societies or issues remained the same at the beginning, during, and at the end of the time period included in the essay prompt. You must explain how the changes and continuities in your essay relate to global processes occurring at the same time. Analyze the causes and effects of the changes and continuities.

The following are some frequently asked questions regarding the continuity and change over time essay:

1. **Does the thesis statement have to appear at the beginning of the essay?** No, the thesis statement may appear at the beginning or at the end of the essay. Since the thesis statement serves as a guide for the essay, however, it is better to place it at the beginning of the essay.

2. **Do I have to write a conclusion to my essay?** Your essay does not need to have a conclusion. If you have sufficient time to meet all the criteria for the essay and write a short conclusion, fine. If you are pressed for time, however, skip the conclusion and proceed to the next question.

3. **What are the most common errors made in the continuity and change over time essay?** One of the most common errors on this essay is the writer's lack of knowledge of world geographical and cultural regions. (For help in this area, consult Chapter 5 in Step 4 of this manual.) Another common error is omission of a discussion of continuities across the time period. Other essays are not answered successfully because they compare only the beginning and the end of the time period in question and fail to address changes and continuities in the middle portion of the period.

The Comparative Essay

The comparative essay question requires you to write an essay that compares and contrasts societies or issues. This question may cover one or more of the Advanced Placement World History time periods. Suggested writing time for the comparative essay is 40 minutes, including a 5-minute prewriting period. In most cases, you will be given several regions and will be asked to compare issues between two of the regions. Some examples of issues that you may be asked to compare are gender roles, political structures, trade, and migrations.

Begin by writing a thesis statement that takes a stand on one aspect of the issues to be compared. Do not simply restate the essay prompt. A statement such as the following, for example, is not an adequate thesis statement: "There are many similarities and differences between the slave trade in the Indian and Atlantic Ocean basins in the period between 1450 and 1750." An adequate thesis statement might read: "While the Indian Ocean slave trade carried slaves from eastern Africa to European-owned plantations in the Indian Ocean between 1450 and 1750, a more vigorous slave trade across the Atlantic between western Africa and the Americas effected profound and enduring changes upon the societies of the Western Hemisphere."

In order to respond adequately, it is necessary to make one or two direct comparisons between the societies or issues addressed. Analyze the direct comparison by showing the causes and effects of similarities and/or differences. An example of a direct comparison is: "Egypt's natural barriers provided a degree of isolation, allowing the Egyptian culture to develop somewhat independently. Unlike Egypt, Sumer was surrounded by few natural barriers, making it vulnerable to frequent invasions and influences from other civilizations and societies."

A good comparative essay will make more than one direct comparison and will include both similarities and differences. Analysis of the regions or issues within the global context will also strengthen the essay.

The following are some commonly asked questions concerning the comparative essay:

1. **What are the most common errors on the comparative essay?** One of the most common errors is failure to answer the right question as a result of not reading the essay prompt carefully. Another very common problem is failure to make at least one direct comparison between the societies or issues addressed in the essay prompt.

2. **Does my essay require an introduction?** No. Many students waste time writing elaborate introductory sentences or paragraphs to the free response questions. The best approach is to state your thesis statement, then defend it with historical details and analyses.

3. **If the essay prompt asks for a comparison between two regions, must I deal with the regions as a whole, or may I compare one country from each region?** Either approach is allowed. You may even treat one region as a whole and deal with the second region through the example of one country.

4. **Is it necessary to know the issues in both regions equally well?** No. As long as you answer all parts of the question, you may write an essay that is stronger in one area than the other.

STEP **4**

Review the Knowledge You Need to Score High

Technological and Environmental Transformations (to 600 B.C.E.)

CHAPTER 5

The World History Environment and Periodization

IN THIS CHAPTER

Summary: Before we begin to consider the scope of the human story, we must first consider the stage on which the story unfolds: the land and the oceans themselves. The Advanced Placement World History course divides the globe into a number of regions that include the following: East Asia, Southeast Asia, South Asia, Central Asia, Southwest Asia (the Middle East) and North Africa, Sub-Saharan Africa, Eastern Europe, Western Europe, North America, Latin America, and Oceania. The map overleaf illustrates the location of these regions. Keep in mind that political boundaries among nations may vary considerably throughout the different periods of history.

Key Terms

An asterisk (*) denotes items listed in the glossary.

civilization*   independent invention

climate*   monsoon*

cultural diffusion*   steppe*

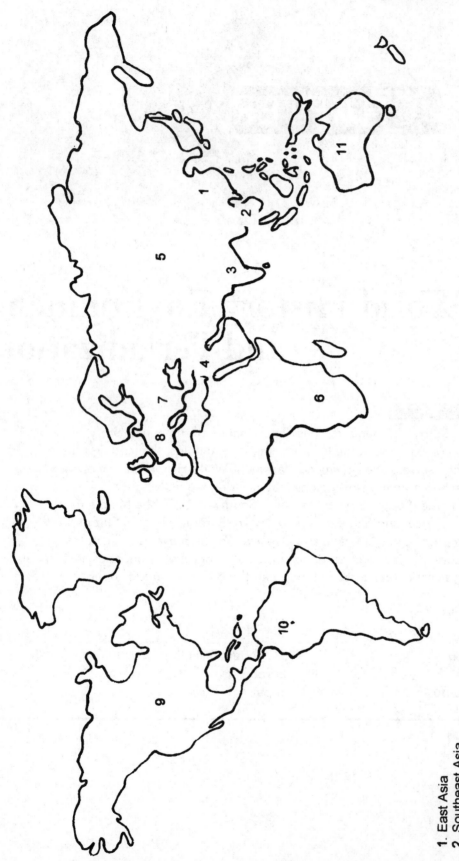

1. East Asia
2. Southeast Asia
3. South Asia
4. Southwest Asia (Middle East) and North Africa
5. Central Asia
6. Sub-Saharan Africa
7. Eastern Europe
8. Western Europe
9. North America
10. Latin America
11. Oceania

Oceans and Seas

The history of the world did not occur in land areas alone; the oceans and seas also have their own stories to tell. Vast migrations of both ancient and modern peoples took place across the waterways of the world; plants, animals, and diseases were exchanged; and competition arose among explorers seeking new lands and merchants pursuing profits. A few points to understand when studying the oceans are:

- The Arctic Ocean, the smallest of the world's oceans, is packed in ice throughout most of the year. Extremely difficult to navigate, it is the location of the famed northwest passage sought by early European explorers. The passage is barely usable because of its ice-bound condition.

- The Indian Ocean, the third largest of the oceans, has seen extensive trade since the people of the Harappan civilization sailed through one of its seas, the Arabian Sea, to trade with Sumer. Throughout history the Indian Ocean has seen Malay sailors and Chinese, Muslim, and European traders use the ocean's **monsoon** winds to guide their expeditions through its waters. Africa also was drawn into this trade. Oftentimes, commercial activity in the Indian Ocean produced intense rivalries, especially among the Dutch, Portuguese, and Muslim sailors in the seventeenth century.

- The Atlantic Ocean became the scene of exchange between the Eastern and Western hemispheres after the voyages of Columbus produced an encounter among European, African, and American peoples. The Caribbean Sea saw the meeting of the three cultures on the sugar plantations of the sixteenth through the eighteenth centuries. The Mediterranean Sea, joined to the Atlantic Ocean, saw the glories of early Middle Eastern and Greco-Roman civilizations. Northern European societies traded in the waters of the North Sea and the Baltic Sea.

- The Pacific Ocean, the world's largest, is dotted with islands that witnessed the ancient voyages of the Polynesian peoples of Oceania. The Bering Sea was the route of the earliest inhabitants of the Americas into those continents. Societies of East and Southeast Asia communicated with one another by means of the Sea of Japan and the South China and East China seas. The Manila galleons of the sixteenth through the nineteenth centuries joined Latin America, the Philippine Islands, and China in trade. World wars saw the use of Pacific islands for strategic purposes.

The chart below illustrates some of the political units and physical features of various world regions.

REGION	EXAMPLES OF MODERN COUNTRIES	MAJOR RIVERS	MAJOR LANDFORMS *CLIMATE*
East Asia	China, Japan, North Korea, South Korea	Yalu River, Huang He River, Chang Jiang River	Mount Fuji, Gobi Desert, Tibetan Plateau
Southeast Asia	Vietnam, Thailand, Laos, Indonesia, Malaysia	Mekong River, Irawaddy River	Ring of Fire
South Asia	India, Pakistan, Nepal, Bhutan, Bangladesh	Ganges River, Indus River, Brahmaputra River	Himalayas, Hindu Kush, Khyber Pass, *monsoons*

continued

REGION	EXAMPLES OF MODERN COUNTRIES	MAJOR RIVERS	MAJOR LANDFORMS *CLIMATE*
Southwest Asia (Middle East) and North Africa	Egypt, Saudi Arabia, Morocco, Israel, Turkey, Iran, Iraq, Afghanistan	Tigris–Euphrates Rivers, Nile River	Zagros Mountains, Arabian Desert, Sahara Desert
Central Asia	Russia, Mongolia, Kazakhstan	Volga River	Gobi Desert, Lake Baikal, Ural Mountains, *steppe*
Sub-Saharan Africa	Nigeria, Somalia, Democratic Republic of Congo, Kenya, South Africa	Congo River, Zambezi River, Niger River	Kalahari Desert, tropical rainforest, Great Rift Valley, Mount Kilimanjaro, Lake Victoria
Eastern Europe	Poland, Slovakia, Lithuania, Croatia	Danube River	Caucasus Mountains, Carpathian Mountains
Western Europe	Spain, United Kingdom, Sweden, Italy, Germany, Austria	Rhine River, Rhone River, Elbe River	Alps, Pyrenees
North America	Canada, United States, Mexico	Mississippi River, Missouri River, St. Lawrence River, Rio Grande River	Rocky Mountains, Canadian Shield, Sierra Madre Mountains
Latin America	Mexico, Cuba, Panama, Brazil, Argentina	Amazon River, Río de la Plata, Paraná	Amazon Rainforest, Andes Mountains, Pampas
Oceania	Australia, New Zealand, Papua New Guinea	Darling River, Murray River	Outback, Great Barrier Reef, Great Dividing Range

Periodization

A unique feature of the Advanced Placement World History course is its division into six periods. It is important for you to familiarize yourself with these periods; the ability to compare and contrast societies, events, and trends within periods will be necessary skills to master the multiple-choice questions as well as the comparative and document-based questions on the AP examination. You will also need to analyze the impact of interactions among societies. Likewise, a grasp of the changes and continuities (those things that stayed the same) between periods is important to success on the multiple-choice questions and the continuity and change over time and document-based questions on the exam. The six AP World History periods are:

- Period 1 Technological and Environmental Transformations (to c. 600 B.C.E.)
- Period 2 Organization and Reorganization of Human Societies (c. 600 B.C.E. to c. 600 C.E.)
- Period 3 Regional and Transregional Interactions (c. 600 C.E. to c. 1450)
- Period 4 Global Interactions (c. 1450 to c. 1750)
- Period 5 Industrialization and Global Integration (c. 1750 to c. 1900)
- Period 6 Accelerating Global Change and Realignments (c. 1900 to the present)

Notice that dates in AP World History use the designations B.C.E. (Before the Common Era) and C.E. (Common Era). These designations correspond to B.C. and A.D., respectively.

AP World History Themes

In each of these six periods, there are five broad themes that the course emphasizes. These are:

- Human-environmental interaction: disease and its effects on population, migration, settlement patterns, and technology
- Cultural development and interaction: religions, belief systems, and philosophies; science and technology; and the arts and architecture
- State-building, expansion, and conflict: political structures and forms of government; empires; nations and nationalism; revolts and revolutions; and regional, transregional, and global organizations and structures
- Creation, growth, and interaction of economic systems: agriculture and pastoralism, trade and commerce, labor systems, industrialization, and capitalism and socialism
- Development and change in social structures: gender roles, family and kinship relations, race and ethnicity, and social and economic class structures

Civilization Versus Society

Another consideration in the AP World History course is the role of societies as well as civilizations. Historians commonly define a **civilization** as a cultural group that displays five characteristics:

- Advanced cities
- Advanced technology
- Skilled workers
- Complex institutions (examples: government, religion)
- A system of writing or recordkeeping

Not all peoples on the earth live in cultural groups that meet these five criteria. Yet inhabitants of societies (cultural groups that do not satisfy all five characteristics of a civilization) also have made significant contributions to the course of world history. One example is that of the highland people of Papua New Guinea, many of whom lack a written language even today, yet who count among the earliest farmers in the world.

Independent Invention Versus Diffusion

Still another consideration in the Advanced Placement World History course is the question of whether **cultural diffusion** or **independent invention** is the more significant method of exchange. For example, in Chapter 6 of this study guide, you will read of the spread of agriculture throughout the globe. In this case, it is the task of the historian to investigate where agriculture arose independently, in addition to tracing its diffusion, or spread, through the migration of agricultural peoples. Also, contact of migratory peoples with one another was responsible for the exchange of ideas and technological inventions in addition to the knowledge of agriculture. Patterns of independent invention compared to those of cultural diffusion will remain a thread woven throughout the story of humankind.

› Rapid Review

The Advanced Placement World History course is unique in its inclusion of both civilizations and societies in its narrative of global history. The division of the course into periods assists you in analyzing global events and trends throughout a specific era by considering comparison, changes, and continuities.

› Review Questions

1. Interactions between Muslims and Europeans during the seventeenth century are most commonly found in
   (A) the Atlantic Ocean
   (B) the Arctic Ocean
   (C) the South China Sea
   (D) the Indian Ocean
   (E) the Pacific Ocean

2. An Advanced Placement World History region that can be classified as a cultural region is
   (A) South Asia
   (B) North America
   (C) Latin America
   (D) Southeast Asia
   (E) Central Asia

3. The study of oceans in world history
   (A) focuses on trans-Atlantic themes
   (B) focuses on the commercial activities of elite classes
   (C) has less impact on global history than the study of land masses
   (D) narrows the study of interaction among global peoples
   (E) coordinates with an emphasis on societies as well as civilizations

4. An example of diffusion rather than independent invention is
   (A) the Sumerian use of the wheel
   (B) the Mayan concept of zero as a place holder
   (C) the origin of the Greek alphabet
   (D) the cultivation of the banana in Southeast Asia
   (E) the origin of monotheism

5. Periodization in the Advanced Placement World History course
   (A) begins with the rise of river valley civilizations in Period One
   (B) assists students in comparing societies and trends within periods
   (C) is irrelevant to the content of document-based questions
   (D) limits the study of continuities between historical periods
   (E) provides even coverage to the millennia of world history

❭ Answers and Explanations

1. **D**—The seventeenth century witnessed intense rivalry among Europeans and Muslims for trade dominance, especially in spices, in the Indian Ocean. The Atlantic Ocean (A) was the scene of interactions among Europeans, Africans, and Native Americans, whereas the Arctic Ocean (B) saw limited trade among various Inuit peoples. The South China Sea (C) was largely the domain of the Chinese. The Pacific Ocean (E) saw limited contacts between Europeans and Pacific Islanders as well as interactions among the Spanish, Chinese, Filipinos, and Indians of South America through the voyages of the Manila galleons.

2. **C**—Latin America embraces the political regions of Mexico, the Caribbean, and South America, with the unifying force a common heritage stemming from speakers of Romance languages. Mexico, for example, belongs politically to North America and culturally to Latin America. South Asia (A), North America (B), Southeast Asia (D), and Central Asia (E) are regions with commonly defined political boundaries.

3. **E**—The study of oceans embraces societies such as Polynesian islanders and Malay peoples in addition to accounts of civilizations. The Indian and Pacific Oceans as well as the Atlantic (A) involve accounts of rich cultural interactions including various social classes (B). Interactions across the ocean waters are no less vital to global history than those across land masses (C), broadening the scope of history (D).

4. **C**—The Greek alphabet originated with the Phoenicians who, through trade, transmitted its knowledge to the Greeks. The Sumerians invented the wheel (A). The Mayans originated the concept of the place holder in the Western Hemisphere (B). Southeast Asia was an area of independent cultivation of the banana (D). The Hebrew people are credited with the origins of monotheism (E).

5. **B**—The organization of the Advanced Placement World History course by periods facilitates comparing events and trends in those periods. Period One begins with the rise of global agriculture (A). Periodization assists students in analyzing the time periods addressed in document-based questions and organizing the study of continuities between time periods (C, D). Periods One and Two are much broader in scope than the other periods in the course, resulting in uneven coverage of the early millennia of world history (E).

CHAPTER 6

Development of Agriculture and Technology

IN THIS CHAPTER

Summary: One of the most significant developments in world history was the independent emergence of agriculture, a process that had already taken place in some locations throughout the Eastern Hemisphere by 8000 B.C.E. The so-called **Agricultural Revolution,** or **Neolithic Revolution,** was in reality more of a slow process resulting from the warming of global temperatures. The accompanying historical period, known as the **Neolithic Age** (or New Stone Age), was named for its characteristic tools made from stone.

Key Terms

Agricultural Revolution*
animism*
artifact*
foraging*
Neolithic Age

Neolithic Revolution
Paleolithic Age
pastoralism*
slash-and-burn cultivation*
specialization of labor*

The Transition from Foraging to Agriculture

At the close of the Paleolithic Age (or Old Stone Age), the transition from **foraging** (hunting and gathering) arose as nomadic groups returned to favorite grazing areas year after year. Perhaps some nomadic peoples made an effort to cultivate those crops that they found most appealing; later they may have transplanted seeds from these same favored crops to other areas through which they traveled. Because hunting required greater physical strength, the early cultivation of plants was probably a task left to women, granting them increased importance among agricultural peoples. Women farmers studied the growth patterns of plants as well as the effect of climate and soil on them. Agricultural development included the domestication of animals as well as the cultivation of crops.

Independent Origins of Agriculture: A Timeline

Key developments in the history of agriculture show the following events in the process:

- Agriculture began sometime after 9000 B.C.E. with the cultivation of grain crops such as wheat and barley in Southwest Asia. Animals such as pigs, cattle, sheep, and goats also were domesticated.
- By 7000 B.C.E. Sudanese Africa and West Africa cultivated root crops such as sorghum and yams.
- Inhabitants of the Yangtze River valley cultivated rice about 6500 B.C.E.
- About 5500 B.C.E., people of the Huang He valley began the cultivation of soybeans and millet. They also domesticated chickens and pigs and, later, water buffalo.
- In Southeast Asia, perhaps around 3500 B.C.E., inhabitants grew root crops such as yams and taro as well as a variety of citrus and other fruits.
- Around 4000 B.C.E., the peoples of central Mexico cultivated maize, or corn, later adding beans, squash, tomatoes, and peppers.
- The principal crop of the Andean region of South America was potatoes, first cultivated around 3000 B.C.E. Maize and beans were added later. The only domesticated animals in the Americas were the llama, alpaca, and guinea pig.

> (*Note to the student:* The multiple-choice questions on the Advanced Placement examination will not require that you know the exact dates included in this timeline. Rather, the dates are given so that you may visualize a pattern of independent invention of agriculture.)

The Spread of Agriculture

After agriculture was established independently in various locations across the globe, the knowledge of crop cultivation spread rapidly. In fact, it was the nature of early agricultural methods that aided the extension of agricultural knowledge. An often-used agricultural method called **slash-and-burn cultivation** involved slashing the bark on trees and later burning the dead ones. The resulting ashes enriched the soil for a number of years. When the soil eventually lost its fertility, however, farmers were forced to move to new territory. By 6000 B.C.E., agriculture had spread to the eastern Mediterranean basin and the Balkans, reaching northern Europe about 4000 B.C.E. These frequent migrations exposed early farmers to new peoples, diffusing both agricultural knowledge and cultural values.

Characteristics of Early Agricultural Societies

Although agriculture required more work than foraging, it had the advantage of producing a more constant and substantial food supply. Consequently, the spread of agriculture not only increased cultural contacts but also produced significant population growth. As populations multiplied, neolithic peoples began to settle in villages. Members of agricultural communities had to cooperate, especially in constructing and maintaining irrigation systems. As villages grew and agriculture continued to supply an abundance of food, not all villagers were needed as farmers. Some inhabitants began to develop other talents and skills such as the manufacture of pottery, metal tools, textiles, wood products, and jewelry. Two early noteworthy agricultural settlements were:

- Jericho (established around 8000 B.C.E.) in present-day Israel. Here farmers produced wheat and barley, while also trading with neighboring peoples in obsidian and salt. Characteristic of Jericho was a thick wall designed to protect the wealthy settlement against raiders.
- Çatal Hüyük (established around 7000 B.C.E.) in Anatolia (present-day Turkey). Residents of this village left **artifacts** representing a variety of craft products indicating an extensive **specialization of labor**. They also traded obsidian with neighboring peoples.

Pastoralism

As agricultural communities arose, **pastoralism** developed in the grasslands of Africa and Eurasia. Pastoralists, or herders, contributed meat and other animal products to the overall food supply, further enlarging neolithic human populations. At times their overgrazing of livestock led to soil erosion. Both agricultural and pastoral peoples exchanged food products and technology.

Early Metallurgy

In addition to the development and spread of agriculture, the Neolithic Age witnessed the origins of metallurgy. The first metal that humans learned to use was copper, with which they cast items such as jewelry, weapons, and tools. Later, neolithic humans learned the use of other metals such as gold and bronze (an alloy of copper and tin), giving rise to the term Bronze Age for the later neolithic period. Still later, the knowledge of ironworking was developed independently in Central Asia and sub-Saharan Africa.

The Culture of Neolithic Societies

As human populations concentrated in permanent settlements, the specialization of labor as well as trade activity resulted in differing degrees of accumulation of wealth. As time progressed, differences in family wealth manifested themselves in the emergence of social classes.

The inhabitants of early agricultural societies observed their environment in order to further their knowledge of the factors necessary to produce a bountiful harvest. Their knowledge of the seasons in relation to the positions of heavenly bodies led eventually to the development of calendars. Interest in the natural world led neolithic humans to celebrate fertility and the cycles of life. Many agricultural and pastoral societies practiced **animism**, or the belief that divine spirits inhabited natural objects such as rocks and trees. In addition, archeologists have unearthed numerous figures representing pregnant goddesses in the ruins of neolithic villages.

The Beginnings of Cities

As population growth resulted in larger settlements, the agricultural world experienced the rise of cities. Urban areas offered further specialization of labor and more sophisticated technology. New roles emerged as cities required administrators, collectors of taxes and tribute, and religious leaders. Cities also acquired influence over larger territories than villages did.

› Rapid Review

The Neolithic Age saw independent origins of agriculture worldwide. As the knowledge of agriculture spread, cultural diffusion marked the ancient world. When crop cultivation produced increasingly larger yields, some farmers specialized in other tasks or crafts. As population concentrations grew increasingly dense, settlements grew into villages and, later, cities. Cities developed a more complex social structure to administer wealth, provide order, and study the meaning of life itself.

› Review Questions

1. Early agriculture in the Americas
   (A) developed as a result of cultural diffusion from the Eastern Hemisphere
   (B) featured the domestication of larger animals than in the Eastern Hemisphere
   (C) began later than in the Eastern Hemisphere
   (D) did not produce the wide variety of crops that the Eastern Hemisphere did
   (E) saw the rise of urbanization earlier than did the Eastern Hemisphere

2. The Agricultural Revolution
   (A) began with an extensive pattern of cultural diffusion
   (B) occurred about the same time throughout the world
   (C) was confined to nonwestern civilization
   (D) was an abrupt process beginning in 8000 B.C.E
   (E) saw the use of agricultural methods that encouraged migration

3. During the Agricultural Revolution, women
   (A) were confined to childbearing duties
   (B) participated in hunting activities with men
   (C) experienced a decrease in status
   (D) were not represented in neolithic art
   (E) observed and studied the agricultural environment

4. The Neolithic Age
   (A) saw the beginnings of urbanization
   (B) saw the process of agriculture carried out without the use of metal tools
   (C) produced societies without class distinctions
   (D) saw a decline in global populations
   (E) witnessed the end of nomadic societies

5. Early urban dwellers
   (A) were dominated by peoples in agricultural settlements
   (B) left the pursuit of religious practices to agricultural peoples
   (C) saw the need for a government
   (D) were exempt from taxation
   (E) were offered few opportunities to carry out specialized tasks

› Answers and Explanations

1. **C**—Agriculture in the Americas began around 5000 B.C.E., whereas that in the Eastern Hemisphere had begun at least 3000 years earlier. Agriculture in the Americas developed independently (A). Animals in the Americas were smaller than those in the Eastern Hemisphere (B). Although food crops in the Americas differed from those in the Eastern Hemisphere, a wide variety, including maize, squash, beans, and cacao, was produced (D). Urban areas such as those of Sumer predated urban areas in the Americas (E).

2. **E**—Slash-and-burn cultivation resulted in the migration of early agricultural peoples as the soil lost its fertility. The Agricultural Revolution developed independently throughout the world (A) and at different times (B). The beginning of agriculture was a gradual process (D) that occurred in both the Eastern and Western hemispheres, although at different times (C).

3. **E**—Women studied the growth of plants and became the first farmers. As such, they were not confined merely to childrearing duties (A). Men handled the more strenuous duties of hunting (B). Women's role as farmers and childbearers gave them an importance in neolithic society (C), a role that was represented in the fertility statues of the Neolithic Age (D).

4. **A**—The first cities arose in Sumer. Some neolithic societies used tools of copper, bronze, and later, iron (B). Societies were often stratified, with elite classes, peasants, and slaves (C). Because of the success of early agriculture, population rose rapidly worldwide during the Neolithic Age (D). Although many nomadic peoples changed to a settled lifestyle in the Neolithic Age, nomadism continues to the present (E).

5. **C**—Government arose from a need to cooperate in major projects such as irrigation and flood control. Early cities tended to embrace and extend their governments to nearby agricultural settlements (A). Religious leaders played a role in early cities (B), residents were required to pay taxes or tribute (D), and specialization of labor was commonplace (E).

Structure of Early Civilizations

IN THIS CHAPTER

Summary: As agricultural villages evolved into cities, some urban areas began to display the characteristics of civilizations (described in Chapter 5). The earliest civilizations in the Eastern Hemisphere arose in Mesopotamia, the Nile valley, the Indus valley, and the Huang He valley; civilizations arose later among the Olmecs in Mesoamerica (Middle America) and the Chavín in the Andes Mountains of South America.

Key Terms

covenant*	polytheism*
cuneiform*	Quetzalcóatl
diaspora*	Ten Commandments
hieroglyphics*	theocracy*
*jati**	Torah*
mandate of heaven*	untouchables*
matrilineal*	*Varna**
monotheism*	*Vedas**
oracle bones*	Yahweh*
patriarchal*	ziggurat*
pharaoh*	

Mesopotamia

The world's earliest civilization arose in the valley of the Tigris and Euphrates rivers in an area the Greeks called Mesopotamia ("Land Between the Rivers"). The cultural achievements of Mesopotamia represented independent innovation, achievements that it passed on to other river valley civilizations in Egypt and, especially, the Indus valley. Around 4000 B.C.E., the inhabitants of Mesopotamia used bronze and copper. By this time they had already invented the wheel and developed irrigation canals to farm the arid lands of their environment.

About 3500 B.C.E., a group of invaders called the Sumerians settled in the southernmost portion of Mesopotamia. The Sumerians developed the first example of writing. Called **cuneiform**, it involved pictures pressed into clay using a wedge-shaped stylus. The pictographs initially stood for objects, but later were refined to represent sounds. The Sumerians also developed a number system based on 60 and studied the movement of heavenly bodies. In architecture, the Sumerians expressed the glories of their civilization and of the many gods of nature that they worshipped by building towers called **ziggurats**. They are credited with relating the first epic in world history, *The Epic of Gilgamesh,* which includes a story of a great flood similar to that of the biblical account in Genesis.

The Tigris and Euphrates rivers were noted for their unpredictable and often violent flooding. Irrigation systems to control flooding and channel water for agricultural use required the cooperation of Mesopotamia's settlements. This need promoted the beginnings of government. Early Mesopotamian government was in the form of city-states, with a city government also controlling surrounding territory.

A social structure headed by rulers and elite classes controlled the land, which was farmed by slaves. Slaves could sometimes purchase their freedom. Sumerian families were **patriarchal**, with men dominating family and public life. Men had the authority to sell their wives and children into slavery to pay their debts. By the sixteenth century B.C.E., Mesopotamian women had begun to wear the veil in public. In spite of these restrictions, Mesopotamian women could sometimes gain influence in the courts, serve as priestesses, or act as scribes for the government. Some worked in small businesses.

A lack of natural protective barriers made Mesopotamia vulnerable to invasion by outsiders; most cities in the region constructed defensive walls. Frequent conflicts among local Sumerian kings over water and property rights weakened the city-states. The Sumerian culture later fell to conquest by the Akkadians and the Babylonians, both of whom spread Sumerian culture. The Babylonian king Hammurabi devised a code of laws that regulated daily life and also provided harsh "an eye for an eye" punishments for criminal offenses. *The Code of Hammurabi* drew distinctions between social classes and genders, administering less severe punishments to elite classes over commoners and men over women for the same offense. After 900 B.C.E., Assyrians and Persians dominated Mesopotamia.

Egypt

About 3000 B.C.E., a second civilization grew up along another river valley, this time the valley of the Nile River in present-day Egypt. In contrast to the unpredictable waters of the Tigris–Euphrates, those of the Nile overflowed once annually, discharging an amount of water that usually varied little from one year to the next. As in Mesopotamia, irrigation projects to channel floodwaters led to the organization of the community and ultimately to the development of political structures. Although several major cities emerged along the Nile, most Egyptian communities were agricultural villages engaged in local trade along the Nile.

The king of Egypt, or **pharaoh**, wielded considerable power. About 2700 B.C.E., the pharaohs began the construction of huge pyramids that served as tombs for themselves and their families. These tombs were decorated with colorful paintings. Like the Sumerians, the Egyptians were **polytheists**, or worshippers of many gods. Their belief in an afterlife led to the practice of mummification to preserve the bodies of pharaohs and, later, those of members of lower classes.

Egyptian society was composed of a number of defined social classes. Within this social structure, however, commoners could enter government service and rise in social status. Egyptian families were patriarchal, with men dominating households and community life. Among the royalty, however, women sometimes acted as regents for young rulers or as priestesses. Other educated women worked as scribes for the Egyptian government.

The Egyptians did not acquire the use of bronze tools and weapons until long after they had reached Mesopotamia. From the Nubian kingdom of Kush, a site of the independent innovation of ironworking, the Egyptians acquired iron implements.

The Egyptians engaged in some trade with the people of Mesopotamia and later with the kingdom of Kush to the south. Some historians believe that Egyptian picture writing, or **hieroglyphics**, was developed from Sumerian cuneiform as a result of trade contacts with Mesopotamia. Cultural diffusion from Egypt produced a Nubian civilization that incorporated Egyptian pyramids, writing, and religion into its own culture. In addition, the Nubian kingdom of Kush invaded Egypt in the eighth century B.C.E. and ruled the Egyptian people for about a century. Throughout most of its early history, however, surrounding deserts protected Egypt from contact with invading peoples, permitting its civilization to develop its own, unique characteristics.

The Indus Valley Civilization

By 2500 B.C.E., another advanced civilization had emerged along the Indus River in present-day Pakistan. Like the Tigris and Euphrates rivers, the Indus River was noted for its unpredictable and often violent pattern of flooding. Among the urban centers that arose along the Indus were Harappa and Mohenjo-Daro. Streets in both cities were laid out along a precise grid, and houses boasted running water and sewage systems.

Much of what historians know about the Indus valley civilization must come from archeological discoveries, because Harappan writing has yet to be deciphered. Archeological findings of Harappan artifacts in Mesopotamia indicate active trade between the peoples of the Indus valley and Sumer by way of the Persian Gulf. Around 1500 B.C.E., the Harappan civilization was overtaken by a group of Indo-European peoples called Aryans. The Harappan civilization which the Aryans conquered had already declined markedly, perhaps as a result of rivers changing their course or a natural disaster such as an earthquake. The blend of the traditional culture of the Indus valley people and that of the Aryans had a profound effect on the future course of Indian history.

Backgrounds of Classical India

The roots of classical India began during the invasions of the Aryans about 1500 B.C.E. From their original home in Central Asia, the Aryans brought a tradition of hunting and cattle-herding; after their arrival in South Asia, however, they adapted the agricultural methods of native peoples. Aryan iron tools facilitated their success in agriculture.

Although the people of the Harappan civilization of the Indus valley possessed a written language, the Aryans did not. Much of our knowledge of the Aryans comes from their oral epics, called the **Vedas**. The *Vedas* were later written down in the Sanskrit language, which remains a prominent language in India today. The influence of the *Vedas* is evident in the term applied to the early classical period of Indian culture, the Vedic Age (1500–1000 B.C.E.). The first Aryan epic, the *Rig-Veda,* is a collection of hymns in honor of the Aryan gods. Other epic literature which shaped Indian culture during the Epic Age (1000–600 B.C.E.) includes the *Ramayana*, the *Mahabharata* (considered the greatest epic poem of India), and the *Upanishads*, a collection of religious epic poems.

Aryan Society

Aryan society was based on a village organization composed of families with patriarchal control. Their society was further organized along a class system. When they invaded the Indus valley, the Aryans, who were fair-complexioned compared to the native people they conquered, perceived the people of the Indus valley as inferior. Therefore, they modified the class system with which they were already familiar in their society to define the new relationship between conqueror and conquered. Society was divided into four distinct classes, or *varna*, based on skin color:

- *Kshatriyas,* or warriors and rulers
- *Brahmins,* or priests
- *Vaisyas,* or merchants and farmers
- *Sudras,* or common workers

The first three classes were composed of Aryans, the fourth of the Dravidians, or the native people of India whom the Aryans encountered at the time of their invasion. During the Epic Age, the first two classes reversed in order of importance. At the very bottom of the social structure was a classless group of **untouchables**. Members of this group were involved in occupations perceived as distasteful, such as handling waste products, carrying out the dead, or butchering animals. As the classes became hereditary they became castes, or rigid social classes that seldom permitted social mobility. Within each caste were numerous subcastes, or *jati*, that further defined Indian society.

The Aryans also introduced to Indian culture their own array of gods and goddesses. Part of their belief system was the veneration of some animals, particularly cattle.

The Shang

The most isolated of the four river valley civilizations was that of the Huang He valley in present-day China. Although the people of the Huang He valley dwelled in a region isolated by deserts, mountains (the Himalayas), and seas, they did engage in some trade with Southwest Asia and South Asia.

The earliest Chinese dynasty that left written records was the Shang dynasty (1766–1122 B.C.E.). A key element of the Shang period was the knowledge of bronze metallurgy. This knowledge, which came to China from Southwest Asia by means of Indo-European migrations, strengthened the Shang war machine. Around 1000 B.C.E., the Shang also became familiar with ironworking. Shang rule was further empowered by the need for central rule to oversee irrigation and flood-control projects along the Huang He River.

During the Shang period, a number of walled cities arose. These urban areas served as cultural, military, and economic centers. Elaborate palaces and tombs were built for Shang rulers.

Examples of early Chinese writing are apparent from a custom of divination using **oracle bones**. When a person sought the advice of the gods on an issue, he or she would visit an oracle, who would scratch the person's question on an animal bone or shell, then heat it. When the oracle bone cracked from the heat, the oracle read the cracks to determine the message from the gods.

Shang society was stratified, with classes of ruling elites, artisans, peasants, and slaves. Families were patriarchal, and the veneration of ancestors was common. The **matrilineal** society that characterized China before the rule of the Shang gradually eroded until women held positions subordinate to those of men.

The Shang dynasty eventually succumbed to the Zhou about 1122 B.C.E. The Zhou claimed that they overthrew the Shang by the will of the gods, which they termed the "**mandate of heaven**." Under the rule of the Zhou, the tradition of central authority that first took root under the Shang continued.

Mesoamerica and Andean South America

Civilizations in the Americas rose later than the river valley civilizations. The civilizations of Mesoamerica and the early societies of the Andes Mountains of South America did not develop in the valleys of major rivers, but rather in a region of smaller rivers and streams near ocean coastlines. Furthermore, the people of the Americas did not know the use of the wheel, nor did they possess large animals to serve as beasts of burden or work animals; the llama of the Andes Mountains was the largest work animal in the Americas from the time of the earliest civilizations until the arrival of the Europeans in the fifteenth century. Human muscle accomplished physical labor in the Americas.

Early Mesoamerican people such as the Olmecs, and later the Maya, constructed lavish pyramids and temples. Like the inhabitants of the river valley civilizations, the people of the Americas were polytheistic, worshipping many gods of nature. Society was stratified, with distinctions among the elite classes of rulers and priests and those of commoners and slaves.

Early Mesoamerican societies provided numerous examples of cultural diffusion. In addition to the transmission of the cultivation of maize, terraced pyramids were commonplace. Regional inhabitants fashioned calendars, the most elaborate being that of the Mayan civilization. The Mayans also had a ball game played on a court. The societies of Mesoamerica also shared the legend of **Quetzalcóatl**, a god who would someday return to rule his people in peace.

In South America, geography and the lack of large pack animals largely prevented communication between the Andean societies and those of Mesoamerica. The cultivation of maize did spread to the Andes, however, while copper metallurgy traveled northward to Mesoamerica. About 900 B.C.E., the Chavín civilization arose in the Andean highlands of present-day Peru. Characterized by a religion that worshipped gods representing crocodiles, snakes, and jaguars, the Chavín built complex temples to honor their gods. Their civilization was located along trade routes that connected western coastal regions to the Amazon rain forest. For a few centuries, Chavín religious unity and trade connections provided a degree of cultural identity to Andean peoples. The rugged terrain of the Andes, however, prevented a central government from unifying the Andean states.

The Hebrews

Along the eastern coast of the Mediterranean Sea lived the Hebrews, another people who profoundly influenced the course of world history.

The concept of **monotheism**, or the worship of one god, is attributed to the Hebrews, or Jews. The Hebrews traced their origins back to Abraham, who is said to have migrated from Mesopotamia to the land of Canaan on the eastern shores of the Mediterranean about 2000 B.C.E. In the account recorded in the Bible, the descendants of Abraham migrated to Egypt. They later left Egypt, embarking on a journey called the Exodus under a leader named Moses. In the biblical account, the Exodus was marked by the giving of the **Ten Commandments**, or moral law of the Hebrews. Returning to the land of Canaan, or Palestine, they established a **theocracy**, or a government ruled directly by God.

The heart of Judaism was a **covenant**, or agreement, between God and Abraham in which **Yahweh** would be their god and the Jews would be his people. The history of this covenant relationship became the basis of the **Torah**, or the Hebrew scriptures.

After years of observing the governments of neighboring kingdoms, the Hebrews established the kingdom of Israel about 1000 B.C.E. with is capital at Jerusalem. The kingdom eventually divided into two kingdoms. The northern kingdom of Israel fell to the Assyrians in 722 B.C.E. Its inhabitants were scattered throughout the far reaches of the Assyrian empire, constituting the first Jewish **diaspora**, or exile. The southern kingdom, called Judah, endured until 586 B.C.E. Conquered by the Chaldeans (from approximately the same territory as the Babylonian Empire), the people of Judah were carried off into captivity into Babylon. After Cyrus conquered the Chaldeans and allowed the Jews to return to Palestine 70 years later, Palestine remained under Persian rule until it became the province of Judea under the Roman Empire in 63 C.E. In 132 C.E., after they rebelled against Roman rule, the Jews were spread throughout the Roman Empire in a second diaspora.

❯ Rapid Review

Beginning with Sumer in Mesopotamia about 3500 B.C.E., civilization grew along the river valleys of the Tigris–Euphrates, Nile, Indus, and Huang He. These civilizations were characterized by community cooperation necessary to manage irrigation and flood control systems. Later their cooperative efforts were further organized to form the beginnings of political institutions. The knowledge of metallurgy led to the refinement of tools, weapons, and objects of art. Writing systems were developed, and social stratification became apparent. In the Americas, civilizations and societies made notable strides in mathematics, astronomy, and architecture.

❯ Review Questions

1. The Egyptian civilization was similar to the Sumerian civilization
   (A) in its reliance on natural defense barriers
   (B) in its system of social stratification
   (C) in its political structure
   (D) in the extent to which its culture was diffused
   (E) in the nature of the flood pattern of its major rivers

2. The earliest civilizations in both the Eastern and Western hemispheres were similar in
   (A) their location at similar latitudes
   (B) their technological knowledge
   (C) their reliance on the flooding of major rivers in their midst
   (D) their practice of polytheism
   (E) the extent of their trade contacts with neighboring peoples

3. The Indus valley civilization
   (A) relied heavily on communal planning
   (B) is best studied through its written records
   (C) was isolated from other river valley civilizations because of surrounding mountains
   (D) declined after the arrival of Aryan invaders
   (E) shared similar flood control concerns with the Egyptians

4. The early civilization with the least developed technology was
   (A) Mesoamerican
   (B) Harappan
   (C) Egyptian
   (D) Sumerian
   (E) Shang

5. The roots of classical India included
   (A) the Aryan written language, or Sanskrit
   (B) the egalitarian Aryan society
   (C) Aryan agricultural knowledge
   (D) a society united by *jati*
   (E) Vedic traditional literature

6. Shang China
   (A) developed numerous artistic works even though they did not know the use of metals
   (B) left no decipherable written records
   (C) was prevented by natural barriers from trading with other early civilizations.
   (D) contributed to the development of central government in China.
   (E) was less urbanized than the Nile valley civilization.

7. Early societies of South America
   (A) were unified under a central government
   (B) were challenged by geographic limitations
   (C) developed societies that had no knowledge of metals
   (D) traded widely with regions to their north
   (E) built upon Mesoamerican cultural traditions

8. Results of cultural diffusion among early civilizations included
   (A) the invention of the wheel
   (B) the legend of Quetzalcóatl
   (C) the cultivation of potatoes
   (D) Harappan sewage systems
   (E) none of the above

› Answers and Explanations

1. **B**—Both Egypt and Sumer had societies comprising various social classes of the elite, peasants, and slaves. Whereas Egypt enjoyed natural defense barriers, Sumer did not (A). Sumer was governed by kings of local city-states, whereas the Egyptian pharaoh was the supreme ruler (C). Although the Egyptians largely developed themselves culturally, Sumerian culture was widely diffused by later conquerors (D). The Nile River flooding was predictable, whereas that of the Tigris and Euphrates rivers was not (E).

2. **D**—All the earliest agricultural civilizations worshipped many gods. They were located in different latitudes (A) and enjoyed different levels of technology (B). The civilizations of the Western Hemisphere did not rely on the flooding of rivers (C). Trade in China and Andean civilizations and societies was limited (E).

3. **A**—The presence of granaries and well-planned street grids in the cities of the Harappan civilization of the Indus valley is evidence of considerable community planning. The writing of the Harappan civilization is so far undecipherable (B). Indus valley peoples bypassed mountain barriers and traded by sea (C). Their civilization had already declined markedly before the arrival of the Aryans (D). Flood patterns of the Indus were unpredictable, whereas those of Egypt were predictable (E).

4. **A**—Early Mesoamerican civilizations did not even have the knowledge of the wheel, whereas the other civilizations mentioned did not have to rely only on human muscle for construction or irrigation projects.

5. **E**—The traditions of the *Vedas* became an integral part of Indian society. Sanskrit, the language of the Aryans, was originally an oral language only (A). Aryan society consisted of a number of classes based on skin color, which would become the foundation of the Hindu caste system (B). Aryans were nomadic peoples who learned of agriculture from the Dravidian people of India (C). The society of classical India was divided by the *jati*, or subcastes of the Hindu caste system (D).

6. **D**—The Shang brought the settlements of northern China under the control of a centralized government. Shang dynasty artisans worked extensively in bronze (A). The Shang were the first Chinese dynasty to leave written records (B). Although natural barriers lessened trade, the Shang carried out some trade with South Asia and Southwest Asia (C). A number of cities arose in China under the Shang (E).

7. **B**—The rugged Andean terraine hindered political unity. Early South American societies were organized into local governments (A) and knew the use of copper (C). Trade with the north was limited because of geographical barriers (D), preventing South American societies from building upon the traditions of Mesoamerica (E).

8. **B**—The legend of Quetzalcóatl diffused throughout early Mesoamerican cultures and civilizations. The invention of the wheel (A) was an independent contribution of the Sumerians. The cultivation of potatoes (C) was limited to the early Andean societies and civilizations. Harappan sewage systems (D) were unique to the people of the Indus valley civilization.

Period 1 Summary: Technological and Environmental Transformations (to c. 600 B.C.E.)

Timeline

8000 B.C.E.	First agricultural villages
4000 B.C.E.	First cities
	Beginning of the cultivation of maize in Mesoamerica
3200 B.C.E.	Beginning of Sumerian dominance of Mesopotamia
3000 B.C.E.	Beginning of agriculture in South America
	Beginning of agriculture in New Guinea
3000 B.C.E.–1000 C.E.	Indo-European migrations
2600-2500 B.C.E.	Pyramid construction in Egypt
2500-2000 B.C.E.	Height of Harappan society in South Asia
2350 B.C.E.	Beginning of regional empires in Mesopotamia
2200 B.C.E.	Beginning of Chinese dynastic rule
2000 B.C.E.	Beginning of the Bantu migrations
1500 B.C.E.	Beginning of Aryan migrations to South Asia
1500-500 B.C.E.	Vedic Age in South Asia
1500 B.C.E.–700 C.E.	Austronesian migrations
1000-970 B.C.E.	Rule of Hebrew King David
900 B.C.E.	Invention of ironworking in sub-Saharan Africa
800 B.C.E.	Establishment of Greek *poleis*
722 B.C.E.	Assyrian conquest of Israel
586 B.C.E.	New Babylonian (Chaldean) conquest of Judah

Key Comparisons

1. Early agriculture in the Eastern Hemisphere versus the Western Hemisphere
2. Pastoral nomadism versus settled lifestyles
3. Political, economic, and social characteristics of the four river valley civilizations
4. Early civilizations of the Eastern and Western hemispheres

Change/Continuity Chart

KEY IDEA

REGION	POLITICAL	ECONOMIC	SOCIAL	CHANGES	CONTINUITIES
East Asia	Dynastic rule Era of the Warring States Mandate of heaven	Rice, millet Bronze crafts Ironworking	Patriarchal societies Oracle bones Stratified society Urbanization	Irrigation Agriculture Bronze metallurgy	Agriculture
Southeast Asia	Regional kingdoms and empires	Root crops Fruit Trade with South Asia	Villages	Agriculture	Agriculture
Oceania	Regional kingdoms	Foraging	Polytheism Animism Tribal organization	Austronesian migrations	Foraging
Central Asia	Tribal governments	Nomadism Trade facilitators	Indo-European migrations	Trade with settled societies	Pastoral nomadism
South Asia	Community planning Aryan invasions	Grains Sewer systems Trade with Sumer	Urbanization Patriarchal societies *Vedas* Sanskrit	Decline of Harappan civilization Regional empires Aryan society	Agriculture Interest in technological advancement Active trade
Southwest Asia	Mesopotamian city-states Code of Hammurabi Kingdom of Israel Persian Empire	Grains Wheel Cuneiform Trade with Indus Valley and Egypt	Urbanization Polytheism Stratified society Slavery Judaism *Epic of Gilgamesh* Phoenician alphabet	Ironworking in Anatolia City-states to empires Conquests of Israel and Judah	Agriculture Irrigation Trade

Region					
North Africa	Pharaohs Kingdoms of Egypt and Kush	Barley Trade with Sumer and Persia Ironworking	Urbanization Village life along the Nile Pyramids Hieroglyphics Polytheism Stratified society	Long-distance trade	Regional kingdoms
Sub-Saharan Africa	Tribal government Regional kingdoms	Root crops Trans-Saharan trade	Polytheism Animism Ancestor veneration Slavery	Sub-Saharan trade Bantu migrations	Regional kingdoms Polytheism
Western Europe	Village governments Greek city-states	Cereal agriculture Ironworking	Agricultural villages Olympic Games	Indo-European migrations	Foraging Agriculture
Eastern Europe	Village governments Greek colonization	Cereal agriculture Ironworking	Agricultural villages	Indo-European migrations	Foraging Agriculture
North America	Tribal government	Foraging Nomadism Cultivation of maize	Village organization Polytheism Shamanism	Migration from Asia Agriculture	Village life Nomadism Polytheism Shamanism
Latin America	City-states Regional governments Andean kingdoms	Limited trade Foraging Cultivation of maize	Stratified society Slavery	Agriculture Olmec civilization Chavín culture	Mesoamerican traditions

PERIOD 2

Organization and Reorganization of Human Societies (c. 600 B.C.E.—c. 600 C.E.)

CHAPTER 8

Rise of Classical Civilizations

IN THIS CHAPTER

Summary: Classical civilizations, defined as those that had enduring influence over vast numbers of people, emerged in China, India, and the Mediterranean region. The first of the classical civilizations began in China. Three Chinese **dynasties** made their mark on the values of traditional Chinese civilization: the Zhou, the Qin, and the Han. In India, the rulers of the Gupta dynasty ushered in the golden age of Indian history. The classical Mediterranean civilizations of Greece and Rome developed political, scientific, and philosophical thought that formed the basis of Western civilization.

KEY IDEA

Key Terms
An asterisk (*) denotes items listed in the glossary.

Alexander the Great	mystery religion*
aristocracy*	*Pax Romana* *
Aristotle	*polis* *
artisan*	*sati* *
democracy*	Silk Roads*
dynasty*	stoicism*
geocentric theory*	Twelve Tables*
Hellenistic Age*	Zoroastrianism*
Indo-Europeans*	

Classical China

The Zhou

Claiming that they possessed the mandate of heaven, or the approval of the gods, the Zhou began to dominate China after the fall of the Shang dynasty. The mandate of heaven would be claimed by future Chinese dynasties as a rationalization for their authority to rule. In power from 1029 to 258 B.C.E., the Zhou:

- Took steps to further centralize the Chinese government.
- Expanded Chinese territory to include the Yangtze River valley. This southern river valley added a fertile rice-growing area to the already rich wheat-producing regions of northern China.
- Produced emperors, calling themselves "Sons of Heaven," who lived lives of luxury.
- Standardized the spoken language.

The Qin

After a period of civil disorder known as the Era of the Warring States, the Zhou were replaced by the Qin dynasty. Under the Qin (221–202 B.C.E.):

- The name of the dynasty, Qin, was applied to the country of China.
- Chinese territory expanded southward as far as northern Vietnam.
- A defensive wall that became the nucleus of the Great Wall was constructed.
- Weights, measures, and coinage were standardized.
- A common written language was standardized.
- The manufacture of silk cloth was encouraged.
- New roads were constructed.

The Han

In 200 B.C.E., the Qin were replaced by the Han, who ruled until 220 C.E. During the rule of the Han dynasty:

- The governmental bureaucracy (ranks of employees) grew stronger.
- Chinese territory expanded into Central Asia, Korea, and Indochina.
- The Chinese civil service exam began.
- Trade along the **Silk Roads** increased.
- A time of peace settled across China.
- Chinese traditions were reinforced through the strengthening of patriarchal society in which the father and other male members of the family were in positions of authority.
- The government oversaw iron production.
- The government sponsored and maintained canals and irrigation systems.
- Society was further stratified, consisting of an elite class (including the educated governmental bureaucracy), peasants and **artisans**, and unskilled laborers (including a small number of slaves).
- Agriculture was improved by the invention of ox-drawn plows and a collar that prevented choking in draft animals.
- Paper was manufactured for the first time.
- Water-powered mills were invented.

Under the Han, the people of China enjoyed a level of culture significantly more advanced than that of other civilizations and societies at that time, a distinction it would maintain until the fifteenth century. So vital were the accomplishments of the Han to Chinese culture that even today the Chinese call themselves the "People of Han."

Classical India

The cultural and social structures of the Vedic and Epic ages formed the basis of the classical civilization of India. Around 600 B.C.E., northern India was divided into sixteen states; one state, Magadha, became prominent. In 327 B.C.E., **Alexander the Great** of Macedonia reached into the Indian subcontinent as far as the Indus River, where he set up a border state, which he called Bactria. Five years later the Mauryan dynasty was founded by a soldier named Chandragupta, an autocratic ruler who developed a large bureaucracy and a large army in addition to promoting trade and communication. Mauryan rulers were the first to unify most of the Indian subcontinent.

The most prominent of the Mauryan rulers was Ashoka (269–232 B.C.E.), the grandson of Chandragupta. Under Ashoka, all of the Indian subcontinent except for the southern tip came under Mauryan control. Known for the brutality of his conquests, Ashoka later moderated his behavior and values, embracing the tolerance and nonviolence of Buddhism while also respecting the values of Hinduism. Like his grandfather Chandragupta, Ashoka encouraged trade and constructed an extensive system of roads, complete with rest areas for travelers. Along these roads, which connected with the Silk Roads, Ashoka spread the ideas of Buddhism.

Ashoka's influence was insufficient to prevent India from dividing into a number of states once again after his death. Invaders from the northwest, the Kushans, ruled India until 220 C.E. Their rule was followed in 320 C.E. by the Guptas, who ushered in the golden age of Indian history.

Gupta India

In contrast to the Mauryans, the Gupta rulers were Hindus. As a result, during Gupta rule, the caste system and the influence of the Brahmins were reinforced. Because of the strict divisions of the caste system, slavery was not widespread. Although Hinduism was the religion of the ruling dynasty, Buddhism was tolerated and Buddhist monks and nuns spread their influence through urban monasteries. The Gupta style of rule was not as centralized as that of the Mauryan Empire, and local rulers were permitted to maintain authority in their respective territories if they submitted to the ultimate rule of the Guptas. Other accomplishments and features of the Gupta dynasty included:

- High-towered temples in honor of the Hindu gods.
- Lavish wall paintings in caves dedicated to the gods. A key example is the Caves of Ajanta in central India.
- The growth of Sanskrit as the language of the educated.
- The discovery of zero as a place holder and the development of "Arabic" numerals, the number system used throughout most of the world today. An innovation of Gupta India, Arabic numerals were so called by the Western world because they were carried from India to the West by means of Arabic caravans.
- The development of the decimal system.
- The strengthening of trade, especially between East and Southeast Asia.
- The deterioration in the status of women; society became increasingly patriarchal. Women gradually lost their right to inherit or own property and were married at a younger age. The custom of *sati* was practiced in some parts of India. *Sati* involved the practice of a widow throwing herself on her husband's funeral pyre. The custom was alleged to bestow honor and purity upon the widow.

- Inoculation against smallpox and sterilization during surgery and in the treatment of wounds.
- Knowledge of plastic surgery and the setting of bones.
- Advances in astronomy such as the prediction of eclipses and the identification of planets.
- The classic Hindu temple complete with courtyards, paintings, and sculptures appeared.

The achievements and knowledge of the Gupta remained part of Indian culture long after the decline of their dynasty.

Persia and the Classical World

Before turning to a discussion of classical Mediterranean civilization, it is necessary to discuss one of the cultures that would significantly influence Mediterranean societies: that of the Persians. The Persians (inhabiting a territory approximate to present-day Iran) counted among the heirs of ancient Mesopotamian civilization. In 550 B.C.E., the Persian conqueror Cyrus the Great had established an empire that encompassed the northern part of Southwest Asia and a portion of northwestern India. The Persian empire was noted for its tolerance toward the customs of conquered peoples. The Persians introduced a new religion called **Zoroastrianism** that held to a belief in a system of rewards and punishments in the afterlife. They spread the knowledge of iron metallurgy throughout their empire and engaged in an active long-distance trade that linked India, Southwest Asia, and Egypt. The Persian Royal Road, complete with relay stations, was a 1600-mile highway linking remote portions of the empire. Persian trade contacts with Greece encouraged artistic and philosophical exchange as well.

Classical Civilization in the Mediterranean: Greece

In addition to the role played by the Persians, the culture of a number of societies in the Mediterranean blended to bring about the civilization of Greece. The island of Crete southeast of the Greek mainland was in contact with the Egyptian civilization by the year 2000 B.C.E. The early Greek civilization, known as Mycenaea, was influenced by that of Crete through contacts with traders in the region. The Greeks were an **Indo-European** people who migrated to the southern portion of the Greek peninsula about 1700 B.C.E. A second wave of Indo-Europeans called the Dorians invaded about 1100 B.C.E., destroying the Mycenaean civilization.

About 800 B.C.E., Phoenician mariners sailed into the Aegean Sea to the east of the Greek mainland. The Phoenicians were largely a seafaring people whose need for accurate recordkeeping in their commercial transactions led them to develop an alphabet of 22 letters representing consonants. The Greeks adapted the Phoenician alphabet, adding symbols for vowel sounds to give the people of the Greek peninsula a common language.

The Importance of Geography

Geography was an important determining factor in the course of Greek history. Separated by mountains and hills, the Greek peninsula was left with little available farmland. At the same time, the peninsula's irregular coastline provided relatively easy access to the sea for Greek settlements. Fishing and trading in the waters of the Aegean became another source to increase the supply of food and other products the Greeks could not provide themselves.

The City-State

The rugged terrain also prevented the easy centralization of communities or government. Greek political organization was based on the city-state, or *polis*, consisting of a city and the surrounding countryside, both under the influence of one government. The two most prominent city-states were Sparta and Athens. Sparta's aristocratic government focused on creating a strong military state, which depended upon the labor of slaves. Athens, by contrast, was initially an aristocracy, but gradually allowed its inhabitants self-rule. The height of Athenian **democracy** occurred during the rule of the aristocrat Pericles (443–429 B.C.E.), and was also considered the golden age of Athens for its achievements in science, philosophy, and the arts. Whereas Sparta's economic life relied on agriculture, the Athenians relied on the sea for their livelihood and engaged in an active trade across the Aegean. The people of Athens, to whom education and artistic expression were important, also depended heavily on slaves. From 500 to 449 B.C.E., Athens and Sparta joined forces to defeat a series of Persian invasions.

After the Persian Wars, Athens grew from a *polis* to an empire. Its dominant status aroused distrust among other *poleis,* including Sparta. From 431 to 404 B.C.E., Athens and Sparta and their allies fought each other for dominance in the Peloponnesian Wars. When Athens suffered a devastating plague during the course of the war, the once proud and flourishing *polis* questioned why its gods had allowed such a great tragedy. The weakened Athens saw defeat at the hands of Sparta.

During the eighth century B.C.E., the population of the Greek city-states increased tremendously, leading the Greeks to seek additional territory. As a result, the Greeks established a number of colonies in Sicily, southern Italy, the eastern Mediterranean, and the Black Sea. These new settlements allowed the Greeks the opportunity to trade grapes and olive oil for products that their rugged terrain could not produce in sufficient quantities, including fish, grain, and honey. Colonies not only served as outlets for population; they also transmitted Greek culture throughout the Mediterranean world.

The Culture of Classical Greece

Throughout the classical period, the various Greek city-states, although often rivals, at the same time shared a common culture. Numerous gods and goddesses, who often displayed human characteristics, formed the basis of Greek religion. The Olympic Games, first held in 776 B.C.E., brought together athletes from across the Greek peninsula to honor their gods. Drama was an integral feature of Greek culture; tragedies explored the relationship between the limitations of humans and the expectations of the gods, whereas comedies often satirized public officials.

Greek philosophy emphasized the power of human reason. The philosopher **Aristotle** wrote on a variety of subjects in politics, arts, and the sciences and became a model of Greek thought by constructing arguments through the use of logic.

Alexander the Great and the Hellenistic Age

When the Greek city-states, or *poleis,* weakened because of their internal conflict in the Peloponnesian War, they captured the attention of Philip, the ruler of the kingdom of Macedon to the north of Greece. When Philip's plans to conquer the Greek *poleis* were cut short by his death, however, his son Alexander stepped in to carry out his father's ambitions. By the time of his death in 323 B.C.E. at the age of 33, Alexander (known as "The Great") had conquered not only the Greek *poleis* but also Egypt, Syria, and Palestine as well as Persia. In South Asia, Alexander proceeded as far as the Punjab across the Indus River when his troops refused to proceed any farther.

Throughout the territories he controlled, Alexander established cities, many named Alexandria in his honor. In order to blend the cultures of Persia and Greece, he married a Persian woman and encouraged his officers to do the same. On his death, however, Alexander's empire was divided among his generals. In spite of these divisions, a relative balance of power was maintained among the remnants of Alexander's former empire as the Greek culture served as its unifying force.

The period of Alexander's rule and that of his generals has been termed the **Hellenistic Age**, named after the influence of the Hellenes, as the Greeks called themselves. The Hellenistic Age was characterized by a blend of the cultures of Greece and the Middle East, particularly Persia. Long-distance trade flourished, establishing communications from the Greek homeland to parts of South Asia and North Africa. Hellenistic philosophy sought personal satisfaction and tranquility. The most popular school of Hellenistic philosophy was **stoicism**. Stoicism taught that men and women should use their powers of reason to lead virtuous lives and to assist others. **Mystery religions** taught that believers who followed their practices would be rewarded with a blissful life in the afterworld. The culture of the Hellenistic world would be adopted by another classical Mediterranean culture, that of the Romans. Among the achievements of the Hellenistic world were:

- Euclidean geometry
- The Pythagorean Theorem
- Studies of human anatomy and physiology by Galen
- The calculation of the circumference of the earth by Eratosthenes

In spite of the significant achievements of scientists and mathematicians of the Hellenistic world, one significant error was promoted during the same era. Contrary to the traditions of Southwest Asia, the Hellenistic astronomer Ptolemy expounded a theory of the nature of the universe which placed the earth at its center. His **geocentric theory**, although incorrect, was widely accepted as truth by the West until the scientific revolution of the seventeenth century.

Classical Civilization in the Mediterranean: Rome

The Hellenistic period ended in 146 B.C.E. with the conquest of the Greek peninsula by Rome. Rome began as a kingdom in central Italy about 800 B.C.E. In 509 B.C.E., the Roman monarch was deposed by the **aristocracy**. The resulting Roman republic began a period of expansion in the Mediterranean world. The defeat of the Phoenician city of Carthage in North Africa during the Punic Wars (264–246 B.C.E.) made Rome master of the Mediterranean Sea. The strong military tradition of the Romans led to power struggles among generals. When one of them, Julius Caesar, came to power in 45 B.C.E., the structures of the Roman republic began to dissolve.

Rome Becomes an Empire

When a conspiracy assassinated Julius Caesar in 44 B.C.E., a period of civil disorder followed, which culminated in 27 B.C.E. with the rule of Octavian, or Augustus Caesar, the grandnephew of Julius Caesar. The period from 27 B.C.E. to 180 C.E. was known as the *Pax Romana*, or Roman Peace. During this more than 200-year period of peace and prosperity:

- A system of public works, including bridges, aqueducts, and roads, served all parts of the empire. Roman roads and sea lanes connected the Roman empire with the Silk Roads of Central Asia.
- Highway banditry decreased.
- A common language, Latin, promoted unity within the empire.
- A common coinage facilitated trade.
- Stadiums were constructed to provide entertainment, such as gladiator contests, for Roman citizens.
- Jesus was born in the Roman province of Judea. The new religion of Christianity spread easily, in part because of the Roman roads.

Roman Government

During the days of the Roman republic, government was centered around the Senate, which was composed primarily of members of the aristocracy. The executive resided in two consuls. When crises occurred, the Senate could appoint a dictator who could hold emergency powers for a period up to 6 months. During the republic, laws were codified, or written down, in the **Twelve Tables**.

Under the Roman Empire, conquered peoples in various parts of the empire were generally allowed a considerable measure of self-rule unless they rebelled against the authority of the emperor. Many inhabitants in conquered provinces, especially those geographically close to Rome, were granted citizenship.

Roman Law

The most lasting contribution of Rome was its system of laws. From the tradition of the Twelve Tables came a desire to extend Roman standards of justice throughout the empire. Among the legal principles established by the Romans were:

- The concept that a defendant is innocent unless proven guilty by a court of law
- The right of defendants to confront their accusers in a court of law
- The right of judges to set aside laws that were unjust

Roman law served to unite not only the peoples of the vast empire, but also left a lasting impact on Western legal tradition.

Roman Culture

Much of the culture of the Romans was adopted from that of the Greeks. The Greek alphabet, a gift of the Phoenicians, was passed on to the Romans, who modified the letters and transmitted the alphabet throughout the various parts of their empire. Many aspects of Greek rational thought, including the works of Aristotle and the philosophical school of Stoicism, became part of Roman life. Greek gods and goddesses, renamed by the Romans, found their way into Roman religious beliefs. Although the Romans were credited with the development of massive arches designed to handle the weight of heavy structures, the architecture of Rome was more a case of cultural diffusion from the Greeks than one of independent invention.

Everyday Life in Greece and Rome

In both classical Mediterranean societies, families were patriarchal, although women in the elite classes of Rome often wielded considerable influence within the family itself. In both Greece and Rome, women sometimes owned property and small businesses. In matters of law, however, women had fewer rights than men. Even Aristotle felt that women should be kept in a subordinate role.

Slavery was commonplace in both Greece and Rome. Aristotle attempted to justify slavery, believing that it was necessary to a thriving society. In some Greek *poleis*, such as Sparta, slaves performed agricultural tasks. In Athens, slaves labored in the silver mines and as household servants. Roman slaves made up as much as one-third of the population. In fact, among the reasons for Roman expansion was the acquisition of slaves from among conquered peoples. Some Roman slaves were used to mine iron and precious metals. Other slaves carried out household duties. Especially prized were educated Greek slaves, who became tutors for the children of Rome's elite class. Slave labor was so widely used by both Greeks and Romans that neither culture found much need for technological advances as labor-saving devices. As a result, the Mediterranean world fell behind the technological level of China and India in the areas of agriculture and manufacturing.

American Civilization

The Maya civilization of the Yucatán Peninsula and present-day Guatemala and Belize reached its height about 300 C.E., building on the cultural traditions of the societies of Mesoamerica. Termed the "Greeks of the Americas" because of their exploration of numerous branches of learning, the Maya:

- Developed a system of writing based on pictographs, or glyphs
- Understood the value of zero as a placeholder
- Studied astronomy and predicted eclipses
- Calculated the length of the year within a few seconds of its actual length

The Maya political organization consisted of small city-states ruled by kings who often fought against one another. Prisoners of war usually ended up as slaves or as sacrifices to the Maya gods.

To the north of the Maya homeland, in the Valley of Mexico, the grand and heavily populated city of Teotihuacán featured pyramids, public buildings decorated with murals, and active marketplaces. The city also served as a center of long-distance trade with coastal peoples and Mayas. To the south of Maya lands, the Mochica people established cities in the central Andes during the first millennium C.E. Inhabitants of these cities cooperated to construct irrigation systems.

❯ Rapid Review

Classical civilizations in China, India, and the Mediterranean forged lasting institutions in their respective regions. China created a complex bureaucracy based on the traditions of family and education. In India, cultural diversity prevailed while a caste system gradually evolved to rigidly organize this diversity. In the Mediterranean, rational thought and the rule of law prevailed during the dominance of the Greeks followed by the Romans.

› Review Questions

1. All of the following Chinese traditions and achievements began under the Han dynasty EXCEPT
   (A) expansion into Central Asia
   (B) paper manufacture
   (C) the civil service exam
   (D) Confucian philosophy
   (E) bureaucratic government

2. The Maya civilization
   (A) was a byproduct of cultural diffusion from earlier Mesoamerican societies
   (B) had a stratified society
   (C) developed a city-state political structure
   (D) all of the above
   (E) none of the above

3. From the time of the Roman republic to the *Pax Romana*
   (A) Rome became increasingly democratic
   (B) the Roman civilization became increasingly weaker
   (C) the territory of Rome continued to expand
   (D) Roman citizenship became increasingly rare
   (E) Greek influence upon Rome became less pronounced

4. Under both the Han and Roman empires
   (A) imperial roads were connected to the Silk Roads
   (B) new territories were added to the empires
   (C) a time of peace settled over both empires
   (D) enduring cultural traditions were established
   (E) all of the above

5. The Hellenistic empire of Alexander
   (A) continued the competition with Persia begun under the Greek *poleis*
   (B) was successful in curbing foreign influence upon Greece
   (C) produced theories that accurately explained the nature of the universe
   (D) blended Mediterranean and Middle Eastern cultures
   (E) strengthened its hold upon the Mediterranean world after Alexander's death

6. During the Gupta dynasty
   (A) Arabic numerals originated in India.
   (B) slavery increased.
   (C) Hinduism and Buddhism became the official religions of India.
   (D) the government of India became more centralized
   (E) the status of women improved

7. The Persians
   (A) were noted for their harsh treatment toward conquered peoples
   (B) continued the traditions of ancient Mesopotamia
   (C) introduced a new religion similar to the structure of Hinduism
   (D) failed to establish a unified empire
   (E) focused their commercial activity on trade with China

8. Greek society
   (A) was unified by the geography of the Greek peninsula
   (B) was disrupted by the conquest of Alexander
   (C) was extended through overseas colonization
   (D) extended the democratic ideal by relying on free labor alone
   (E) organized its faith around a monotheistic religion

› Answers and Explanations

1. **D**—Confucian philosophy was introduced after the fall of the Zhou dynasty. The Han dynasty expanded Chinese territory, including adding territory from Central Asia (A). Paper manufacture was developed (B) and the civil service exam was (C) introduced under the Han. Chinese government under the Han depended on the use of administrators to assist in governing its vast empire (E).

2. **D**—The Mayans adopted their calendar, the cultivation of maize, the legend of Quetzalcóatl, and other features of earlier Mesoamerican civilizations (A). They had a society composed of several social classes (B) and organized their government around several local city-states (C).

3. **C**—The territory of the Roman Empire expanded greatly during this time period. Rome became less democratic as the empire evolved (A). The *Pax Romana* marked the height of Roman civilization; decline began after this period (B). During this period, inhabitants of nearby Roman provinces were offered citizenship (D). Roman culture continued to preserve the Hellenistic traditions on which it was built (E).

4. **E**—All of the above. Roman roads connected to the Silk Roads, allowing trade between the Roman Empire and Han China (A). Both empires expanded significantly during their duration (B). Both experienced a time of relative peace when their respective cultures flourished (C), allowing the establishment of enduring traditions in philosophy, language, and government (D).

5. **D**—Alexander united the cultures of both Greece and the Middle East, particularly Persia, in his empire. Competition between Greece and Persia, therefore, was not a characteristic of his empire (A). The nature of Alexander's empire was to blend foreign cultures with that of the Greeks (B). Ptolemy embraced the geocentric view (C). Alexander's empire was divided by his generals and did not continue after his death (E).

6. **A**—Arabic numerals originated in Gupta India but were given their name because they were carried to the Western world by Arab caravans. The Hindu caste system lessened the need for slavery (B). Although the Gupta tolerated Buddhism, they embraced Hinduism as their own religion and promoted its acceptance (C). The Indian government was less centralized under the Gupta than it had been under Mauryan rulers (D). Women had a more inferior status, exemplified by the practice of *sati* (E).

7. **B**—The Persian conquest of Mesopotamia continued the transmission of Mesopotamian culture. They were noted for tolerance toward conquered peoples who did not rebel against Persian rule (A). In contrast to Hinduism, the new religion of Zoroastrianism was a religion of rewards and punishments in the afterlife (C). The Persians unified their empire through the Royal Road (D), which focused on trade with neighboring peoples in India, Southwest Asia, and Egypt (E).

8. **C**—Colonization spread the knowledge of Greek culture throughout the Mediterranean world. The mountains of the Greek peninsula prevented Greeks from uniting (A). Alexander continued the traditions of Greece (B). Greek society relied heavily on slave labor (D). Its religion was polytheistic, with gods and goddesses who displayed human characteristics (E).

Origins of World Belief Systems

IN THIS CHAPTER

Summary: The period from 8000 B.C.E. to 600 C.E. saw the beginnings of many of the world's major belief systems. Both Hinduism and Buddhism originated in India. The philosophies of Confucianism and Daoism profoundly affected traditional Chinese culture. In the Middle East, the Hebrew faith gave the world the concept of **monotheism**. Christianity emerged from the Hebrew belief in a **Messiah**, or a savior from sin. Followers of Jesus as the Messiah spread their faith throughout the Roman world.

KEY IDEA

Key Terms

Analects	Messiah
animism*	*moksha**
*bodhisattvas**	New Testament*
Brahmin*	*nirvana**
*dharma**	pope*
disciple	reincarnation*
Edict of Milan*	shamanism*
filial piety*	*yin* and *yang**
*karma**	

Polytheism

Both nomadic and early agricultural peoples often held to a belief in many gods or goddesses, or polytheism. The ancient river valley civilizations in the Eastern Hemisphere, as well as the early civilizations in the Americas, believed in numerous gods and goddesses representing spirits or objects of nature. The Greeks and Romans also believed in an array of deities who represented natural phenomena but at the same time took on humanlike qualities. Some early peoples practiced a form of polytheism called **animism**, or a belief that gods and goddesses inhabited natural features. Animism was widespread among many societies in Africa and in the Pacific islands of Polynesia. **Shamanism**, a form of animism, expressed a belief in powerful natural spirits that were influenced by shamans, or priests. Shamanism remained a common practice in Central Asia and the Americas.

Hinduism

Hinduism is a belief system that originated in India from the literature, traditions, and class system of the Aryan invaders. In contrast to other world religions, Hinduism did not have a single founder. As a result, the precepts and values of Hinduism developed gradually and embraced a variety of forms of worship. Hinduism took the polytheistic gods of nature that had been central to the worship of the **Brahmins**, or priests, then changed their character to represent concepts.

According to Hindu belief, everything in the world is part of a divine essence called Brahma. The spirit of Brahma enters gods or different forms of one god. Two forms of the Hindu deity are Vishnu, the preserver, and Shiva, the destroyer. A meaningful life is one that has found union with the divine soul. Hinduism holds that this union is achieved through **reincarnation**, or the concept that after death the soul enters another human or an animal. The person's good or evil deeds in his or her personal life is that person's *karma*. Those who die with good *karma* may be reincarnated into a higher caste, whereas those with evil *karma* might descend to a lower caste or become an animal. If the soul lives a number of good lives, it is united with the soul of Brahma. Upon achieving this unification, or *moksha*, the soul no longer experiences worldly suffering.

Hinduism goes beyond a mystical emphasis to effect the everyday conduct of its followers. The moral law, or **dharma**, serves as a guide to actions in this world. *Dharma* emphasizes that human actions produce consequences and that each person has obligations to the family and community.

The Hindu religion reinforced the Indian caste system, offering hope for an improved lifestyle in the next life, especially for members of the lower castes. Those of the upper castes were encouraged by the prospect of achieving *moksha*. Hinduism also extended the Aryan custom of venerating cattle by considering cattle as sacred and forbidding the consumption of beef.

In time, Hinduism became the principal religion of India. Carried by merchants through the waters of the Indian Ocean, Hindu beliefs also spread to Southeast Asia, where they attracted large numbers of followers. During the first century C.E., there were already signs of Indian influence in the societies of the islands of the Indian Ocean and in the Malay peninsula. Some rulers in present-day Vietnam and Cambodia adopted the Sanskrit language of India as a form of written communication.

Buddhism

The second major faith to originate in India was Buddhism. In contrast to Hinduism, Buddhism had a founder in an Indian prince named Gautama, born about 563 B.C.E. Troubled by the suffering in the world, Gautama spent six years fasting and meditating on its cause. After he determined that suffering was the consequence of human desire, he began traveling to spread his beliefs. At this time Gautama became known as the "Buddha," or the "enlightened one."

Although later followers would consider Buddha a god, Buddha did not see himself as a deity. Rather, he stressed the existence of a divine essence. Buddhism sought self-control and stressed the equal treatment of peoples from all walks of life. The Buddhist faith, therefore, opposed the caste system.

Buddhism shared with Hinduism the concept of reincarnation but in a different perspective. Buddhist belief held that a series of reincarnations would lead the faithful follower to ever higher levels toward the ultimate goal, which was *nirvana*, or a union with the divine essence.

The popularity of Buddhism emerged from its acceptance of men and women from all ranks of society. At first Buddhism spread through the efforts of monks and nuns who established religious communities in northern India. Located along trade routes, Buddhist monasteries served as lodging for traders, who learned of the teachings of Buddhism through contact with Buddhist monks and nuns. Contact with Hellenistic culture produced the Gandhara Buddhas, a syncretic sculpture combining the symbol of the Buddha with the exaltation of the human body typical of Hellenistic culture. In time, merchants carried the doctrines of Buddhism along the Silk Roads and other trade routes. Initially, Buddhist popularity was strengthened when the Mauryan emperor Ashoka adopted its beliefs. The faith, however, did not enjoy a long-term period of popularity in India because of opposition from Hindu Brahmins and the later promotion of Hinduism by Gupta emperors. Buddhism spread along the trade routes to become popular in Southeast Asia and East Asia, especially in Sri Lanka, Japan, Korea, and China. In China, Buddhism blended with Confucianism to reinforce the concept of patriarchal families. As it spread to other locales, Buddhism developed the belief of *bodhisattvas*, which held that, through meditation, ordinary people could reach *nirvana*.

Confucianism

Out of the disorder of the Era of Warring States after the fall of the Zhou dynasty came a number of philosophies designed to create order in China. Among these philosophies was Confucianism, named after its founder Confucius, or Kúng Fu-tse (551–478 B.C.E.). Confucius believed that the source of good government was in the maintenance of tradition; tradition, in turn, was maintained by personal standards of virtue. These included respect for the patriarchal family (**filial piety**) and veneration of one's ancestors.

Confucius also believed that governmental stability depended on well-educated officials. To this end, he required his followers to study history and literature from the Zhou dynasty to determine the value of these subjects for government officials. Some of the students of Confucius compiled his sayings into the **Analects**, a work which also served to educate the Chinese bureaucracy or government officials. The Han dynasty appreciated Confucian philosophy because it supported order and submission to the government. The civil service examination that developed during the Han dynasty was based on the *Analects* and the course of study developed by Confucius. The Confucian values of veneration of one's ancestors and respect for the patriarchal family, as well as good government staffed by a responsible, well-educated bureaucracy, became basic traditions that defined Chinese culture.

Daoism

Another philosophy that developed in response to the Era of Warring States was Daoism. Its founder was Lao-zi (or Lao-tsu), who is believed to have lived during the fifth century

B.C.E. The philosophy adapted traditional Chinese concepts of balance in nature, or *yin* (male, assertive) and *yang* (female, submissive). According to Daoist philosophy, human understanding comes from following "The Way," a life force which exists in nature.

In contrast to the Confucian respect for education and for orderly government, Daoism taught that political involvement and education were unnecessary. Rather, in time, the natural balance of the universe would resolve most problems. Chinese thought and practice gradually blended both Confucianism and Daoism to include a concern for responsibility for the community and time for personal reflection.

Judaism

Unlike other religions of the period, notably Buddhism and Christianity, Judaism was not a missionary religion. Although the Jews had lived in Babylon for seventy years, with some Jews remaining after most of the former captives returned to Babylon, they did little to attempt to convert non-Jews. From the Jewish faith, however, would come another major world religion: Christianity.

Christianity

A key element of Judaism was the belief that God had promised to send the Jews a **Messiah**, or a savior from their sins. Some of the early Jews felt that that promise was fulfilled when Jesus was born in the Roman province of Judea about 4 to 6 B.C.E. As an adult, Jesus and his 12 **disciples**, or followers, went throughout the land of Judea, preaching the forgiveness of sins. Jesus was also called Christ, meaning "anointed." When Jesus' teachings were feared as a threat to Roman and Jewish authority, he was tried and put to death by crucifixion. His followers believed that he was afterwards resurrected from the dead. This belief fueled their religious zeal.

The network of Roman roads facilitated the spread of Christianity throughout the empire. Missionaries, traders, and other travelers carried the Christian message of forgiveness of sins and an afterlife in heaven for those who believed in Jesus as their savior from sin. The greatest missionary of the early Christian church was Paul of Tarsus. A Roman citizen, he undertook three missionary journeys throughout the Roman Empire in the first century C.E. Accounts of Jesus' life in addition to the missionary efforts of Paul and other followers of Jesus are found in the New Testament of the Christian Bible.

Several Roman emperors considered Christianity a threat to their rule. Although some, such as Diocletian, persecuted the Christian church, it continued to grow. In 313, the Roman Emperor Constantine changed the position of earlier Roman emperors regarding Christianity. In the **Edict of Milan** he permitted the practice of Christianity in the Roman Empire. Christianity became the official religion of the Roman Empire in 381 under the Emperor Theodosius.

After its adoption as the state church of Rome, Christianity in the west began developing an organization under the leadership of the bishop of Rome, or **pope**. In addition to priests who served local churches, monks and nuns withdrew from society to devote their time to prayer and meditation. As it spread throughout the Roman world, Christianity gained popularity because of its appeal to all social classes, especially the poor. Women received new status as Christianity taught that men and women were equal in matters of faith. After the fall of the western Roman Empire, Christianity spread to northern Europe, the Balkans, and Russia.

› Rapid Review

Although polytheism was the most common religious belief among early agricultural and nomadic peoples, a number of major belief systems arose before 600 C.E. Monotheism was the gift of Judaism, which, in turn, became the source of the Christian religion. In India, two faiths—Hinduism and Buddhism—emerged from the diverse social structure of South Asia. In China, Confucianism and Daoism blended family and political order with the balance of nature to define Chinese philosophical thought.

› Review Questions

1. Both Hinduism and Buddhism
   (A) supported the caste system
   (B) revered women
   (C) became increasingly popular in India
   (D) all of the above
   (E) none of the above

2. Christianity
   (A) remained a religion of the Roman Empire
   (B) taught the forgiveness of sins through faith in Jesus
   (C) was not a missionary religion
   (D) failed to utilize the public works of the Roman Empire
   (E) gained an early popularity among Roman rulers

3. Confucianism and early Buddhism
   (A) became the dominant philosophy of their respective regions
   (B) emphasized the importance of effective government
   (C) included a belief in *nirvana*
   (D) did not believe that their founders were gods
   (E) elevated the status of women

4. Daoism and Confucianism
   (A) agreed on the importance of education
   (B) disagreed on the need for personal reflection
   (C) taught that active political involvement was essential to a stable society
   (D) agreed on how to address the turmoil after the fall of the Zhou dynasty
   (E) based their teachings on Chinese traditions

5. The Silk Roads were especially instrumental in the spread of
   (A) polytheism
   (B) Confucianism
   (C) Daoism
   (D) Buddhism
   (E) Judaism

6. During the period of the late Roman Empire, Christianity
   (A) experienced a change in its official status
   (B) declined in numbers because of persecutions
   (C) became less organized as the empire fell
   (D) appealed primarily to elite classes
   (E) denied the equality of women in matters of faith

7. Hinduism
   (A) was based on traditions of the Harappan civilization
   (B) addressed the consequences of one's behavior
   (C) offered no hope for members of lower castes
   (D) became secondary to Buddhism among the religions of India
   (E) gained little acceptance outside India

8. Buddhism
   (A) became the most popular faith in India
   (B) was the adopted faith of Gupta rulers
   (C) opposed Confucian ideals of patriarchal families
   (D) changed over time from transmission by traders to its spread through the services of monasteries
   (E) changed over time to teach that common people could reach *nirvana*

› Answers and Explanations

1. **E**—None of the above. Whereas Hinduism supported the caste system, Buddhism did not (A). Buddhism showed respect for women; Hinduism did not (B). Only Hinduism became increasingly popular in India (C).

2. **B**—Forgiveness of sins was a central teaching of Christianity. Christianity spread beyond the borders of the Roman Empire to Africa and Asia (A). Christian missionaries, especially Paul of Tarsus, actively promoted their faith (C). Missionary efforts were facilitated by the system of Roman roads (D). Roman emperors tended to fear the new religion and some of them, especially Diocletian, persecuted Christians. Later Roman emperors such as Constantine and Theodosius treated Christians favorably (E).

3. **D**—Neither Confucius nor the Buddha believed himself to be a god. Later Buddhists, however, sometimes deified the Buddha. Although Confucianism became the dominant philosophy throughout most of Chinese history, Buddhism lost popularity to Hinduism (A). Only Confucianism emphasized the importance of effective government (B). The concept of *nirvana* was a Buddhist belief only (C). Confucianism kept women in a subordinate position (E).

4. **E**—Confucianism embraced the traditions of centralization of government and veneration of ancestors, whereas Daoism used the concepts of *yin* and *yang* to explain its teachings. Confucianism stressed the importance of education (A), whereas Daoism taught personal reflection (B). Confucianism encouraged active political involvement (C). Confucianism sought to end political turmoil by creating educated leaders, whereas Daoism held to the belief that eventually the problems following the fall of the Zhou would be resolved by the balance of nature (D).

5. **D**—Buddhism was spread primarily by traders who followed the Silk Roads. Polytheism (A) was found in numerous locations worldwide and was not spread along the Silk Roads. Confucianism (B) spread to Korea and Japan, areas not included in the Silk Roads. Daoism (C) was essentially a Chinese philosophy. Judaism (E) remained a faith of the Middle East and of Jewish diaspora communities; it was not a religion that actively sought converts.

6. **A**—During the late Roman Empire, Christianity became the official religion of the Roman Empire. Persecution only increased its numbers (B). During the latter days of the empire, the Christian religion was acquiring a detailed organization from parish priest to pope (C). The new religion appealed to members of all classes, especially the poor (D) and treated women and men with respect and equality in matters of faith (E).

7. **B**—Hinduism held its followers responsible for their actions. It was based on the traditions of the Aryan society (A). Offering lower classes the hope of reaching *moksha* (C), Hinduism became popular in Southeast Asia as well as India (E). It became the dominant religion of India (D).

8. **E**—The Buddhist belief of *bodhisattvas,* developed after the faith spread out from India, taught that common people could reach *nirvana.* Buddhist women were allowed to become nuns (A). Hinduism was adopted by the Gupta (B). In China, Buddhism eventually blended with Confucianism to support the concept of patriarchal families (C). Over time, Buddhism changed from spreading through contacts with Buddhist monasteries to being spread by traders (D).

CHAPTER 10

Interactions in the Late Classical Period

IN THIS CHAPTER

Summary: The classical period came to an end with the weakening and fall of the empires of Rome, Han China, and Gupta India to invaders. The fall of the three great classical empires showed a number of similarities. At the same time, the late classical period featured increased interactions among the classical empires and other peoples of Asia, the Indian Ocean basin, and the Mediterranean world.

Key Terms

Hsiung-nu   Silk Roads*
Huns   White huns
*latifundia**

Han China

The Han dynasty of China began to decline around 100 C.E. Among the causes of its decline were:

- Heavy taxes levied on peasants
- The decline of interest in Confucian intellectual goals
- Poor harvests
- Population decline from epidemic disease
- Social unrest, particularly by students
- A decline in morality
- Weak emperors and the increased influence of army generals

- Unequal land distribution
- A decline in trade
- Pressure from bordering nomadic tribes

As political, economic, and social decay befell Han China, Daoism gained a new popularity. In 184, the Yellow Turbans, a Daoist revolutionary movement, promised a new age of prosperity and security which would be initiated by magic. Buddhism also spread as Chinese cultural unity was dissolving.

The decay of the Han Empire made it difficult for the Chinese to resist nomadic invaders living along their borders. These invaders, or **Hsiung-nu**, had for decades been raiding Han China, prompting the Chinese to pay them tribute to prevent further invasions. By 220, however, Han China's strength had deteriorated to the point that it could no longer repel a final thrust by the invading Hsiung-nu, who then poured into the empire. The fall of Han China was followed by centuries of disorder and political decentralization until Chinese rulers in the northern part of the country drove out the invaders. In 589, the Sui dynasty ascended to power and continued to establish order in China. In spite of significant threats to Chinese civilization, it did ultimately survive. Confucian tradition endured among the elite classes, and the nomads eventually assimilated into Chinese culture.

Rome

The golden age of Rome—the *Pax Romana*—came to a close with the death of Marcus Aurelius in 180. Historians have noted a number of causes of the decline and fall of Rome including:

- Ineffective later emperors concerned more with a life of pleasure than a desire to rule wisely
- The influence of army generals
- The decline of trade
- Increasingly high taxes
- A decreased money flow into the empire as conquests of new territory ceased
- Population decline as a result of epidemic disease
- Poor harvests
- Unequal land distribution
- Social and moral decay and lack of interest in the elite classes
- Roman dependence on slave labor
- The recruitment of non-Romans into the Roman army
- The vastness of the empire, rendering it difficult to rule
- Barbarian invasions

Attempts to Save the Roman Empire

As the Roman Empire declined economically, small landowners were frequently forced to sell their land to the owners of large estates, or *latifundia*. The self-sufficiency of the *latifundia* lessened the need for a central authority such as the Roman emperor. Furthermore, the economic self-sufficiency of the estates discouraged trade among the various parts of the empire and neighboring peoples. The decline in trade eventually produced a decline in urban population.

Some emperors tried desperately to save the empire. Diocletian (ruled 284–305) imposed stricter control over the empire and declared himself a god. When the Christians refused to worship him, Diocletian heightened persecutions against them. The Emperor Constantine (ruled 312 to 337) established a second capital at Byzantium, which he renamed Constantinople. Converting to Christianity, Constantine allowed the practice of the faith in Rome. Although the western portion of the empire steadily declined, the eastern portion, centered around Constantinople, continued to thrive and carry on a high volume of long-distance trade.

The last measure that weakened the western Roman Empire originated in the steppes of Central Asia. In the fifth century, the nomadic **Huns** began migrating south and west in search of better pasturelands. The movement of the Huns exerted pressure on Germanic tribes who already lived around the border of the Roman Empire. These tribes, in turn, overran the Roman borders. By 425, several Germanic kingdoms were set up within the empire; by 476, the last western Roman emperor was replaced by a Germanic ruler from the tribe of the Visigoths.

The eastern portion of the empire did not fall at the same time as the western empire. One reason for its endurance was that it saw less pressure from invaders. Located on the Bosporus, it was the hub of numerous trade routes and a center of art and architecture. Neighboring empires—most notably the Parthians and, after 227, the Sassanids—served as trade facilitators. Not only did they preserve the Greek culture, but they continued to bring Indian and Chinese goods and cultural trends to the eastern, or Byzantine, empire. The Byzantine Emperor Justinian (ruled 527 to 565) attempted to capture portions of Rome's lost territory. Justinian's efforts were largely in vain, however, as the western empire increasingly fragmented into self-sufficient estates and tiny Germanic kingdoms. Trade and learning declined, and cities shrank in size. The centralized government of Rome was replaced by rule based on the tribal allegiances of the Germanic invaders.

Gupta India

The fall of Gupta India to invading forces was less devastating than that of Han China or Rome. By 500, Gupta India endured a number of invasions by the White Huns, nomadic peoples who may have been related to the Huns whose migrations drove Germanic peoples over the borders of the Roman Empire. Simultaneously, the influence of Gupta rulers was in decline as local princes became more powerful. Until about 600, the nomads drove farther into central India. India fragmented into regional states ruled by the princes, who called themselves Rajput.

Although political decline occurred as a result of invasions, traditional Indian culture continued. Buddhism became less popular, while Hinduism added to its number of followers. Traditional Indian culture met another challenge after 600 in the form of the new religion of Islam.

Other Contacts with Classical Civilizations

Although the civilizations of Han China, Gupta India, Greece, and Rome dominated world history during the classical period, other societies and civilizations came into contact with and were influenced by them. Indian merchants drew the people of Southeast Asia into long-distance trade patterns. Contacts between India and Southeast Asia were further broadened by the spread of Buddhism and Hinduism from India to Southeast Asia.

Trade contacts also drew Africa into the classical Mediterranean world. South of Egypt lay the kingdom of Kush. The Kushites had long admired Egyptian culture and adapted their own writing system from Egyptian hieroglyphics. Kush also was a center of the independent invention of iron smelting. About 750 B.C.E., as Egypt weakened, Kush conquered Egypt. Kush, in turn, was defeated by the Christian kingdom of Axum about 300 C.E. Axum and its rival, the kingdom of Ethiopia, traded with parts of the Roman Empire along the eastern Mediterranean. Greek merchants had carried Christianity to Ethiopia in the fourth century C.E.

Silk Road Trade

One of the most far-reaching of the contacts between classical civilizations and other societies was the contact of the pastoral nomads of Central Asia with established societies. Central Asian herders often served as trade facilitators along the famed **Silk Roads** that linked trade between China and urban areas in Mesopotamia in the last millennium B.C.E. During the time of the Roman Empire, the Silk Roads were extended to the Mediterranean world. Named for their most prized trade commodity, the Silk Roads also were noted for the exchange of a variety of other goods between East and West. Nomadic peoples frequently supplied animals to transport goods along the Silk Roads. The Silk Roads served as an artery that transported not only trade goods but also religious beliefs, technology, and disease.

Indian Ocean Trade

The Silk Roads included not only land routes across Central Asia and Europe but also sea lanes in the Indian Ocean. Chinese pottery was traded along with Indian spices and ivory from India and Africa. The Indian Ocean trade network, which included the South China Sea, involved mariners from China, Malaysia, Southeast Asia, and Persia. Sailors used the seasonal monsoon winds to chart their course and carry out voyages that linked sections from East Africa to Southern China.

Trans-Saharan Trade

A third principal trade route in classical times was one across the Sahara. One of the most significant developments in the trade across the Sahara was the use of the camel and the development of the camel saddle. It is possible that the camel arrived in the Sahara from Arabia in the first century B.C.E. Early Saharan trade patterns included the exchange of salt and palm oil. During the days of the Roman Empire, North Africa also supplied Italy with olives and wheat, and with wild animals.

› Rapid Review

Although they ultimately fell to nomadic invaders, the classical civilizations of China, India, and the Mediterranean produced traditions that stamped an enduring mark on world cultures. Major world belief systems spread throughout Eurasia. The Silk Roads, Indian Ocean network, and trans-Saharan routes linked the Eastern Hemisphere into the foundations of a global trade network.

› Review Questions

1. During the classical period, Africa
   (A) was cut off from global trade patterns
   (B) repelled Christian missionary efforts
   (C) lost contact with classical civilizations
   (D) saw new technology used in trans-Saharan travel
   (E) saw the arrival of Buddhist missionaries

2. The declining years of Han China and the Roman Empire shared all of the following EXCEPT
   (A) a decline in morality
   (B) epidemic disease
   (C) assimilation of invading peoples into imperial culture
   (D) unequal land distribution
   (E) decline in trade

3. Attempts to save the Roman Empire from ruin included
   (A) the division of the *latifundia*
   (B) initial acceptance of Christianity followed by increased persecution
   (C) the emancipation of Roman slaves
   (D) the establishment of a new capital in the eastern empire
   (E) reducing the size of the empire

4. The eastern portion of the Roman Empire
   (A) successfully restored the boundaries of the western empire under Justinian
   (B) competed with the Parthians and Sassanids for trade
   (C) was a center of trade, art, and architecture
   (D) unlike the western portion, did not experience pressure from invaders
   (E) was cut off from contact with cultures from the east

5. The decline of Gupta India
   (A) saw the increased power of local princes
   (B) resulted in the decline of traditional Indian culture
   (C) unlike Rome, did not result in the fragmentation of the country
   (D) occurred without pressure from invading peoples
   (E) resulted in a decline in the popularity of Hinduism

6. Silk Road trade
   (A) flourished in spite of constant interferences from nomadic tribes
   (B) was confined to land routes across Asia
   (C) bypassed Mesopotamia
   (D) established links between the empires of Han China and Rome
   (E) linked North Africa with Rome

7. Indian Ocean trade
   (A) linked all areas of the Indian Ocean basin except Africa
   (B) saw mariners utilize the geographic forces of the Indian Ocean
   (C) declined with the fall of classical empires
   (D) failed to establish connections with land routes
   (E) concentrated on trade among neighboring peoples rather than long-distance trade

8. The decline of Han China
   (A) saw the end of Chinese established traditions
   (B) like Rome, saw invaders permanently dominate the empire
   (C) witnessed Daoism, rather than Confucianism, gaining popularity
   (D) was the end of Chinese dynastic rule
   (E) resulted in the decline of Buddhism in China

› Answers and Explanations

1. **D**—The camel saddle was especially important to trans-Saharan trade during the classical era. Africa traded with Rome (C) and was connected to Indian Ocean trade (A). Christianity entered Axum and Ethiopia during this period (B). Buddhism did not reach Africa (E).

2. **C**—Although barbarian invaders assimilated into the Chinese culture, the same did not occur after the fall of Rome. The remaining four choices were common to both empires in their period of decline.

3. **D**—In order to tap into the wealth of the eastern empire, Constantine established a new capital at Constantinople, the former Byzantium. During Rome's decline the *latifundia* became larger, not smaller (A). Persecutions of Christians were followed by acceptance of the religion, then by official status under Theodosius (B). Romans continued to rely on slavery (C). The empire lost size during the declining years, but not as a result of a deliberate effort to reduce its territory (E).

4. **C**—The Byzantine Empire was a cultural center. Justinian's efforts were only partially successful in temporarily restoring some of the boundaries of Rome (A). The Parthians and Sassanids acted as trade facilitators (B). The eastern empire experienced some pressure from invaders, but not nearly to the extent that the western portion did (D). The eastern empire was a hub of trade routes that offered cultural exchange with peoples to the east (E).

5. **A**—After the fall of the Gupta dynasty, India was fragmented (C) into local principalities. Indian culture, however, remained intact (B), and Hinduism remained the dominant religion of India (E). Like Rome, Gupta India experienced pressure from invaders (D).

6. **D**—The Roman roads connected to the routes of the Silk Roads. Nomadic tribes often assisted travelers and traders along the Silk Roads, providing horses, camels, and supplies (A). The Silk Roads also embraced the sea lanes of the Indian Ocean (B) and went through Mesopotamia (C). Although North Africa traded with the Roman Empire, its routes were not included among the Silk Roads (E).

7. **B**—Mariners used the monsoon winds to facilitate travel in the Indian Ocean. Africa was connected to Indian Ocean trade (A). Trade in the Indian Ocean continued after the fall of classical empires, especially after the entry of Islam into the region (C). The waters of the Indian Ocean facilitated long-distance trade from China to Africa (E) and connected with land routes from China to Rome (D).

8. **C**—Daoism enjoyed a resurgence of prosperity as Han China declined, whereas Confucianism declined in popularity. Although Chinese traditions suffered initially, they rebounded after the fall of the Han (A). Invaders eventually assimilated into the Chinese culture (B). Chinese dynastic rule would continue into the early twentieth century (D). Buddhism gained popularity in China after the fall of the Han (E).

PERIOD 2 Summary: Organization and Reorganization of Human Societies (c. 600 B.C.E.–c. 600 C.E.)

Timeline

509 B.C.E.	Establishment of the Roman republic
480–221 B.C.E.	Era of the Warring States in China
336–323 B.C.E.	Rule of Alexander of Macedon (the Great)
330 B.C.E.	Conquest of Achaemenid Empire by Alexander
20 B.C.E.–180 C.E.	*Pax Romana*
4 B.C.E.–29 C.E.	Life of Jesus Christ
300–1100 C.E.	Mayan civilization
Third–first centuries B.C.E.	Spread of Buddhism and Hinduism from South Asia
206 B.C.E.–220 C.E.	Han dynasty
320–550 C.E.	Gupta dynasty
476 C.E.	Fall of the western Roman Empire

Key Comparisons

1. Political, economic, and social characteristics of the empires of Rome, Han China, and Gupta India
2. Exchanges in the Indian Ocean versus those in the Mediterranean Sea
3. The expansion and appeal of Buddhism, Hinduism, and Christianity
4. The origins, philosophies, and goals of Confucianism and Daoism
5. The decline and fall of Han China, Rome, and Gupta India
6. Trans-Saharan versus Silk Roads trade

Change/Continuity Chart

KEY IDEA

REGION	POLITICAL	ECONOMIC	SOCIAL	CHANGES	CONTINUITIES
East Asia	Dynastic rule Mandate of heaven Centralized government Great Wall Civil service exam	Rice, millet Bronze crafts Ironworking Silk production Silk Road trade Paper	Urbanization Patriarchal societies Stratified society Confucianism Daoism	Development of philosophy	Chinese traditions of Confucianism, family Dynastic rule Ancestor veneration Mandate of heaven
Southeast Asia	Chinese Influence	Root crops Fruit Trade with South Asia	Urbanization Hinduism Buddhism	Adaptations of Chinese culture Hinduism and Buddhism Urbanization	Agriculture
Oceania	Regional kingdoms	Foraging	Polytheism Animism Tribal organization	Development of kingdoms	Foraging Austronesian migrations
Central Asia	Tribal governments Chinese influence Migrations toward classical empires	Nomadism Trade facilitators	Indo-European migrations	Trade facilitators Invasion of classical empires	Pastoral nomadism Shamanism
South Asia	Community planning Mauryan and Gupta dynasties	Grains Indian Ocean trade	Urbanization Patriarchal societies Hinduism Varna Buddhism Inoculation *Sati*	Hinduism Buddhism Caste system Dynasties	Agriculture Interest in technological advancement Active trade *Vedas* Sanskrit
Southwest Asia	Persian Empire Hellenistic Empire	Grains Wheel Cuneiform Trade with Indus Valley and Egypt Camel saddle	Urbanization Polytheism Stratified society Judaism Zoroastrianism Christianity	Development of major religions	Agriculture Irrigation Trade Judaism Zoroastrianism

North Africa	Pharaohs Kingdoms of Kush, Axum, Ethiopia	Barley Trade with Sumer and Persia Ironworking Salt/palm oil Use of camel saddle Trade with Rome	Urbanization Village life along the Nile Pyramids Hieroglyphics Polytheism Stratified society Christianity	Long-distance trade Decline of Egyptian civilization Christianity	Regional kingdoms Village life along the Nile
Sub-Saharan Africa	Regional kingdoms	Root crops Trans-Saharan trade Ivory trade/ Indian Ocean	Polytheism Animism	Indian Ocean trade Sub-Saharan trade	Regional kingdoms Polytheism Ancestor veneration Bantu migrations
Western Europe	Athenian democracy *Poleis* Hellenistic Empire Roman Empire	Greek trade/colonization Silk Roads trade Roman roads Decline of trade and learning	Phoenician alphabet Olympic games Greek drama Greek philosophy Hellenistic thought *Pax Romana* Latin Roman law Christianity	Fall of Roman Empire	Greco-Roman culture
Eastern Europe	Byzantine Empire Justinian's attempts to recover Roman territory Code of Justinian	Agriculture Center of trade	Greek learning Christianity	Urbanization and trade in Byzantium	Greco-Roman culture
North America	Tribal government Regional empires	Maize Nomadism Some trade iwth Mesoamerica	Village organization Polytheism	Trade expansion	Village life Nomadism Polytheism Shamanism
Latin America	City-states Mayan civilization Andean societies and civilizations	Maize, potato Llama, alpaca Obsidian, jade Limited trade	Urbanization Quetzalcóatl Stratified society Zero Astronomy Calendar	Pyramids Ceremonial buildings Mayan astronomy	Mesoamerican traditions Shamanism Ancestor veneration

PERIOD 3

Regional and Transregional Interactions (c. 600–c. 1450)

CHAPTER 11

The Rise and Spread of Islam

IN THIS CHAPTER

Summary: As the empires that lent their grandeur to the classical period of early civilization fell into decline, the barren desert of the Arabian Peninsula witnessed the development of a belief system that evolved into a religious, political, and economic world system. *Dar al-Islam,* or the house of Islam, united sacred and secular institutions.

Key Terms

An asterisk (*) denotes items listed in the glossary.

Allah*	*minaret**
arabesque	mosque*
astrolabe*	Muslim*
Battle of Tours*	People of the Book*
caliph*	*Quran**
Dar al-Islam*	Ramadan*
Five Pillars*	*shariah**
Hadith*	Shi'ite*
hajj*	Sufis*
harem*	sultan*
hijrah*	Sunni*
jihad*	*umma**
Ka'aba*	zakat
Mamluks*	

The World of Muhammad

The Arabian peninsula into which Muhammad was born in 570 was a hub of ancient caravan routes. Although the coastal regions of the peninsula were inhabited by settled peoples, the interior region provided a homeland for nomadic tribes called Bedouins. Located in the interior of the peninsula was the city of Mecca, which served both as a commercial center and as the location of a religious shrine for the polytheistic worship common to the nomadic peoples of the peninsula. Pilgrims were in the habit of visiting Mecca and its revered shrine, the **Ka'aba**, a cubic structure that housed a meteorite. The merchants of Mecca enjoyed a substantial profit from these pilgrims.

Muhammad, an orphan from the merchant class of Mecca, was raised by his grandfather and uncle. He married a wealthy local widow and businesswoman named Khadija. About 610, Muhammad experienced the first of a number of revelations that he believed came from the archangel Gabriel. In these revelations he was told that there is only one God, called "**Allah**" in Arabic. (Allah was one of the gods in the Arabic pantheon.) Although the peoples of the Arabian peninsula had already been exposed to monotheism through Jewish traders and Arabic converts to Christianity, Muhammad's fervent proclamation of the existence of only one god angered the merchants of Mecca, who anticipated decreased profits from pilgrimages if the revelations of Muhammad were widely accepted. In 622, realizing that his life was in danger, Muhammad and his followers fled to the city of Yathrib (later called Medina), about 200 miles northwest of Mecca. Here Muhammad was allowed to freely exercise his role as prophet of the new faith, and the numbers of believers in the new religion grew. The flight of Muhammad from Mecca to Medina, called the *hijrah*, became the first year in the Muslim calendar.

In Medina, Muhammad oversaw the daily lives of his followers, organizing them into a community of believers known as the *umma*. The well-being of the *umma* included programs concerning all aspects of life, from relief for widows and orphans to campaigns of military defense.

In 629, Muhammad and his followers journeyed to Mecca to make a pilgrimage to the Ka'aba, now incorporated as a shrine in the Islamic faith. The following year they returned as successful conquerors of the city, and in 632, they again participated in the *hajj*. In 632, Muhammad died without appointing a successor, an omission that would have a profound effect on the future of Islam.

The Teachings of Islam

The term Islam means "submission," while the name **Muslim**, applied to the followers of Islam, means "one who submits." Muhammad viewed his revelations as a completion of those of Judaism and Christianity and perceived himself not as a deity but as the last in a series of prophets of the one god, Allah. He considered Abraham, Moses, and Jesus also among the prophets of Allah. According to the teachings of Islam, the faithful must follow a set of regulations known as the **Five Pillars**. They include:

- *Faith.* In order to be considered a follower of Islam, a person must proclaim in the presence of a Muslim the following statement: "There is no god but Allah, and Muhammad is his prophet."
- *Prayer.* The Muslim must pray at five prescribed times daily, each time facing the holy city of Mecca.

- *Fasting.* The faithful must fast from dawn to dusk during the days of the holy month of Ramadan, a commemoration of the first revelation to Muhammad.
- *Alms-giving.* The Muslim is to pay the **zakat,** or tithe for the needy.
- *The* hajj. At least once, the follower of Islam is required to make a pilgrimage to the Ka'aba in the holy city of Mecca. The faithful are released from this requirement if they are too ill or too poor to make the journey.

The revelations and teachings of Muhammad were not compiled into a single written document until after his death. The resulting **Quran,** or holy book of the Muslims, was completed in 650. In addition, the sayings of Muhammad were compiled into the books of the **Hadith.** After the death of Muhammad the **shariah,** or moral law, was compiled. In addition to addressing issues of everyday life, the *shariah* established political order and provided for criminal justice.

The Split Between the Sunni and the Shia

After the death of Muhammad in 632, the *umma* chose Abu-Bakr, one of the original followers of Muhammad, as the first **caliph,** or successor to the prophet. The office of caliph united both secular and religious authority in the person of one leader. When the third caliph, Uthman of the Umayyad family, was assassinated, Ali, the cousin and son-in-law of Muhammad, was appointed caliph. Soon controversy arose over his appointment. As time progressed, the disagreement became more pronounced, resulting in a split in the Muslim world that exists to the present. After the assassination of Ali in 661, the **Shia** sect, believing that only a member of the family of Muhammad should serve as caliph, arose to support the descendants of Ali. The **Sunni,** who eventually became the largest segment of Islam, believed that the successor to the caliphate should be chosen from among the *umma,* or Muslim community, and accepted the earliest caliphs as the legitimate rulers of Islam.

The Early Expansion of Islam

Shortly after the death of Muhammad, the new religion of Islam embarked upon a rapid drive for expansion. Unlike the Buddhist and Christian religions, which expanded by means of missionary endeavor and commercial activity, Islam at first extended its influence by military conquest. Islam spread swiftly throughout portions of Eurasia and Africa:

- Within a year after the death of Muhammad, most of the Arabian Peninsula was united under the banner of Islam.
- Persia was conquered in 651 with the overthrow of the Sasanid dynasty.
- By the latter years of the seventh century, the new faith had reached Syria, Mesopotamia, Palestine, and Egypt.
- At the same time, Islam extended into Central Asia east of the Caspian Sea, where it competed with Buddhism.
- During the eighth century, Muslim armies reached present-day Tunisia, Algeria, and Morocco; Hindu-dominated northwest India; and the Iberian peninsula (present-day Spain and Portugal).

The earliest Muslim conquerors were not as concerned with the spread of religious belief as they were with the extension of power for the Muslim leaders and people.

The Umayyad Caliphate

After the assassination of Ali in 661, the Umayyad family came to power in the Islamic world. Establishing their capital at Damascus in Syria, the Umayyad were noted for the following:

- An empire that emphasized Arabic ethnicity over adherence to Islam.
- Inferior status assigned to converts to Islam.
- Respect for Jews and Christians as "**People of the Book.**" Although required to pay taxes for charity and on property, Jews and Christians were allowed freedom of worship and self-rule within their communities.
- Luxurious living for the ruling families, which prompted riots among the general population.

These riots among the general population led to the overthrow of the Umayyad by the Abbasid dynasty in 750. Although most of the Umayyad were killed in the takeover, one member of the family escaped to Spain, where he established the Caliphate of Cordoba.

The Abbasid Caliphate

The Abbasids, originally supported by the **Shi'ites (Shia)**, became increasingly receptive to the Sunni also. Establishing their capital at Baghdad in present-day Iraq, the Abbasids differed from the Umayyad in granting equal status to converts to Islam. Under the Abbasids:

- Converts experienced new opportunities for advanced education and career advancement.
- Trade was heightened from the western Mediterranean world to China.
- The learning of the ancient Greeks, Romans, and Persians was preserved. Greek logic, particularly that of Aristotle, penetrated Muslim thought.
- The Indian system of numbers, which included the use of zero as a place holder, was carried by caravan from India to the Middle East and subsequently to Western Europe, where the numbers were labeled "Arabic" numerals.
- In mathematics, the fields of algebra, geometry, and trigonometry were further refined.
- The **astrolabe**, which measured the position of stars, was improved.
- The study of astronomy produced maps of the stars.
- Optic surgery became a specialty, and human anatomy was studied in detail.
- Muslim cartographers produced some of the most detailed maps in the world.
- The number and size of urban centers such as Baghdad, Cairo, and Córdoba increased.
- Institutions of higher learning in Cairo, Baghdad, and Córdoba arose by the twelfth century.
- In the arts, calligraphy and designs called **arabesques** adorned writing and pottery.
- New architectural styles arose. Buildings were commonly centered around a patio area. **Minarets**, towers from which the faithful received the call to prayer, topped **mosques**, or Muslim places of worship.
- Great literature, such as poetic works and *The Arabian Nights,* enriched Muslim culture. Persian language and literary style was blended with that of Arabic.
- Mystics called **Sufis**, focusing on an emotional union with Allah, began missionary work to spread Islam.

Although responsible for much of the advancement of Islamic culture, the Abbasids found their vast empire increasingly difficult to govern. The dynasty failed to address the problem of succession within the Islamic world, and high taxes made the leaders less and less popular.

Independent kingdoms began to arise within the Abbasid Empire, one of them in Persia, where local leaders, calling themselves "**sultan**," took control of Baghdad in 945. The Persians were challenged by the Seljuk Turks from central Asia, who also chipped away at the Byzantine Empire. The weakening Persian sultanate allied with the Seljuks, whose contacts with the Abbasids had led them to begin converting to Sunni Islam in the middle of the tenth century. By the middle of the eleventh century, the Seljuks controlled Baghdad. In the thirteenth century, the Abbasid dynasty ended when Mongol invaders executed the Abbasid caliph.

It was the Seljuk takeover of Jerusalem that prompted the beginnings of the Crusades in 1095 (see Chapter 13). Divisions within the Muslim world allowed Christians from Western Europe to capture Jerusalem during the First Crusade. Under Saladin, however, Muslim armies reconquered most of the lost territory during the twelfth century.

Al-Andalus

The flowering of Islamic culture became particularly pronounced in *al-Andalus,* or Islamic Spain. In 711, Berbers from North Africa conquered the Iberian peninsula, penetrating the European continent until their advance was stopped about 200 miles south of Paris at the **Battle of Tours** in 732. Allies of the Umayyad dynasty, the caliphs of *al-Andalus* served to preserve Greco-Roman culture, enhancing it with the scientific and mathematical developments of the Muslim world. The Caliphate of Córdoba boasted a magnificent library and free education in Muslim schools. Interregional commerce thrived, while Arabic words such as *alcohol, álgebra,* and *sofá* were added to the Spanish vocabulary, and Muslim styles such as minarets, rounded arches, and arabesques were used in Spanish art and architecture.

Islam in India and Southeast Asia

Between the seventh and twelfth centuries, Muslims expanded their influence from northwest India to the Indus Valley and a large portion of northern India. Centering their government at Delhi, the rulers of the Delhi Sultanate extended their power by military conquest, controlling northern India from 1206 to 1526. Unsuccessful at achieving popularity among the Indians as a whole because of their monotheistic beliefs, the Muslim conquerors found acceptance among some Buddhists. Members of lower Hindu castes and untouchables also found Islam appealing because of its accepting and egalitarian nature. Although militarily powerful, the Delhi Sultanate failed to establish a strong administration. It did, however, introduce Islam to the culture of India.

In Southeast Asia, Islam spread more from commercial contacts and conversion than from military victories. By the eighth century, Muslim traders reached Southeast Asia, with migrants from Persia and southern Arabia arriving during the tenth century. Although the new faith did not gain widespread popularity among Buddhist areas of mainland Southeast Asia, the inhabitants of some of the islands of the Indian Ocean, familiar with Islam from trading contacts, were receptive to the new faith. Hinduism and Buddhism remained popular with many of the island peoples of the Indian Ocean. At the same time, however, Islam also found a stronghold on the islands of Malaysia, Indonesia, and the southern Philippines.

Islam in Africa

The spirit of *jihad*, or Islamic holy war, brought Islam into Africa in the eighth century. Wave after wave of traders and travelers carried the message of Muhammad across the sands of the Sahara along caravan routes. In the tenth century, Egypt was added to the Muslim territories. The authoritarian rulers of African states in the savannas south of the Sahara Desert adapted well to the Muslim concept of the unification of secular and spiritual powers in the person of the caliph. By the tenth century, the rulers of the kingdom of Ghana in West Africa converted to Islam, followed in the thirteenth century by the conversion of the rulers of the empire of Mali to the east of Ghana. Although widely accepted by the rulers of these regions, the common people preferred to remain loyal to their traditional polytheistic beliefs. When they did convert to Islam, they tended to blend some of their traditional beliefs and practices with those of Islam. Some Sudanic societies were resistant to Islam because their matrilineal structure offered women more freedom than did the practice of Islam.

Along the east coast of Africa, Indian Ocean trade was the focal point that brought Islam to the inhabitants of the coastal areas and islands. East African cities such as Mogadishu, Mombasa, and Kilwa became vibrant centers of Islam that caught the attention of Ibn Battuta, an Arab traveler who journeyed throughout the world of Islam in the fourteenth century. Islam did not experience much success in finding converts in the interior of Africa. In East Africa, as in the western portion of the continent, rulers were the first to convert to Islam, followed much later, if at all, by the masses. Women in eastern Africa already experienced more freedoms than did their Muslim counterparts, a fact that made them resistant to the new faith.

The Mamluk Dynasties

With the destruction of Islamic power in Baghdad at the hands of the Mongols (see Chapter 14), the **Mamluk** dynasties provided the force that made Egypt a center for Muslim culture and learning. The Mamluks were converts to Islam who maintained their position among the caliphs by adhering to a strict observance of Islam. By encouraging the safety of trade routes within their domain, the Mamluks contributed to the prosperity of Egypt during the fourteenth and fifteenth centuries until internal disorder led to their takeover in the sixteenth century by the Ottoman Turks (see Chapter 16).

The Role of Women in Islamic Society

The role of women in Islam underwent considerable change from the time of Muhammad to the fifteenth century. In the early days of Islam, women were not required to veil and were not secluded from the public; these customs were adopted by Islam after later contact with Middle Eastern women. The seclusion of the **harem** originated with the Abbasid court. From the time of Muhammad onward, Muslim men, following the example of Muhammad, could have up to four wives, provided that they could afford to treat them equally. Women, by contrast, were allowed only one husband.

In many respects, however, Islamic women enjoyed greater privileges than women in other societies at the same time. Both men and women were equal before Allah, and female infanticide was forbidden. Women could own property both before and after marriage. In some circumstances, Islamic women could initiate divorce proceedings and were allowed to remarry if divorced by their husband. As time progressed, however, the legal privileges enjoyed by Islamic women were counterbalanced by their seclusion from the public, a situation designed to keep women, especially those from the urban elite classes, away from the gaze of men. This isolation often created barriers against the acceptance of Islam, especially among African women. Furthermore, both the *Quran* and the *shariah* established a patriarchal society.

Slavery in *Dar al-Islam*

Islamic law forbade its followers from enslaving other Muslims, except in the case of prisoners of war. Neither was the position of a slave hereditary; Muslims were frequently known to free their slaves, especially if they converted to Islam during their period of servitude. Children born to a slave woman and a Muslim man were considered free.

› Rapid Review

From the seventh to the fifteenth centuries, Islam served as a unifying force throughout many parts of Asia, Europe, and Africa, contributing to the cultural landscape of all three continents. Islam preserved the learning of the Greeks, Romans, and Persians, blending it with the artistic, scientific, and mathematical knowledge of its own culture. Educational opportunities were extended and urban centers established as *Dar al-Islam* extended its influence into the everyday lives of the inhabitants of the Eastern Hemisphere.

› Review Questions

1. With regard to the doctrines of Islam in the period 600–1450,
   (A) the concept of monotheism was unknown to the inhabitants of the Arabian Peninsula prior to Muhammad's teachings
   (B) their teachings of equality made them more popular among the general population of Africa than among African rulers
   (C) they were embraced by members of the lower Hindu castes in India because of their emphasis on equality
   (D) they found widespread acceptance among Buddhists of both Central Asia and Southeast Asia
   (E) they were transmitted more frequently through missionary endeavor than through commercial contacts or conquest

2. The area in which Islam showed the most profound change during the seventh to the fifteenth centuries was in
   (A) the position of the caliph
   (B) its treatment toward People of the Book
   (C) the development of the *shariah*
   (D) the status of slaves
   (E) the role of women

3. One of the weaknesses of the early Muslim empires was
   (A) intolerance of the legal traditions of non-Muslim peoples
   (B) disregard for the cultural traditions of conquered peoples
   (C) failure to resolve questions of succession
   (D) insistence on conversion of non-Arabs within the empire
   (E) indifference to the Sunni/Shi'ite split

4. The Abbasid dynasty
   (A) created a social rift between Arabs and new converts
   (B) was more interested in strengthening Arab power than in gaining converts
   (C) healed the rift between Sunnis and Shi'ites
   (D) discouraged commercial activity in an effort to focus on missionary endeavor
   (E) proved the high point of Muslim cultural achievement

5. Which of the following qualifies as a primary source on the teachings of Muhammad?
   (A) The *Quran*
   (B) The *Hadith*
   (C) The Five Pillars
   (D) The *umma*
   (E) *The Arabian Nights*

6. Muhammad
   (A) made provisions for the future leadership of Islam
   (B) established clear class distinctions for Islamic society
   (C) built on the religious traditions of the Arabian peninsula
   (D) went against established gender distinctions in the practice of his faith
   (E) spoke out against military conquest as a vehicle for the extension of Islam

7. The Five Pillars
   (A) are inattentive to distinctions in social class
   (B) are included in the *Quran*
   (C) require religious instruction as an entrance to the Islamic faith
   (D) provide unity within Islam
   (E) address both religious and secular matters

8. As a new faith, Islam gained strength
   (A) within portions of the former Roman Empire
   (B) when adherence to Arabic ethnicity was emphasized over adherence to Islam
   (C) first in Mecca, then throughout the Arabian peninsula
   (D) because of rules of succession established by the first caliphs
   (E) in East Asia

› Answers and Explanations

1. **C**—Although the general population in India tended to cling to Hinduism, the lower castes and the untouchables often embraced Islam because it offered them the equality that the caste system did not. Monotheism (A) had already been introduced to the Arabian Peninsula by Jewish traders and Arab Christians. Islam was more popular among African rulers (B) than among the general population. In both Central Asia and Southeast Asia (D), Islam competed with Buddhism for followers. Although the Sufis (E) were active in missionary work during the Abbasid era, the main avenues of Islamic expansion were through military conquest and commercial contacts.

2. **E**—The role of women changed significantly from the early days of Islam; contacts with other peoples introduced the veiling of women and their seclusion from society, both customs absent in the early Islamic culture. The position of the caliph (A) as both spiritual and secular leader remained fairly constant throughout the caliphate. Throughout the period of the caliphate, the People of the Book (B) were respected by Muslim leaders. The precepts of the *shariah* remained consistent throughout the period (C). The status of slaves (D) as a nonhereditary class did not change during the caliphate.

3. **C**—Failure to resolve questions of succession led to the continued split between Sunnis and Shi'ites (E). Early Muslim empires tolerated both the legal systems (A) and the cultural traditions (B) of non-Muslim peoples within the empire, and non-Islamic peoples were not required to convert (D).

4. **E**—With its preservation of Greco-Roman and Persian cultures and its own dissemination of knowledge and promotion of urbanization, the Abbasid dynasty proved the golden age of Islamic culture. The Abbasids accepted new converts on an equal basis with Arabs (A). Conversion was a primary goal of the Abbasids (B). The Sunni/Shi'ite split continues to the present (C). Missionary zeal did not diminish the commercial interests (D) of the Abbasids, especially in the Mediterranean world and Indian Ocean trade.

5. **B**—The *Hadith* was a written compilation of the sayings of Muhammad, qualifying them as a primary source. The *Quran* (A) is a compilation of the revelations said to have been given to Muhammad by the archangel Gabriel. The Five Pillars (C) evolved as regulations exacted of every Muslim. The *umma* (D) is the term for the community of the faithful, and *The Arabian Nights* (E) is a literary work of the Abbasid period.

6. **C**—The god Allah was already among the gods in the Arabic pantheon. Monotheism was practiced by the Jewish and Christian minorities living on the Arabian peninsula. In failing to name a successor, Muhammad did not make provisions for the future leadership of Islam (A). Muhammad came from a modest background but married into a family of wealthy merchants, indicating a disregard for social distinctions, a policy that was carried out in the requirement of Muslims to give alms to the poor (B). Women of the Arabian peninsula were allowed to engage in commerce, a tradition that was carried on in early Islam (D). The *umma* established by Muhammad included programs for campaigns of military defense (E).

7. **D**—The first pillar requires only a simple statement of faith, a requirement that serves to unify Islam. No formal religious instruction is required by this statement (C). The Five Pillars make provisions for the welfare of the poor in Islamic society (A). The *Quran* was written down after the Five Pillars were established (B). The Five Pillars are concerned with religious matters only, whereas the *shariah* includes matters of everyday life (E).

8. **A**—In the eighth century, Islam had extended to Spain, which had been a part of the Roman Empire. Islam became more unified after it changed the policy of the Umayyads to reflect an emphasis on acceptance of the faith over Arabic ethnicity (B). The people of Mecca accepted Islam only after Muhammad's reconquest of the city (C). The first caliphs conflicted over the choice of a successor to Muhammad because of the prophet's failure to appoint a successor (D). Early Islam did not spread to East Asia (E).

CHAPTER 12

The Expansion of China

IN THIS CHAPTER

Summary: The political disorder following the collapse of the Han dynasty was reversed by the establishment of centralized government under the Sui dynasty (589–618). The brief period of Sui rule was followed by the power-ful Tang (618–907) and Song (960–1279) dynasties. Although the era of the Tang was characterized by trade and agricultural expansion, that of the Song produced significant technological advances. At the same time, the Song emphasized Chinese tradition, including the patriarchal family and Confucian teachings.

KEY IDEA

Key Terms

*abacus**	kowtow*
*bakufu**	Neo-Confucianism*
*bushi**	*samurai**
*bushido**	scholar-gentry*
celadon	*seppuku*
*daimyo**	serf*
flying money	Shinto*
footbinding*	*shogun**
Gempei Wars	shogunate*
Grand Canal	tea ceremony*
junks*	tribute*

The Tang Dynasty

Internal disorder preceded the rise of the Tang dynasty in 618. The Tang conquered central Asia to the eastern border of Bactria (present-day Afghanistan), including portions of Tibet, Manchuria, and South Vietnam. In order to solidify control of their vast empire, the Tang used diplomacy and also strengthened the Great Wall to ward off the advances of nomadic peoples. The expanding Tang empire centered on a bureaucracy influenced by the **scholar-gentry** and by Confucian perceptions of effective government. During both the Tang and Song eras, the Chinese civil service examination was strengthened.

In spite of the emphasis placed by the Tang government on Confucian principles, Buddhism gained acceptance in China during the Tang period. Buddhism's popularity among both elite and peasant groups resulted in an initial acceptance of the faith by Tang rulers. Thousands of monasteries populated by Buddhist monks and nuns dotted the Chinese landscape under early Tang rule. Especially supportive of Buddhism was Empress Wu (ruled 690–705), who supported Buddhist art and sculpture and attempted to promote the faith as a state religion. As imperial tax exemptions and private gifts of property to Buddhist monasteries increased their wealth, the Tang began to fear the increasing power of Buddhism. Consequently, later Tang rulers placed restrictions on gifts of land and money to Buddhist monasteries, a policy that weakened the influence of the Buddhist faith in China. As Buddhism declined in power and wealth, Confucianism gained in popularity as an expression of Chinese tradition.

The Decline of the Tang

Following the pattern of earlier Chinese dynasties, the Tang dynasty weakened as internal rebellion spread through the empire. At the same time, the Tang were plagued by invasions of nomadic peoples along their northern borders. By the ninth century, these nomads had placed themselves in control of large portions of northern China. Civil disorder reigned between the fall of the Tang in 907 and the accession of the Song in 960.

Achievements of the Tang

Under Tang rule:

- Trade and travel along the Silk Roads was protected.
- Contacts with Islamic peoples increased.
- Ocean-going ships were improved, increasing interest in ocean trade.
- Chinese **junks** were among the world's best ships and Chinese merchants dominated trade in the Indian Ocean.
- Paper money was introduced to China.
- Letters of credit, or **flying money**, facilitated long-distance trade.
- Urban areas grew in size.
- Canals and irrigation systems increased agricultural productivity. The Tang extended the Chinese canal system to supplement the **Grand Canal**, a 1,100-mile waterway constructed under the Sui to ease trade by connecting northern and southern China.
- Large estates were broken up and land redistributed.
- Gunpowder was invented.
- Short stories and poetry were popular.
- Tea and fast-growing rice were imported from Vietnam.
- Population growth in the rice-growing south surpassed that of the millet-growing north.

The Song Dynasty

In 960, China was overtaken by the Song dynasty. From its beginnings, the Song dynasty was unable to completely control the Khitan, a nomadic people to the north of the empire that had already assimilated much of Chinese culture. Throughout its 300-year rule of China, the Song had to pay **tribute** to the Khitan to keep them from conquering additional Song territory.

Under the Song dynasty many Chinese traditions were strengthened. For example:

- Civil service exams were emphasized as a prerequisite for government posts.
- Greater prestige was granted to the scholar-gentry.
- **Neo-Confucianism** arose as a blend of Confucian and Buddhist values. The new philosophy promoted the application of Confucian respect for authority and family to the everyday life of all levels of Chinese society, a feature that made it attractive to Chinese rulers. At the same time, the traditional aspect of Neo-Confucianism heightened the tendency of the Chinese elite classes to withdraw from contact with other peoples. Neo-Confucianism also reinforced gender and class distinctions.

The Song emphasis on the importance of the scholar-gentry over the military weakened its ability to withstand the threat of Khitan conquests of its northern borders. The cost of tribute paid to the Khitan burdened the Song economy as a whole, and especially the peasant class. Efforts at reform ended in the late eleventh century when Neo-Confucians reestablished Chinese tradition.

The faltering Song Empire now faced another threat: invasion by the Jurchens, another nomadic group. The Jurchens had overthrown the Khitan and settled in the region north of the Song Empire. They continued their conquest by dominating most of the basin of the Huang He (Yellow) River and causing the Song to retreat southward. The Song continued to thrive in the basin of the Yangtze River until 1279, during this time achieving noteworthy cultural and technological advances.

The Achievements of the Song

During the rule of the Song dynasty:

- Overseas trade begun under the Tang continued.
- Artists expressed themselves through landscape paintings.
- Warfare saw the use of catapults to hurl bombs and grenades. Armies and ships used flame-throwers and rocket launchers.
- Printing with movable type was developed.
- Compasses were used in ocean navigation.
- The **abacus** was developed to aid counting and the recording of taxes.
- The practice of **footbinding** spread among the elite classes. Later, lower classes would often adopt the custom as well.
- The concept of the patriarchal family intensified.

The Extension of China's Influence

The reestablishment of tradition among the Chinese during the Tang and Song dynasties did not prevent Chinese culture from expanding to other regions in the East. Throughout the period, Japan built on its previous contacts with Chinese culture, while Vietnam and Korea forged new ones.

Japan

During the seventh century C.E., Chinese culture reached Japan. Attempts by the Japanese emperor to mimic the form of Chinese bureaucracy resulted in Japan's adoption of both Confucian thought and Chinese written characters. Buddhism mixed with **Shinto**, the traditional Japanese belief system that revered spirits of nature and of ancestors.

Aristocratic rebellion against the complete adoption of Chinese ways led to the restoration of the elite classes and the establishment of large estates in Japan. Local aristocrats began to acquire their own military. As the power of the Japanese emperor steadily gave way to that of aristocrats in the capital at Kyoto, the power of local lords in the countryside increased. Rather than providing land and labor for the imperial court, local lords ran their own tiny kingdoms. The Japanese countryside saw the construction of fortresses protected by earthen walks and ditches similar to the moats used by European fortresses (Chapter 13).

The small states into which Japan was divided by the eleventh century were led by *bushi*, who not only administered their territories but also maintained their own military. Armed military troops called *samurai* served the *bushi*. Periodically, the *samurai* also were expected to serve in the capital to protect the emperor from bandits. Armed with curved swords, they engaged in battles in which they shouted out the details of their family heritage before engaging in conflicts.

The rise of the *samurai* gradually moved Japan toward a style of feudalism with some similarities to that of Western Europe during the same period. A *samurai* code of honor called **bushido** developed. This code included the practice of **seppuku**, or disembowelment, a form of suicide used by defeated or disgraced warriors to maintain family and personal honor. Japanese peasants gradually became **serfs** bound to the land and considered property of the local lord.

By the twelfth century, powerful families such as the Fujiwara allied themselves with local lords. During the late twelfth century, a series of conflicts called the **Gempei Wars** placed peasants against the *samurai*. The Japanese countryside was destroyed. As a result of the Gempei Wars, in 1185 a powerful family, the Minamoto, established the **bakufu**, or military government. Although the emperor and his court remained, real power now resided in the Minamoto family and their *samurai*. As imperial government broke down, the Japanese increasingly distanced themselves from Chinese Confucian ways.

The Shogunate

During the thirteenth and fourteenth centuries, real Japanese authority lay in the hands of prominent families who, in turn, controlled military leaders called *shoguns*. A period of civil disorder in the fourteenth century lessened the power of both the emperor and the **shogunate**. The resulting power vacuum allowed the *bushi* vassals to acquire lands that they then divided among their *samurai*. The *samurai* were required to pledge loyalty to their lord and provide him with military assistance when needed. Further court rebellions from 1467 to 1477 culminated in the division of Japan into approximately 300 tiny kingdoms, each ruled by a warlord called a **daimyo**.

Japanese warrior culture changed as the code of *bushido* lost its dominance in the fifteenth and sixteenth centuries. Large castles of stone and wood began to dot the Japanese landscape. Poorly trained peasant armies armed with pikes became a major fighting force of *daimyo* armies.

Gradually, some *daimyo* began to impose a degree of centralization upon their vassals and peasants. Taxes were collected to fund public projects such as the improvement of irrigation systems. Trade between villages arose and blossomed into long-distance trade, including trade with China. Merchant and artisan guilds arose; both men and women participated in these organizations. The strengthening of trade in Japan promoted the use of a common currency that assisted the centralization of the Japanese state.

Although trade revived in Japan, Japanese art also was developing its characteristic traditions. Although much Japanese art was an imitation of Chinese models, Japanese artists created their own style in sketches done in ink. Both Shintoism and Buddhism were reflected in two additional examples of Japanese artistry: the **tea ceremony** and decorative gardens.

Korea

Chinese influences in Korea can be traced back as far as the fourth century B.C.E., when the knowledge of metallurgy and agriculture spread from China to the Korean peninsula. In the latter part of the Han dynasty, Chinese settlers moved into Korea. Through these contacts Chinese culture, especially Buddhism, found a path into Korea. Chinese writing, which was later modified and made more suitable to the Korean language, was introduced. Confucian classics were read by Korean scholars.

Tang rulers defeated Korean peoples who resisted Chinese rule. The Silla kingdom of Korea, however, routed Tang forces. In 668, the Chinese withdrew from Korea in exchange for an arrangement that made the Silla vassals of the Tang and required them to pay tribute. After the Tang withdrew, the Silla united Korea.

The Silla studied Chinese customs and willingly performed the **kowtow** (a ritual bow) to the Chinese emperor. They introduced the Chinese civil service exam to Korea. The Silla made tribute payments that allowed them to participate in the Chinese trade network and in educational systems with Vietnamese, Japanese, and other Eastern peoples. Korean cultural and commercial opportunities, therefore, expanded. Buddhism became popular, especially with the Korean elite classes. Techniques of porcelain manufacture made their way from China to Korea; the Koreans modified Chinese porcelain to produce **celadon** bowls with a characteristic pale green color.

The Mongol invasion of Korea in the thirteenth century interfered with cultural contacts between Korea and China. When the Mongols were cast from Korea in 1392, Korea once again established contacts with the Chinese.

Vietnam

Southeast Asians displayed a somewhat different response to the introduction of Chinese culture than the peoples of East Asia had. While the Viets admired the technological advances and political ideals of the Chinese, at the same time they highly valued their own independence. Before the time of the Qin dynasty, the Viets carried on an active trade with the people of southern China. The Viets gradually brought the lands of the Red River valley under their control and began intermarrying with the peoples of present-day Cambodia and others in Southeast Asia. In contrast to the Chinese, the Viets had a different spoken language, lived in villages rather than establishing large urban areas, and based their society on the nuclear family. Vietnamese women enjoyed more privileges than women in China. Additionally, Buddhism gained greater popularity in Vietnam than in China.

When Han rulers attempted to annex South China into their empire, they encountered opposition from the Viets. Initially requiring the payment of tribute from the Viets, the Han conquered them in 111 B.C.E. Under Han rule the Viets adopted Chinese agricultural and irrigation techniques, the Confucian concept of veneration of ancestors, and the extended family structure. In spite of their admiration of some aspects of Chinese culture, however, the Viets periodically staged rebellions against Chinese rule. After the fall of the Tang in 907, they staged a major protest, which in 939 resulted in Vietnamese independence. After their independence was secured, the Viets continued the Confucian civil service examinations, which had earlier been disbanded. Vietnamese conquests of neighboring peoples succeeded largely because of the military organization and technology they had adopted from the Chinese.

› Rapid Review

The Tang and Song dynasties proved to be an era of active long-distance trade contacts and unprecedented technological innovation in China. During this era, China extended its borders to intensify the diffusion of its culture to regions such as Japan, Korea, and Vietnam. At the same time that China was broadening its influence, it was repeatedly plagued by nomadic invaders from the north such as the Khitan and the Jurchens. The necessity of addressing the problem of nomadic invasions became China's next great challenge.

› Review Questions

1. Confucianism
   (A) became more popular in Vietnam than in Korea
   (B) was rejected as an acceptable philosophy by the Japanese
   (C) combined with Buddhism to create a cultural bridge between China and Korea
   (D) brought greater freedom to Vietnamese women
   (E) blended well with Shintoism to forge Japanese artistic traditions

2. Which was NOT an achievement of the Tang dynasty?
   (A) the solution to the problem of nomadic peoples along China's border
   (B) the adoption of products from Vietnam
   (C) an emphasis on long-distance trade
   (D) irrigation
   (E) advances in the technology of warfare

3. The position of Chinese women
   (A) resulted in greater freedoms under Neo-Confucianism
   (B) changed markedly between the seventh and thirteenth centuries
   (C) was defined by Confucianism
   (D) was more restrictive under the Tang than under the Song
   (E) declined in regions where Buddhism was popular

4. Japanese feudalism
   (A) brought a temporary end to internal conflicts
   (B) increased the power of the emperor
   (C) revolved around the power of the *samurai* as warlords
   (D) saw the beginnings of a centralized Japan
   (E) united peasant and elite classes

5. Compared to the Viets, the Chinese were more
   (A) agrarian
   (B) ethnically diverse
   (C) interested in trade
   (D) urbanized
   (E) interested in preserving their own culture

6. Compared to Korean attitudes toward the Chinese, the Japanese
   (A) more greatly appreciated the centralization of the Chinese government
   (B) were more devoted to Confucianism
   (C) were more favorable to the civil service examination
   (D) demonstrated a desire to show respect to the Chinese emperor
   (E) were similar in their desire to become part of the Chinese trading system

7. The position of the Chinese scholar-gentry
   (A) was mimicked by the Japanese
   (B) was admired by the Vietnamese
   (C) weakened efforts to curb nomadic invasions
   (D) declined during the Song dynasty
   (E) was not supported by Confucian philosophy

8. Buddhism became more popular among China's neighbors than in China itself because
   (A) Buddhism reinforced Confucian gender roles
   (B) Buddhism weakened the power of the Chinese emperor
   (C) Buddhism reinforced a stratified society
   (D) Buddhism did not originate in China
   (E) Buddhism emphasized centralized government

› Answers and Explanations

1. **C**—The Confucian civil service exam was adopted by the Koreans and Confucian classics were studied by Korean scholars. Also, Buddhist thought gained popularity among Koreans. Confucian thought was accepted more readily in Korea than in Vietnam, which strongly preferred Buddhism (A). Buddhism gained acceptance among the Japanese (B), blending with traditional Japanese Shinto beliefs to influence Japanese gardens and tea ceremonies (E). Among the distinct differences between the Vietnamese and Chinese were the restrictions placed on Chinese women (D).

2. **A**—The Tang were unable to permanently resolve the problem of nomadic peoples along their northern borders. Tea and fast-growing rice were adopted from Vietnam (B). Long-distance trade increased contacts with other peoples in the East (C). China became increasingly urbanized under the Tang (D). Tang inventions included gunpowder (E).

3. **C**—Confucianism strengthened the concept of the patriarchal family, which placed women in a position subordinate to men. Neo-Confucianism, which applied Confucian principles to everyday life, did nothing to elevate the status of women (A). Although Chinese women enjoyed a few opportunities to participate in business ventures during Tang rule (D), the basic position of women as inferior to men changed little over the centuries in this patriarchal society (B). Buddhism tended to elevate the position of women in society (E).

4. **D**—Efforts of the *daimyo* in the later years of feudalism to adopt a common currency and fund public works led to the beginnings of a centralized Japanese state. Internal conflicts between warlords and also between peasants and warlords (E) marked Japanese feudalism (A).

5. **D**—Especially by the Song era, urbanization became a trademark of Chinese civilization. The Viets lived almost entirely in villages. Although agriculture was common to both societies, Chinese urban life made its culture less agrarian than that of the Viets (A). The Vietnamese custom of intermarrying with the peoples of other societies in Southeast Asia made their society more ethnically diverse than that

of the Chinese (B). Both societies traded widely, often with each other (C). Both also were intent on preserving their own culture (E).

6. **E**—Both Japan and Korea benefited by participation in the Chinese trading system. The Japanese rejected the centralization of the Chinese government as unsuitable for their society (A). Of the two belief systems borrowed from China, Buddhism became more accepted in Japan (B). The Chinese civil service exam was used in Korea rather than in Japan (C). The Koreans, not the Japanese, performed the kowtow to the Chinese emperor (D).

7. **C**—Under the Song, the relative importance placed on the scholar-gentry over that of the military weakened efforts to curb the threat of nomads along China's northern border. Neither the Japanese (A) nor the Vietnamese (B) developed a class of scholar-gentry. The position of the scholar-gentry strengthened under the Song (D), which capitalized on Confucian philosophy of effective education to support the scholar-gentry (E).

8. **D**—Originating in India, Buddhism was not so strongly associated with Chinese culture as Confucianism. Buddhism was more accepting of women than Confucianism with its defined gender roles (A). Buddhism favored a more egalitarian society (C). Buddhist belief did not strive to undermine the power of the emperor (B) and supported the political system of the country, whether centralized or decentralized (E).

CHAPTER 13

Changes in European Institutions

IN THIS CHAPTER

Summary: In the centuries after the fall of the Roman Empire, Western Europe underwent a period of political, economic, and social upheaval that continued until about 900. The one stabilizing force throughout most of Western Europe was the Roman Catholic Church. Only in Spain, dominated by Muslim influences, did the learning of the Greeks and Romans thrive in Western Europe.

Key Terms

*benefice**	*Magna Carta**
chivalry*	manorialism*
excommunication*	medieval*
feudalism*	Middle Ages*
fief*	moldboard plow
Gothic architecture*	parliament*
investiture*	vassal*

Manorialism and Feudalism in Western Europe

Even before the fall of the Roman Empire, declining prosperity in the final years of the empire had caused small landowners to sell off their land holdings to the owners of large estates. Although some peasants relocated to urban areas, others remained to work the land, receiving protection from their landlords in exchange for their agricultural labor. As trade continued to decline and political order disintegrated, **manorialism** became more widespread. When a wave of Vikings from Scandinavia invaded Europe in the ninth century, Western Europeans turned to **feudalism** to provide a means of protection.

Feudalism was a political, economic, and social system. Throughout most areas of Western Europe, nobles or landlords offered **benefices**, or privileges, to **vassals** in exchange for military service in the lord's army or agricultural labor on the lord's estate. Often the benefice was a grant of land, called a **fief**. Feudalism was structured so that a person could enjoy the position of a noble with vassals under him and, at the same time, serve as vassal to a noble of higher status. Knights, similar in their role to the *samurai* of Japan, were vassals who served in the lord's military forces. Like the *samurai*, the knights of Western Europe followed an honor code called **chivalry**. In contrast to the *samurai* code of *bushido*, however, chivalry was a reciprocal, or two-sided, contract between vassal and lord. Whereas the code of *bushido* applied to both men and women of the *samurai* class, chivalry was followed only by the knights.

Occupying the lowest rank on the **medieval** European manor were serfs, whose labor provided the agricultural produce needed to maintain the self-sufficiency of the manor. The life of serfs was difficult. In addition to giving the lord part of their crops, they had to spend a number of days each month working the lord's lands or performing other types of labor service for the lord. The agricultural tools available to them were crude. Only after the invention of the heavy **moldboard plow** in the ninth century did they possess a tool adequate to turn the heavy sod of Western Europe. Serfdom was different from slavery; serfs could not be bought or sold and could pass on their property to their heirs.

The Beginnings of Regional Governments

At the same time that feudalism provided protection to the inhabitants of Western Europe, the people known as the Franks rose in prominence in the region of present-day northern France, western Germany, and Belgium. The Franks were the descendants of the Germanic tribe that overran Gaul (present-day France) after the fall of Rome. By the fifth century, the Franks had converted to Christianity. From the time of the ninth century onward, some areas of Western Europe saw the strengthening of regional kingdoms such as that of the Franks.

Rulers of northern Italy and Germany also gained prominence by the tenth century. Eventually, in an effort to connect with the classical empire of Rome, they began to call their territory the Holy Roman Empire. As the French philosopher Voltaire later commented, however, it was "neither holy, nor Roman, nor an empire." The new empire was but a fraction of the size of the original empire of the Romans. In spite of its grand claims, northern Italy continued to be organized into independent city-states, and Germany into numerous local states also overseen by feudal lords. While providing a measure of unity for a portion of Europe during the **Middle Ages**, the long-term political effect of the Holy Roman Empire was to delay the unification of both Germany and Italy into separate states until the end of the nineteenth century.

In England, an alternate form of feudalism took hold as a result of the Norman invasion of 1066. In that year, the Duke of Normandy, later called William the Conqueror, arrived in England from his province of Normandy in northern France. Of Viking descent, William transplanted his form of feudalism to England. Rather than following a complex structure of lords and vassals, William imposed a feudal structure that required all vassals to owe their allegiance directly to the monarch.

The Growth of Parliamentary Government in England

The political structure of medieval England further distinguished itself by imposing limitations on the power of the monarchy, and establishing one of the earliest parliamentary governments. Even under the English style of feudalism, nobles continued to hold considerable influence. In 1215, in an effort to control the tax policies of King John, English nobles forced John to sign the *Magna Carta*. This document endowed the English nobility with basic rights that were later interpreted to extend to the other English social classes as well. The first English **parliament**, convened in 1265, also was an extension of feudal rights of collaboration between king and vassals. The first meeting of this representative body saw its division into a House of Lords representing the clergy and nobility and a House of Commons elected by urban elite classes. Parliaments also arose in Spain, France, Scandinavia, and parts of Germany.

Renewed Economic Growth

Although Western Europe experienced political disorder during the medieval period, by the ninth century the former Roman Empire began to witness signs of renewed economic growth and technological innovation. Contacts with the eastern portion of the former Roman Empire and with people of Central Asia had brought the moldboard plow into use in Western Europe. Also, the military effectiveness of the medieval knight was improved through the introduction of the stirrup.

Improved agricultural techniques resulted in population growth, a trend that also increased the size of urban areas. Warmer temperatures between 800 and 1300 also contributed to urban revival. Landlords often extended their landholdings, sometimes paying serfs a salary to work these new lands. A degree of security returned to Western Europe as many of the Vikings, now Christian, ceased their raids and became settled peoples. In present-day France, palace schools were established to educate local children.

The Crusades

The Crusades between the Western and Eastern worlds and between Christianity and Islam opened up new contacts. As a result of their campaigns to retake the Holy Land from the Seljuk Turks, Western Europeans were exposed to the larger and more prosperous urban areas of the Byzantine Empire with their magnificent examples of Eastern architecture. The Crusades also introduced the West to sugarcane, spices, and luxury goods such as porcelain, glassware, and carpets from the Eastern world. Trade between East and West increased, although it proved an unbalanced trade; while the West was attracted to the fine goods of the East, the Eastern world displayed little interest in the inferior trade items offered by the West. Western appreciation for the treasures of the East was not universal, however. During the Fourth Crusade, merchants from Venice expressed their intense rivalry with Eastern merchants by looting the city of Constantinople.

As Western Europe widened its knowledge of other peoples through trade, its growing population also extended into neighboring areas. After settling down in Europe during the tenth century, the Vikings explored the northern Atlantic, inhabiting Iceland and establishing temporary settlements in Greenland and the northeastern portion of North

America. Seeking new agricultural lands, the people of Western Europe also pushed into areas of Eastern Europe.

Conflicts Between Church and State

While Western Europeans engaged in commercial rivalries with other societies, a second rivalry had developed in Western Europe: one between church leaders and monarchs. Throughout the Middle Ages, the church had sometimes taken the role of a feudal lord, owning large landholdings. In some cases, the growing wealth of the Roman Catholic Church served as a temptation for priests and monks to set aside their spiritual responsibilities to concentrate on the acquisition of material possessions.

Conflicts between church leaders and secular leaders arose over the issue of **investiture**. Lay investiture was a process by which monarchs appointed church bishops. Especially intense was the controversy between Pope Gregory VII (1073–1085) and Holy Roman Emperor Henry IV, which culminated with the **excommunication** of Henry IV. Henry's subsequent confession demonstrated that, in this instance, the pope had gained the upper hand.

The Role of Women in Medieval European Society

Throughout the Middle Ages, Western European women carried out traditional roles of homemaker and childcare provider. It is possible that among the elite classes, the position of women declined over that of earlier ages as the code of chivalry reinforced ideas of women as weak and subordinate to men. Women who resided in medieval towns were allowed a few privileges such as participation in trade and in some craft guilds. Convents also offered some women opportunities for service in their communities. For the most part, however, medieval European women were expected to serve as reflections of their husbands.

The High Middle Ages in Western Europe

By the eleventh century, significant changes occurred in Western Europe to indicate the region's gradual emergence from the relative cultural decline of the medieval period. Termed the High Middle Ages, the eleventh to the fifteenth centuries saw the following changes in Western European society:

- **Gothic architecture**—Cathedrals with tall spires and arched windows with stained glass reflected Muslim designs and Western architectural technology.
- Increased urbanization—The size of Western European cities still could not compare with the much larger urban areas of China.
- The rise of universities.
- A decline in the number of serfs on the manor. Some serfs received wages to work in new agricultural lands, while others fled to towns. A serf who remained in a town for a year and a day was considered a free person.
- The emergence of centralized monarchies.

- The strengthening of nation-states. The Hundred Years' War (1337–1453) increased the power of both France and England and is also considered by many historians as the end of Europe's medieval period.
- Increased Eurasian trade.
- The growth of banking.
- New warfare technology such as gunpowder and cannon that made castles increasingly obsolete.

The renewal of economic and intellectual vigor and the tendency toward centralized regional political authority marked the beginning of a new era on the European continent.

› Rapid Review

The decline of Roman authority in Western Europe resulted in the rise of feudalism as a system of protection. Feudalism in Western Europe bore some similarities to Japanese feudalism. Although Western European feudalism created local governments, in some areas of Europe, such as France, regional kingdoms arose. Characteristic of feudal Europe was a persistent conflict between popes and kings concerning secular authority. Many European women continued in traditional roles. By the eleventh century, Western Europe demonstrated signs of revival as universities were established, trade increased, and some serfs began to leave the manor.

› Review Questions

1. In contrast to Japanese feudalism, Western European feudalism
   (A) included women in the feudal relationship
   (B) created a reciprocal relationship between lord and vassal
   (C) was based on a noncontractual relationship
   (D) did not lead to centralized regional governments
   (E) endured for a longer period

2. Early medieval Europe's strongest state was
   (A) the Papal States
   (B) England
   (C) France
   (D) the Holy Roman Empire
   (E) Spain

3. The period of greatest population decline in Europe during the Middle Ages was
   (A) from the tenth to the thirteenth centuries
   (B) the fourteenth century
   (C) the fifth and sixth centuries
   (D) the fifteenth century
   (E) the eighth century

4. During the Middle Ages, the concept of limited government was seen most clearly in
   (A) France
   (B) Germany
   (C) England
   (D) Italy
   (E) Spain

5. Which statement describes Europe between the ninth to fifteenth centuries?
   (A) The consolidation of Germanic kingdoms into a single Germanic state
   (B) The end of pressure from migratory peoples
   (C) Steady decline of educational opportunities
   (D) European retreat from contact with neighboring societies
   (E) The expansion of the Eastern world into Western Europe

6. Trade during the medieval period
   (A) weakened in the Baltic regions as continental routes broadened
   (B) placed the power of the merchant classes in competition with monarchical power
   (C) shifted away from the Mediterranean basin after the fall of Rome
   (D) placed Europe within the Muslim commercial network
   (E) was balanced between Eastern and Western markets

7. The fifteenth century was characterized by
   (A) the beginnings of nation-states in Italy and Germany
   (B) the strengthening of nation-states in England and France
   (C) decentralization of political power in Spain
   (D) the establishment of Western European political tradition in the Middle East
   (E) the establishment of parliamentary tradition in England and France

8. Medieval Europe
   (A) extended local schools found on the manor
   (B) developed new banking institutions from multicultural contacts
   (C) saw the rise of universities after the conclusion of the Hundred Years' War
   (D) produced urban areas that rivaled those of Eastern empires
   (E) produced uniquely Christian architectural forms

› Answers and Explanations

1. **B**—Feudalism in Western Europe was based on a reciprocal, or mutual relationship of responsibility between lord and vassal, whereas Japanese feudalism exacted obedience from the *samurai* regardless of the responsibility of the *daimyo*. European chivalry was binding to the knights only, whereas Japanese *bushido* applied to both men and women of the *samurai* class (A). The European relationship between lord and vassal was based on a contract, whereas the Japanese *bushido* was based on *samurai* honor (C). Although Japanese feudalism did not lead to the establishment of regional governments, Europe saw the prominence of centralized regional governments in France, England, and the Holy Roman Empire (D). Japanese feudalism lasted far longer (into the nineteenth century) than did Western European feudalism, which ended by the mid-fifteenth century (E).

2. **D**—The Holy Roman Empire brought a measure of unity to central Europe, essentially embracing the city-states of northern Italy and the principalities of Germany. The Papal States consisted of a small territory in the central Italian peninsula (A), whereas Spain remained under Islamic control until the late fifteenth century (E). Both England (B) and France (C) saw the beginnings of regional governments that did not compare in size with that of the Holy Roman Empire.

3. **B**—European population declined drastically during the fourteenth century because of the devastation of the bubonic plague. This decline was reversed during the fifteenth century (D). European population saw a steady rise between the tenth to the thirteenth centuries as a result of the introduction of new crops and farming methods (A). Although European population declined somewhat after the fall of Rome in the fifth century (C), this decline was not as dramatic as that of the fourteenth century. Population growth was fairly steady in the eighth century (E).

4. **C**—England witnessed the signing of the *Magna Carta* in 1215 and the first parliament in 1265, both placing limits on the power of the monarchy. France remained under the control of mon-

archs (A), whereas Spain remained under the influence of the Muslim caliphate; the gradual reconquest of Spain left the country under monarchical control (E). Germany (B) and Italy (D), not yet united as nation-states, were part of the Holy Roman Empire.

5. **E**—From 711 to 1492, portions of Spain were dominated by the empire of Islam. Silk Roads trade continued to forge contacts between East and West, and contact with the Eastern world escalated as a result of the Crusades (D). German provinces were not united into a single German state (A). The Vikings moved into Europe, not forming settled communities on a large scale until about the year 1000 (B). By the ninth century, palace schools had arisen in Western Europe, and by the eleventh century several universities were in operation (C).

6. **D**—During the Muslim occupation of Spain, al-Andalus became part of the Muslim trade network. During the European Middle Ages, trade increased in the Baltic regions (A) and continued in the Mediterranean basin, even though it weakened after the fall of Rome (C). Merchant classes tended to prefer the stability that monarchs could bring to the commercial world (B). Trade was not balanced between Eastern and Western markets. Although the West favored the luxury goods of the East, the West produced little of interest to Eastern merchants (E).

7. **B**—The end of the Hundred Years' War in 1453 saw the strengthening of the concept of the nation-state in both France and England. Italy and Germany were not organized into nation-states until the late nineteenth century (A). Power in Spain was centralized under both Muslim rule and under Christian rulers as they began the reconquest (C). The Middle East was uninterested in the establishment of Western political traditions (D). Parliamentary government was introduced to England before the fifteenth century, but was not a feature of France at that time period (E).

8. **B**—Letters of credit used in the Chinese and Muslim worlds became forerunners of the Western European banking institution in the Middle Ages. Medieval European manors did not usually provide schools for manor children (A). Universities had already begun to appear in various parts of Europe by the twelfth century (C). Eastern urban areas, especially those in China, tended to be much larger than those in Western Europe (D). Christian churches adapted arches and decorative designs from the Muslim world (E).

CHAPTER 14

Interregional Trade and Exchange

IN THIS CHAPTER

Summary: Throughout the period from 600 to 1450, global contacts gradually increased. In Eurasia, the Mongols served as trade facilitators between East and West. In Africa, the migrations of **Bantu-speaking peoples** not only altered the nature of African society but also led to new contacts between African and Arab peoples in the eastern portions of sub-Saharan Africa. Indian Ocean trade networks enriched contacts between African and Asian peoples. The eastern portion of the Roman Empire gradually lost territory to the Turks as Western Europe built upon Islamic and Greco-Roman traditions to forge a new society on the European continent.

Key Terms

age grade*
astrolabe*
Austronesian*
Bantu-speaking peoples*
Black Death*
caravel*
griots*
Hanseatic League
kamikaze*
Khan*
lateen sail*
Malay sailors*

Maori*
metropolitan*
Middle Kingdom*
Ming dynasty
Mongol Peace*
perspective*
Renaissance*
stateless society*
steppe diplomacy*
syncretism*
Yuan dynasty

The Mongols

The Song dynasty was overcome in the thirteenth century by the Mongols, a society of pastoral nomads from the steppes of Central Asia. By the end of their period of dominance in the fifteenth century, the Mongols had conquered China, Persia, and Russia, controlling the largest land empire in history. In establishing their empire, the Mongols facilitated the flow of trade between Europe and Asia and brought bubonic plague to three continents.

Accomplished horsemen, the Mongols typified the numerous nomadic bands that migrated throughout Central Asia in search of grazing lands for their livestock. To supplement the meat and dairy products provided by their herds, the Mongols traded with settled agricultural peoples for grain and vegetables. The basic unit of Mongol society was the tribe; when warfare threatened, tribes joined together to form confederations. Although men held tribal leadership roles, Mongol women had the right to speak in tribal councils. Throughout their history, the Mongols were masters of the intrigues of **steppe diplomacy**, which involved alliances with other pastoral groups and the elimination of rivals, sometimes rivals within one's own family.

Early Mongol influence on China had begun as early as the twelfth century, when the Mongols defeated an army from Qin China sent to repel their advances. The leader credited with organizing the Mongols into an effective confederation was Temujin, who was renamed Chinggis Khan when he was elected the ultimate ruler, or ***Khan***, of the Mongol tribes in 1206. A master at motivating the Mongol tribes, Chinggis Khan managed to break individual clan loyalties and construct new military units with allegiance to himself as their leader.

In addition to their unparalleled horsemanship, the Mongols became masters of the shortbow. Mongol contact with the Chinese also introduced them to other weapons of war such as the catapult, gunpowder, cannons, flaming arrows, and battering rams. By the time that Chinggis Khan died in 1227, the Mongols controlled an empire that extended from northern China to eastern Persia.

As they consolidated their empire, the Mongols were more preoccupied with collecting tribute than with administering their newly acquired territories. They were generally tolerant toward the religious beliefs and practices of the people they conquered and sometimes eventually adopted the dominant religion of their subject peoples.

Expansion of the Mongol Empire into Russia

The Mongol conquests continued after the death of Chinggis Khan, reaching Russia by 1237. From that year until 1240 the Mongols, or Tartars as the Russians called them, executed the only successful winter invasions of Russia in history. Cities that resisted Mongol advances saw their inhabitants massacred or sold into slavery. The once-prosperous city of Kiev was burned to the ground. The effects of the Mongol occupation of Russia were numerous:

- The Mongols set up a tribute empire called The Golden Horde.
- Serfdom arose as peasants gave up their lands to the aristocracy in exchange for protection from the Mongols.
- Moscow benefited financially by acting as a tribute collector for the Mongols. When neighboring towns failed to make their tribute payments, the princes of Moscow added their territory to the principality of Moscow.
- They strengthened the position of the Orthodox Church by making the **metropolitan**, or head of the Orthodox Church, the head of the Russian church.
- Mongol rule kept Russia culturally isolated from Western European trends such as the Renaissance. This isolation denied Russia opportunities to establish both commercial and cultural contacts with the West, in a situation that fostered misunderstanding through the modern period.

After establishing their presence in Russia, the Mongols went on to their next goal: the conquest of Europe. After an attempted conquest of Hungary in 1240 and raids in Eastern Europe, the Mongols withdrew to handle succession issues in their capital of Karakorum in Mongolia. The proposed conquest of Europe never materialized.

The Mongols in Persia

After abandoning their plans to add Europe to their empire, the Mongols turned to conquest within the world of Islam. In 1258, the city of Baghdad was destroyed and Persia added to the portion of the Mongol Empire known as the Ilkhanate. Among the approximately 800,000 people slaughtered in the capture of Baghdad was the Abbasid caliph. With his murder, the Islamic dynasty that had ruled Persia for about 500 years ended. Another group of Islamic peoples, the Seljuk Turks, had been defeated by the Mongols in 1243, weakening their dominance in Anatolia. The resulting power vacuum facilitated the conquest of Anatolia (present-day Turkey) by the Ottoman Turks in the fifteenth century. The Mongol threat to the Islamic world ended in 1260 at the hands of the Mamluks, or slaves, of Egypt.

The Mongols in China

In China, the Mongols under the leadership of Kubilai Khan, a grandson of Chinggis Khan, turned their attention to the remnants of the Song Empire in the southern part of the country. By 1271, Kubilai Khan controlled most of China and began to refer to his administration of China as the **Yuan dynasty**. The Yuan dynasty would administer China until its overthrow by the **Ming dynasty** in 1368. Under Mongol rule:

- The Chinese were forbidden to learn the Mongol written language, which was the language of official records under the Yuan dynasty.
- Intermarriage between Mongols and Chinese was outlawed.
- The Chinese civil service examination was not reinstated.
- Religious toleration was practiced.
- Chinese were allowed to hold positions in local and regional governments.
- Mongol women enjoyed more freedoms than Chinese women, refusing to adopt the Chinese practice of footbinding. Mongol women also were allowed to move about more freely in public than were Chinese women. Toward the end of the Yuan dynasty, however, the increasing influence of Neo-Confucianism saw greater limits placed on Mongol women.
- The Yuan used the expertise of scholars and artisans from various societies.
- Foreigners were welcome at the Yuan court. Among visitors to the Mongol court were the Venetian Marco Polo and his family. Marco Polo's subsequent account of his travels, perhaps partially derived from other sources, increased European interest in exploring other lands.
- Merchants were accorded higher status in the Mongol administration than they had under the Chinese.
- The suppression of piracy furthered maritime trade.
- Attempts at expansion culminated in the unsuccessful invasions of Japan in 1274 and 1280 and a brief occupation of Vietnam. The attempted invasions of Japan were turned back by treacherous winds known to the Japanese as divine winds, or **kamikaze.**

By the mid-fourteenth century, the court of Kubilai Khan weakened as it became more concerned with the accumulation and enjoyment of wealth than with efficient administration. Banditry, famine, and peasant rebellion characterized the last years of the Yuan until their overthrow by a Chinese peasant who founded the Ming dynasty.

The Impact of Mongol Rule on Eurasia

The most significant positive role of the Mongols was the facilitation of trade between Europe and Asia. The peace and stability fostered by the Mongol Empire, especially during the **Mongol Peace** of the mid-thirteenth to the mid-fourteenth centuries, promoted the exchange of products that brought increased wealth to merchants and enriched the exchange of ideas between East and West. Along the major trade routes, merchants founded diaspora communities that fostered cultural exchange. Among them were Jewish communities along the Silk Roads and the Mediterranean in addition to settlements of Chinese merchants in Southeast Asia. New trading posts and empires encouraged European peoples to later invest in voyages of exploration.

Long-distance travel increased. Ibn Battuta, a Moroccan Muslim scholar, travelled throughout the Muslim world, including Central Asia, China, Southeast Asia, Spain, and East Africa. His journal, as well as the writings of Marco Polo, became valuable resources in the study of cultural exchange in the thirteenth and fourteenth centuries.

Another exchange brought about unintentionally by the Mongols proved devastating to Europe, Asia, and Africa: the spread of bubonic plague. It is possible that the plague entered Mongol-controlled territories through plague-infested fleas carried by rats that helped themselves to the grain in Mongol feedsacks. The bubonic plague, known also in Europe as the **Black Death**, spread across the steppes of Central Asia to China, where it contributed to the weakening and eventual fall of the Yuan dynasty. In the mid-fourteenth century, the plague also spread throughout the Middle East, North Africa, and Europe. The disease followed Eurasian and African trade routes as merchants carried it from city to city and port to port. As many as 25,000,000 people may have died from plague in China, and Europe lost about one third of its population; the Middle East also suffered a large death toll. Significant loss of life among Western European serfs helped deal a final blow to manorialism in that region. Some plague-devastated areas required 100 years or more to recover population losses and economic and urban vigor.

Further Nomadic Influences

With the decrease of Mongol dominance in Eurasia came a final nomadic thrust by Timur the Lame, or Tamerlane, a Turk from Central Asia. Although his capital city at Samarkand was noted for architectural beauty, his conquests were known only for their incredible brutality. From the mid-1300s until his death in 1405, Tamerlane spread destruction across Persia, Mesopotamia, India, and a part of southern Russia. His death marked the final major thrust of nomadic peoples from Central Asia into Eurasia.

Encounter and Exchange in Africa: The Bantu Migrations

Sub-Saharan Africa witnessed an exchange of ideas, technology, and language through the migrations of the Bantu-speaking peoples. About 2000 B.C.E., small numbers of agrarian peoples from the edge of the rain forest in present-day Nigeria began migrating from their homeland, perhaps as a result of population pressures. The migrations escalated throughout the period from 500 B.C.E. to 1000 C.E., and continued until about 1500 C.E.

As the Bantu peoples migrated southward and eastward throughout sub-Saharan Africa, they spread the knowledge of the agricultural techniques that they brought from their homeland. Following the course of the Congo River, they farmed the fertile land along riverbanks at the edges of the rain forest. Their contacts with foraging peoples of central Africa taught them the techniques of cattle-raising. As they migrated, the Bantu also spread the knowledge of ironworking. Historians are unsure whether their skills in ironworking were learned from previous contact with the ironworkers of Kush or were acquired by independent innovation. Whatever the reason, the spread of iron agricultural implements facilitated crop cultivation throughout sub-Saharan Africa.

The Bantu acquired an additional source of nutrition with the arrival of the banana on the African continent. Carried from Southeast Asia through the Indian Ocean to Madagascar by the **Malay sailors** about 400 C.E., the banana reached the African continent through interactions between the descendants of the Malay sailors and African peoples. After its arrival on the African continent, the banana spread throughout sub-Saharan Africa in a reverse pattern to that of the migratory Bantu. Today, the inhabitants of Madagascar speak a language belonging to the same **Austronesian** linguistic group as Malaysian tongues.

Interactions in East Africa

The Bantu migrations also resulted in the spread of the Bantu languages. By the thirteenth century, the Bantu had reached the eastern coast of Africa, where they came into contact with Arab traders. The interactions between the two groups of people forged the **syncretism** of the Bantu and Arabic languages into the Swahili tongue. Swahili remains a major African language to the present.

Bantu Society and Government

The Bantu also contributed their social and political organization to the heritage of sub-Saharan Africa. With the village as the basis of Bantu society, **stateless societies** emerged as the political organization of the Bantu. Stateless societies were organized around family and kinship groups led by a respected family member. Religion was animistic, with a belief in spirits inhabiting the natural world. Early Bantu societies did not have a written language; oral traditions were preserved by storytellers called *griots*.

Bantu society centered around the **age grade**, a cohort group that included tribal members of the same age who shared life experiences and responsibilities appropriate to their age group. Woman's role as a childbearer was highly respected, and women shared in agricultural work, trade, and sometimes military duties. All property was held communally; individual wealth was determined not by the acquisition of property but by the acquisition of slaves.

China and Europe in the Indian Ocean

The disruption of overland trade routes fostered by the decline of Mongol power in Eurasia produced increased commercial vigor in the Indian Ocean. China's Ming dynasty (1368–1644) responded to the fall of the Yuan dynasty by a renewed focus on Indian Ocean trade. In the early fifteenth century, the Ming sent out massive expeditions into the Indian Ocean to display the glories of the **Middle Kingdom**. In addition to exploring the Indian Ocean, the Chinese expedition entered the Persian Gulf and the Red Sea, carrying with them Chinese porcelain and other luxuries to trade for local merchandise. The expeditions were led by Zheng He, a Chinese general of the Muslim faith.

In 1433, the voyages of Zheng He were abruptly called to an end by the Ming emperors. Confucian scholars had long resented the notoriety that Zheng He enjoyed by virtue of his voyages. To this resentment the Ming emperors now added fear of the cost of the expeditions, taking the opinion that the money would be better spent on resisting the continuing Mongol threat against China's borders and on constructing a new capital at Beijing. Although China now returned to its more traditional policy of isolation, Ming emperors continued to engage in regional trade in Southeast Asia.

The Rise of Western Europe

As the Chinese withdrew from world commercial dominance, the nations of Western Europe stepped in to fill the void. By the 1400s, European regional monarchies possessed the political power and financial resources to allow them to investigate the world beyond their borders. European technology had become more sophisticated, and commercial activity in urban areas contributed to its financial stability. European visitors to the Mongol court learned of advances in Asian technology such as the printing press, gunpowder, and the magnetic compass.

In spite of the increased economic vitality enjoyed by Europeans in the early modern era, there remained a serious imbalance of trade between Europe and the East. Although many Europeans craved the luxury goods of the East, Europe offered very few products attractive to the peoples of the East. Europe's trade goods consisted mainly of items such as wool, honey, salt, copper, tin, and animals for Eastern zoos. The unfavorable balance of trade between Europe and the East meant that Europeans frequently had to pay for their luxury items in gold, a situation that drained Europe of its gold supply.

Although Europe experienced an unfavorable balance of trade with the East, several trading cities in northern Europe capitalized on regional commerce and formed the **Hanseatic League**. By the thirteenth century, this trade association was active in the Baltic and North Sea regions. Eventually both the Hanseatic League and Italian ships from Mediterranean waters extended their commercial activity to the manufacturing centers of Flanders.

The Renaissance

By the beginning of the fifteenth century, the city-states of northern Italy were experiencing a renewed interest in the learning and artistic styles of the Greco-Roman world. This rebirth of learning, or **Renaissance**, owed its origins partly to interactions with the Muslim world. European contacts with the Middle East during the Crusades, the preservation of Greco-Roman learning by the Muslims during their occupation of Spain, and Islamic and European interactions in the weakening Byzantine Empire invigorated the revival of learning and trade characteristic of the Renaissance. Furthermore, the northern Italian city-states had become wealthy from their role in supplying goods for the Crusaders and in transporting them across the waters of the Mediterranean.

The Renaissance spirit differed from that of the European Middle Ages by focusing on life in this world rather than in the afterlife. Many Renaissance paintings continued to feature religious subjects; but, at the same time, there was an additional emphasis on paintings of people and nature. Renaissance painting also was characterized by the use of **perspective** and a greater variety of colors.

Early European Explorations

By the early 1400s, European explorations outside the Mediterranean had been primarily confined to the Atlantic islands of the Azores, Madeiras, and the Canaries. Europeans also had carried out some explorations along the western coast of Africa. Lack of European technological expertise prevented further explorations into the waters of the Atlantic. Contacts with Chinese and Arab merchants introduced Europeans to the magnetic compass, the **astrolabe**, and the **caravel**, a lighter vessel with a **lateen sail** and a steerable rudder.

Voyages of exploration soon changed focus to colonization as Spain and Portugal settled the Canary and Madeira Islands and the Azores. The crop initially grown on these islands was sugar, which had been introduced to Europeans by Middle Eastern peoples during the Crusades. Slaves were brought from northwestern Africa to work the plantations.

Oceania

Two regions that by 1450 remained outside the global network were the Americas and Oceania. (The Americas will be discussed in Chapter 15.) After 600 C.E., the peoples of Polynesia were involved in migration and expansion from island to island in the Pacific. From their base in the islands of Fiji, Samoa, and Tahiti, Polynesians in canoes sailed northward to the uninhabited islands of Hawaii. For several centuries, Polynesians continued to spread throughout the Hawaiian Islands, establishing agricultural and fishing villages. Inhabitants set up regional kingdoms with a highly stratified class system.

About 1200, another group of Polynesians migrated to the islands of present-day New Zealand. The **Maori**, as these migrants came to be called, learned to adapt to the colder environment of their new home. The Maori set up a stratified society that included slaves.

› Rapid Review

One of the most significant forces in history throughout the mid-fifteenth century was the movement of the Mongols into Russia, the Middle East, and China. While they were responsible for the massacre of hundreds of thousands of peoples who resisted them, especially in the Middle East, the Mongols deserve credit for forging strong trade connections between Europe and Asia. While the Mongols were establishing their presence in Eurasia, the Bantu-speaking peoples were continuing their migrations throughout sub-Saharan Africa, spreading the knowledge of agriculture and ironworking. Their contacts with Arabs in eastern Africa gave birth to a new language: Swahili. In the Indian Ocean, China engaged in massive expeditions, which were abruptly halted about the time that Europe entered the global trade network. Still outside the global network were Polynesia and the Americas. The inhabitants of Polynesia and the Americas interacted with other peoples in their own regions.

› Review Questions

1. Mongol rule in Russia and China differed in that
   (A) in China, the Mongols maintained Chinese traditions of isolation from foreigners
   (B) Eurasian trade routes under Mongol protection connected Russia more than China to Western European trade routes
   (C) the Mongols became more involved in administration in China than in Russia
   (D) the Mongols were more interested in controlling trade in China than they were in Russia
   (E) Russia advanced culturally under Mongol rule while China became backward

2. Historians studying linguistic syncretism would be most interested in
(A) the voyages of the Malay sailors
(B) the writings of Renaissance philosophers
(C) the Polynesian migrations
(D) the Bantu migrations
(E) the Yuan dynasty

3. The Black Death
(A) was most devastating in North Africa
(B) originated in Europe
(C) changed the course of political institutions
(D) spread solely along routes of Mongol conquest
(E) produced large loss of life in India

4. The Yuan dynasty was brought down by all of the following EXCEPT
(A) foreign resistance to the Mongol Peace
(B) bubonic plague
(C) economic distress
(D) inefficient administration
(E) a breakdown in internal security

5. The Renaissance
(A) was a movement of uniquely Western origins
(B) began in the Eastern Roman Empire
(C) was a result of the Crusades
(D) represented a complete break from medieval traditions
(E) was a period of classical tradition rather than independent innovation

6. European exploration through the mid-fifteenth century
(A) produced intense rivalries with East Asian civilizations
(B) placed merchants in conflict with monarchs
(C) suffered from a lack of technological expertise
(D) depended upon the knowledge of the Eastern world
(E) created trade connections that increased Europe's gold supply

7. Under Mongol rule in China
(A) Japan and Vietnam were brought under Mongol control
(B) Chinese women were placed in a more subordinate position
(C) Chinese educational traditions were maintained
(D) Chinese regional rulers were allowed to govern
(E) in contrast to Chinese tradition, scholars were despised

8. The influence of nomadic peoples in Eurasia
(A) created a reciprocal relationship between nomads and settled peoples
(B) ended with the Mongols
(C) delayed the interaction of global commercial networks
(D) brought efficient administration to Eurasia
(E) brought increased religious intolerance to Eurasia

› Answers and Explanations

1. **C**—The Mongols were more involved in profiting from Russian tribute and trade than in administering the Russian people; in China, the Mongols established the Yuan dynasty to rule their subjects. In China, the Mongols encouraged the use of foreign advisers (A). China was part of Eurasian trade routes protected by the Mongols, whereas the Mongols kept Russia isolated from Western European routes (B). The Mongols controlled both Chinese and Russian trade (D). Russia became more culturally and economically backward under Mongol rule, whereas China continued to thrive (E).

2. **D**—The Bantu migrations resulted in the new language of Swahili, which represented syncretism between Bantu languages and Arabic. Although the Malay sailors spread their Austronesian tongue from Malaysia to Madagascar, the resulting language of Madagascar was not a linguistic blend (A). The writings of the Renaissance philosophers were not particularly useful in studying language transmission (B). The Polynesian migrations were not noted for creating linguistic blends (C). The Yuan dynasty actively prevented linguistic syncretism by enacting laws that forbade the Chinese from learning the Mongol language (E).

3. **C**—The Black Death helped bring down the Yuan dynasty and also was a factor in the end of Western European feudalism. The Black Death was more devastating in China, Europe, and the Middle East than in North Africa (A). It also did not drastically affect India, which was to the south of the most traveled trade routes in the fourteenth century (E). The Black Death originated in Central Asia, spreading first to China (B). Although the Mongols were the initial transmitters of the bubonic plague, the disease also spread along Mediterranean routes not reached by the Mongols (D).

4. **A**—The Mongol Peace of the mid-thirteenth to the mid-fourteenth centuries promoted trade connections rather than foreign resistance. The Yuan dynasty fell because of the distress and population losses of the bubonic plague (B) and inefficient administration (D), which resulted in economic problems (C) and highway banditry (E) in China.

5. **C**—Among the results of the Crusades was renewed Western interest in the splendid cities of the East. Also, the wealth obtained by Italian city-states resulted from acting as suppliers of provisions and transportation for Crusaders. Beginning in the northern Italian city-states (B), the Renaissance was a revival of the Greco-Roman culture that had been preserved by the Muslims in Spain and in the eastern portions of the former Roman Empire (A). Although it dwelled on subjects in this world, the Renaissance continued some medieval traditions by featuring some art of a religious nature (D). Whereas the Renaissance represented a return to the Greco-Roman classics, the use

of perspective and new varieties of color in Renaissance painting represented independent innovation (E).

6. **D**—The technological improvements that propelled Europe into the Age of Exploration were borrowed and adapted from the Arabs and Chinese (C). In the mid-fifteenth century, Europe and East Asia had not yet developed intense rivalries (A). Merchants tended to support monarchs because of the political and economic stability they brought to Europe (B). Trade imbalances between East and West caused Europeans to pay for many of their goods in gold, which drained the continent of much of its supply of gold (E).

7. **D**—The Mongols relied on China's regional rulers to help provide an efficient administration. Twice the Mongols failed in their attempt to invade Japan, while Vietnam came under Mongol domination only briefly (A). Mongol culture placed women in a more dominant role than did the Chinese (B). The Chinese civil service exam was not reinstated under Mongol rule (C). Scholars from other societies, however, were brought into China and their works were admired (E).

8. **A**—Nomadic peoples frequently supplemented their diet by trading for the agricultural products of settled peoples. Nomads also sometimes provided horses and camels for trading along established routes. Nomadic influence ended with the invasion of Tamerlane (B). The nomadic Mongols increased the volume of Eurasian trade (C), but they were not noted for their administrative skills (D). The Mongols and other nomadic peoples tended to tolerate religious differences in Eurasia (E).

CHAPTER > 15

Empires in the Americas

IN THIS CHAPTER

Summary: Before the voyages of Columbus and the conquests of the Spanish, the civilizations and societies of the Americas developed in isolation from the remainder of the world. Within the Western Hemisphere, many of the peoples of the Americas engaged in long-distance as well as regional trade. When the Europeans arrived in the Americas, they encountered not only societies with their own rich traditions but also mighty empires that dazzled their conquerors.

KEY IDEA

Key Terms

Anasazi	Mississippians
*ayllus**	*mita**
*calpulli**	Moundbuilders
Chimor	parallel descent*
*chinampas**	Quechua*
Inca*	*quipus**
Mexica*	Toltecs

Pre-Columbian Mesoamerica

After the decline of Teotihuacán and of the Mayan civilization, nomadic peoples such as the **Toltecs** moved into central Mexico. Establishing a capital at Tula in the mid-tenth century, the Toltecs created an empire in central Mexico. Their empire included the city of Chichén Itzá in the Yucatán peninsula. The Toltecs carried on long-distance trade, exchanging obsidian from northern Mexico for turquoise obtained from the **Anasazi** people in present-day southwestern United States. Another legacy of the Toltecs was the legend of the god Quetzalcóatl, a tradition that would circulate among the various inhabitants of Mesoamerica.

Moundbuilders of North America

A second major concentration of pre-Columbian Native Americans was found among the **Moundbuilders** of North America from about 700 to 1500 C.E. Also called the **Mississippians**, these early Americans established their settlements along major rivers such as the Mississippi and the Ohio. Agricultural people, they constructed large earthen mounds that served as burial places or ceremonial centers. Among the most well-known and largest mounds are those found at Cahokia, in present-day southern Illinois. Some historians believe that the pyramid shape of these mounds suggests contact between the Mississippians and the early peoples of Mesoamerica.

The Rise of the Aztecs

When the Toltec empire fell in the mid-twelfth century, perhaps to invaders, another people called the Aztecs, or **Mexica**, were a nomadic people migrating throughout central Mexico. By the mid-thirteenth century, they had settled in the valley of Mexico, establishing their capital city at Tenochtitlán about 1325. Constructed on an island in the center of Lake Texcoco, Tenochtitlán was linked to the mainland by four causeways. To provide additional land for farming, the Aztecs fashioned *chinampas*, or platforms constructed of twisted vines on which they placed layers of soil. These garden plots floated in the canals that ran through the city of Tenochtitlán. Maize and beans became the staple crops of the Aztecs. Like other Mesoamerican peoples, they engaged in agriculture and construction without the use of the wheel or large beasts of burden.

By the mid-fifteenth century, the Aztecs had emerged as the dominant power of central Mexico. After conquering neighboring peoples, the Aztecs established a tribute empire. The Aztec military seized prisoners of war for use as human sacrifices. Although seen in other Mesoamerican and South American societies, human sacrifice was most widely practiced among the Aztecs. Sacrifices were carried out atop truncated, or trapezoid-shaped, pyramids in the Mesoamerican tradition. The Aztecs also worshipped the numerous gods of nature of their Mesoamerican predecessors, among them Quetzalcóatl and the rain god Tlaloc. The chief Aztec god was their own deity, Huitzilopochtli, the god of the sun. Human sacrifices were dedicated to this regional god in the belief that the gods were nourished by the sacrifice of human life. Another aspect of Aztec religious life was its calendar, which was similar to that of the Mayas.

Aztec society was stratified, with classes of nobles, peasants, and slaves, who were often war captives. The social structure was further organized into clans, or *calpulli*, that began as kinship groups but later expanded to include neighboring peoples. Economic life included a marketplace under government regulation that featured items obtained by long-distance trade. Records were kept through a system of picture writing, or hieroglyphics.

Women who died in childbirth were granted the same honored status as soldiers who died in battle. Aztec women who displayed a talent for intricate weaving also were highly regarded. Although Aztec women were politically subordinate to men, they could inherit property and will it to their heirs.

The Incas

Around 1300, about the time that the Aztecs were moving into the central valley of Mexico, the Incas, or **Quechua**, rose to power in the Andes Mountains of western South America. Their empire, or Twantinsuyu, became a model of organization. Building on the contributions of previous Andean societies, the Incas mastered the integration of diverse peoples within their empire.

The immediate predecessors of the Inca were the **Chimor**, who established a kingdom along the western coastal region of South America from 900 until the Incas conquered them in 1465 by taking over their irrigation system. At the same time, the southern Andean homelands were inhabited by a number of peoples, among them several *ayllus*, or clans, that spoke the Quechua language. About 1438, under the direction of their ruler, or **Inca**, called Pachacuti, they gained control of the large area around Lake Titicaca. On the eve of its conquest by the Spanish, the Inca Empire extended from present-day Colombia to the northern portion of Argentina. As a tribute empire it required its subjects to supply the *mita*, or labor on government-controlled lands.

The Structure of the Inca Empire

The most noteworthy achievement of Inca rulers was their ability to integrate approximately 11 million people of diverse cultural and linguistic backgrounds under one empire. Unlike the Aztecs, who ruled conquered peoples harshly, the Incas incorporated the conquered into their way of life. The Quechua language was purposely spread throughout the empire to serve as a unifying force. Inca rulers sent groups of Quechua-speaking people to settle throughout the empire to protect it from uprisings among conquered peoples. Another Inca strategy was to settle conquered peoples in an area far from their original homeland. The royal family forged marriage alliances that prevented rivals from obtaining power within their empire.

Although ruins of other urban areas have been discovered, the center of the empire was the capital city of Cuzco. Accurate imperial records were maintained without a system of writing by devices called *quipus*. *Quipus* were groups of knotted cords, with the knots of various sizes and colors to represent categories of information, such as finances or religion. The Incas further strengthened the organization of their empire by a dual system of roads, one running across the Andes highlands and the other across the lowlands. Way stations were set up about a day's walking distance apart to serve citizens and armies traveling these roads.

Inca Society and Religion

A polytheistic people, the Incas centered their worship around the sun god, while the creator god, or Viracocha, was also a key element of Inca religion. Local deities were worshipped as well. Society was organized into clans called *ayllus*. Women carried out traditional child-care roles, worked in fields, and achieved special recognition for their skill in weaving cloth for religious and state use. Inheritance was organized along lines of **parallel descent**, with inheritances passed along through both male and female sides of the family.

The Incas based their economy on the cultivation of the potato. They cultivated maize as a supplemental crop. State regulation of trade left little opportunity for long-distance trade, and there was not a separate merchant class among the Incas.

› Rapid Review

Although the Aztecs built upon Mesoamerican tradition to establish a powerful empire in the valley of Mexico, the Andean highlands also saw the emergence of an extremely native empire in the centuries before European conquest. The Aztecs ruled other peoples with brutality, whereas the Incas concentrated on integrating subject peoples into their empire. Aztec peoples engaged in long-distance trade, while the Incas were noted for the careful organization of their empire and their system of roads. In addition to the natives of Mesoamerica and Andean America, native peoples of the Mississippian culture of North America also constructed large mounds used for ceremonial and burial purposes.

› Review Questions

1. Both the Aztecs and Incas
   (A) allowed women a significant role in public life
   (B) were originally nomadic people
   (C) had an egalitarian social structure
   (D) built on the traditions of their predecessors
   (E) integrated conquered peoples into their empire

2. Aztec and Incan religions
   (A) restricted the worship of subject peoples
   (B) stressed a personal relationship with their gods
   (C) placed women in a subordinate position
   (D) widely practiced human sacrifice
   (E) reflected the agrarian nature of their respective societies

3. The natives of North America
   (A) built empires on the scale of those of Mesoamerica
   (B) demonstrated no signs of contact with Mesoamerican or Andean societies or civilizations
   (C) established tribute empires
   (D) used architectural designs similar to those of Mesoamerica
   (E) were known for their widespread expertise in irrigation

4. Which of the American societies altered their environment most extensively?
   (A) The Aztecs
   (B) The Mississippians
   (C) The Toltecs
   (D) The Incas
   (E) The Chimor

5. The Aztec and Incan civilizations differed most significantly in their
   (A) religious institutions
   (B) technological skill
   (C) system of recordkeeping
   (D) social structure
   (E) economic structure

6. Trade among the peoples of the Americas
   (A) united the Chimor and Inca people
   (B) was most similar in the Aztec and Toltec societies
   (C) was facilitated in the Andes by geography
   (D) remained local
   (E) was discouraged by the inhabitants of Mesoamerica

7. Which of the American peoples was closest to the Persians in their administrative style?
   (A) The Mayas
   (B) The Mississippians
   (C) The Aztecs
   (D) The Toltecs
   (E) The Incas

8. Both the Aztecs and Incas
   (A) entered into marriage for political reasons
   (B) gained the cooperation of subject peoples
   (C) showed limited signs of urbanization
   (D) lacked a merchant class
   (E) were tribute empires

› Answers and Explanations

1. **D**—The Aztecs built on a number of Mesoamerican traditions, including polytheism, architectural patterns, the use of a calendar, and the legend of Quetzalcóatl. The Incas continued the use of irrigation systems used by the Chimor, practiced polytheism, and organized their society into *ayllus*. Although Aztec and Incan women were valued as bearers of children and weavers and both could will property to their heirs, public life was male-dominated in both civilizations (A). Whereas the Aztecs were nomads, the Incas were a settled people (B). Both had a stratified social structure (C). Only the Incas integrated conquered peoples into their empire (E).

2. **E**—Two of the chief gods in the Aztec pantheon were the gods of the sun and of rain; Incan worship centered around the sun. Neither the Aztecs nor the Incas resisted the religious beliefs of subject peoples (A). Their religions were based on the appeasement of the gods, not upon a personal relationship with them (B). Aztec and Incan religions did not place women in a subordinate position. Aztec women were respected for their childbearing roles and Inca women received recognition for their skill in weaving cloth for religious use (C). Whereas the Incas occasionally practiced human sacrifice, only the Aztecs sacrificed human beings routinely (D).

3. **D**—The pyramid-shaped mounds of the Mississippian culture were similar to the truncated pyramids of Mesoamerican and Andean societies. This observation has led some historians to suggest contact between the Mississippian culture and those of Mesoamerica and the Andes (B). The natives of North America did not establish tribute empires (C). While they sometimes built up regional confederations, they did not establish empires like those of Mesoamerica (A). Although some southwestern tribes used irrigation, the Mississippian culture, found in humid climates and located along river valleys, did not (E).

4. **A**—The Aztecs extensively altered the environment of the central valley of Mexico by building Tenochtitlán on an island in the center of a lake and by constructing causeways to link the city to the mainland. They also constructed *chinampas* to increase the amount of agricultural land. The mounds of the Mississippians (B), the pyramids of the Toltecs (C), the roads of the Incas (D), and the irrigation systems of the Chimor (E), although noteworthy adaptations, did not involve the extensive environmental modifications as did the building of Tenochtitlán.

5. **C**—Although the Aztecs had a system of picture writing, the Incas, who did not develop a writing system, used *quipus* to record information. Both civilizations were polytheistic, worshipping gods of nature (A). Technological skill was demonstrated by the Aztecs' construction of Tenochtitlán and by their pyramids, while the Incas also constructed pyramids in addition to their dual system of roads (B). Both had stratified societies (D) and an economy based largely on agriculture (E).

6. **B**—Both the Aztecs and Toltecs participated in long-distance trade. Rather than trade with the Chimor, the Incas conquered their society (A). The rugged Andes hindered trade among Andean societies (C). Although the Incan government did not sponsor long-distance trade (D), both regional and long-distance trade were common in Mesoamerica (E).

7. **E**—Like the Persians, the Incas were adept at integrating subject peoples into their empire as long as their subjects refrained from rebellion. Both the Incas and the Persians also constructed roads to serve as communication links to the various parts of their empires. The Aztecs were noted for their exceptionally harsh treatment of conquered peoples (C). The Toltecs (D) and Mayas (A) did not demonstrate the imperial organizational skills of the Incas, while the Mississippians did not establish an empire (B).

8. **E**—Both collected tribute from subject peoples. Only the Incas entered into marriage alliances for political reasons (A). The Aztecs were despised by subject peoples (B). Both developed urban centers, most notably their capital cities of Tenochtitlán and Cuzco (C). Only the Incas lacked a merchant class (D).

PERIOD 3 Summary: Regional and Transregional Interactions (c. 600 C.E.–c. 1450)

Timeline

570–632	Life of Muhammad
618–907	Tang dynasty in China
622	The *hijra*
711–1492	Muslim occupation of Spain
750–1258	Abbasid dynasty
960–1279	Song dynasty in China
1054	Schism between the eastern and western Christian churches
1066	Norman invasion of England
1096	First Crusade
Eleventh–thirteenth century	Kingdom of Ghana
Eleventh–fifteenth century	Swahili cities in East Africa
Twelfth–fifteenth century	Kingdom of Great Zimbabwe
Twelfth–sixteenth century	Kingdom of Axum
Thirteenth century	Beginning of chiefdoms in Oceania
Thirteenth–fifteenth century	Empire of Mali
1206–1526	Sultanate of Delhi
1211	Beginning of Mongol conquests
1271–1295	Marco Polo's travels to China
1279–1368	Yuan dynasty
1289	Founding of the Ottoman dynasty
1304–1369	Life of Ibn Battuta
1325	Founding of Tenochtitlán by the Mexica (Aztecs)
1330s	Beginnings of bubonic plague in China
1337–1453	Hundred Years' War
1347	Beginnings of bubonic plague in the Mediterranean world
1368–1644	Ming dynasty
Fourteenth–seventeenth century	Kingdom of Kongo
1405–1433	Zheng He's voyages in the Indian Ocean
1441	Beginning of the Portuguese slave trade in Africa

Key Comparisons

1. Feudalism in Japan and Western Europe
2. Mongol rule in Russia and China
3. Muslim Spain and feudal Europe
4. The spread of Islam and the spread of Buddhism
5. Chinese and European presence in the Indian Ocean
6. Urban areas in the Islamic world, non-Islamic Europe, and China
7. Acceptance of Islam in Africa and Europe
8. Mesoamerican and Andean civilizations
9. Polynesian, Viking, and Bantu migrations
10. Gender roles in early Islam and under the caliphate

Change/Continuity Chart

KEY IDEA

REGION	POLITICAL	ECONOMIC	SOCIAL	CHANGES	CONTINUITIES
East Asia	Japanese feudalism Tang/Song dynasties Mongols Yuan dynasty Ming dynasty	Gunpowder Long-distance trade Technology Flying money Zheng He expedition Grand Canal	Urbanization Neo-Confucianism Buddhism Movable type Celadon pottery Bubonic plague	Japanese shogunate Neo-Confucianism Chinese expansion into Vietnam Mongol domination in China	Nomadic threats Confucianism Footbinding Patriarchal family Shinto
Southeast Asia	Expansion of China into Vietnam	Malay sailors	Islam	Islam	Hinduism Buddhism
Oceania	Regional kingdoms	Agriculture Fishing	Polytheism Polynesian migrations Stratified society	Settlement of Hawaii	Isolation from global trade network
Central Asia	Mongols Steppe diplomacy Tamerlane	Silk Roads trade Moldboard plow	Maori Mongol Peace Women have a voice in tribal councils	Mongol dominance Islam Isolation of Russia from Western Europe	Pastoral nomadism Steppe diplomacy Buddhism
South Asia	Delhi Sultanate Rule of Tamerlane	Arabic numerals Indian Ocean trade	Caste system Islam	Islam	Hinduism Caste system
Southwest Asia	Crusades Mongol destruction of Baghdad	Malay sailors Long-distance trade	Islam Veiling of women *Shariah* *Umma* Bubonic plague	Rise of Islam, Sunni/Shi'ite split, transfer of knowledge of sugarcane to Europeans	Nomadic tribes
North Africa	Regional kingdoms Islam, Mamluk dynasties	Trans-Saharan trade, gold, salt Ironworking	Slavery Travels of Ibn Battuta Bubonic plague	Islam	Trans-Saharan trade

Region					
Sub-Saharan Africa	Stateless societies Islam	Indian Ocean Trade in ivory, ebony, animal skins Trade with Portugal Ironworking	Bantu migrations Swahili *griots* Age grades	Islam Introduction of banana cultivation by Malay sailors	Christianity Slavery Bantu migrations
Western Europe	Feudalism Holy Roman Empire Attempted Mongol incursions Islamic Spain Investiture conflict	Manorialism Moldboard plow Rise of universities Bubonic plague Mediterranean trade routes Hanseatic League	Feudalism Population growth Viking invasions Urbanization Renaissance Palace schools	Islam Increased urbanization and trade Decline of feudalism Renaissance	Christianity Feudalism
Eastern Europe	Byzantine Empire Mongol invasion Seljuk and Ottoman incursion	Expansion of Western Europe Serfdom Trade in fur and timber Hanseatic League	Serfdom Viking invasion	Mongol invasion Viking invasion Serfdom	Eastern Orthodox Christianity Byzantine trade networks
North America	Regional tribal organization	Agriculture Fishing Trade with Mesoamerica	Anasazi and Mississippian cultures Mounds	Trade with Mesoamerica	Isolation from global trade networks
Latin America	Aztec and Incan empires	*Chinampas* Long-distance and regional trade Calendar Incan roads *Quipus*	Human sacrifice Polytheism Quetzalcóatl Parallel descent *Mita* Weaving *Ayllus, capulli*	Aztec and Incan empires	Isolation from global trade networks

PERIOD 4

Global Interactions (c. 1450–c. 1750)

CHAPTER 16

Empires and Other Political Systems

IN THIS CHAPTER

Summary: About 1450, a major global transition took place with the withdrawal of the Chinese from global interactions and the rise of European dominance. The Byzantine Empire fell to the power of the Ottoman Turks, an empire which by 1750 was in decline. Russia emerged from Mongol control to forge an empire under the rule of the Romanovs. New patterns of world interactions formed as societies of the Eastern and Western hemispheres exchanged cultural traditions across the Atlantic Ocean.

KEY IDEA

Key Terms
An asterisk (*) denotes items listed in the glossary.

absolute monarchy*
boyars*
Cossacks*
criollos (creoles)*
devshirme*
divine right*
Dutch learning*
encomienda*
Enlightenment*
Estates-General*
Glorious Revolution*
Hagia Sophia
Janissaries*
Jesuits*
Manchus*
mercantilism*

mestizos*
Mughal dynasty
mulato (mulatto)*
nation-state*
parliamentary monarchy*
peninsulares*
purdah*
Qing dynasty
Reconquista (Reconquest)*
repartamiento*
sovereignty*
Taj Mahal
Tokugawa Shogunate
Treaty of Tordesillas*
viceroyalty*

Spain and Portugal in the Americas

In the mid- and late fifteenth century, events that took place on the Iberian peninsula culminated in an encounter between Western Europe and the Americas. This encounter profoundly altered the government and society of the peoples of the Americas. In the mid-fifteenth century, Portuguese establishment of a navigation school increased exploration of the western and eastern coasts of Africa. The knowledge and wealth obtained from these ventures created further interest in expeditions of exploration and colonization. In Spain, the marriage of Fernando of Aragón and Isabel of Castile in the mid-fifteenth century united the kingdoms of Aragón and Castile. This union gave its support to three significant events in Spanish history in 1492:

- The *Reconquista* (**Reconquest**) of former Spanish territory from the Muslims with the fall of Granada.
- The expulsion of Jews who refused to convert to Christianity. Spain would suffer serious economic repercussions with the removal of the Jews, who were some of its most well-educated and skilled people.
- The first voyage of Columbus. The unification of central Spain and the end of warfare with the Muslims freed the Spanish monarchs to turn their attention to voyages of exploration.

The Spanish-sponsored voyage of Ferdinand Magellan, beginning in 1519, not only circumnavigated the globe but also gave Spain a basis for its colonization of the Philippines in the late sixteenth century.

Spain's Empire

Control in the Caribbean

Spain's interests in the Americas began in the Caribbean. During his second voyage in 1493, Columbus established a colony on Santo Domingo. In the sixteenth century, the Spaniards took control of Puerto Rico and Cuba and settled Panama and the northern coast of South America. Spanish control of these regions introduced European diseases to the Native Americans, an exchange that significantly decreased the native population. The Spanish crown granted Caribbean natives to the conquerors for use as forced labor.

Conquest in the Americas

In the fifteenth century, the once mighty empires of the Aztecs and Incas fell to the Spaniards. Tales of riches in the interior of Mexico led the Spaniard Hernán Cortés to attempt the conquest of the Aztec Empire. The Spaniards were aided in their venture by several factors:

- Indian allies from among native peoples who had been conquered by the Aztecs.
- The legend of Quetzalcóatl—Moctezuma II, the Aztec leader at the time of the conquest, believed that Cortés may have been the god who was expected to return to Mesoamerica.
- Superior Spanish weaponry.
- The assistance of Malinche (called Doña Marina by the Spanish), an Aztec woman who served as interpreter between the Spanish and the Aztecs.
- Smallpox—introduced into the Aztec Empire by one infected member of the Cortés expedition, it caused the death of thousands.

On the completion of the Aztec conquest in 1521, the capital city of Tenochtitlán was burned to the ground and a new capital, Mexico City, was constructed on its site. The Spaniards then continued their conquests into north central Mexico, Guatemala, and Honduras.

The Spaniards also turned their attention to the region of the Andes Mountains of western South America. By 1535, Francisco Pizarro had conquered the rich Inca Empire, already weakened by years of civil war. The Spaniards then sent expeditions from northern Mexico into what is now the southwestern portion of the United States. From 1540 to 1542, Francisco de Coronado reached as far north as what is now Kansas in an unsuccessful search for seven mythical cities of gold. Further campaigns of exploration led to the conquest of Chile and the establishment of the city of Buenos Aires in present-day Argentina. By the late sixteenth century, the Spaniards had set up about 200 urban centers in the Americas.

Despite constant threats from Caribbean pirates, Spanish galleons carried loads of gold and silver across the Atlantic Ocean to Spain, where the influx of such large quantities of the precious metals caused inflation of the Spanish economy. Eventually, inflation spread throughout Europe. Until the eighteenth century, the Manila galleons sailed the Pacific, transporting silver from the mines of Spain's American colonies to China to trade for luxury goods.

The pursuit of gold and adventure was not the sole motive for the founding of a Spanish colonial empire. Another goal was the desire to spread the Roman Catholic faith to native peoples. Roman Catholic religious orders such as the **Jesuits**, Dominicans, and Franciscans established churches and missions where they educated the Indians and taught them the Christian faith. The Roman Catholic faith became an integral element in the society of the Spanish colonies.

The right of the Spaniards to govern their American colonies was established by papal decree through the **Treaty of Tordesillas** (1494). This agreement divided the newly discovered territories between the Catholic countries of Spain and Portugal by drawing an imaginary line around the globe. Spain received the right to settle the lands to the west of the line drawn through the Western Hemisphere, and Portugal those to the east. Spanish government in the Americas was a massive bureaucracy controlled from Spain by the Council of Indies. The council was further divided into two **viceroyalties**, one centered in Mexico City and the other in Lima, in present-day Peru.

The economic structure of Spain's American colonies was the *encomienda* system. *Encomiendas* were grants from the Spanish crown that allowed the holders to exploit the Indians living on the land they controlled. In Peru, the exploitation of Indians took the form of the *mita,* or forced labor, especially in the silver mines. After Father Bartolomé de las Casas spoke out against the mistreatment of the Indians, the *encomienda* system was restructured as the *repartamiento*. The new system allowed a small salary to be paid to Indian laborers.

Spanish American Society

Spanish American society took on a hierarchical structure. Four basic classes emerged:

- *Peninsulares*—colonists born in Europe. The *penisulares* initially held the most powerful positions in colonial society.
- *Criollos* (creoles)—colonists born in the Americas of European parents. Generally well-educated and financially secure, the creoles would eventually become colonial leaders and organizers of colonial independence movements.
- *Mestizos*—people of mixed European and Indian ancestry.
- *Mulatos* (mulattos)—people of mixed European and African ancestry. The *mestizos* and *mulatos* occupied the lowest political and social positions in Spanish American society.

Families in the Spanish and Portuguese American colonies were patriarchal. Women were expected to devote themselves to traditional household and childbearing duties. Lower-class women worked in the fields and sometimes managed small businesses. Women could control their dowries, however, and also could inherit property.

Portugal's Empire

The Portuguese colony of Brazil became the first colony based on a plantation economy. Founded by Pedro Cabral in 1500, Brazil was settled in 1532 by Portuguese nobles. Sugar plantations using Indian labor arose; when the Indians died of European diseases, slaves were brought from Africa. Labor in Brazilian gold mines also was supplied by Indians and African slaves. Society in Brazil followed a hierarchy similar to that of the Spanish colonies, and Roman Catholicism was introduced by Jesuit missionaries. In addition to Brazil, the Portuguese Empire included colonies and trade outposts in Africa and Asia.

The Ottoman Empire

The Mongol invasion of eastern Anatolia in 1243 led to the collapse of the Seljuk Turks and the subsequent rise of the Ottoman Turks. The Ottomans migrated into Anatolia to fill the vacuum left by the Seljuks. Named after their leader Osman Bey, the Ottomans established an empire centered around Anatolia. By the late fourteenth century, much of the Balkans were added to the Ottoman Empire.

In 1453, the Ottomans completed their conquest of the city of Constantinople. The Christian church of **Hagia Sophia** was converted into an elaborate mosque, palaces were constructed in the city, and the defense system of Constantinople was repaired. After the conquest of Constantinople, the Ottomans united most of the Arab world by adding Syria, Egypt, and the rest of North Africa to their empire. In the fifteenth century, they became a major naval power until they suffered a decisive defeat by a combined Venetian and Spanish fleet at the Battle of Lepanto in 1571. As late as 1688, the Ottomans threatened the Austrian capital of the Hapsburg dynasty. This siege was not as devastating, however, as a previous siege against Vienna in 1529.

The Ottoman Empire was focused on warfare. Beginning in the middle of the fifteenth century, its armies were largely composed of soldiers called **Janissaries**. Janissaries were Christian boys who were captured and enslaved. Sometimes the boys were turned over to the Ottomans by their own parents in the hope that the education given to them would lead to a prominent position in the Ottoman Empire. The selection process for the Janissaries was called *devshirme;* it placed the boys with Turkish families to learn their language and the teachings of Islam.

Women in Ottoman society maintained a subordinate role to their fathers and husbands. Although some women in lower classes became involved in trade and small businesses, Ottoman women as a whole were given very little opportunity to acquire an education or participate in politics. Instead, Ottoman women, especially those in elite classes, were restricted by the wearing of the veil and, in some cases, seclusion within the harem.

Ottoman Decline

By the late seventeenth century, the vast Ottoman Empire was so difficult to administer that it fell into a gradual decline. As opportunities to add new territories ran out because of the strengthening military power of other Muslims and of Christians, the Ottomans lost their ability to maintain their large army and bureaucracy. Taxes charged to the lower classes were raised as Ottoman rulers became more and more corrupt. The inflationary trend that affected Europe as a result of the influx of gold and silver in Spain also produced inflation within the Ottoman territories. The Ottomans fell behind in warfare technology because of their reliance on huge weaponry intended for siege tactics. Ignoring the value of Western technological innovations, the Ottomans also disregarded the growing power of Western Europe, a policy that hastened its decline.

Mughal India

In 1526, Babur, a descendant of Mongols and of Turks, migrated from the steppes of central Asia to the Indian subcontinent. The founder of the **Mughal dynasty** had lost his kingdom in Central Asia; by 1528, he had used his superior gunpowder technology to conquer a large portion of northern India and had founded a dynasty that would last to the mid-nineteenth century.

The greatest leader of the Mughal dynasty was Akbar (ruled 1560–1605). Throughout his reign, he brought more of northern and central India under his control, established a bureaucracy, and patronized the arts. He encouraged cooperation between Hindus and Muslims in India.

Akbar also broke with Hindu and Muslim tradition regarding the treatment of women in society. He encouraged widows to remarry and outlawed *sati,* the practice among Hindu elite classes of burning women on their husband's funeral pyre. Akbar also encouraged merchants to arrange market days for women only so that those following the practice of **purdah**, or confinement in their homes, would have an opportunity to participate in public life. By the declining years of the Mughal Empire, however, the improvements in the position of women had largely been discontinued.

Mughal art and architecture often blended Muslim styles with those of other societies. Mughal artists were known for their miniatures, some of which included Christian religious subjects. Mughal architecture blended the white marble typical of Indian architecture with the arches and domes of the Islamic world. Probably the most well-known architectural structure of the Mughal era was the **Taj Mahal**, constructed by Shah Jahan as a tomb for his wife, Mumtaz Mahal.

The cost of warfare and defensive efforts to protect the northern borders of the Mughal Empire contributed to its decline. Later Mughal rulers failed to bridge the differences between Muslims and Hindus. Centralized government broke down as India returned to numerous local political organizations. The decline of centralized authority opened doors for the entrance of foreign powers, especially the British.

Monarchies in France and England

In the sixteenth century, European monarchies expanded their power dramatically. Characteristics of these monarchies were:

- The maintenance of strong armies
- The establishment of elaborate bureaucracies
- High taxes to support the frequent wars on the European continent

In France, a system of **absolute monarchy** arose as monarchs stopped convening the **Estates-General**, the medieval parliament. In addition to the characteristics of monarchs listed above, absolute monarchs believed in a concept called the **divine right** of kings. Divine right held that monarchs were granted their right to rule by God. Territorial expansion was a goal of the strong military that the absolute monarchies assembled. The most noteworthy of European absolute monarchs was Louis XIV of France (1643–1715), who not only adhered to the doctrine of divine right but also lived extravagantly in his palace at Versailles outside Paris. Keeping with absolutist tradition, Louis XIV also spent huge sums on the military in order to carry out numerous wars to expand French territory.

The prevailing economic theory of the day, called **mercantilism**, encouraged nations to export more than they imported and promoted the founding of colonies. Colonies provided raw materials and ready markets for the manufactured goods produced by the mother country.

The English developed a different model of monarchy in the seventeenth century: **parliamentary monarchy**. Although ruled by a centralized government, England limited the power of its monarchs with a parliament in which they shared power with representatives chosen by voters from the elite classes. The English Civil War (1642–1649) and the **Glorious Revolution** of 1689 placed the power of parliament over that of the king. The English parliament met regularly without the consent of the monarch and also retained the authority to tax and appropriate tax revenues.

The Development of European Nation-States

Government in Europe was organized around the **nation-state**. Well suited to a continent composed of various cultural groups, a nation-state is defined as a political unit that:

- Governs people who share a common culture, including a common language
- Has definite geographic boundaries
- Enjoys **sovereignty**

European nation-states were governed by either absolute or parliamentary monarchs. The number of nation-states on the small European continent, however, created rivalries and divisions that often led to war.

The Russian Empire

Russia followed the path of absolute monarchy after the final expulsion of the Mongols in 1480. The Mongol occupation of Russia produced a nation with a weakened emphasis on education, and also depressed trade and manufacturing. Under the tsars Ivan III (the Great) and Ivan IV (the Terrible), Russia expanded from the eastern border of Poland into western Siberia across the Ural Mountains. Russian pioneers called **Cossacks** were sent to the newly conquered territories, taking over land previously held by Asian nomads. In the process of expanding its borders, Russia added a substantial Muslim minority to its population.

The death of Ivan IV without an heir paved the way for the emergence of the Romanov dynasty. In 1613, the Russian nobles, or **boyars**, selected Mikhail Romanov as Russia's new tsar, beginning a dynasty that ruled until 1917. The new tsar continued Russian expansion, adding part of the Ukraine around Kiev and also southern territory that extended to the frontier of the Ottoman Empire. Later Romanovs created state control over the Russian Orthodox Church.

Peter the Great

In 1700, the Russian Empire remained agricultural to a larger extent than East Asian empires or Western European nations. Peter I (the Great), who ruled from 1689 to 1725, launched a new era in Russian history by opening up the country to Western influence. On a trip to Western Europe in a vain attempt to enlist support against the Turks, Peter acquired an appreciation for Western science and technology. When he returned to Russia, he took

Western craftsmen with him. In order to bolster trade, Peter fought a war with Sweden in which he not only greatly reduced the military power of Sweden but also gained for Russia a warm water port on the Baltic Sea. Peter also moved his capital from Moscow to a new city on the Baltic that he named St. Petersburg. He then created a navy for Russia. Continuing his policy of westernization, Peter required boyars to shave their beards and wear Western clothing. He also brought the ballet from France to Russia and allowed women of elite classes to attend public events for the first time.

In spite of his interest in Western technology, Peter the Great did not accept Western democratic trends. Unimpressed with parliamentary government, he continued to favor absolute monarchy. He set up controls over his subjects by creating a secret police and encouraged the continuation of serfdom. Serfdom, which differed from slavery in binding laborers to the land only, kept the Russian economy focused on agriculture, in spite of the westernization policies of Peter the Great.

Catherine II (the Great), who ruled from 1729 to 1796, continued the expansionist and westernization policies of Peter. Laws restricting serfs were harsher than before. Catherine upheld the concept of absolute monarchy but also brought ideas of the **Enlightenment** (see Chapter 19) to Russia. She reduced severe punishments for crimes in order to bring the Russian justice system more in line with that of Western Europe and encouraged Western art and architecture. Catherine added new territory in the Crimea, Alaska, and northern California to the Russian Empire.

Ming China

The Ming dynasty was founded by Zhu Yuanzhang, a warlord who had assisted in the expulsion of the Mongols from China. The Ming dynasty, which reacted against Mongol rule by returning to Chinese tradition, lasted from 1368 to 1644. Under Ming rule:

- The revered position of the scholar-gentry was restored.
- The Confucian-based civil service exam was reinstated and expanded. Women, however, continued to be banned from taking the exam.
- Public officials who were corrupt or incompetent were beaten publicly.
- Thought control, or censorship of documents, was sanctioned by the government.
- Neo-Confucianism, which supported strict obedience to the state, increased its influence.
- Women continued to occupy a subordinate position in the strongly patriarchal society.

Between 1405 and 1423, the Ming dynasty, under the leadership of Zheng He, engaged in several major expeditions of exploration and trade. Designed to impress the remainder of the Eastern Hemisphere with the glories of Ming China, the Zheng He expeditions sailed through the Indian Ocean, the Arabian Sea, and the Persian Gulf. By the 1430s, however, the scholar-gentry had persuaded Ming leaders that the expeditions were too costly in light of the need to spend the empire's funds on restraining continued Mongol threats to China's northern border.

In the late sixteenth century, Jesuits such as the scholar Matteo Ricci were allowed to enter China. More interested in the Jesuits' transmission of scientific and technological knowledge than in Christian theology, the Ming Chinese allowed some Jesuits to remain in China throughout the Ming era.

During the last 200 years of the Ming dynasty, China was ruled by incompetent rulers. The maintenance of dams, dikes, and irrigation systems was neglected, and nomadic peoples continued to exert pressure along the Great Wall. In 1644, the Jurchen, or **Manchus**, a nomadic people on China's northern borders, conquered the Ming dynasty. The new **Qing dynasty** ruled until the early twentieth century as the last Chinese dynasty.

Japan

While the Ming dynasty isolated itself from most foreigners, Japan went through periods of both isolation and acceptance of Western influence. In 1603, the Tokugawa family gained prominence when one of its members acquired the title of *shogun*. Ruling Japan from the city of Edo (present-day Tokyo), the **Tokugawa Shogunate** brought a degree of centralized authority to Japan. Large estates of many of the *daimyo* were broken up and taken over by the Tokugawa family.

Europeans entered Japan in 1543 when Portuguese sailors shipwrecked and were washed up on the shore of the southern island of Kyushu. Additional visits from European traders and missionaries brought Western technology, including clocks and firearms, into Japan. The use of firearms changed Japanese warfare from feudal to modern and assisted the Tokugawa in maintaining their authority. When Christian missionaries arrived to bring Roman Catholicism to the Japanese, the Tokugawa at first protected them from Buddhist resistance. In the late 1580s, however, the Tokugawa stifled Buddhist resistance to their authority. Christianity was perceived as a threat to Tokugawa authority, and Christian missionaries were ordered to leave Japan. Japanese Christians were persecuted and executed. By 1630, foreign trade was allowed only in a few cities and Japanese ships were banned from trading or sailing across long distances. By the 1640s, only the Dutch and Chinese were allowed to trade through the port of Nagasaki. Contacts with the Dutch allowed the Japanese to keep informed about Western developments (**Dutch learning**) and adopt those they considered appropriate to Japanese goals.

› Rapid Review

Western Europe developed models of both absolute and parliamentary monarchy as its advanced technology strengthened its position as a world leader. Russia built a large empire whose rulers continued repressive policies and a system of serfdom that perpetuated Russian backwardness begun under Mongol rule. Spain and Portugal established empires in Mesoamerica and South America, while England and France vied for colonial dominance in North America. The Ottoman Empire conquered the Byzantine Empire, but by the early seventeenth century, could not keep up with Western technological advances and was on a path of decline. Ming China and Tokugawa Japan displayed varying responses to foreign influence. At the conclusion of the period, the Chinese pursued a policy of isolation from foreigners, whereas Japan allowed limited Western influence in order to avail itself of Western technology. Mughal India at first brought centralized government that softened relations between Hindus and Muslims; then later it broke up into regional governments that created openings for foreign intervention.

› Review Questions

1. Mercantilism
   (A) did not affect empires that were not based in Europe
   (B) brought long-term prosperity to Europe
   (C) encouraged the importation of foreign goods
   (D) supported free trade
   (E) sparked further rivalries among European nations

2. In the early eighteenth century, the political system where citizens enjoyed the greatest amount of self-rule was
   (A) Japan
   (B) Russia
   (C) France
   (D) England
   (E) the Ottoman Empire

3. Both the Russian Empire and Ming China
   (A) became increasingly more traditional after the expulsion of the Mongols
   (B) improved the position of women in the period 1450–1750
   (C) established policies that were a reaction to the Mongol presence in central Asia
   (D) cooperated with the established religions in their respective countries
   (E) enjoyed a surge of renewed industrial growth after the collapse of the Mongol Empire

4. A comparison of the reactions of Japan and China to European influence in the period 1450–1750 shows that
   (A) the Chinese persecuted Christian missionaries about the same time that the Japanese gave them some acceptance
   (B) Japan saw the need for knowledge of Western developments, but China did not
   (C) both excluded foreigners from trading at their ports.
   (D) European philosophy was accepted, but Western technology was not
   (E) both tolerated European influence in their culture in order to actively participate in global trade

5. Compared to the Spanish Empire, that of the Portuguese
   (A) developed a more egalitarian society
   (B) was more global in its extent
   (C) was less influenced by the Roman Catholic Church
   (D) developed a better relationship with Indian inhabitants
   (E) was more strictly controlled by the government in Europe

6. The Mughal Empire
   (A) failed to ease tensions between Hindus and Muslims in India
   (B) controlled the entire Indian subcontinent
   (C) terminated in the return of a traditional centralized government to India
   (D) produced art and architecture that reflected syncretism
   (E) placed women in a more subordinate position than before Mughal rule

7. The Ottoman Empire
   (A) weakened because its technology fell behind that of Europe
   (B) unlike the Mughal Empire, was not a gunpowder empire
   (C) was unsuccessful in controlling European territory
   (D) reached its height around 1750
   (E) prohibited the use of forced labor

8. The nation-state
   (A) was embraced by the Ottoman Empire
   (B) arose in Europe because of its diversity of cultural groups
   (C) was incompatible with absolute monarchies
   (D) was not limited to definite borders
   (E) promoted harmony among Europeans

› Answers and Explanations

1. **E**—Inherent in mercantile philosophy was the need for colonies, a necessity that provoked international rivalries. Answer (A) is incorrect because the Ottoman Empire suffered from the inflationary trend in the Eastern Hemisphere caused by Spain's acquisition of wealth from its colonies. Spain's wealth caused a European depression rather than long-term prosperity (B). Mercantilism encouraged exports rather than imports (C) and government participation in economic matters rather than free trade (D).

2. **D**—In the early 1700s, England had already established the sovereignty of Parliament, whose members were elected by the elite classes. Russia (B) and France (C) were under the authority of absolute monarchs who ruled without parlia-

mentary authority. Japan (A) was ruled by the authoritarian Tokugawa Shogunate, and the Ottoman Empire remained under the authority of the sultan (E).

3. **C**—The emperors of Ming China returned to Confucian traditions and by the 1430s had entered a period of isolation as a response to Mongol threats along China's northern borders. Russia reacted to the previous Mongol occupation by establishing absolute rule and expanding its territories to include land previously held by Asian nomadic peoples. Although Ming China became increasingly more traditional, Russia eventually entered into a period of increased westernization (A). Although Russia allowed women more participation in public events, the subordinate position of women in China was continued by the strict Confucian and Neo-Confucian policies under the Ming (B). Although the Ming cooperated with Confucianists and Neo-Confucianists because of their respect for governmental authority, Russian tsars placed the Russian Orthodox Church under their authority (D). China's period of industrial expansion had occurred previously under the Song, whereas Russia would only begin to industrialize to some extent under Peter the Great (E).

4. **B**—Although both countries entered into a period of isolation, Japan maintained some contact with Western ways through trade with the Dutch. In the 1580s, Japan persecuted Christian missionaries while China gave them some acceptance (A). China retained two ports for foreigners, whereas Japan kept only the port of Nagasaki open to trade with the Dutch and Chinese (C). Western philosophy was not embraced by either country, but there was interest in Western technology, particularly firearms in Japan and clocks in China (D). Both countries were more interested in regional than in long-distance trade (E).

5. **B**—Although the Spanish Empire embraced only the Philippines and the Americas, the Portuguese Empire included Brazil, outposts in Africa and India, and trading posts throughout the Indian Ocean and East Asia. Both the Spanish and Portuguese colonial empires had a stratified society (A). Both were Roman Catholic empires with active missionary efforts; both nations had submitted to the pope's authority in accepting the Treaty of Tordesillas (C). Both empires first used Indians as forced labor (D). The Spanish Empire was more strictly regulated by its Council of the Indies in Spain (E).

6. **D**—Mughal art and architecture reflected Christian themes and Persian and Indian architectural structures. Under Akbar, cooperation between Muslims and Hindus was encouraged (A). The Mughals controlled the northern and central portions of India (B). Their rule ended in the return of traditional regional government in India (C). Under some Mughal rulers, *sati* was forbidden and widows were encouraged to remarry (E).

7. **A**—The Ottoman decline was hastened because of Ottoman reluctance to embrace Western technology of the time period. Both the Ottomans and Mughals were gunpowder empires (B). The Ottomans gained control of Hungary and some parts of the Balkans (C), but was in decline by 1750 (D). The *devshirme* system enslaved the Janissaries (E).

8. **B**—Nation-states are organized around cultural groups, a characteristic of Europe. The Ottoman Empire included numerous cultural groups under one empire (A). Many of the European nation-states were ruled by absolute monarchs (C). By definition, a nation-state must have definite geographical boundaries (D). The different nation-states in Europe contributed to conflict (E).

CHAPTER 17

Hemispheric Exchange

IN THIS CHAPTER

Summary: The period from 1450 to 1750 was one of increased global exchange. While some regions such as China gradually withdrew from long-distance trade, the volume of trade in the Indian Ocean increased with the entry of Europeans into waters that already saw bustling commercial activity among Indian, Muslim, and African peoples. To the trade of the Eastern Hemisphere were added vast interchanges between the Eastern and Western hemispheres across the Atlantic Ocean.

KEY IDEA

Key Terms

capitalism*

caravel*

Columbian Exchange*

factor*

northwest passage*

Trading Companies

As European nation-states grew more powerful and involved in colonial expansion, their governments formed trading companies. The governments of Spain, the Netherlands, England, and France gave regional monopolies to these companies. Among the two most prominent companies were the British East India Company, which concentrated on trade in India and North America, and the Dutch East India Company, which focused on trade with Indonesia. With the origin of the great trading companies came increased consumption of eastern products such as coffee, tea, and sugar. The growth of trade and commerce fostered the growth of **capitalism**, an economic system that is based on the private ownership of property and on investments with the hope of profit.

European Explorations

Technological inventions such as the **caravel**, magnetic compass, and astrolabe, adopted from the eastern world by the Europeans in the early fifteenth century, facilitated the entrance of Europe into expeditions of exploration. Portugal had already sailed along the western coast of Africa in the early fifteenth century, trading gold and crude iron pots for spices and slaves. The voyage of Vasco da Gama around the Cape of Good Hope to India in 1498 broke the Muslim and Italian monopolies on trade with the Middle East, East Asia, and Southeast Asia. One Portuguese expedition was blown off course and landed in Brazil, giving Portugal a claim to territory in the Western Hemisphere. The Portuguese continued their commercial interests by setting up forts and trading posts on the eastern African coast and also in India at the port of Goa. Portugal also traded in the port of Malacca in Indonesia. From the Chinese port of Macao it entered into trade between Japan and China.

Columbus's rediscovery of the Americas for Spain in 1492 was followed by the Magellan expedition's circumnavigation of the globe, which gave Spain claim to the Philippine Islands. In the sixteenth century, the states of northern Europe joined in voyages of exploration. The defeat of the Spanish Armada by the English navy in 1588 made England the foremost naval power among the European nations.

Both the French and the British turned their attentions to North America, creating rivalries that erupted in warfare in the latter part of the eighteenth century. In 1534, France claimed present-day Canada. In the seventeenth century, the French established settlements and fur-trading outposts in the Ohio and Mississippi River valleys. During the sixteenth century, the British had explored the Hudson Bay area of North America in search of a **northwest passage** to the Indies. In the seventeenth century, England established colonies along the east coast of North America to provide the raw materials and markets that were a part of its mercantilist policy.

The Netherlands, which had recently won its independence from Spain, set up colonies in North America and, for a brief time, in Brazil. The Dutch demonstrated their power in the Indian Ocean by removing the Portuguese competition in Indonesia in the early seventeenth century. In 1652, they established Cape Colony, a settlement at the southern tip of Africa, using it primarily as a supply station for ships sailing to Indonesia.

The Columbian Exchange

The voyages of Columbus to the Americas initiated a system of exchange between the Eastern and Western hemispheres that had a major impact on the Atlantic world. The **Columbian Exchange** was a trade network that exchanged crops, livestock, and diseases between the two hemispheres. Tobacco was introduced to the Eastern Hemisphere. American food crops such as maize and sweet potatoes spread to China and parts of Africa. White potatoes spread to Europe, and manioc to Africa. The introduction of new food crops tended to boost population growth in the Eastern Hemisphere. Coffee, sugarcane, wheat, rice, and bananas made their way across the Atlantic from the Eastern to the Western Hemisphere. The indigenous people of the Americas, however, were largely uninterested in the food crops introduced by Europeans. Sugarcane cultivation was eventually transferred to Brazil and the Caribbean islands, and raw sugar was sold to the Eastern Hemisphere.

The Columbian Exchange brought livestock such as cattle, horses, sheep, and pigs to the Americas. The horse revolutionized the lifestyle of the nomadic Plains Indians of North America by facilitating the hunting of buffalo.

Epidemic disease also found its way to the Americas through the Columbian Exchange. Prior to the voyages of Columbus, the peoples of the Americas had lived in virtual isolation from the rest of the world, a situation that prevented their exposure to the diseases of the populations of the Eastern Hemisphere. When Europeans arrived in the Americas, they brought with them common diseases to which the Native Americans had developed no immunity: diseases such as smallpox, measles, tuberculosis, and influenza. Within 50 years after the voyages of Columbus, approximately 90 percent of American native peoples had died, most of them from epidemic disease.

Patterns of World Trade

By the seventeenth century, Europeans had established ports in East Asia, Southeast Asia, India, and the west coast of Africa. In general, involvement in international trade positively affected local and regional economies. In areas where direct trade was not possible, Europeans negotiated special economic rights. In Russia, Western European shippers known as **factors** established agencies in Moscow and St. Petersburg. In the Ottoman Empire, Western European traders formed colonies within the city of Constantinople where they were granted commercial privileges.

Regions Outside the World Trade System

Until the eighteenth century, large regions of the world lay outside the international trade system. China relied primarily on regional trade, channeling most of its commercial activity through the port of Macao. One reason for China's limits on trade with Europe was disinterest in European products. As a result, Europeans paid for the few items they purchased from China with silver, which was the basis of the Chinese economy. England and the Netherlands compensated for the expense of acquiring fine Chinese porcelain by developing their own porcelain modeled after Chinese patterns. Tokugawa Japan also prohibited foreign trade except for limited commercial activity with the Dutch and Chinese through the port of Nagasaki.

Other world regions carried on only limited long-distance trade. Russia traded primarily with the nomads of Central Asia until the eighteenth century, when it began trading grain to the West. The Ottomans, who dismissed the impact of European technology, showed little enthusiasm for trade with the West. Mughal India encouraged trade with the West but was more preoccupied with imperial expansion. Whereas some trading ports were established by Europeans along Africa's west coast, Europeans were deterred from entering the continent by the risk of contracting malaria and by the lack of navigable rivers.

› Rapid Review

The increased level of exchange between the Eastern and Western hemispheres began with the voyages of Columbus. Crops, livestock, and diseases changed the demographics on both sides of the Atlantic. Colonies furthered the interchange between the two hemispheres. Some areas such as Japan and China remained largely outside global trade networks, whereas regions such as Russia and the Ottoman Empire concentrated on regional trade.

› Review Questions

1. European explorations
   (A) were dependent on European technological innovation
   (B) promoted harmony among the nations of Europe
   (C) sought to break established trade monopolies
   (D) concentrated on the Americas
   (E) interfered with the growth of capitalism

2. The Columbian Exchange
   (A) improved the nutrition of American indigenous peoples
   (B) did not involve Africa
   (C) drew the world's oceans into an active trade network
   (D) produced both positive and adverse effects on world population
   (E) did not affect East Asia

3. The English and French engaged in rivalries over territory in
   (A) Indonesia
   (B) China
   (C) North America
   (D) East Africa
   (E) western Africa

4. The region with the greatest number of colonial and commercial competitors was
   (A) the western coast of Africa
   (B) Indonesia
   (C) the Caribbean islands
   (D) the Philippines
   (E) Japan

5. The Netherlands established commercial or colonial interests in all of the following areas EXCEPT
   (A) southern Africa
   (B) South America
   (C) western Africa
   (D) North America
   (E) Japan

6. Which of the following regions sustained trade patterns that were the most different from the others before the eighteenth century?
   (A) Japan
   (B) Indonesia
   (C) China
   (D) Mughal India
   (E) Russia

7. Which crop arrived in the Americas as part of the Columbian Exchange and later became a key product of the Americas?
   (A) Tobacco
   (B) Sugar
   (C) Sweet potatoes
   (D) Bananas
   (E) Manioc

8. As a result of hemispheric trade between 1450 and 1750,
   (A) the entire globe was linked by numerous active trade routes
   (B) European governments lost influence to the power of the great trading companies
   (C) the work of African artisans found new markets
   (D) the Ottoman Empire strengthened its hold on European territory
   (E) European wealth and commercial dominance increased

› Answers and Explanations

1. **C**—The Portuguese more than other nations attempted to break the trade monopolies of the Muslims and Italian merchants in the Indian Ocean and succeeded with the voyage of Da Gama. The English also sought a northwest passage to the East in order to break up trade monopolies. European technology depended on inventions from the Muslim and Chinese worlds (A). Exploration promoted rivalry rather than harmony among the nations of Europe, as in the case of competition between England and Spain that led to the defeat of the Spanish Armada (B). Europeans concentrated on African and Indian Ocean trade as well as trade with the Americas (D). Trade strengthened capitalism (E).

2. **D**—While the influx of added nutrients tended to increase populations of the Eastern Hemisphere, American indigenous populations were devastated by disease. American natives were not widely interested in the food crops of Europeans (A). Africa benefited from the introduction of manioc from the Americas (B), whereas sweet potatoes enriched the diets of the Chinese (E). The Columbian Exchange centered on trade across the Atlantic Ocean (C).

3. **C**—Rivalries between France and England were intense in North America. The French were not involved in Indonesian trade (A), or in trade with China (B) or East Africa (D). Neither nation established trade in western Africa during this time period (E).

4. **B**—Indonesian trade involved Muslims, Chinese, Dutch, Portuguese, East African, Southeast Asian, and English traders. The western coast of Africa was primarily the domain of Portugal (A). The Caribbean islands were opened up to Portuguese, English, and French trade (C). The Philippines were controlled by Spain (D), and Japan limited European trade with the Portuguese, then allowed trade only with the Dutch and Chinese (E).

5. **C**—The Portuguese, not the Dutch, established trade contacts in western Africa. The Dutch established Cape Colony in southern Africa as a way station (A) and briefly carried on trade in Brazil (B). The Dutch had a colony in North America for a few years (D) and established trade relations with Tokugawa Japan (E).

6. **E**—Russian trade was local and regional during this time period. Japan (A) and China (C) both engaged in regional trade and in limited long-distance trade. Indonesian trade actively involved a number of European and eastern nations (B), whereas Mughal India encouraged long-distance trade but was too preoccupied with internal expansion to become fully involved in commercial interests (D).

7. **B**—Sugar was transferred from the Middle East to the Mediterranean, then to Brazil and the Caribbean islands, where it became a major export crop to the Eastern Hemisphere. Tobacco (A), sweet potatoes (C), and manioc (E) were exchanged from the Western Hemisphere, whereas bananas (D) were an exchange that originated in the Eastern Hemisphere.

8. **E**—European profits and global dominance increased as a result of its interests in exploration, trade, and colonization. Many regions such as Russia, Japan, China, Mughal India, parts of Africa, and the Ottoman Empire were outside global trade networks (A). The great trading companies were controlled by their respective governments (B). African trade involved primarily slaves, with little global interest in African art (C). The Ottoman Empire, uninterested in technological advances, continued its decline (D).

CHAPTER 18

Systems of Slavery

IN THIS CHAPTER

Summary: As the Columbian Exchange united the Eastern and Western hemispheres across the Atlantic Ocean, the exchange of human beings created a new interaction between Africa and the Western Hemisphere. Slave systems, already a part of life in African kingdoms, became a part of life in the Western world. The result was the unification of three cultures—African, European, and American—in the Americas.

Key Terms

impressment*   Middle Passage*
indentured servitude*   triangular trade*

The Beginnings of the Atlantic Slave Trade

Portugal's quest for gold and pepper from African kingdoms brought it into contact with systems of slave trade already in existence in Africa. The subsequent development of the trans-Atlantic slave trade was an extension of trade in human beings already carried out by Africans enslaving fellow Africans. The slave trade within Africa especially valued women slaves for use as household servants or as members of the harem.

The long-existent trans-Saharan trade had already brought some African slaves to the Mediterranean world. In the mid-fifteenth century, Portugal opened up direct trade with sub-Saharan Africa. Portuguese and Spanish interests in the slave trade increased when they set up sugar plantations on the Madeira and Canary Islands and on São Tomé. The first slaves from Africa arrived in Portugal in the mid-1400s. Europeans tended to use Africans as household servants.

Trade in gold, spices, and slaves brought the Portuguese into contact with prosperous and powerful African kingdoms, among them Kongo, Benin, Mali, and Songhay. Mali and Songhay had already become wealthy Muslim kingdoms enriched by the trans-Saharan gold–salt trade that had been in existence for centuries. In Kongo and Benin, Portugal was interested in Christianizing the inhabitants in addition to establishing trade relations. In the late fifteenth century, the rulers of Kongo had converted to Christianity; a few years later the nonruling classes were also converted.

Characteristics of African Kingdoms

Many of the African kingdoms encountered by the Portuguese had developed their own political and court traditions. African monarchs often ruled with the assistance of governing councils and had centralized governments with armies that carried out the state's expansionist policies. Artisans produced works in ivory and ebony and, in Benin, also in bronze. Active trade existed not only in slaves but also in spices, ivory, and textiles. Slaves usually were prisoners of war or captives from African slave raids that were carried out against neighboring kingdoms and villages.

The Trans-Atlantic Slave Trade

After Native Americans died in phenomenal numbers from European diseases, European colonists in the Americas turned to Africans as forced labor. West Africans, already skilled in agricultural techniques, were especially sought by Europeans for labor on the sugar plantations of Brazil and the Caribbean and in the rice fields of the southern colonies of British North America. The trans-Atlantic slave trade reached its peak during the eighteenth century. The slave trade was part of a **triangular trade** that involved three segments:

- European guns and other manufactured goods were traded to Africans for slaves. (Guns were then used by Africans to capture more slaves.)
- Slaves were transported from Africa to South America or the West Indies. This **Middle Passage** across the Atlantic placed the slaves in shackles in overcrowded and unsanitary slave ships.
- Sugar, molasses, and rum produced by slave labor were traded to Europe for manufactured goods, and the cycle resumed.

Slaves who crossed the Atlantic came from western and central Africa, particularly from Senegambia, Dahomey, Benin, and Kongo. As many as 25 percent of the slaves who came from central Africa died on the long march to the coast to be loaded onto slave ships. Perhaps 20 percent of slaves died on the Middle Passage from illness or suicide. If supplies ran low aboard ship, some slaves were thrown overboard.

Of the approximately 9 to 11 million slaves who crossed the Atlantic, only about 5 percent reached the colonies of British North America. Most of the slaves who eventually reached North America did not arrive directly from Africa, but first spent some time in the West Indies in the Caribbean Sea. The rigors of sugar production in the Caribbean islands and in Brazil required especially large numbers of slaves.

Once in the Americas, African slaves blended their culture with that of the Western Hemisphere. Particularly noteworthy was their introduction of African religions to the Americas. Slaves from West Africa often continued to practice Islam in addition to native

African beliefs, while others created a syncretism of native African practices and beliefs and those of Christianity.

Slavery in Eastern and Southern Africa

Not all slave routes originating in Africa crossed the Atlantic or led to Europe. The cities of eastern Africa traded with the interior of the continent for gold, ivory, and slaves. Many of these slaves were transported to the Middle East, where they became household servants or members of harems. Other slaves in the Indian Ocean system were used on European plantations on islands in the Indian Ocean. Africans from the Swahili coast, Arabs, and Indians also set up plantation colonies along the eastern coast of Africa and on the islands of the Indian Ocean.

In southern Africa, the Cape Colony established by the Dutch in 1652 depended on slave labor. The first slaves arrived from Indonesia and Asia, but later the Dutch enslaved Africans.

Effects of the Slave Trade on Africa

The African slave trade profoundly altered the demographics of Africa. Family life was disrupted as more males than females were transported across the Atlantic for the heavy work required on plantations. In some areas of Africa, populations were reduced by one half. The slave trade increased African dependency on the importation of European technology, lessening the technological development of African kingdoms.

Other Forms of Servitude

In addition to their involvement in both the Mediterranean and trans-Atlantic slave trades, Europeans used other forms of servitude such as **impressment** and **indentured servitude**. Impressment involved the seizure of sailors from foreign vessels. Indentured servants were required to work for a master for a specific number of years in exchange for passage to a European colony such as the English colonies of northeastern North America.

› Rapid Review

Europeans did not initiate the African slave trade but tapped into slave trade systems already in place. Europeans involved in the slave trade encountered wealthy and powerful African kingdoms. Although the main focus of the African slave trade in the seventeenth and eighteenth centuries occurred across the Atlantic, there also was an active slave trade in the Indian Ocean. The slave trade significantly reduced the populations of some areas of Africa and created a dependence on European goods.

❯ Review Questions

1. African kingdoms in the period from 1450 to 1750
   - (A) featured monarchs who ruled without advisors
   - (B) frequently enslaved their own people
   - (C) like the Chinese, were not interested in European trade goods
   - (D) ruled without the use of military units
   - (E) were involved in the slave trade before the arrival of Europeans

2. Compared to the trans-Atlantic slave trade, that of eastern Africa
   - (A) involved only European nations
   - (B) acquired slaves from coastal areas only
   - (C) did not involve central Africa
   - (D) became a model for European slave systems
   - (E) also involved the plantation system

3. Within Africa, the slave trade
   - (A) increased African dependence on European nations
   - (B) decreased the value of women slaves
   - (C) had little effect on central African kingdoms
   - (D) promoted unity among African kingdoms
   - (E) concentrated on western Africa

4. Historians searching for the earliest models of European plantation slavery would need to study
   - (A) plantation society on Indian Ocean islands
   - (B) the history of the Madeira and Canary Islands
   - (C) sugar plantations in the West Indies
   - (D) cotton plantations in British North America
   - (E) slavery among the Dutch in Cape Colony

5. The African slave trade
   - (A) had no ties to Middle Eastern trade
   - (B) was frequently the result of African rivalries
   - (C) was abolished by the Dutch in southern Africa
   - (D) was limited to the Atlantic Ocean
   - (E) replaced trade in gold and ivory

6. The trans-Atlantic slave trade
   - (A) produced average mortality rates of over 50 percent along the Middle Passage
   - (B) carried the majority of slaves to North America
   - (C) increased after the establishment of sugar plantations
   - (D) was separate from triangular trade patterns
   - (E) carried more women than men

7. When the Portuguese first became involved in the slave trade
   - (A) they were uninterested in Christianizing African peoples
   - (B) they were interested primarily in gold and spices
   - (C) they were amazed at the poverty of African kingdoms
   - (D) they created the African slave trade
   - (E) they bypassed trade relations with sub-Saharan Africa

8. Sugar plantations
   - (A) were initially founded in the Caribbean
   - (B) required fewer slaves than the cotton and rice fields of North America
   - (C) were the ultimate destination of the first Portuguese slaves
   - (D) especially valued slaves from western Africa
   - (E) competed with triangular trade

› Answers and Explanations

1. **E**—Trans-Saharan and Middle Eastern trade routes existed before 1450. African monarchs tended to rule with councils of advisors (A). Africans seldom enslaved their own people, usually enslaving prisoners of war or captives from raiding parties on neighboring tribes or kingdoms (B). African traders became dependent on European goods they received in exchange for slaves (C). Armies were important to expanding African kingdoms (D).

2. **E**—Both the trans-Atlantic and eastern African trade routes took slaves to European-run plantations. Eastern African slave trade involved Africans, Indians, and Arabs also (A). It involved both coastal and island areas (B). Slaves were captured from central Africa before being taken to the coast (C). European plantation systems became models for those of other cultural groups (D).

3. **A**—Guns purchased from European nations were used by Africans to acquire more slaves within Africa. Within Africa, slave women were valued as household servants (B). Central African kingdoms were often the source of slaves for trade across the oceans and within Africa (C). The slave trade increased African rivalries (D) and involved most parts of Africa (E).

4. **B**—The earliest models of European plantations were established on the Madeira and Canary Islands. Plantations in the Indian Ocean (A), the West Indies (C), British North America (D), and Cape Colony (E) occurred later.

5. **B**—African rulers often raided neighboring villages in order to secure the wealth and power of slaves. Indian Ocean trade took slaves from East Africa to the Middle East (A). The Dutch enslaved Africans in Cape Colony (C). The Indian Ocean was another site of active slave trade (D). The slave trade took place along with the trade in gold and ivory (E).

6. **C**—The sugar plantations of the Caribbean and Brazil were the primary destination of the trans-Atlantic slave trade. Middle Passage mortality rates averaged about 20 percent (A). Only about 5 percent of slaves crossing the Atlantic were sent to North America (B). It was part of the triangular trade (D) and involved more men than women (E).

7. **B**—Portugal was interested in the gold and spice trade before it was concerned with the slave trade. The Portuguese were interested in bringing Christianity to Africa (A). They found wealthy and powerful African kingdoms (C), and tapped into already existing slave routes (D). Portugal increased trade relations with sub-Saharan Africa (E).

8. **D**—Western Africans were already accomplished farmers. The first sugar plantations were founded off the coast of Africa (A). They required the most slaves of any crop because of the rigors of sugar cultivation (B). The first Portuguese slaves were destined for the households of Europe (C). Sugar plantations were part of the triangular trade (E).

Cultural and Intellectual Changes

IN THIS CHAPTER

Summary: The transformations in the formation of empires, in the slave trade, and in hemispheric connections took place against a backdrop of cultural and intellectual changes. In Europe, a spirit of religious reform created new religious denominations and promoted education. A scientific revolution provided new explanations for the nature of the universe, while Enlightenment philosophers analyzed the nature of political relationships. Enlightenment ideas spread through Europe, Russia, and the Western Hemisphere.

KEY IDEA

Key Terms

Catholic Reformation
(Counter-Reformation)*
commercial revolution*
Deism*
empirical research*
Enlightenment*
excommunication*
heliocentric theory*
indulgence*
laissez-faire economics*

natural laws*
Ninety-Five Theses
Northern Renaissance*
philosophes*
predestination*
Protestant Reformation*
Scientific Revolution*
Society of Jesus

The Protestant and Catholic Reformations

The Renaissance, which began in the city-states of northern Italy, gradually spread to the states of northern Europe. The **Northern Renaissance** was characterized by a more intense religious devotion than the Italian Renaissance. In 1517, to finance the restoration of St. Peter's Basilica in Rome, the Roman Catholic Church authorized the sale of **indulgences**. Indulgences were documents that granted the purchaser the forgiveness of sins. A German priest and former monk named Martin Luther nailed the **Ninety-Five Theses**, or statements for debate, to the door of the Castle Church in Wittenberg in present-day Germany. Luther's studies of the Bible had led him to believe that salvation was obtained only through faith in Jesus Christ as the savior of the world from sin and was not dependent on following Church practices and traditions. Roman Catholic opposition to Luther's teachings led to his eventual **excommunication** from the Roman Catholic Church. Luther's ideas spread widely throughout Europe as a result of the introduction of movable type, an adaptation of Chinese printing technology, by Johannes Gutenberg in the mid-fifteenth century. Gutenberg also used the new printing technology to produce *The Gutenberg Bible*, written in Latin, about 1455.

The **Protestant Reformation** gained popularity not only for its religious teaching but also because of the political climate in Europe in the sixteenth century. A new wave of nationalism was sweeping through Europe, including the German states, which were part of the Holy Roman Empire. Many Germans resented the authority of the pope and welcomed Protestantism for this reason. Protestantism also looked more favorably on Christian participation in commercial and money-making ventures than did Roman Catholicism, a factor that contributed to the **commercial revolution** of the early modern period.

The Spread of Protestantism

A second Protestant Reformation occurred in England when Henry VIII of England broke with the Roman Catholic Church over the pope's refusal to annul his first marriage, which had not produced a male heir. Under Henry's daughter Elizabeth I, England officially recognized Protestantism. Another Protestant, John Calvin, preached the concept of **predestination**, which held that God had predetermined those people who would be saved. Calvinism spread not only through much of western and northern Europe but also to North America through the migrations of the Puritans.

The Catholic Reformation

The Protestant Reformation produced a movement within the Roman Catholic Church to consider Protestant charges against it. As a result of the **Catholic Reformation (Counter-Reformation)**, a church assembly, the Council of Trent, abandoned the sale of indulgences, but preserved traditional Roman Catholic beliefs and practices. A new religious order, the Jesuits, or **Society of Jesus**, was organized to serve as the missionary and educational arm of the Church. The Jesuits engaged widely in missionary work in the Americas and in Asia, taking both Christianity and the knowledge of European culture and technology to those continents.

The Results of the Protestant Reformation

In addition to spreading the belief in salvation by faith alone, the Protestant Reformation:

- Increased European questioning of political authority
- Strengthened the authority of monarchs as papal power decreased
- Encouraged education as Protestants wanted their children to be able to read the Bible
- Improved the status of women within marriage as religious writers encouraged love between husband and wife
- Created new Protestant churches

The Scientific Revolution

The seventeenth and eighteenth centuries saw another kind of revolution: one in scientific thought. Among the key debates of science was a dialogue concerning the nature of the universe. Copernicus, a Polish scientist, abandoned the geocentric theory of Ptolemy to prove that the sun was the center of the solar system (the **heliocentric theory**). The Italian scientist Galileo used a telescope to confirm the discoveries of Copernicus and to study planetary motion and gravity. As a result of his studies, Galileo was taken to court by the Roman Catholic Church and required to publicly recant his theories. A German scientist, Johannes Kepler, discovered the elliptical pattern of planetary motion, whereas Isaac Newton established the basic principles of motion and described the forces of gravity.

New knowledge also was obtained concerning the human body. Vesalius of Belgium studied human anatomy. The Englishman John Harvey explained the circulatory system.

The Revolution in Scientific Thought

The **Scientific Revolution** supported additional research. René Descartes encouraged the educated to develop a skeptical approach to learning. Francis Bacon advocated **empirical research** based on observations and carefully obtained data. Western science took on a nature distinct from scientific thought in East Asia. In contrast to Chinese scientific thought, which generally dealt with specific facts that were practical in nature, Western scientific thought formulated general laws of nature that had roots in Islamic and Greek philosophy. Also characteristic of Western scientific thought were principles that could be utilized for the improvement of humankind.

The Enlightenment

The revolution in science led to a revolution in thought regarding the nature of politics, economics, and society. The **Enlightenment** involved the application of human reason to improve society. Behind the movement was the belief that human beings were basically good and that education and reason could improve their condition even further. Childhood was recognized as a separate stage of growth, and children's toys and books appeared for the first time. Like the Protestant Reformation, the Enlightenment supported marriages based on love, a concept that raised the status of women in family life.

The Beginning and Spread of Enlightenment Thought

The Enlightenment began with the *philosophes*, or French philosophers, many of whom discussed their ideas at Parisian meetinghouses called salons. As the movement spread throughout Europe, Russia, and Europe's colonies in the Americas, the Enlightenment continued to support scientific advances. Some Enlightenment thinkers followed a scientific philosophy called **Deism**, which held that there was a god who created the earth, then left it to operate by **natural law**.

Enlightenment Political Thought

Political philosophers such as the Englishman John Locke and the Frenchman Jean Jacques Rousseau wrote of a social contract in which governments ruled by the consent of the governed to ensure the preservation of the natural rights of humankind. Criminologists advocated rehabilitation for criminals, whereas Mary Wollstonecraft of England spoke out for political rights for women. The Scottish economist Adam Smith wrote *The Wealth of Nations* (1776), in which he set forth the principles of *laissez-faire* **economics**. Smith's philosophy held that government regulation of the economy should be minimal in order to allow the free operation of the laws of supply and demand. Denis Diderot of France compiled the *Encyclopédie,* which included the scientific and social scientific knowledge of the Enlightenment.

❯ Rapid Review

The period from 1450 to 1750 witnessed three major cultural and intellectual revolutions. The Protestant Reformation defied established church traditions and taught salvation by faith alone. The Scientific Revolution explained the nature of the universe and encouraged research. Another movement, the Enlightenment, believed in the basic goodness of humanity and spoke of natural rights that formed the philosophy behind the political revolutions of the eighteenth century.

❯ Review Questions

1. Both the Protestant Reformation and the Enlightenment
   (A) questioned political authority
   (B) lowered the status of women
   (C) upheld church traditions
   (D) relied on reason over faith
   (E) remained confined to Europe

2. The Protestant Reformation
   (A) strengthened the authority of the papacy
   (B) spread because of advances in Chinese and European technology
   (C) became the basis of Enlightenment thought
   (D) diminished the achievements of the commercial revolution
   (E) was carried by Jesuits to the Western Hemisphere

3. All of the following describe the Scientific Revolution EXCEPT that
   (A) it emphasized the value of research
   (B) it described the nature of the universe
   (C) some of its beliefs were openly opposed by the Roman Catholic Church
   (D) it was modeled on Chinese philosophy
   (E) it believed in the overall goodness of humanity

4. Enlightenment thought
   (A) resulted in harsher punishments for criminals
   (B) treated children as miniature adults
   (C) resembled Renaissance thought
   (D) was not embraced by the women's movement
   (E) introduced economic theories that supported mercantilism

5. The Protestant and Catholic reformations were alike
   (A) in their attitudes toward money-making
   (B) in their reliance on church councils
   (C) in their views toward papal authority
   (D) in their abandonment of church traditions
   (E) in their emphasis on education

6. The Scientific Revolution and the Enlightenment
   (A) both held that reason could be used to improve humanity
   (B) broke completely with classical traditions
   (C) supported the ideas of the Roman Catholic Church concerning the nature of the universe
   (D) were global movements
   (E) continued medieval traditions

7. Which of the following is NOT a finding of the Scientific Revolution or the Enlightenment?
(A) Planetary motion
(B) Heliocentric theory
(C) Movable type
(D) The circulatory system
(E) The social contract

8. Which of the following concepts of the period 1450 to 1750 did NOT rely on natural laws?
(A) Predestination
(B) Deism
(C) *Laissez-faire* philosophy
(D) The social contract
(E) The theory of gravity

› Answers and Explanations

1. **A**—Some Europeans favored the Protestant Reformation because it opposed the political and religious authority of the pope. Enlightenment political thinking questioned the authority of governments not established by the consent of the governed. Both improved the status of women by emphasizing the element of love within marriage. Feminists such as Mary Wollstonecraft spoke out in favor of women's rights (B). The Enlightenment placed human reason above church traditions, whereas the Protestant Reformation also challenged them (C). The Protestant Reformation relied on faith over reason (D). The Protestant Reformation spread to North America, whereas the Enlightenment also spread to Russia (E).

2. **B**—The Chinese invention of movable type and the European printing press facilitated the production of documents that spread Reformation thought. The Protestant Reformation weakened the authority of the papacy with regard to both religious and secular matters (A). Reformation theology was based on faith rather than on natural laws (C). Protestantism favored participation in commercial ventures (D). The Jesuits spread Roman Catholicism, not Protestantism, to the Western Hemisphere (E).

3. **D**—Chinese ideas differed from the principles of the Scientific Revolution in not being concerned with the application of science to everyday society. The Scientific Revolution stressed the value of data and research (A) and broke with ancient traditions to describe the nature of the universe (B). The heliocentric theory was initially opposed by the Roman Catholic Church (C). The Scientific Revolution was based on the concept that science could improve the condition of humanity, which was basically good (E).

4. **C**—The philosophy of both the Renaissance and the Enlightenment was based on reason. Enlightenment thought advocated rehabilitation for criminals (A). It treated childhood as a separate stage in life (B). Mary Wollstonecraft, an Enlightenment thinker, spoke out on behalf of political rights for women (D). *Laissez-faire* economics differed from mercantilism, which involved government regulation of the economy (E).

5. **E**—Both reformations valued education as a tool to spread their beliefs. The Protestants were more accepting of Christians in money-making activities than were the Roman Catholics (A). The Roman Catholic Church depended on church councils to establish official church doctrines, whereas the Protestant Reformation taught independence from church traditions and practices (B). Although the Roman Catholic Church relied on papal authority, the Protestant churches did not (C). Although the Protestants abandoned some church traditions, the Roman Catholic Church reaffirmed them in their councils (D).

6. **A**—Both believed that science had a practical role in society. Greek thought influenced both movements (B). Both disagreed with the Roman Catholic Church over the nature of the universe (C). Neither movement directly influenced the Eastern world (D). Both broke with medieval traditions of faith over reason (E).

7. **C**—Movable type, influenced by Chinese printing, was developed in Europe in the 1450s, before the Scientific Revolution or the Enlightenment. The other choices were new to the Scientific Revolution or the Enlightenment.

8. **A**—Predestination was the belief of John Calvin that God had chosen which people would receive salvation and which would not. Deism held that the creator god had left the world to operate according to natural laws (B). *Laissez-faire* economics was based on the natural laws of supply and demand (C). The social contracts of both Locke and Rousseau involved the preservation of natural rights (D), whereas Newton's theory of gravity was based on the natural laws of the universe (E).

PERIOD 4 Summary: Global Interactions (c. 1450–c. 1750)

Timeline

1453	Fall of the eastern Roman Empire
1464–1591	Empire of Songhay
1492	The Reconquest (Spain)
	First voyage of Christopher Columbus
1494	Treaty of Tordesillas
1497–1498	Vasco da Gama's voyage to India
1517	Beginning of the Protestant Reformation
1519–1521	Spanish conquest of Mexico
1526–1858	Mughal dynasty (India)
1532–1540	Spanish conquest of Peru
1545–1563	Council of Trent
1588	Defeat of the Spanish Armada
1603–1867	Tokugawa Shogunate (Japan)
1613	Beginning of the Romanov dynasty of Russia
1643–1715	Reign of Louis XIV of France
1644–1911	Qing dynasty (China)

Key Comparisons

1. European versus Asian monarchs
2. Empires in Africa, Asia, and Europe
3. European versus Asian economic systems
4. Reactions of Japan versus China to Western influence
5. Slavery versus serfdom
6. Trade in Mughal India versus Ming China
7. Russian versus Ottoman interaction with the West
8. Gender roles in Ming China versus Western Europe
9. Transatlantic versus Indian Ocean trade
10. Western European versus Asian and Ottoman technology

Change/Continuity Chart

KEY IDEA

REGION	POLITICAL	ECONOMIC	SOCIAL	CHANGES	CONTINUITIES
East Asia	Ming/Qing dynasties Tokugawa Shogunate	Japanese trade with the Dutch Chinese trade through Macao	Patriarchal society Population increase	Columbian Exchange (China) Christianity Chinese withdrawal from world trade	Ming dynasty Confucianism Neo-Confucianism
Southeast Asia	Regional kingdoms	Indian Ocean trade European plantations	Slavery Islam	Increased European trade Columbian Exchange	Muslim trade Islam Hinduism
Oceania	Regional kingdoms	Agriculture Fishing	Exposure to epidemic disease	Some European explorations	Relative isolation
Central Asia	Steppe diplomacy Russian Empire	Pastoral nomadism Westernization of Russia	Serfdom Tribal units	Russian expansion	Mongol threats to China
South Asia	Mughal dynasty Entry of the British	European trading empires	Miniatures Temporary improvement in women's status Taj Mahal	Columbian Exchange Return to local governments	Indian Ocean trade Islam Hinduism
Southwest Asia (Middle East)	Ottoman Empire	Decline of trade with the West	Slaves from North Africa Harem	Columbian Exchange Ottoman decline	Slavery Islam
North Africa	Regional kingdoms	Gold–salt trade	Slavery Islam	Columbian Exchange	Trans-Saharan slave trade Islam

Region					
Sub-Saharan Africa	Regional kingdoms Cape Colony founded	Bronze, ivory, gold, slaves, ebony Indian Ocean trade	Trans-Atlantic slave trade Christianity	Reduced population Columbian Exchange Dependence on European technology	Islam Tribal allegiances Slavery within Africa Native religions
Western Europe	*Reconquista* Defeat of the Spanish Armada Expulsion of the Jews from Spain	Growth of capitalism Slave trade Exploration Inflation Scientific Revolution	Population increase Reformation Enlightenment	Columbian Exchange	Renaissance
Eastern Europe	Fall of Byzantium Ottoman rule	Agriculture	Serfdom	Columbian Exchange Islam	Serfdom Orthodox Christianity
North America	Colonization	Fur trade Plantations	Slavery Triangular trade Indentured servants	Columbian Exchange European presence	Foraging Nomadism Polytheism
Latin America	Colonization	Mining Sugar plantations	Slavery Social classes Triangular trade	Columbian Exchange European conquest	Polytheism

Industrialization and Global Integration (c. 1750–c. 1900)

CHAPTER 20

The Industrial Revolution and Social Changes

IN THIS CHAPTER

Summary: The period between 1750 and 1900 was one of radical change, especially in the West, Russia, Japan, and China. Political revolutions occurred in the Americas, France, and China. The global population increase caused in part by the Columbian Exchange was followed by a revolution in industry that began in England.

KEY IDEA

Key Terms

An asterisk (*) denotes items listed in the glossary.

capital*
domestic system*
economic liberalism*
enclosure movement*
entrepreneurship*
factors of production
gold standard*
Industrial Revolution*

laissez-faire economics*
limited liability corporation*
Meiji Restoration*
Russo-Japanese War*
Second Industrial Revolution*
Sino-Japanese War
stock market*
zaibatsu*

The Industrial Revolution

The change in the production of manufactured goods from the home to the factory began in the English textile industry in the mid-eighteenth century. The **Industrial Revolution** built on innovations in agriculture that had brought improved farming methods such as crop rotation, scientific breeding of livestock, and the application of fertilizers. A result of increased agricultural output was the **enclosure movement**. Large landholders fenced pastures that previously had been left open for common use, creating a sizable population of landless laborers. England's growing position in global trade contributed to the pursuit of manufacturing interests. The English government supported industrialization by passing laws and instituting policies that promoted its growth. In addition, England possessed the **factors of production:**

- Land (including natural resources such as coal and iron ore)
- Labor (including thousands of dispossessed farmers from southeastern England evicted from their land as a result of the enclosure movement)
- **Capital** (banking and investment interests capable of funding the costs of factories and machinery)
- **Entrepreneurship** (groups of individuals with the knowledge of combining land, labor, and capital to establish factory production)

The technological advance that initiated the transition of manufacturing from home to factory was the steam engine, invented by James Watt of Scotland in the 1770s. Accompanying factory production were changes in transportation and communication such as the telegraph, canals, steamships, and railroads, all of which served to speed up the movement of goods and information.

Expansion of Financial Institutions

To promote industrial investments, financiers offered a variety of services, including insurance, **stock markets**, and **limited liability corporations**. Many favored the use of the **gold standard** to promote financial stability. The globalization of industrialization gave rise to **transnational companies** such as the United Fruit Company and the Hongkong and Shanghai Banking Corporation. These financial innovations owed their origin to the economists Adam Smith and John Stuart Mill. Both Smith's *laissez-faire* **economics** and Mill's **economic liberalism** held that government intervention in and regulation of the economy should be minimal.

Social Changes Brought by Industrialization

The factory system brought a number of changes to family life and society:

- Work was carried out outside the home, a situation that separated family members.
- Factory workers were required to follow schedules and to arrive at work at a specified time.
- Factories required workers to adhere to strict rules.
- Work was done to the noise of machines.
- The pace of work was generally more rapid than at home.
- Women lost manufacturing jobs carried out under the **domestic system**. They were expected to return to the traditional roles of homemaker and childcare provider.
- Social status began to be determined more by wealth than by family position in society.
- Early industrial cities were generally crowded, unsanitary, and poorly lit, with no police protection.

After 1850, the nature of the industrial setting changed somewhat:

- Workers in Western societies received higher wages and shorter working hours, allowing more leisure time activities.
- With the increase in leisure time came popular interest in the theater and in sports.
- Additional employment opportunities arose in secretarial work and sales. Some of these jobs were filled by women, especially those who were unmarried.
- The mass production of clothing made it more affordable, allowing the general population to wear similar fashions.
- Popular consumption of manufactured goods led to advertising campaigns.

The Spread of Industrialization

After England industrialized, other Western nations soon followed. By the 1820s, Belgium and France had begun to industrialize, and a few years later the United States and Germany began factory production. About 1850, the **Second Industrial Revolution** applied the use of electricity and steel to the industrial process. By the end of the nineteenth century, Russia, Egypt, and Japan had become industrialized nations. Common to industrialization in Western nations, Russia, and Japan was the development of railroads, with Russia and the United States constructing transcontinental railways.

Industrialization in Russia

As the Western nations began to industrialize, Russia remained backward in technology. The emancipation of the serfs in 1861 aided Russia in the transition from a predominantly agricultural to a more industrialized society. Government support for industry led to the construction of a trans-Siberian railroad that linked the European portion of Russia with the Pacific world. By the later years of the nineteenth century, factories had arisen in Moscow and St. Petersburg. Government-sponsored programs at the turn of the century improved the Russian banking system and applied high tariffs to protect industry. By the beginning of the twentieth century, Russia ranked fourth in the world in steel production.

Industrialization in Japan

During the first half of the nineteenth century, Japan continued to be governed by the Tokugawa Shogunate. Technologically backward to the industrialized West, Japan emerged from its relative isolation after the 1854 arrival of an expedition from the United States under the command of Commodore Matthew Perry. In 1856, Japan opened two ports to trade with the United States. Shortly thereafter, Great Britain, the Netherlands, and Russia were granted similar concessions.

Some of the Japanese *samurai* favored an end to Japan's isolation. In 1868, the Japanese chose a new emperor named Mutsuhito, or "Meiji," meaning "Enlightened One." The **Meiji Restoration** ended feudalism in Japan and centralized its government. The Meiji government sent key *samurai* to Western Europe and the United States to study Western technology, government, and economics. In the 1870s, the Meiji government abolished the position of *samurai*, and in the 1880s, created a bicameral parliament along Western models.

Japanese social and political changes were accompanied by rapid industrialization. Banks were set up, and the Japanese army and navy were modernized. Key to the success of Japanese industry was strong government support. State-sponsored railroads, steamships, and factories were built. Heavy taxes imposed on Japanese citizens supported industry. By the 1890s, many of the textile mills and other factories were sold off to private investors who formed conglomerates called **zaibatsu**.

In spite of Japan's rapid industrialization, the islands were not fully equipped for industrialization. Japan lacked significant coal and iron ore deposits essential to carry on an industrial economy. By the beginnings of the twentieth century, Japan remained dependent on the West for raw materials and technology.

In the 1890s, Japan's need for raw materials for its industries prompted a quest for empire. In 1895, Japan defeated China in the **Sino-Japanese War**, which was fought over control of Korea. Japan's influence in Korea also led to the **Russo-Japanese War** of 1904–1905, in which Japan defeated Russia. In 1910, Japan annexed Korea.

Social Changes in Industrial Japan

The influence of industrialization introduced a number of Western practices to Japan. Public primary education was offered to all children. The Japanese adopted the metric system, clocks, and the Western calendar. Western haircuts became the fashion for Japanese men. In spite of these adaptations to Western ways, however, few Japanese adopted Christianity, and Shinto and Confucianism became even more popular. Family life also maintained its traditions; Japanese women retained their traditional roles of wives and mothers in a patriarchal family.

Industrialization in Egypt

Under the leadership of its ruler Muhammad Ali, Egypt began to industrialize in the early nineteenth century. In order to lessen Egypt's dependence on the Ottomans, Muhammad Ali built up the Egyptian military. He also brought in European advisers to build up industries. To fund the new industries, Egyptian peasants were required to grow cotton and wheat to export to industrialized nations. When Muhammad Ali levied high tariffs on imported goods, the British objected and forced him to discontinue the duties. Egypt's new industries were unable to compete with British manufacturers, and became dependent on lower-priced manufactured goods from Great Britain.

> Rapid Review

Beginning in Great Britain, the Industrial Revolution spread throughout Western Europe and the United States, altering society and family life. After abolishing serfdom in 1861, Russia began to industrialize, constructing a trans-Siberian railroad to link European Russia to the Pacific coast. The Perry expedition to Japan in 1854 prompted Japan to open its doors to industrialization. Japan ended feudalism and established a centralized empire that built up an industrial sector by the end of the nineteenth century. Japan, however, remained poor in natural resources, a situation that furthered its quest for empire to acquire resources to run its industries. In Egypt, attempts at industrialization met with limited success because of the intervention of Great Britain.

› Review Questions

1. Efforts at industrialization in Russia and Japan were similar in that
   (A) both began in the early nineteenth century
   (B) both followed the termination of long-established institutions
   (C) both countries developed more centralized governments
   (D) both depended on the textile industry
   (E) both countries widely adopted Western practices

2. In the early years of industrial development
   (A) women in Japan emerged from traditional roles
   (B) husbands and wives were given more opportunities to work together
   (C) married women had more opportunities for clerical jobs
   (D) British women lost jobs in domestic manufacturing
   (E) families enjoyed improved housing

3. Common to most early industrial nations was the development of
   (A) steel manufacturing
   (B) railroads
   (C) *zaibatsu*
   (D) unions
   (E) low tariffs

4. Japan's greatest challenge to industrialization was
   (A) its inefficient banking system
   (B) its geography
   (C) lack of government cooperation
   (D) the continued presence of the shogunate
   (E) competition between the government and the *zaibatsu*

5. The Industrial Revolution in Great Britain
   (A) was facilitated because of the enclosure movement
   (B) followed a similar revolution in the United States
   (C) initiated an interest in global trade
   (D) received little government support
   (E) produced a revolution in agriculture

6. Industrialization in Egypt
   (A) gave new freedoms to lower classes
   (B) decreased Egypt's dependency on the West
   (C) resulted from disharmony in the Muslim world
   (D) was accomplished without government support
   (E) narrowed the technological gap between the Muslim world and the West

7. In the early nineteenth century, Russia remained backward to Western nations because of
   (A) a history of tsarist opposition to westernization
   (B) its decentralized government
   (C) its lack of a labor force
   (D) its lack of natural resources
   (E) its continuation of serfdom

8. After the Perry expedition to Japan
   (A) Japan refused to open ports to Western nations
   (B) the *samurai* opposed trade relations with the West
   (C) industrialization was accompanied by imitation of Western governments
   (D) traditional Japanese religion lost popularity
   (E) Japan abandoned its desire for empire

› Answers and Explanations

1. **B**—Prior to industrialization, Russia abolished serfdom and Japan ended feudalism. Both countries began to industrialize in the latter part of the nineteenth century (A). Whereas Japan developed a more centralized government about the time that it industrialized, the Russian government was already centralized (C). Whereas textile mills were a part of early Japanese industrialization, Russia was more dependent upon the production of steel (D). Whereas the Japanese adopted many Western practices, the Russians did not (E).

2. **D**—Many British women had worked in domestic industries prior to the transition to factory production. Women in Japan continued their traditional roles (A). The Industrial Revolution produced less togetherness as married women retained their roles in the home while their husbands worked in factories (B). Married women retained traditional roles in the home (C). Initially, housing in industrialized cities was unsanitary, crowded, and dangerous (E).

3. **B**—Railroads were a common feature of industrialized nations, with Russia's trans-Siberian railroad and the U.S. transcontinental railroad serving as examples. Steel manufacturing was a feature of Russian industry (A). The *zaibatsu* pertained to Japanese industry (C). Unions arose in the West as industrialization progressed (D). High tariffs protected the industries of some nations (E).

4. **B**—Japan's geography did not provide the country with an abundance of needed resources. Japan developed an efficient banking system (A) and enjoyed government support (C). The shogunate was terminated about the time that Japan industrialized (D). The Japanese government cooperated with the *zaibatsu* (E).

5. **A**—The enclosure movement provided the needed labor force to facilitate industrialization. The Industrial Revolution in Britain preceded that in the United States (B). An interest in world trade preceded British industrialization (C). British industry received government backing (D). It followed an agricultural revolution (E).

6. **C**—Egyptian industrialization resulted from the desire of Muhammad Ali to become more independent from Ottoman influence. Peasant classes were forced to grow crops for export (A). When Great Britain interfered with Egyptian industrialization, Egypt became more dependent on the West (B). Industrialization was the project of Egyptian leader Muhammad Ali (D). Not completely successful, Egyptian efforts at industrialization did not narrow the technological gap (E).

7. **E**—Serfdom, not abolished until 1861, kept Russia an agricultural nation. Both Peter the Great and Catherine the Great had favored westernization (A). Russian government was highly centralized under the tsars (B). Its large population provided an ample labor force (C), and it possessed the necessary resources for industrialization (D).

8. **C**—Japan instituted a bicameral parliament based on Western models. Japan opened two ports to Western nations (A). Some *samurai* favored trade relations with the West (B). Christianity did not find much support among the Japanese, while Shinto gained somewhat in popularity (D). Industrialized Japan continued on a quest for empire, in part to provide the country with needed natural resources (E).

CHAPTER 21

Demographic and Environmental Developments

IN THIS CHAPTER

Summary: The Industrial Revolution brought a number of changes in the environments of industrialized nations. A population increase in the West, China, and Japan during the eighteenth century provided the labor force needed by the factory system but also added new challenges. Industrial pollution plagued urban areas. Migration between the Eastern and Western hemispheres enriched the cultural makeup of the Americas.

KEY IDEA

Key Terms

*Maori**   romanticism*
pogrom*   theory of natural selection
quantum physics   theory of relativity

The Population Revolution in the West

In the middle of the eighteenth century, the population of Western Europe increased dramatically. Among the causes of this increase were the end of episodes of epidemic disease and the improved diets resulting from increased consumption of potatoes. Infant mortality rates decreased, whereas larger numbers of healthy adults resulted in a higher birth rate. Larger populations provided a ready labor supply for the new factories.

Industrialization also contributed to patterns of migration. Substantial numbers of people, especially young adults, migrated from the country to the city in search of employment in factories, upsetting the makeup of the traditional Western family. Another pattern of migration involved the movement of the middle class away from the central city to emerging suburbs.

After 1850, urbanization continued in the West; in Great Britain and other Western countries the majority of the population resided in cities. Accompanying a drop in death rates was a lowering of birth rates. Families no longer felt as great a need to produce large families to serve as laborers on family farms. Contributing to falling death rates were more hygienic practices used during childbirth following Louis Pasteur's discovery of the germ theory of disease in the 1880s.

Population Growth in the Non-Western World

Population growth was not restricted to the Western world. In the nineteenth century, the population of Latin America doubled. The cultivation of the sweet potato in China increased population to levels that stressed the country's economy and resources, demonstrating a need for improvement in agricultural methods and technology in China. Also in the nineteenth century, Japan experienced a population explosion because of improvements in nutrition and medical care. Like China, Japan felt the strain in natural resources caused by its growing population. The increased consumption of the potato in the nineteenth century also produced significant population increases in Russia.

Urban Populations and Environments

Sudden population growth was only one of the problems encountered by industrialized urban areas in the West and in Japan. Water supplies were contaminated by human sewage and industrial waste. The dark skies resulting from coal-produced smoke hovering over industrial cities contributed to frequent cases of rickets, a disease of the bones caused by underexposure to sunlight.

Patterns of Migration and Immigration

Migration in the period between 1750 and 1914 took on various forms. Western Europeans continued to colonize and settle regions of the Americas, India, Africa, the Pacific, and Southeast Asia well into the eighteenth century. Settler colonies not only brought about rivalries between Europeans and native peoples but also, as in the Columbian Exchange of the sixteenth and seventeenth centuries, exposed indigenous peoples to European diseases. Among the victims of European diseases were the **Maoris** of New Zealand, whose population was reduced by about one third, and native Hawaiians, over half of whom fell to diseases such as tuberculosis and syphilis. The decimation of the Hawaiian population created a need for imported workers; in the late 1800s, workers from China and Japan arrived in the Hawaiian Islands and transmitted their culture to the islands.

The need for labor in various regions of Latin America in the late nineteenth century produced a flood of immigration from Europe to Brazil and Argentina. Many of the newcomers to Brazil were immigrants from Portugal and Italy who came to work on Brazil's coffee plantations. Because of the physical strength required to carry out plantation labor, most of these migrants were male, leaving women to remain in their home countries and assume new roles in their society. Some of these Italian immigrants returned to Italy part of the year to work the crops there, but others remained in Latin America permanently, adding a European flair and a new diversity to Brazil and Argentina. In the early years of the twentieth century, Russians, Germans, and Jews also contributed to the immigrant population of Latin America. Many of the Jewish immigrants were refugees from **pogroms**, or mass persecutions, of Jews in Russia.

Many immigrants became victims of racial and ethnic prejudice in their new environment. For example, after anti-Chinese riots broke out in some communities in the western United States, the U.S. Congress passed the Chinese Exclusion Act of 1882, which prevented most Chinese immigration.

Changes in the Educational and Artistic Environment

As the inhabitants of Western industrial cities gradually acquired more leisure time, there was a growing interest in scientific knowledge and theories as well as in new methods of literary and artistic expression. In early-nineteenth-century literature and the arts, a new manner of expression called **romanticism** explained human experiences and nature through the use of emotion rather than reason. In 1859, Charles Darwin proposed his **theory of natural selection**, which stated that living species had evolved into their current forms by the survival of the fittest species. Darwin's ideas remained controversial because they conflicted with the biblical account of creation. In 1900, the German physicist Max Planck discovered that light and energy flow in small units that he named "quanta," establishing the discipline of **quantum physics**. In 1916, Albert Einstein, also a German physicist, formulated his **theory of relativity**, which argued that time and space are relative to one another. Social scientists used experimental data to explain human behavior; Sigmund Freud of Vienna explained new theories of the workings of the human mind and developed the technique of psychoanalysis.

› Rapid Review

Improvements in medical practices and sanitation as well as widespread consumption of the potato increased populations in various world regions. The crowded populations of industrial cities presented new problems in housing developments. Although medical knowledge improved throughout the years from 1750 to 1914, pollution in industrial urban areas presented new health issues. Colonization brought new contacts between East and West, including the spread of epidemic disease. At the same time, European immigrants to the Western Hemisphere contributed customs that enriched the cultural landscape of the Americas. Increased leisure time created popular interest in science and the arts.

› Review Questions

1. In the late nineteenth century, Chinese and Japanese laborers were sought in
   (A) Hawaii
   (B) Argentina
   (C) Mexico
   (D) Western Europe
   (E) India

2. Among common migration patterns in the nineteenth century was
   (A) migration from Latin America to Mediterranean Europe
   (B) middle-class migration from countryside to city
   (C) the discontinuation of settler colonies
   (D) migration for religious reasons
   (E) migration of lower classes from cities to suburbs

3. Disease transmission between 1750 and 1914
   (A) resulted in new employment opportunities for East Asian immigrants
   (B) did not effect Oceania
   (C) produced increased mortality rates during childbirth
   (D) saw thousands of Europeans die from exposure to native diseases of the Americas and East Asia
   (E) was unaffected by industrial factors

4. Population patterns in the nineteenth century
   (A) showed growth restricted to the Western world
   (B) showed limited growth among working classes
   (C) showed decline in East Asia and growth in Western Europe
   (D) were the result of increased Western efforts to produce large families to provide farm labor
   (E) were affected by the Columbian Exchange of the previous period

5. New scientific and artistic expressions in the West in the nineteenth century
   (A) supported traditional beliefs
   (B) relied on reason in literary expression
   (C) created new frontiers in physics
   (D) relied on observation rather than experiments to explain human behavior
   (E) found no interest among the general population

› Answers and Explanations

1. **A**—High mortality rates among Hawaiians when exposed to European diseases caused a need for workers from China and Japan. The other four responses were not destinations of major immigrations from China and Japan.

2. **D**—Notable was the migration of Russian Jews to the West as a result of pogroms directed toward them. The period saw migration from Mediterranean Europe to Latin America (A). Members of the lower classes tended to move from the countryside to the cities (B). Settler colonies continued to be inhabited by Europeans (C). Middle classes tended to migrate from cities to suburbs (E).

3. **A**—Immigrants from Japan and China found employment in Hawaii because of Hawaiian population decline from epidemic disease. The Maoris of New Zealand were decimated by European diseases (B). Improved sanitation methods decreased childbirth mortality (C). Europeans introduced the diseases that killed native populations (D). Industrial pollution blocked out sunshine, a situation that made inhabitants of industrial cities susceptible to rickets (E).

4. **E**—Food crops from the Americas, especially the potato, were responsible for the nutritional improvements that contributed to population growth as late as the eighteenth and nineteenth centuries. This population growth affected non-Western (C) as well as Western nations (A). Working classes also benefited from increased nutrients and improved health care (B). As more families moved from the country to the city, there was less of a tendency to produce large families (D).

5. **C**—The quantum theory and the theory of relativity were two frontiers in physics formulated during the period. The theory of natural selection is one example of an idea that broke with traditional beliefs (A). Romanticism relied on emotion rather than reason (B). The new science relied on experimental data (D). The general public became increasingly aware of new ideas in science and literature (E).

CHAPTER 22

World Trade

IN THIS CHAPTER

Summary: The manufactured goods of the industrialized West and the raw materials used to produce them became a primary focus of world trade in the period between 1750 and 1900. In the Atlantic world, trade largely revolved around the plantation system and the economic exploitation of the newly independent nations of Latin America (see Chapter 23). Methods of extracting natural resources from subject nations changed as railroads and roads were constructed to transport raw materials from the interior of colonies to port areas for eventual transport to Europe. Instead of small, independent farm plots owned and cultivated by native peoples, large plantations arose to replace them. On these new agricultural units, native peoples of Africa, India, and Southeast Asia produced crops necessary to the industrialized nations of Europe.

Key Terms

extraterritoriality*
guano*
Monroe Doctrine*
Opium War*
Qing dynasty
spheres of influence*

Suez Canal*
Tanzimet reforms*
Treaty of Nanking*
Wahhabi rebellion*
Young Turks*

Latin American Trade

The profitable sugar plantations of the Caribbean and Brazil were at the heart of Latin American trade with Europe. Brazil also produced cotton and cacao for European use, and during the late eighteenth century, its seaports were opened to world trade. Trade increased the importation of slaves to the Portuguese colony.

As Latin American independence movements drew to a close in the 1820s, the United States stepped forward to monitor future trade with its southern neighbors. The **Monroe Doctrine** (1823) announced the intention of the United States to maintain a "hands off" policy with regard to European colonization in the Americas. Great Britain already had trade agreements with the Spanish colonies since the eighteenth century. It now foresaw the newly independent Latin American republics as future trade partners and supported the Monroe Doctrine. A more active trade began with Britain trading manufactured goods to Latin America, especially Brazil, in exchange for raw materials. In the late nineteenth century, the United States, France, and other nations also traded with Latin America.

By the end of the nineteenth century, active trade was carried on in Cuban tobacco and sugar; Brazilian sugar and coffee; Mexican copper, silver, and henequen; Peruvian **guano;** Chilean grain and copper; and Argentinian beef, grain, hides, and wool. Beef exports increased dramatically after the invention of the refrigerated railroad car in the late nineteenth century. Also in the late nineteenth century, as European nations established colonies and increased industrial production, demand for Latin American rubber, especially from Brazil, increased.

Large landholders who exported sugar and hides especially benefited from foreign trade, whereas local independent traders often had to compete with cheaper and better quality foreign goods. As a result, Latin America became increasingly dependent on the importation of foreign goods, whereas power and wealth concentrated in the hands of large landholders. Foreign investments provided Latin America with necessary capital but also with industry and transportation largely under foreign control. Global trade with the Americas increased after the Panama Canal opened in 1914.

Trade with the Islamic World

Although trade with Latin America increased markedly in the middle and latter years of the nineteenth century, foreign trade with the Ottoman Empire continued on a path of gradual decline. The empire was increasingly weakened by successful independence revolts of its subject peoples, including the Greeks in 1820 and the Serbs in 1867. In the early nineteenth century, the **Wahhabi rebellion** attempted to restore Ottoman strength by insisting upon a return to more traditional Islam and strict adherence to *shariah* law. Contributing to Ottoman weakness was the empire's disinterest in industrialization, which led minority groups such as Christians and Jews within the Ottoman Empire to carry on their own trade with Western European nations for manufactured goods. The artisans who produced goods using the domestic system had difficulty competing with European imports.

The threat of European competition produced a wave of political and economic reform from 1839 to 1876 that opened the Ottoman Empire more to Western influence. The **Tanzimet reforms** facilitated trade, but they came too late to make sweeping changes in the Ottoman economy. Further reform efforts by the **Young Turks** failed to achieve permanent change. The corruption of later Ottoman rulers and decreased agricultural revenue took their toll. In return for foreign loans to bolster its faltering economy, the Ottoman Empire was made economically dependent on European imports and influence. Europeans were granted the privilege of **extraterritoriality**, which allowed Europeans in Ottoman commercial centers to live according to their own laws rather than those of the Ottomans.

Egyptian commerce also suffered from European competition. Muhammad Ali's insistence on increasing cotton production diverted farmers from grain production and made Egypt dependent upon the export of a single crop. A decline in the price of cotton worldwide could have devasted the Egyptian economy. By 1869, however, Egyptian trade strengthened because a canal opened across the Isthmus of Suez. Connecting the Mediterranean and Red seas, the **Suez Canal** made Egypt a significant commercial and political power between Europe and its colonies in Africa and Asia.

Qing China and the Opium Trade

In 1644, the weakened Ming dynasty was overtaken by the Manchus, a largely nomadic people who lived north of the Great Wall. The new dynasty, calling itself **Qing**, lifted Ming restrictions against foreign travel. Chinese merchants took an increasingly active part in overseas trade, and foreign merchants traded with China through the port of Canton. Trade in Chinese tea, silk, and porcelain brought in large quantities of silver, which was the basis of the Chinese economy. By the nineteenth century, international trade based in southern China was especially profitable.

One of China's chief trading partners, Great Britain, became increasingly concerned over having to pay large amounts of silver for Chinese luxury goods. British merchants solved the trade imbalance by trading Indian opium to China. Indian opium, which was of a higher quality than Chinese-grown opium, took such a hold on Chinese society that soon the Chinese were forced to pay for the product with large quantities of their silver. In addition to this trade reversal, millions of Chinese became addicted to opium, a situation that affected work and family responsibilities. When the Qing emperor took measures to block the opium trade, war broke out in 1839 between China and Great Britain. British victory in the **Opium War** and another conflict in the 1850s resulted in the opening of China to European trade. The **Treaty of Nanking** (1842) that ended the Opium War made Hong Kong a British colony and opened up five ports to foreign commerce instead of only the port of Canton. Opium continued to flow into China. By 1900, more than ninety ports were open to foreign trade. Foreign **spheres of influence** were drawn up in China; within these territories, the controlling nation enjoyed special trade privileges as well as the right of extraterritoriality.

Russia and World Trade

Russia continued to occupy a backward position in trade and technology. The Russians exported some grain to western Europe in exchange for Western machinery. By 1861, the desire to compete with Western nations in world trade prompted Russia to emancipate its serfs. Still, Russia lagged behind in export crops as the emancipation of the serfs left a labor force that used outdated agricultural methods.

Japanese Entrance into World Trade

The second Perry expedition to Japan in 1854 opened two ports to trade with the United States. Later, the Netherlands, Great Britain, and Russia initiated trade relations with Japan. As Japan industrialized, it depended on imports of Western equipment and raw materials, especially coal.

The End of the Trans-Atlantic Slave Trade

The combination of Enlightenment thought, religious conviction, and a slave revolt in Haiti led to the end of the trans-Atlantic slave trade. The British ended their participation in the slave trade in 1807, then worked to get the cooperation of other slave importers to the Americas to end their part in the slave trade. While Britain seized hundreds of slave ships, Cuba and Brazil, with the cooperation of African rulers, continued to import huge numbers of slaves. The trans-Atlantic slave trade did not end until 1867.

› Rapid Review

Although the trade in human beings across the Atlantic was coming to an end, other avenues of trade appeared worldwide. Latin America, Russia, the Islamic world, and Japan developed an increased dependency on Western technology. China saw its favorable balance of trade reversed as its silver supply was diminished to purchase Indian opium from Great Britain. By the beginning of the twentieth century, European products dominated global trade routes.

› Review Questions

1. As a result of the Opium War,
   (A) the Qing dynasty overtook the Ming
   (B) Great Britain acquired Hong Kong
   (C) the Chinese silver supply was restored
   (D) the importation of opium to China increased
   (E) foreign spheres of influence were abolished

2. The end of the trans-Atlantic slave trade
   (A) was resisted by Great Britain
   (B) received widespread support of African kings
   (C) began with Brazil
   (D) occurred about the same time as the emancipation of Russian serfs
   (E) was initiated by the United States

3. The country least dependent on Western technology in the early nineteenth century was
   (A) the Ottoman Empire
   (B) Japan
   (C) Russia
   (D) China
   (E) Argentina

4. As a result of Latin America's trade relationship with the United States and Great Britain,
   (A) Latin America became dependent on United States and European manufactured goods
   (B) Latin America began to industrialize
   (C) local independent trade flourished in Latin America
   (D) land was redistributed
   (E) peasants benefited from trade more than did large landowners

5. The Ottoman Empire
   (A) refused to accept foreign loans
   (B) resisted economic reforms
   (C) supported policies that benefited local artisans
   (D) saw trade between non-Muslims and European merchants
   (E) increased agricultural profits in the nineteenth century

6. Egyptian trade
   (A) was dependent on the exportation of a single crop
   (B) did not suffer from competition with Europe
   (C) improved as a result of Muhammad Ali's policies
   (D) weakened after the opening of the Suez Canal
   (E) was independent of world export prices

7. Latin American trade
   (A) decreased after the 1820s
   (B) caused Great Britain to support the Monroe Doctrine
   (C) depended on the increased slave trade of the late nineteenth century
   (D) relied on exports of manufactured goods
   (E) increased local wealth by supplying inexpensive foreign imports

8. World trade in the period 1750 to 1900
   (A) brought greater prosperity to China than to the West
   (B) decreased the economic power of the West
   (C) strengthened Latin America's trade position
   (D) concentrated on the Atlantic Ocean
   (E) benefited Western colonial powers

› Answers and Explanations

1. **B**—The Treaty of Nanking (1842) made Hong Kong a British colony. The Qing overtook the Ming in 1644, while the Opium War occurred between 1839 and 1842 (A). China's silver supply was drained to purchase opium (C) and was not immediately restored since the opium trade continued after the war (D). Foreign spheres of influence were set up after the war (E).

2. **D**—Both ended in the 1860s. Great Britain initiated the end of the trans-Atlantic slave trade (A) (E). Brazil continued to support the slave trade (C) with the approval of many African kings (B).

3. **D**—China continued to resist the intrusion of Western technology, whereas the Ottoman Empire (A) and countries of Latin America (E) became increasingly dependent on it. After the Meiji restoration, Japan depended on Western technology, sending students to the West to learn of its use (B). Russia purchased machinery from the West (C).

4. **A**—The United States and Europe encouraged Latin America to provide them with raw materials rather than build factories (B), a situation

that kept Latin America dependent on U.S. and European manufactured goods. Local traders were forced to compete with less expensive imports (C). Land remained in the hands of a few large landholders (D), who benefited the most from the wealth brought in by trade (E).

5. **D**—Most European trade carried on within the Ottoman Empire was on the part of Jewish and Christian merchants. The Ottoman Empire accepted some loans from the West (A) in spite of enacting some economic reforms within the empire (B). Local artisans suffered because of the influx of better and less expensive European goods (C). Agricultural revenue declined (E).

6. **A**—Egyptian trade depended on the exportation of cotton. It suffered because of the influx of European goods (B) and was dependent on world cotton prices (E). Muhammad Ali's insistence on a single cash crop hindered Egyptian trade (C). Trade improved after the opening of the Suez Canal (D).

7. **B**—Great Britain supported the Monroe Doctrine to improve its relations with Latin America so that it could actively trade with the

Latin American nations. Latin American trade increased after the independence movements of the 1820s (A). The slave trade ended in the late nineteenth century (C). Latin American nations imported manufactured goods (D). Local artisans suffered because of the importation of European goods (E).

8. **E**—Much of world trade in this period benefited Western colonial powers, who imposed their manufactured goods on the developing world, increasing the economic power of the West (B). China suffered an outflow of silver because of the opium trade (A). Latin America became dependent on U.S. and European manufactured goods (C). Trade was active in the Indian and Pacific oceans in addition to the Atlantic (D).

CHAPTER 23

Political Revolutions

IN THIS CHAPTER

Summary: In the period between 1750 and 1900, the Industrial Revolution was joined by political revolutions. Enlightenment philosophies that society could improve through education and reason led to revolution in the British North American colonies, France, and Haiti in the latter part of the eighteenth century and early nineteenth century. Additional Latin American independence movements flourished in the early nineteenth century. In China, the Qing dynasty faced local revolts as it gradually declined.

KEY IDEA

Key Terms

Bill of Rights
bourgeoisie*
Boxer Rebellion*
Code Napoleon*
communism*
Congress of Vienna
conscription*
conservatism*
Declaration of Independence
Declaration of the Rights of Man
   and of the Citizen*
Declaration of the Rights of
   Woman and of the Female*
estates*
Estates-General*

feminism*
Gran Colombia*
Jacobins*
Jamaica Letter
liberalism*
maroon societies*
natural rights*
proletariat*
queu
radicalism*
Reign of Terror*
Revolutions of 1848*
self-strengthening movement*
separation of powers*

The American Revolution

The revolt for independence in the British North American colonies was the child of Enlightenment philosophers, most notably the Englishman John Locke. Locke spoke of a **social contract** in which the people relinquished some of their rights to the government in order to establish order. Governments had the responsibility of safeguarding the "unalienable" rights of "life, liberty, and property." If a government did not preserve these rights, the people had the right to overthrow it and establish a new government.

Britain's North American colonies had gradually developed their own identity since their founding in the early seventeenth century. The colonists particularly resented British policies that levied taxes on them without allowing them their own representative in Parliament. Higher taxes were imposed in 1763 after the end of the French and Indian War (the American phase of the **Seven Years' War**) as a result of British efforts to receive colonial reimbursement for part of the expense of the war that the British had fought on the colonists' behalf. The aftermath of war also brought British restrictions against colonial migration into territories west of the Appalachians once held by the French, territories the British considered unsafe for settlement because of potential conflicts with Native Americans in the area.

The American Revolution began in 1775 as a result of efforts from colonial leaders well versed in Enlightenment thought. In 1776, the colonists set up a government that issued the **Declaration of Independence**, a document modeled after the political philosophies of John Locke. Its author, Thomas Jefferson, altered the **natural rights** identified by John Locke to include "life, liberty, and the pursuit of happiness." With the aid of the French, the British colonists were victorious in 1781. In 1787, the new United States of America wrote a constitution insuring the **separation of powers** and the **system of checks and balances**, both ideas of the Enlightenment philosopher Montesquieu. A **Bill of Rights** added a statement of individual liberties in keeping with Enlightenment principles. Voting rights were increased to embrace more white male voters; by the 1820s, property rights for voting had been abolished in the new states. Neither the Declaration of Independence nor the United States Constitution addressed the issue of slavery.

The French Revolution

Enlightenment thinking also contributed to a revolution in France. In the late eighteenth century, French society was divided into three classes, or **estates**:

- First Estate—the clergy, comprising a little more than 1 percent of the population, and paying no taxes.
- Second Estate—the nobility, comprising slightly more than 2 percent of the population, and paying only a few taxes.
- Third Estate—the remainder of the population, made up of merchants, artisans, and peasants. The peasants were burdened with heavy taxes and labor requirements that were carryovers from feudal days. The middle class, or **bourgeoisie**, were the merchants, artisans, and professionals who became the driving force of the revolution.

Representatives of the three estates met in the **Estates-General**, the French legislative assembly. In 1789, however, the French monarchs had not called the Estates-General into session for 175 years. Revolution broke out because of:

- Bourgeoisie desire for a wider political role
- Bourgeoisie wish for restraints on the power of the clergy, monarchy, and aristocracy
- Population growth
- Poor harvests in 1787 and 1788

When King Louis XVI was forced to call a meeting of the Estates-General in 1789 in order to raise taxes, the bourgeoisie insisted on changing the voting rules in the Estates-General from one vote per estate to one vote per representative. The king was forced to agree to the new voting arrangement as rioting broke out in Paris. On June 14, 1789, the Bastille, a Parisian political prison, was stormed by a Paris mob. The incident liberated only a handful of prisoners but became the rallying point of the French Revolution.

The new bourgeoisie-dominated National Assembly issued the **Declaration of the Rights of Man and of the Citizen**, a document whose content bore a resemblance to clauses in the Declaration of Independence and the United States Constitution. The French declaration identified natural rights as "liberty, property, security, and resistance to oppression." A new constitution guaranteed freedoms of the press and of religion and increased voting rights. Olympe de Gouges countered the French declaration of rights with her **Declaration of the Rights of Woman and of the Female**.

The Reign of Terror

In 1792, the revolution entered a more radical phase known as the **Reign of Terror** as the monarchy was abolished, with Louis XVI executed on the guillotine. Under the leadership of a radical club known as the **Jacobins**, thousands were executed during the Reign of Terror. A new constitution provided **universal male suffrage** and universal military **conscription**.

The revolutionaries had to repel foreign armies of Prussia, Russia, Austria, and Great Britain that attempted to preserve the French monarchy. Eventually, the European armies were driven from France, and revolutionaries added new territory in the Netherlands, Germany, and Italy. A wave of nationalism spread throughout France.

The Final Stage

The republican gains of the French Revolution came to an end in 1799 with the rise to power of army general Napoleon Bonaparte. Napoleon limited the power of the legislative assembly and returned authoritarian rule to France. Napoleon also:

- Censored speech and the press
- Codified laws in **Code Napoleon**
- Granted religious freedom
- Established universities
- Denied women basic rights

Napoleon declared himself the emperor of a new French empire in 1804. The major powers of Europe fought a number of wars against Napoleon's armies. An 1812 French invasion of Russia led to a decisive defeat for Napoleon, largely as a result of the harsh Russian winter. The European alliance defeated Napoleon in 1814 and again, decisively, in 1815. Although it was a setback for the revolutionary principles in France, Napoleon's empire spread the ideals of the revolution outside France and created a spirit of nationalism throughout Europe.

The Aftermath of the Napoleonic Wars

After the final defeat of Napoleon in 1815, European leaders met at the **Congress of Vienna** to restore legitimate monarchs to the thrones of Europe and to create a balance of power. The purpose of the balance of power was to prevent France or any other European nation from dominating the continent again. This spirit of **conservatism** kept Europe largely at peace until the end of the nineteenth century. Other political movements gained strength: **liberalism** sought protection for the rights of propertied classes, whereas **radicalism** wanted broader suffrage and social reforms on behalf of the lower classes. In 1848, a series of revolutions again swept through Europe, bringing the end of monarchy in France. The liberal **Revolutions of 1848** largely failed, however, to bring permanent reform to Europe. Nationalist stirrings in Italy and Germany united the various political units in both regions. The unification of Italy was completed in 1870, while German unification occurred a year later in 1871.

The Haitian Revolution

The revolutions in the British North American colonies and in France inspired a revolt in the French Caribbean island colony of Saint-Dominigue, or Haiti. The Haitian Revolution was the first incident in world history in which black slaves successfully rebelled against their enslavers. Haiti's colonial economy was based on the production of sugar. Haitian society was divided among slave workers on the sugar plantations, free people of color, and French colonists. During the French Revolution, tensions increased between white inhabitants and free people of color. In 1791, Haitian slaves took advantage of this division to rebel. Under the leadership of a free black named Toussaint L'Overture, the rebellion succeeded, and in 1804 the island declared its independence as the republic of Haiti.

Other Latin American Revolts and Independence Movements

Enlightenment ideas and a succession crisis in Spain created an opportune moment for the realization of independence in Spain's colonies. The placement of Napoleon's brother on the throne of Spain instead of the Spanish king caused the American colonists to question the identity of Spain's ruler. Consequently, independence revolutions broke out in the Americas.

Mexican Independence

In Mexico, the Creole Father Miguel de Hidalgo called on *mestizos* and Indians to assist him in a rebellion against Spain in 1810. The Creoles, fearing the social reforms that might materialize from *mestizo* and Indian involvement, initially abandoned the independence movement. After Hidalgo was executed, the Creoles rejoined the cause under Augustín de Iturbide, a Creole officer. In 1821, Mexico declared its independence from Spain. In 1824, Mexico became a republic. The Central American states, which had been a part of Mexico, divided into separate independent nations in 1838.

The South American Phase

In the northern part of South America, the Creole Simón Bolívar centered his movement for independence against Spain in Caracas. His **Jamaica Letter** (1815) expressed his hope that freedom from Spanish rule would ultimately insure prosperity for Latin America. By 1822, he had liberated Colombia, Ecuador, and Venezuela, uniting these regions into the nation he called **Gran Colombia**. Regional differences led to the eventual breakup of the new nation.

In the southern portion of South America, José de San Martín emerged as the independence leader from Río de la Plata (present-day Argentina). Río de la Plata declared its independence in 1816. San Martín then crossed into Chile to assist in its liberation. By 1823, all of Spanish America had declared its independence and established republics in all the new nations except Mexico. Independence, however, did not bring prosperity to Latin America, as Bolívar had hoped.

Independence in Brazil

The Portuguese colony of Brazil followed a pattern for independence different from that of the other Latin American countries. In 1807, when the French invaded Portugal, the Portuguese royal family fled to Brazil. The colony of Brazil acquired a status equal to that of Portugal. When Napoleon was defeated, the Portuguese king was recalled and left his son Dom Pedro regent in Brazil.

In 1822, Dom Pedro declared Brazil independent after realizing that Brazil was about to lose its representative in the Portuguese parliament. Unlike the other Latin American nations, Brazil did not have to endure a prolonged independence movement. Brazil became a monarchy, and the institution of slavery was left untouched in the newly independent country.

Maroon Societies

Some slaves in Latin America also resisted their colonial government, especially in Brazil and the Caribbean. Runaway slaves who had fled the plantations established their own communities. In the Caribbean, these **maroon societies** often located in remote areas in the mountains of Jamaica and Hispaniola and in the islands of the Guianas. Initially intended to provide havens for future escaped slaves, some of the maroon societies eventually were granted independence from colonial rulers.

The Delcine of Qing China

The Manchus who entered China as the Qing dynasty in 1644 had been exposed to Chinese culture as a result of years spent living along the northern Chinese border. The Qing continued Chinese traditions such as the civil service examination and patriarchal family structure. Female infanticide increased. Women were confined to traditional household duties, while women from peasant families also worked in the fields or in village marketplaces. The Manchus required Chinese men to distinguish themselves from them by wearing a **queu**, or braided ponytail.

Although the Qing attempted to control the consolidation of large tracts of land, they had little success. The gap between rural peasants and rural gentry increased. Some men of the gentry began to let their fingernails grow extremely long to indicate that they did not have to do any physical labor.

By the end of the eighteenth century, the Qing dynasty was in decline. The civil service examination had often given way to obtaining governmental posts through bribery. Dams, dikes, and irrigation systems were in disrepair. Highway bandits were a problem in some areas of China. The importation of opium (see Chapter 22) caused conflicts with Great Britain.

The increased influence of foreign powers on Chinese society and China's defeat in the Opium War produced widespread rebellion in south China in the 1850s and early 1860s. This rebellion resulted from the inability of the Qing to repel foreign influence in China. The **Taiping Rebellion** advocated programs of social reform, more privileges for women, and land redistribution. When the scholar-gentry realized that the rebellion was reaching to the heart of Chinese tradition, it rallied and ended the rebellion.

Later Qing officials attempted to spare the Chinese economy by carrying out a **self-strengthening movement** that encouraged Western investments in factories and railroads and modernized the Chinese army. Reform movements were crushed, however, under the rule of the dowager empress Cixi. The **Boxer Rebellion** (1898–1901) was a revolt against foreigners that was backed by Qing rulers. The rebellion, which culminated in the execution of foreigners in China, was put down by a coalition force from Europe, the United States, and Japan.

Socio-Political Movements: Feminism, Marxism, and Socialism

Feminism

In the eighteenth century, **feminist** movements began to seek political, social, and economic gains for women. Among the goals of these movements were access to higher education and the professions and the right to vote. By 1914, Scandinavian countries and some states in the United States had granted women the right to vote. Within a few years, women's suffrage had extended to all states in the United States and to Great Britain and Germany.

Marxism

The socio-political theories of the German Karl Marx became significant in Russian history. Marx taught that all history was the result of a class struggle between the bourgeoisie, or middle class, and the **proletariat**, or working class. According to Marx, the proletariat would eventually revolt and establish a "dictatorship of the proletariat" that would insure social and political freedom. When this occurred, there would no longer be a need for the state, which would wither away. The result would be pure **communism**, or a classless society.

Less extreme forms of **socialism** emerged in European nations as socialist parties arose in Germany, France, and Austria. Many Europeans were fearful of the revolutionary nature of some socialist movements. Socialism in Germany, France, and Austria brought changes such as the recognition of labor unions and disability and old-age insurance.

> Rapid Review

The spirit of the Enlightenment produced revolutions in the British North American colonies, France, and Latin America. Reaction against foreign intervention and the weakness of the Qing dynasty culminated in local revolts in China that weakened centuries-old dynastic rule in that country. Accompanying political revolution was an increasingly vocal movement to grant political rights to women in the Western world. Socialism attempted to create working conditions and societies that would improve the condition of humanity, whereas the Marxist brand of socialism defined a class struggle whose ultimate purpose was the abolition of government.

› Review Questions

1. The American and the French revolutions were alike in all the following ways EXCEPT
   (A) they both brought increased political power for women
   (B) they were prompted by issues of taxation
   (C) they both involved representation in their respective legislatures
   (D) they produced documents that defined similar natural rights
   (E) they were based on Enlightenment thought

2. The Haitian Revolution was the only revolution of the period 1750 to 1900 that was initiated and fought by
   (A) Creoles
   (B) *mestizos*
   (C) slaves
   (D) foreign mercenaries
   (E) elite classes

3. The Brazilian independence movement
   (A) resulted in the abolition of slavery
   (B) produced a republic for Brazil
   (C) involved a prolonged struggle with Portugal
   (D) followed a pattern similar to that of other Latin American independence movements
   (E) was the result of the Napoleonic wars

4. The declining years of the Qing dynasty saw
   (A) the influence of foreign nations
   (B) invasion by nomadic people north of the Great Wall
   (C) the long-term acceptance of the self-strengthening movement
   (D) the end of the opium trade
   (E) the return to tradition by new dynastic rule

5. Marxism
   (A) became the model for socialism in Western European nations.
   (B) anticipated revolution in agrarian societies
   (C) advocated centralization of the state
   (D) became a factor in the French Revolution
   (E) saw history as a series of class struggles

6. Political, economic, and social change from 1750 to 1900
   (A) saw sweeping changes in political rights for women
   (B) was generally led by members of the lower classes
   (C) included reaction against foreign influence in China and Mexico
   (D) brought increased prosperity to Latin America
   (E) brought republican government throughout the Americas

› Answers and Explanations

1. **A**—Although the French Revolution increased women's political rights somewhat until the rule of Napoleon, no political rights were gained by women as a result of the American Revolution. The French Revolution was a reaction of the Third Estate against taxation, while the American Revolution was a protest against taxation without representation in the British Parliament (B). The French revolt also involved the degree of representation of the Third Estate in the Estates-General (C). The Declaration of Independence and the Declaration of the Rights of Man and of the Citizen spoke of similar natural rights (D). Both were based on Enlightenment thought, especially that of Locke and Rousseau (E).

2. **C**—The Haitian Revolution was initiated by black slaves. The other responses are incorrect.

3. **E**—Brazil saw an opportunity to raise its status to the level of Portugal as a result of the French occupation of the Portuguese throne, a situation that ultimately led to its independence. It did not abolish slavery (A) and produced a monarchy for Brazil (B). It did not involve a prolonged struggle for independence (C), thereby following a different pattern from that of other Latin American independence movements (D).

4. **A**—The Opium War was a case of foreign involvement in China. The Qing were the last nomadic invaders of China during the seventeenth century (B). The self-strengthening movement produced only temporary changes (C). The opium trade continued after the Opium War (D). The end of dynastic rule was a turn away from Chinese tradition (E).

5. **E**—Marx saw history as a series of struggles between the bourgeoisie and the proletariat. Socialism in Europe outside Russia took on a milder form (A). Marx anticipated revolution in industrialized countries (B) and advocated overthrow, rather than centralization, of the state (C). Marxism was not defined until after the French Revolution (D).

6. **C**—Both the Mexican and Chinese revolts were in part reactions against foreign involvement. Women did not see significant changes in their political rights (A). Most revolutions were led by the middle classes (B). Independence did not bring increased prosperity to Latin America (D). Brazil established a monarchy after independence (E).

Western Imperialism

IN THIS CHAPTER

Summary: The strengthening of European nation-states and the technological changes brought by the Industrial Revolution gradually began to erode the European balance of power achieved by the Congress of Vienna. As European nation-states competed for power, they turned to colonies to supply them with raw materials and with markets for their manufactured goods. The rivalries among European nations were carried out in the territories of non-Western nations. The United States also realized its imperialist ambitions in Latin America and the Pacific.

KEY IDEA

Key Terms

Berlin Conference*
Boer War*
Boers*
economic imperialism*
Great Trek
imperialism*
Indian National Congress*

Manifest Destiny
Raj
Sepoy Rebellion*
sepoys*
Social Darwinism*
Spanish-American War*

The Background of Imperialism

Imperialism, or the quest for empire, was in part a result of the Industrial Revolution. The mechanization of industry and resulting improvements in transportation brought new demands for raw materials, such as palm oil as a machine lubricant and rubber for tires. The industrial age also:

- Produced military weaponry such as the machine gun and the repeating rifle, which gave Western nations a military advantage over developing nations.
- Saw the application of steam to ships. Steamships could travel previously unnavigable rivers, allowing Europeans to reach the interior regions of continents.
- Brought the application of science to the study of health, resulting in preventative measures against the threat of malaria, a common tropical disease to which most Europeans were not immune.

In addition to the impact of industrialization, the concept of **Social Darwinism** contributed to the race for colonies. Social Darwinism was the application of Charles Darwin's theory of natural selection to society to justify the conquest by European nations of non-Western societies.

The Role of Nationalism

Nationalism, or intense pride in one's national culture, also contributed to the new imperialism of the nineteenth and early twentieth centuries. Nationalism served as both a positive and negative force. In 1870, a common language and culture resulted in the unification of the Italian city-states into one nation. The following year, the German principalities also joined to form a single nation-state. In the mid-nineteenth century, the United States followed a policy of **Manifest Destiny** that led to its expansion from the Atlantic to the Pacific.

Within the Austrian Empire, by contrast, were a number of nations with different languages, religions, and institutions. Among them were Poles, Croatians, Czechs, Slovaks, and Hungarians. The Russian Empire also was ethnically diverse, including not only Slavs but also Turks, Poles, Finns, Estonians, and Jews, as well as other ethnic groups. Its diversity led Russia to try to impose the Russian language on all its subject peoples.

The Scramble for Colonies

The main regions of European colonization were India and Africa. British influence in India began as commercial activity during the declining years of the Mughal Empire. The breakup of Mughal rule resulted in minor disputes among local princes. The British took advantage of this situation to help settle disputes, thereby gradually gaining greater influence in India. The Seven Years' War (1756–1763), which also was fought in Europe and North America, was the first global war. It brought the British and French into conflict in India. British victories over the French in India gave them control of the country. Many of the Indian soldiers, or **sepoys**, were attracted to the higher-paying British army. India gradually emerged as Britain's key source of raw materials and main colonial market for Britain's manufactured goods.

British Colonial Society in India

The British who went to India created a stratified society with Europeans occupying the highest positions. English became the language of instruction in Indian schools. The British **Raj** (the Sanskrit name for the British government in India) set up telegraph lines to facilitate communications with Great Britain, and railways to carry troops and raw materials. For the most part, the British did not train the Indians in the use of the new technology that they brought to India. With the cooperation of the Western-educated Indian leader Ram Mohun Roy, the British outlawed *sati*.

British rule over India tightened after the 1857 **Sepoy Rebellion**. The cause of this revolt of Indian soldiers in the British army was the issue of new rifles that required the soldiers to use their teeth to tear open the cartridges. These ammunition cartridges were lubricated with animal fat. Muslims, who did not eat pork, were offended by grease that came from animal fat, while Hindus objected to grease from the fat of cattle. Even though the procedure for opening the cartridges was changed, the sepoys rebelled against British authority. The revolt was put down in 1858, but not before several hundred British men, women, and children were massacred.

Schools and universities established by British and American missionaries created an educated class of Indians with a strong nationalist sentiment. In 1885, they founded the **Indian National Congress**, which promoted a greater role for Indians in their country's government. The new organization also sought harmony among Indians of diverse religious and social groups.

Imperialism in South Africa

The first European colonial presence in present-day South Africa was the Dutch way station established at Cape Colony in 1652. Eventually, the Dutch, or **Boers**, moved into the interior of the continent. There they enslaved the inhabitants, the Khoikhoi. Interracial mixing produced the South Africans known as "colored" today.

During the wars of the French Revolution, the British captured Cape Town and annexed it in 1815. A conflict between the Boers, who were slaveholders, and the British over the end of slavery caused many Boers to leave Cape Colony. Their migration, called the **Great Trek** (1834), took the Boers into the interior of South Africa. There they clashed with the Bantu peoples, especially the powerful Zulu. Under the leadership of their leader, Shaka, the Zulu nation fought back against Dutch, then British, rule, only to be defeated by the more advanced British technology.

In the 1850s, the Boers established two republics in the interior of South Africa: the Transvaal and the Orange Free State. When diamonds were discovered in the Orange Free State in 1867, the imperialist businessman Cecil Rhodes and other British moved into the Boer republics. In spite of war between the Boers and the British from 1880 to 1881 that ended in Boer victory, the British continued to pour into South Africa. Migration was especially intense after gold was discovered in the Transvaal in 1885. Continued tension between the British and the Boers culminated in the **Boer War** of 1899 to 1902. After this conflict, the Boers began a period of dominance over native South Africans. In 1902, the individual Boer republics maintained their self-governing status as they were united into the Union of South Africa, controlled by Great Britain.

The Partition of Africa

Intense rivalries among European nations played out on the African continent. As the need for raw materials and colonial markets arose, Africa was divided among European colonial powers. The **Berlin Conference** of 1884–1885 partitioned Africa into colonies dominated by Great Britain, France, Portugal, Spain, Germany, Belgium, and Italy. Only Liberia and

Ethiopia were not colonized by Europeans. Absent from the Berlin Conference were representatives from any African nation.

The divisions of the Berlin Conference were carried out without regard for ethnic and cultural groups. Boundaries dividing the territorial possessions of one European power from another often cut through ethnic and cultural groups, placing members of a single group in different colonies dominated by different European powers. Traditional African life was disrupted as Europeans imposed on the continent their concept of the nation-state as the unit of government. These colonial divisions would affect African life to the present.

As in India, European imperialist powers in Africa contributed railways, roads, and other public works to the African landscape. Hospitals were set up and sanitation improved. Most of the improvements were intended initially for the welfare of the European colonists. As in India, Europeans in Africa failed to train natives to use the new technology they brought to the continent.

European businesses set up plantations and required local African natives to work long hours at extremely low wages to produce export crops for European benefit. Work on European plantations prevented Africans from tilling their home and village plots, a situation that led to decreased food supplies and malnutrition for their families.

Imperialism in Southeast Asia

Prior to the new imperialism of the nineteenth century, most of Southeast Asia consisted of independent kingdoms. The Malay States (present-day Malaysia) and Burma (presently Myanmar) came under British rule. Indochina was colonized by the French and the East Indies (now Indonesia) by the Netherlands. Siam (present-day Thailand) was the only Southeast Asian country that did not fall to imperialist ambitions. When native populations provided an insufficient labor supply, Europeans brought in immigrants from India and China.

Economic Imperialism

Another pattern of imperialist control was seen primarily in Hawaii and Latin America: **economic imperialism**. Economic imperialism involved the exertion of economic influence rather than political control over the region. In Hawaii, American companies exported Hawaiian-produced goods such as sugar and pineapple. Beginning in the early nineteenth century, missionaries from New England brought Christianity and education to the Hawaiians. Europeans and Americans also brought Western diseases to the islands, killing over half the population. Chinese and Japanese workers were brought in to work on Hawaiian plantations. American planters in Hawaii urged the United States to annex the islands. In 1898, the Hawaiian ruler was overthrown, and Hawaii was annexed to the United States.

The increase in Latin American trade (see Chapter 22) attracted North American and European investors. Businesses based in the United States, Great Britain, France, and Germany invested in Latin American banks, utilities, mines, and railroads. After World War I, U.S. business interests dominated in the region. The nations and islands of Latin America exported food products and raw materials and imported manufactured goods. Western perpetuation of this Latin American trade pattern kept Latin America dependent on the industrialized West.

In Cuba, U.S. economic imperialism turned to territorial acquisition. U.S. businesses had long invested in Cuban sugar and tobacco plantations. When the Cubans rebelled against Spanish rule in 1895, U.S. businessmen became concerned about their Cuban investments. When the U.S. battleship *Maine* exploded in Havana harbor, the United States went to war against Spain. U.S. victory in the **Spanish-American War** (1898) resulted in Spanish cession of Puerto Rico and Guam to the United States and the U.S. purchase of the Philippines. Cuba became an independent republic subject to control by the United States. The United States was now a world power.

U.S. Interests in Central America and the Caribbean

The nations of Central America and the Caribbean, both dependent on foreign loans, often were threatened by foreign intervention when they could not repay their loans. The United States intervened in Cuba three times during the early twentieth century. During the same period, U.S. troops occupied the Dominican Republic, Nicaragua, Honduras, and Haiti. U.S. support for Panamanian independence led to the construction and opening of the Panama Canal in 1914.

› Rapid Review

European nations colonized India and Africa, providing benefits such as improved medical care and more advanced infrastructures including better roads and railways. Most improvements were intended more for the benefit of imperialist nations than for native peoples. African village organization was disrupted as European nations divided the continent without regard to ethnic patterns, a practice that proved devastating to Africa's future. Southeast Asia, except for Siam, came under the control of a number of European powers. Economic imperialism supported the interests of United States and European businesses and created continued dependence of nonindustrialized nations on the industrialized world.

› Review Questions

1. Imperialism in the late nineteenth and early twentieth centuries was a result of all the following EXCEPT
   (A) nationalism
   (B) militarism
   (C) industrialization
   (D) Social Darwinism
   (E) socialism

2. Economic imperialism
   (A) did not lead to direct political control over new territories
   (B) led to colonial dependence upon industrialized nations
   (C) was the most common imperialist model in Africa
   (D) led to industrialization of Latin America
   (E) led to close political ties between Latin American and European nations

3. Which of the following pairs of nations and their imperialist interests is NOT correct?
   (A) United States–Cuba
   (B) Great Britain–India
   (C) Japan–Hawaii
   (D) Germany–Africa
   (E) The Netherlands–South Africa

4. The new imperialism of the late nineteenth and early twentieth centuries
   (A) brought technology created for the benefit of subject peoples
   (B) created an egalitarian society in India
   (C) resulted in some effects similar to those of the Columbian Exchange
   (D) strengthened African village traditions
   (E) led to increased cooperation between the United States and the governments of Latin America

5. South Africa
   (A) was subjected more to economic imperialism than political control
   (B) saw British enslavement of native peoples
   (C) became an egalitarian society under Dutch rule
   (D) saw the beginnings of racial divisions during colonial rule
   (E) was not subject to European competition because of its lack of natural resources

6. Nationalism
   (A) brought tolerance for diversity within the Russian Empire
   (B) eased tensions within the Austrian Empire
   (C) delayed the unification of both Italy and Germany
   (D) worked against U.S. expansionist policy
   (E) served as both a unifying and a divisive force

7. European imperialism was facilitated by all the following EXCEPT
   (A) medical advances
   (B) the abolition movement
   (C) the invention of the steam engine
   (D) improved European weaponry
   (E) the desire for commercial plantations

8. Colonialism in India
   (A) was facilitated by the breakup of the Mughal Empire
   (B) brought an end to tensions between Muslims and Hindus
   (C) brought greater self-rule to the subcontinent after the Sepoy Rebellion
   (D) decreased nationalist feelings among Indians
   (E) destroyed the Indian educational system

› Answers and Explanations

1. **E**—Socialism was a political movement that had no bearing on imperialism. Nationalism (A) and militarism (B) connected to imperialism by promoting the glories of one's nation. Industrialization created a need for raw materials and markets that was supplied by colonies (C), whereas Social Darwinism provided the rationalization for industrialized countries to dominate the natives of developing regions (D).

2. **B**—Economic imperialism led to dependence on the imperialist country to provide manufactured goods. Sometimes, as in the case of the United States and Hawaii, economic imperialism led to direct political control (A). Direct political control was the common imperialist model in Africa (C). It led to Latin America's continuation as a supplier of raw materials rather than an industrialized region (D). It led to close economic, but not political, ties between Latin American and European nations (E).

3. **C**—The United States, not Japan, had imperialist interests in Hawaii. The other pairs are correct.

4. **C**—Hawaii is an example of native death from exposure to diseases brought by foreigners, as in the case of the diseases brought to the Americas through the Columbian Exchange. The new imperialism brought technology intended for the benefit of the imperialist nations (A). It created a stratified society in India (B). African village traditions were weakened by imperialism (D). The United States became an imperialist power to many Latin American nations (E).

5. **D**—Social divisions based on race and skin color began in South Africa under Dutch rule. South Africa was subjected more to political control by the Dutch and British (A). The Dutch, not the British, enslaved native Africans (B). The Dutch stratified society according to the degree of African descent (C). The discovery of gold and diamonds in the later nineteenth century increased European competition in South Africa (E).

6. **E**—Nationalism served to unite Italy and Germany (C), but divided the Austrian (B) and Russian empires (A). Nationalism was the driving force behind Manifest Destiny (D).

7. **B**—The abolition movement created conflict between the Boers and British in South Africa. Medical advances brought effective treatments for malaria, which aided imperialism (A). The invention of the steam engine allowed Europeans to navigate rivers to the interior of continents (C). Improved weaponry gave them power over developing societies (D), and the desire for commercial plantations prompted the use of non-Western peoples as suppliers of raw materials (E).

8. **A**—The breakup of the Mughal Empire facilitated the entrance of Britain into India. Tensions between Muslims and Hindus were heightened by the British, leading to the Sepoy Rebellion (B). After the rebellion, British rule tightened (C), increasing nationalist sentiment among the Indians (D). The British improved the Indian educational system (E).

PERIOD 5 Summary: Industrialization and Global Integration (c. 1750–c. 1900)

Timeline

1750s	Beginnings of the Industrial Revolution in England
1756–1763	Seven Years' War
1768–1780	Voyages of Captain James Cook in the Pacific Ocean
1775–1781	American Revolution
1788	Founding of the first European colony in Aus..alia
1789–1799	French Revolution
1793–1804	Haitian Revolution
1799–1814	Rule of Napoleon Bonaparte
1805–1848	Rule of Muhammad Ali in Egypt
1807	End of the British slave trade
1810–1825	Independence wars in Latin America
1814–1815	Congress of Vienna
1839–1842	Opium War in China
1839–1876	Tanzimet era
1848	Publication of the *Communist Manifesto*
1850–1864	Taiping Rebellion
1854	Matthew Perry's expedition to Tokyo
1857	Sepoy Rebellion
1861	Abolition of serfdom in Russia
1861–1865	U.S. Civil War
1865	Abolition of slavery in the United States
1867	Establishment of the Dominion of Canada
1868	Meiji Restoration (Japan)
1869	Opening of the Suez Canal
1870	Unification of Italy
1871	Unification of Germany
1884–1885	Berlin Conference
1888	Abolition of slavery in Brazil
1898–1899	Spanish-American War
1899–1902	Boer War

Key Comparisons

1. The Industrial Revolution in Europe, Russia, and Japan
2. Revolutions: American, French, and Haitian
3. Responses to Western influence in China, Japan, India, and the Ottoman Empire
4. Nationalism in Italy and Germany
5. Nationalism in the Austrian Empire and Russia
6. Imperialism in Africa and India
7. Forms of imperialism in Africa and Latin America
8. Roles of European women in upper and middle classes versus women in lower classes
9. Trade in the Atlantic and Indian Ocean basins
10. Trade in Western Europe and the Ottoman Empire

Change/Continuity Chart

REGION	POLITICAL	ECONOMIC	SOCIAL	CHANGES	CONTINUITIES
East Asia	Meiji Restoration Opium War Taiping Rebellion	Spheres of influence Self-strengthening movement Industrialization *Zaibatsu*	Crowded industrial cities Population growth	Dependence on Western technology Bicameral parliament (Japan)	Patriarchal society Shinto Confucianism Buddhism Lack of resources (Japan)
Southeast Asia	Western imperialism	Plantation economy	Influx of Chinese and Japanese	European and East Asian influence	Agriculture Indian Ocean trade
Oceania	Regional kingdoms	Agriculture in Australia	European settlement of Australia and New Zealand	European colonization European diseases	Agriculture Fishing Foraging
Central Asia	Russian expansion Pogroms	Nomads Industrialization Trans-Siberian railway	Emancipation of serfs Russian assimilation of ethnic groups	Abolition of serfdom Industrialization	Tsarist rule Agriculture
South Asia	British Empire Sepoy Rebellion Indian National Congress	Plantation economy Opium trade Hospitals Railroads	End of *sati* English instruction	End of Mughal rule Western political influence	Muslim/Hindu tensions Indian Ocean trade Caste system
Southwest Asia (Middle East)	Ottoman rule Tanzimet reforms Young Turks	Export of raw materials Disinterest in trade	Harem Patriarchal society Islam Wahhabi rebellion	Western influence Extra-territoriality	Ottoman decline
North Africa	Rule of Muhammad Ali European influence Berlin Conference	Suez Canal Industrialization Cotton as a single crop	Islam	Industrialization Foreign influence	Agriculture

continued

Change/Continuity Chart (continued)

REGION	POLITICAL	ECONOMIC	SOCIAL	CHANGES	CONTINUITIES
Sub-Saharan Africa	Imperialism Boer War Berlin Conference	Plantation economy Western technology Gold Diamonds	Ethnic tension Great Trek Strain on village life Sanitation Railroads	Western influence Disruption of village life	Agriculture Slave trade
Western Europe	French Revolution Code Napoleon Unification of Italy and Germany Socialism	Industrial Revolution Jobs for lower class women	Social Darwinism Abolition of the slave trade Crowded cities Feminism	Industrialization Emancipation of slaves Increased suffrage	Traditional gender roles Agriculture
Eastern Europe	Pogroms Austrian Empire Partition of Poland	Agriculture	End of serfdom	Emancipation of serfs	Agriculture Nationalist sentiment
North America	American Revolution Annexation of Hawaii Spanish-American War Monroe Doctrine	Industrial Revolution End of plantation economies	Abolition of slavery Feminism	Industrialization U.S. Civil War	Agriculture Immigration
Latin America	Independence movements Mexican and Haitian revolutions	Economic imperialism Panama Canal	Immigration from Europe Abolition of slavery	Republican government Monroe Doctrine	Sugar plantations Catholicism Agriculture Poverty Social stratification

Accelerating Global Change and Realignments (c. 1900 to the present)

CHAPTER 25

Revolution, World Wars, and Depression

IN THIS CHAPTER

Summary: Because of European competition for colonies in Africa, India, and Southeast Asia, the delicate balance of power that had existed in Europe after the Congress of Vienna gradually eroded. European rivalries negotiated new alliances that led to warfare, while conditions in Russia culminated in a new form of government. Mexico underwent a liberal revolution and Chinese dynastic rule ended with the fall of the Qing. The economic devastation of World War I led to global depression and extremism in the form of fascist ideology. The conclusion of World War II brought the end of the period of European dominance and the rise of two superpowers: the United States and the Soviet Union.

Key Terms

An asterisk (*) denotes items listed in the glossary.

Allied Powers*	Pan-Slavic movement*
Anschluss*	Potsdam Conference*
appeasement*	reparations*
British Commonwealth*	Revolution of 1905*
Central Powers*	Russo-Japanese War*
Duma*	Russification*
fascism*	Spanish Civil War*
Great Depression	Tehran Conference*
Holocaust*	Treaty of Brest-Litovsk*
League of Nations*	Treaty of Versailles*
mandate*	United Nations*
Mexican Revolution	Yalta Conference*

Revolutions in Mexico and China

Revolution in Mexico

In 1876, Porfirio Díaz was elected president of Mexico. For the next 35 years, he continued the economic growth of the rule of his predecessor, Benito Juárez. Díaz encouraged foreign investment, industries, and exports. In contrast to other Latin American countries such as Argentina and Brazil, Mexico was not the destination of many immigrants; its population, therefore, was largely native. Often economic growth did not benefit the peasants and working classes. Opponents of Díaz were arrested or exiled and election fraud was common.

In 1910, the middle class began a movement for election reform. Soon joined by workers and peasants, the reform movement escalated into a 10-year-long rebellion known as the Mexican Revolution. The revolution ended in a new constitution that guaranteed land reform, limited foreign investments, restricted church ownership of property, and reformed education.

Revolution in China

The leaders of the movement that brought down the Qing dynasty were Western-educated reformers who wanted to model China's government along Western lines. Sun Yat-sen, one of the movement's chief leaders, also intended to carry out reforms to benefit peasants and workers. Although they admired some aspects of Western society, the revolutionaries envisioned a China free of foreign imperialists. In 1911, opposition to Qing reliance on Western loans for railway improvements led to a final rebellion that toppled the Qing in 1912. Centuries of Chinese dynastic rule had come to an end.

The Background of World War I

Three forces interacted to set the scene for World War I:

- Nationalism—an intense pride in one's nation and its people
- Imperialism—the acquisition of colonies
- Militarism—the maintenance of standing armies

Added to these three forces was a system of entangling alliances that complicated international relations in the event of war.

The immediate cause of World War I was the assassination of Archduke Francis Ferdinand and his wife in Sarajevo, Bosnia, by a Serbian nationalist protesting against the Austrian annexation of Bosnia. In the aftermath of the assassinations, Germany supported Austria in a declaration of war against Serbia. Serbia, a Slavic nation, was in turn linked to Russia's ethnic policies. By the early twentieth century, Russia's policy of **Russification**, or insistence on the acceptance of Russian culture by its various ethnic groups, had broadened into a **Pan-Slavic movement** that was designed to bring all Slavic nations into a commonwealth with Russia as its head. Russia, therefore, began to mobilize its troops in defense of Serbia.

Within a few weeks after the assassination at Sarajevo, the system of European alliances had brought the world into war. Two alliances faced off against each other: the **Central Powers** of Germany, Austria-Hungary, the Ottoman Empire, and Bulgaria; and the **Allied Powers** of Great Britain, France, Russia, Italy, Japan, and later, the United States. **British Commonwealth** members Canada, Australia, and New Zealand took an active part fighting on the Allied side. In 1917, China also declared war on Germany. Subject peoples of Europe's colonies in Asia and Africa participated in the war as combatants and support personnel. Many colonial peoples hoped to be granted independence as a result of their war efforts.

Throughout the early war years the U.S. government sold arms to the Allies, while U.S. bankers lent money to the Allied nations. In 1917, the United States was drawn into World War I by two events: Germany's declaration of unrestricted submarine warfare and Great Britain's interception of the Zimmermann Telegram. The telegram proposed that, if Mexico would enter the war as an ally of Germany, the German government would assist Mexico to recover the territory it had lost to the United States as a result of the Mexican War. U.S. entry into World War I provided the Allies with additional supplies and freshly trained troops, two factors that helped turn the tide of war in favor of the Allies.

Revolution in Russia

Nationalism and a mutual desire to control Korea led to war between Russia and Japan in 1904. When the **Russo-Japanese War** ended in Russian defeat in 1905, an uprising known as the **Revolution of 1905** forced Tsar Nicholas II to allow the **Duma,** or Russian Parliament, to convene. When Nicholas abolished the Duma a few weeks later, small groups of radicals began planning the overthrow of tsarist rule.

In March 1917, Russia's decline as a world power, peasant dissatisfaction, political repression, and the human and financial costs of World War I brought about the end of tsarist rule. After a weak provisional government failed to maintain social order, a second revolution in October 1917 brought the Bolsheviks, or Communists, into power. The new government, led by V. I. Lenin, decided that Russia was too devastated by revolution to continue the war. In March 1918, Russia and Germany signed the **Treaty of Brest-Litovsk,** which ceded vast amounts of Russian territory to Germany.

Between 1918 and 1921, Russia was engaged in a civil war in which the Bolsheviks, or Red Army, solidified their power over supporters of tsarist rule and wealthy landowners. The opposing forces, or White Army, were supported by troops from the United States, France, Great Britain, and Japan.

The Peace Settlements

Several peace treaties were signed following the war's end in November 1918; the most well known was the **Treaty of Versailles** between most of the Allied nations and Germany. As a result of the Treaty of Versailles:

- A war guilt clause placed total blame for the war on Germany.
- Germany was assigned **reparations** payments of $33 billion.
- Germany lost its colonies.
- Alsace and Lorraine were returned to France.
- Germany's military power was severely limited.
- The coal-rich Rhineland was demilitarized.
- A **League of Nations** was established to work for international peace. The dream of U.S. President Woodrow Wilson, the League's future impact was weakened when the United States refused to join. (The United States later signed a separate peace treaty with Germany.) Also, Germany and Russia were forbidden to join the League.

Other Outcomes of World War I

Because of World War I:

- An entire generation of young European men was almost wiped out.
- Italy and Japan were angered at not receiving additional territory.
- The Ottoman Empire was reduced to the area of present-day Turkey.
- China lost territory to Japan and became a virtual Japanese protectorate.
- The Austro-Hungarian Empire was dissolved.
- The new nations of Yugoslavia, Hungary, and Czechoslovakia were formed from Austria-Hungary. All three nations contained within their borders a variety of ethnic groups with their own nationalist aspirations.
- Russia lost territory to Romania and Poland. Finland, Latvia, Estonia, and Lithuania gained their independence.
- Poland was restored to the European map. A Polish Corridor was created to give Poland an outlet to the Baltic Sea.
- The Ottoman Empire was divided into **mandates** with Great Britain controlling Iraq and Pakistan, and France acquiring Syria and Lebanon.

The Great Depression

The cost of war in Europe devastated the economies of European nations on both sides of the conflict. When Germany announced it was unable to make its reparations payments to the former Allies, Great Britain and France were unable to fully honor repayment of their war debts to the United States. The agricultural sector in Europe and the United States suffered from overproduction that resulted in a decline in farm prices. Farmers in Western Europe and the United States borrowed to purchase expensive farm equipment. Overproduction also resulted in lower prices on plantation-grown crops in Africa and Latin America.

As the economic situation in Europe worsened, banks began to fail. In 1929, when the economy and banking systems in the United States also crashed, the United States was unable to continue its loans to European nations. Global trade diminished, creating massive unemployment not only in Europe and the United States but also in Japan and Latin America.

The economic distress of the **Great Depression** created various reactions in the political arena. In the West, new social welfare programs broadened the role of government. In Italy and Germany, fascist governments developed. Japan's search for new markets was accompanied by increased imperial expansion.

World War II

Prelude to War

The fragmented political order that was the legacy of World War I combined with the economic distress of the Great Depression created the second global conflict of the twentieth century. Fascist governments (nationalist, one-party authoritarian regimes) arose in Germany and Italy. The Nationalist Socialist (Nazi) Party of Adolf Hitler sought to redress the humiliation Germany had suffered in the Treaty of Versailles and to expand German territory. **Fascism** in Italy under Benito Mussolini hoped to restore the lost glories of the state. In Japan, competition among extreme nationalists led to the rise of military rule in the 1930s.

Military expansionist policies during the depression created the stage for war:

- In 1931, the Japanese invaded Manchuria. The goal was to create a buffer zone between the Soviet Union and the Japanese and to make Manchuria's coal and iron deposits available to resource-poor Japan.
- In 1935, Hitler began to rearm Germany.
- In 1935, Mussolini invaded Ethiopia.
- In 1936–1939, the **Spanish Civil War** brought into power the fascist regime of Francisco Franco. It served as a dress rehearsal for World War II, as Germany and Italy aided Franco, while the Soviet Union sent supplies and advisers to his republican opponents. Pablo Picasso expressed his view of the horrors of the Spanish Civil War in his painting *Guernica*.
- In 1937, the Japanese invaded China, whose opposition was a threat to their presence in Manchuria. The event signaled the beginning of World War II in Asia.
- In 1938, Hitler proclaimed *Anschluss*, or the unification of Austria with Germany.
- In 1938, Hitler annexed the Sudetenland, the German-speaking Western portion of Czechoslovakia.
- In 1938, the Munich Conference followed a policy of **appeasement**, in which Great Britain and France accepted Hitler's pledge to not take any further territory.
- In 1939, Hitler annexed all of Czechoslovakia.
- In 1939, Hitler signed a nonaggression pact with the Soviet Union.
- On September 1, 1939, Hitler attacked Poland, marking the beginning of World War II in Europe.

The Opposing Sides

Two opposing sides arose, with the major powers including:

- The **Axis Powers**—Germany, Italy, and Japan.
- The **Allied Powers**—Great Britain, France, and the Soviet Union.

The Course of War

World War II was fought in two theaters: the Pacific and the European, which included the Middle East and Africa. In an effort to control the oil reserves of Southeast Asia, Japan seized Indochina from France and attacked Malaysia and Burma. When the United States imposed an embargo against Japan as a result of these actions, Japan retaliated by attacking the U.S. fleet anchored at Pearl Harbor, Hawaii, on December 7, 1941. The Japanese attack brought the United States and its greater industrial power into the war on the side of the Allied powers.

The early years of the war showcased Axis strength. In 1941, the tide began to turn in favor of the Allies when Hitler undertook an unsuccessful winter invasion of Russia and the United States entered the war. When Hitler was forced to withdraw his forces from Russia in 1942, Soviet armies began their advance through Eastern Europe and into Germany. After deposing Mussolini, Allied forces pushed into France and met in Germany in April 1945. Hitler's subsequent suicide was followed by Allied victory in Europe in May 1945.

After victory in Europe, the Soviet Union assisted in the Allied effort against Japan. After the U.S. use of atomic bombs against the Japanese cities of Hiroshima and Nagasaki, the Japanese surrendered in August 1945, ending World War II.

The Cost of the War

World War II took a devastating toll in human life, killing about 35 million people, including about 20 million in the Soviet Union. The **Holocaust**, Hitler's elimination of European Jews in gas chambers, took the lives of 6 million. Other groups such as Gypsies, Slavs, political prisoners, and Jehovah's Witnesses were also sent to extermination camps during the Holocaust. More than 300,000 were killed by the Japanese offensive in China, most of them in the city of Nanking. The fire bombings of Japanese cities and of the German city of Dresden added tens of thousands to the death toll. Nearly 80,000 were killed in Hiroshima, and tens of thousands were killed in Nagasaki.

Designing the Peace

World War II peace settlements began before the war had ended:

- In 1943, at the **Tehran Conference**, the Allied powers decided to focus on the liberation of France, allowing the Soviet Union to move through the nations of Eastern Europe as it advanced toward France. The Soviet Union, therefore, gained ground and influence in Eastern Europe.
- In 1945, at the **Yalta Conference**, the Soviet Union agreed to join the war against Japan in exchange for territory in Manchuria and the northern island of Japan. The Yalta Conference also provided for the division of Germany into four zones of occupation after the war.
- In 1945, the **Potsdam Conference** gave the Soviets control of eastern Poland, with Poland receiving part of eastern Germany. It made the final arrangements for the division of Germany and also divided Austria.

After the war had ended:

- The United States occupied Japan.
- Korea was divided into U.S. and Soviet occupation zones.
- China regained most of its territory, but fighting between Nationalist and Communist forces resumed.
- Latvia, Lithuania, and Estonia became Soviet provinces.
- Czechoslovakia, Hungary, Bulgaria, and Romania were occupied by the Soviet Union.
- Colonies renewed their independence efforts.
- European world dominance ended.
- A new international peace organization, the **United Nations**, was created in 1945, with the United States among its key members.
- International dominance remained in the hands of two superpowers—the United States and the Soviet Union.

› Rapid Review

The forces of nationalism, imperialism, and militarism combined with entangling defense alliances produced the first global war of the twentieth century. Postwar peace settlements created new nations without consideration of ethnic differences within those nations. The Treaty of Versailles left Germany economically and militarily devastated and humiliated by the war guilt clause. The costs of war ruined regional economies and world trade, creating a depression that reached most regions of the world. Out of the despair of the Great Depression arose new political institutions, including fascism in Germany and Italy and military rule in Japan. The world found itself at war for the second time in the twentieth century. Millions died in the Holocaust, while the atomic age was launched with the bombings of Hiroshima and Nagasaki. The lessons of war created an attempt at a new world order that included a stronger international organization, the United Nations.

› Review Questions

1. World War I was considered a global conflict because
   (A) it involved battles on every continent
   (B) it was fought in both European and Pacific theaters
   (C) the warring powers held colonies that participated in the war
   (D) it began in Europe, whose culture dominated the globe in the early twentieth century
   (E) it involved both Europe and the United States

2. Russia's role in twentieth-century global conflicts included all of the following EXCEPT
   (A) an ethnic-based alliance with Serbia
   (B) providing opportunity for Germany to turn its attention to France
   (C) participation in the formation of the League of Nations
   (D) creating opportunities for postwar influence in Eastern Europe
   (E) participation in the war against Japan

3. Spain did not participate in World War II because
   (A) its republican government feared a fascist coup
   (B) it was still recovering financially from World War I
   (C) it feared communist domination
   (D) it had just endured a civil war
   (E) it was angered over the provisions of the Treaty of Versailles

4. The Allied policy toward Hitler in the 1930s can best be described as one of
   (A) confrontation
   (B) appeasement
   (C) containment
   (D) indifference
   (E) support

5. All of the following are true of communism after World War II EXCEPT that
   (A) it produced a division in Korea
   (B) Eastern European countries were subjected to Soviet occupation
   (C) it spread to largely agricultural regions
   (D) it altered the territory of Poland
   (E) it created a pause in the civil war in China

6. In contrast to the period following World War I, that following World War II
   (A) did not produce a single defining peace treaty
   (B) produced an international organization with fewer powers of enforcement
   (C) saw immediate independence for Europe's African colonies
   (D) disregarded the Soviet war effort
   (E) created new colonial possessions

7. The nation that rose in power during World War I but declined in power during World War II was
   (A) Great Britain
   (B) Japan
   (C) Russia
   (D) the Ottoman Empire
   (E) Austria

8. The nation that saw a consistent rise in global influence during both world wars was
   (A) Germany
   (B) Poland
   (C) China
   (D) France
   (E) the United States

9. The French Revolution of 1789 and the Chinese revolt of 1911 were alike in that
   (A) they were initiated by the lower classes
   (B) they were not nationalist independence movements
   (C) they ended immediately in dictatorship
   (D) they failed to achieve their goals
   (E) they were a response to foreign intervention

10. Both the Mexican revolts of 1821 and 1910
   (A) were initially Creole-backed movements
   (B) ended in the immediate establishment of a republic
   (C) resulted in territorial losses within a few years after the revolt
   (D) involved resistance to foreign influence
   (E) were independence movements

› Answers and Explanations

1. C—The European nations possessed Asian and African colonies that participated in the war in hopes of being granted independence. No World War I battles were fought in Australia or South America (A). World War II was fought in both European and Pacific theaters (B). European dominance alone did not give the war its global status (D), nor did the involvement of only Europe and the United States (E).

2. C—Because of its early withdrawal from the war and its communist regime, Russia was not allowed to join the League of Nations. Russia's Pan-Slavic movement hoped to unite all Slavic peoples, including the Serbs (A). Russia's early withdrawal from the war allowed Germany to devote its full attention to the defeat of France and other Allies (B). As the Soviet Union pushed toward France and Germany in the final months of World War II, it moved through Eastern Europe, establishing its presence in that region (D). At the Yalta Conference, Stalin agreed to join the war against Japan (E).

3. D—The Spanish Civil War occurred between 1936 and 1939. During World War II, Spain was already fascist (A). It had not participated in World War I (B, E). Its fascist government was firmly in power in 1939 (C).

4. B—An example is the Munich Conference, which allowed Hitler to annex the Sudetenland in exchange for a pledge to refrain from taking additional territory. Containment (C) was the U.S. policy against communism.

5. E—After World War II, the Chinese civil war, which had been put on hold, resumed. Korea was divided into north and south, with the north under communism (A). In the final months of the war, the Soviet Union occupied many European nations (B), most of them agricultural rather than industrial nations (C). The Soviet Union received part of eastern Poland, while Poland received part of eastern Germany in exchange (D).

6. A—World War II peace arrangements were formulated through a series of conferences rather than through one major treaty such as the Treaty of Versailles. The United Nations was a more effective organization than the League of Nations (B). Europe's African colonies did not begin receiving independence until the 1950s (C). The Soviet Union was included in the Yalta and Potsdam conferences (D). No new colonial possessions were created after World War II (E).

7. B—Japan rose in power, especially in East Asia, during World War I, but its empire ended after World War II. Great Britain (A) and Austria (E) declined in power as a result of both wars. Russia (C) declined in power during World War I, but emerged from World War II as a superpower. The Ottoman Empire ended after World War I (D).

8. E—The United States emerged as a major world power after World War I and a superpower after World War II. The power of European nations declined markedly during both wars (A, B, D). After World War II, China remained involved in a civil war (C).

9. B—Neither revolution desired independence from a colonial power. The French Revolution was initiated by the bourgeoisie, and the Chinese revolt by the Western-educated middle class (A). The French Revolution ended in the ultimate dictatorship of Napoleon, whereas the Chinese revolution at first attempted to model China's government after Western republics (C). The French Revolution reached its goal of ending absolute monarchy, while the Chinese revolt ended Qing rule (D). Although the French Revolution did not involve a response to foreign intervention, the Chinese Revolution was in part a reaction against foreign involvement in China under the Qing (E).

10. **D**—The 1821 revolution was an independence movement against Spain, while the 1910 revolution came about in part because of foreign influence during the rule of Díaz. The 1821 revolt was initially backed by *mestizos*, whereas the later revolt was Creole-backed from its beginning (A). The Mexican republic was established in 1824, three years after the end of the earlier revolt (B). Although the 1910 revolt did not result in territorial loss, the earlier revolution saw the separation of the Central American republics a few years later (C). The earlier revolt was an independence movement, whereas the second was a liberal revolt (E).

CHAPTER 26

The Cold War and the Postwar Balance of Power

IN THIS CHAPTER

Summary: The decades following World War II were dominated by the relationship between the two superpowers: the United States and the Soviet Union. During the postwar period, the superpowers were almost always on the verge of warfare. As former colonial possessions gained independence, many of them sought aid from the United States or the Soviet Union. As the Soviets extended their dominion throughout Eastern Europe, Asia, and Cuba, the United States attempted to contain communist expansion.

Key Terms

Afrikaners*
Alliance for Progress*
apartheid*
ayatollah*
Berlin Wall
brinkmanship*
coalition*
Cold War*
collectivization*
containment*
Cuban Missile Crisis
Cultural Revolution*
Five Year Plans*
Geneva Conference*

genocide*
glasnost*
Government of India Act
Great Leap Forward*
Guomindang*
Iron Curtain
Korean Conflict
kulaks*
Marshall Plan*
May Fourth Movement*
New Economic Policy (NEP)*
nonalignment*

North Atlantic Treaty
Organization (NATO)*
*perestroika**
Prague Spring*
purges*
Red Guard*

Sandinistas*
Six-Day War*
Solidarity*
Tiananmen Square*
Truman Doctrine*
Warsaw Pact*

The Beginnings of the Cold War

British Prime Minister Winston Churchill described the new postwar world order by stating that an "**iron curtain**" dividing free and communist governments had fallen across Europe. In order to prevent communist-dominated nations east of the Iron Curtain from spreading totalitarianism, the United States sponsored a program of European recovery known as the **Marshall Plan** (1947). The program provided loans to European nations to assist them in wartime recovery. The U.S. policy of **containment** of communism was set forth in 1947 in the **Truman Doctrine**. When Greece and Turkey were threatened by communism, U.S. President Truman issued his policy, which pledged U.S. support for countries battling against communism.

In 1946, Great Britain, France, and the United States merged their occupation zones into a unified West Germany with free elections. In 1947, Western attempts to promote economic recovery by stabilizing the German currency resulted in a Soviet blockade of Berlin—the divided city located within the Russian zone of occupation. For nearly eleven months, British and U.S. planes airlifted supplies to Berlin until the Soviets lifted the blockade.

Two opposing alliances faced off during the **Cold War** era. The **North Atlantic Treaty Organization (NATO)**, led by the United States, was founded in 1949. NATO allied Canada, the United States, and most of Western Europe against Soviet aggression. The Soviet Union responded with an alliance of its eastern European satellites: the **Warsaw Pact**. U.S.–Soviet rivalry intensified in 1949, when the Soviet Union developed an atomic bomb.

The Cold War escalated to military confrontation in 1950 when North Korean forces invaded South Korea. North Korea eventually received the backing of the Soviet Union and Communist China, while a United Nations **coalition** led by the United States supported South Korea. The **Korean Conflict** ended with the establishment of the boundary between the two Koreas near the original line.

The Beginnings of Decolonization

After the end of World War II, most European nations and the United States decided that their colonies were too expensive to maintain. Within the colonies, renewed nationalist sentiments led native peoples to hope that their long-expected independence would become a reality. In 1946, the United States granted the Philippines their independence. France was alone in wanting to hold on to its colonies in Algeria and Indochina.

Africa

In 1957, Ghana became the first African colony to gain its independence. By 1960, French possessions in West Africa were freed, and the Belgian Congo was granted independence. Independence movements in the settler colonies of Algeria, Kenya, and Southern Rhodesia took on a violent nature. By 1963, Kenya was independent; in 1962 a revolt in Algeria also had ended colonial rule in that country. Southern Rhodesia became the independent state of Zimbabwe in 1980, and in 1990, Namibia (German Southwest Africa, which had been made a mandate of South Africa in 1920) became the last African colony to achieve independence.

In South Africa, the white settler population was divided almost equally between **Afrikaners** and English settlers. Although the white settlers were a minority, by 1948 the Afrikaners had imposed upon South Africa a highly restrictive form of racial segregation known as **apartheid**. Apartheid prohibited people of color from voting and from having many contacts with whites. The best jobs were reserved for whites only. Apartheid continued after South Africa gained its independence from Great Britain in 1961.

Egypt won its independence in the 1930s; meanwhile, the British continued to maintain a presence in the Suez Canal zone. After Egypt's defeat in the Arab–Israeli War of 1948, the Egyptian military revolted. In 1952, King Farouk was overthrown; in 1954, Gamal Abdul Nasser was installed as ruler of an independent Egypt. In 1956, Nasser, backed by the United States and the Soviet Union, ended the influence of the British and their French allies in the Suez Canal zone.

In 1967, Nasser faced a decisive defeat once again in the **Six-Day War** with Israel. His successor, Anwar Sadat, strove to end hostilities with Israel after a nondecisive war with Israel in 1973. Sadat's policy of accepting aid from the United States and Western Europe has been continued by his successor, Hosni Mubarak, who came to power after the assassination of Sadat by a Muslim fundamentalist.

The Effects of Decolonization

Independence did not bring peace or prosperity to most of the new African nations. New states tended to maintain colonial boundaries, meaning that they often cut through ethnic and cultural groups. Sometimes ethnic conflicts turned violent, as in the tribal conflicts in the territories of the former Belgian Congo and the Biafra secessionist movement in southeastern Nigeria.

Soviet Communism

After the Russian civil war, which lasted from 1918 to 1921, Lenin moved quickly to announce a program of land redistribution and a nationalization of basic industries. When his initial programs culminated in industrial and agricultural decline, Lenin instituted his **New Economic Policy (NEP)**. The NEP permitted some private ownership of peasant land and small businesses; it resulted in an increase in agricultural production.

In 1923, Russia was organized into a system of socialist republics under a central government and was renamed Union of Soviet Socialist Republics. The republics were under the control of the Communist Party. When Lenin died in 1924, Joseph Stalin eventually became the leader of the Soviet Union. Stalin's regime was characterized by **purges**, or the expulsion or execution of rivals. Especially targeted were the **kulaks**, wealthy peasants who refused to submit to Stalin's policy of **collectivization**. Collectivization consolidated private farms into huge collective farms worked in common by farmers. Farmers were to share the proceeds of the collective farms and also to submit a portion of the agricultural products to the government. Millions of kulaks were executed or deported to Siberia. Even after farmers accepted collectivization, however, lack of worker initiative prevented it from being successful.

Stalin had greater success in improving Soviet industry. He set up a series of **Five Year Plans** that concentrated on heavy industry. By the end of the 1930s, the Soviet Union was behind only Germany and the United States in industrial capacity.

The Expansion of Soviet Rule

During the final weeks of World War II, the Soviet Union liberated Eastern Europe (except Yugoslavia and Greece) from Nazi rule. By 1948, these areas, except for Greece, had communist governments. Yugoslavia's communist rule under Marshall Tito did not become a part of the Soviet bloc, attempting instead to forge a style of communism more responsive to its citizens.

In 1956, a Hungarian revolt against repressive Soviet rule was put down by Soviet tanks. When large numbers of East Germans began migrating to West Berlin, the **Berlin Wall** was constructed in 1961 to stem the tide of refugees. In **Prague Spring** (1968), Czech leader Alexandr Dubcek stood up against Soviet oppression, abolishing censorship; the result of his efforts was Soviet invasion. Only in Poland was Soviet rule somewhat relaxed; religious worship was tolerated and some land ownership allowed. In the late 1970s, **Solidarity**, Poland's labor movement, challenged the Soviet system.

Soviet Rule after Stalin

In 1956, Nikita Khrushchev rose to power in the Soviet Union. Criticizing Stalin's ruthless dictatorship, Khrushchev eased up on political repression. In 1962, Soviet construction of nuclear missiles in Cuba brought days of tense confrontation between Khrushchev and U.S. President Kennedy. Khrushchev ultimately backed down, and the missiles were removed. The **Cuban Missile Crisis** was a classic example of **brinkmanship**, or the Cold War tendency of the United States and the Soviet Union to be on the brink of war without actually engaging in battle. Also during Khrushchev's regime, the rift between the Soviet Union and Communist China widened.

The Later Decades of the Twentieth Century

In December 1979, the Soviet Union invaded Afghanistan to support communist combatants in Afghanistan's civil war. The Soviets withdrew their forces in 1989 after failing to establish a communist government for Afghanistan.

In the 1980s, economic setbacks and the military power of the United States produced a reform movement within the Soviet Union. The new Soviet leader, Mikhail Gorbachev, reduced Soviet nuclear armaments. His reform program revolved around the concepts of *glasnost* and *perestroika. Glasnost,* meaning "openness," allowed Soviet citizens to discuss government policies and even criticize them. *Perestroika* was an economic reform program that permitted some private ownership and control of agriculture and industry. Foreign investments were allowed, and industry was permitted to produce more consumer goods.

Latin America

Mexico emerged from its revolution with a one-party system. The Partido Revolucionario Institucional (PRI) dominated Mexican politics for seventy years.

In Argentina, government was under the control of military leaders who wanted to industrialize the country. Some of them were fascist sympathizers, among them Juan Perón and his wife, Evita. Although Perón raised the salaries of the working classes, his government controlled the press and denied civil liberties to its citizens. When he died in 1975, Argentina continued to be ruled by military dictators. In 1982, a short war with Great Britain over the Falkland Islands resulted in Argentine defeat.

From 1934 to 1944, and from 1952 to 1959, Cuba was ruled by dictator Fulgencio Batista. U.S. trade relations with Cuba gave it an influence over the island nation. In 1959, the Cubans revolted against the corruption of the Batista regime, replacing it with the rule of a young revolutionary lawyer named Fidel Castro. During the revolution, Batista lost the support of the United States because of his corrupt government.

Shortly after assuming power in Cuba, Castro proclaimed himself a Marxist socialist. He seized foreign property and collectivized farms. In 1961, Castro terminated relations with the United States and gradually aligned Cuba with the Soviet Union. Also in 1961, the United States sponsored an unsuccessful invasion of Cuba by Cuban exiles. Cuba's dependence on the Soviet Union led to the missile crisis of 1962.

Throughout Central America, U.S. businesses such as United Fruit invested in national economies, resulting in a U.S. presence often resented by Central Americans. In Nicaragua, the **Sandinistas** carried out a protest against U.S. intervention that resulted in a socialist revolution in the 1980s.

The United States attempted to contain communism in Latin America by supporting governments that professed adherence to democratic principles. It also sponsored programs such as the **Alliance for Progress**, begun in 1961 and intended to develop the economies of Latin American nations. By the final decades of the twentieth century, the United States changed its position to one of less intervention in Latin America. Under the Carter administration, the United States signed a treaty with Panama that eventually returned control of the Panama Canal to Panama. By the 1980s, the United States was again assuming a more direct role in Central America. In 1990, the United States helped end the Noriega government, which was known for its authoritarianism and control of the drug trade.

Decolonization of India

Indian independence from Great Britain was accomplished largely through the efforts of Mohandas Gandhi, who believed in passive resistance to accomplish his goals. In 1935, the British Parliament passed the **Government of India Act**, which increased suffrage and turned provincial governments over to Indian leaders. Indian independence was delayed by the insistence of some Muslims on a separate Muslim state. In 1947, the British granted India its independence; India followed a path of **nonalignment** with either superpower.

At the same time that India received its independence, the new nation of Pakistan was created. Pakistan was then divided into eastern and western regions separated by over 1,000 miles of Indian territory. A few years later, Burma (Myanmar) and Ceylon (Sri Lanka) also gained independence. Unequal distribution of wealth between the two Pakistans ended in civil war in the early 1970s; in 1972, East Pakistan became the independent nation of Bangladesh.

Conflict in Palestine

The Holocaust strengthened international support for a homeland for the Jews. As the Nazis continued their policy of **genocide** against the Jews, immigration to Palestine increased. When Arab resistance turned to violence against Jewish communities in Palestine, the British placed restrictions on Jewish immigration. In 1948, the United Nations partitioned Palestine into Jewish and Arab countries; the independent state of Israel was proclaimed. Almost immediately, war broke out as Arabs protested the partition. A Jewish victory resulted in the eventual expansion of the Jewish state at the expense of hundreds of thousands of Palestinian Arabs who were exiled from their homes.

Iran

In 1979, the U.S.-backed Iranian government of Reza Shah Pahlavi was overthrown by Islamic fundamentalists. The middle classes were opposed to the shah's authoritarian and repressive rule; Iran's *ayatollahs*, or religious leaders, opposed the shah's lack of concern for strict Islamic observance. Iran also was suffering from a fall in oil prices prior to the 1979 revolution.

The new Iranian ruler, the Ayatollah Khomeini, rejected Western culture as satanic, and imposed strict Islamic law, including the veiling of women, on Iran. Saddam Hussein, leader of Iraq, took advantage of Iranian weakness by annexing its oil-rich western provinces. When peace came in 1988, Iran was devastated economically.

Postrevolutionary China

One of the key leaders of the 1911–1912 revolt against the Qing dynasty was Western-educated Sun Yat-sen. He briefly ruled China's new parliamentary government until he relinquished his place to warlord rule. After World War I, the **May Fourth Movement** (1919) attempted to create a liberal democracy for China. In the same year, Sun Yat-sen and his followers reorganized the revolutionary movement under the **Guomindang**, or Nationalist Party. Marxist socialism also took hold in China, however; and in 1921, the Communist Party of China was organized. Among its members was a student named Mao Zedong.

After the death of Sun Yat-sen in 1925, Jiang Jieshi (Chiang Kai-shek) seized control of the Guomindang. A 1927 incident in which the Guomindang executed a number of communists in Shanghai so enraged the communists that civil war broke out. Except for the years during World War II, the Chinese civil war lasted until 1949, when Mao Zedong's communists, whose land reforms gained peasant support, were victorious. After their defeat, Jiang Jieshi's forces fled to the island of Taiwan (Formosa) off the coast of China, while Mao proclaimed the birth of the People's Republic of China on the Chinese mainland.

After gaining control of China, the communists contained secessionist attempts in Inner Mongolia and Tibet; some Tibetan opposition exists to the present. China also supported North Korea in its conflict with South Korea in the 1950s.

Once in power, Mao began organizing China along Soviet models. Farms were collectivized, leading to lack of peasant initiative and a decrease in agricultural production. Eager to increase the participation of rural peoples, Mao instituted the **Great Leap Forward**, which attempted to accomplish industrialization through small-scale projects in peasant communities. The Great Leap Forward proved a resounding failure.

In 1960, Mao was replaced as head of state, although he retained his position as head of the Communist Party. The new leaders, Zhou Enlai and Deng Xiaoping, instituted some market incentives to improve the Chinese economy. In 1965, Mao launched his **Cultural Revolution**, a program that used student **Red Guard** organizations to abuse Mao's political rivals. Especially targeted were the educated and elite classes; universities were closed. Opposition from Mao's rivals led to the end of the Cultural Revolution, whereupon relations were opened between China and the United States.

In 1976, both Zhou Enlai and Mao Zedong died, paving the way for the leadership of Deng Xiaoping. Deng discontinued collective farming and allowed some Western influence to enter China. His government did not, however, permit democratic reform, as shown in the government's suppression of students demonstrating for democracy in **Tiananmen Square** in 1989.

Vietnam

After World War II and the end of Japanese occupation of Vietnam, France was eager to regain its former colony. During Japanese occupation, however, Vietnamese nationalism had materialized under the leadership of Marxist-educated Ho Chi Minh. In 1945, in a document whose preamble echoed that of the U.S. Declaration of Independence, Ho Chi Minh proclaimed the independence of the nation of Vietnam.

Ho Chi Minh's party, the Viet Minh, had control over only the northern part of the country. The French, aided by Great Britain, occupied most of the south and central portions. In 1954, the Vietnamese defeated the French. The **Geneva Conference** (1954) gave the Viet Minh control of the northern portion of the country while providing for elections throughout Vietnam in two years. With U.S. support, Ngo Dinh Diem was installed as the president of South Vietnam. The required free elections were not held, and pockets of communist resistance, the Viet Cong, continued to exist in the south.

When Diem's government proved corrupt and ineffective, the United States arranged for his overthrow. By 1968, hundreds of thousands of U.S. troops were fighting in Vietnam. In 1973, the United States negotiated an end to its involvement in Vietnam; in 1975 the government in the south fell, and all of Vietnam was under communist control. The neighboring countries of Laos and Cambodia also fell to communism.

› Rapid Review

The postwar world saw the emergence of two superpowers: the United States and the Soviet Union. The Cold War period was one of constant threats of aggression between the superpowers as the Soviet Union sought to expand communism and the United States sought to contain it. Communism spread outside the Soviet Union to Eastern Europe, China, Southeast Asia, North Korea, and Cuba.

After World War II, most colonial possessions gradually achieved their long-awaited independence. Newly independent nations often aligned themselves with either the United States or the Soviet Union. Other nations such as India, however, chose the independence of nonalignment. New nations often experienced conflicts that continue to the present; the first Arab–Israeli war occurred immediately after the establishment of the nation of Israel, and sub-Saharan Africa has experienced a continuing history of ethnic strife.

› Review Questions

1. Which communist leader is most often associated with purges against his rivals?
   (A) Lenin
   (B) Sun Yat-sen
   (C) Mao Zedong
   (D) Stalin
   (E) Deng Xiaoping

2. An example of brinkmanship is found in
   (A) the Cuban Missile Crisis
   (B) the Arab–Israeli War
   (C) the Iran–Iraq War
   (D) the Cultural Revolution
   (E) the Korean War

3. The country that was most interested in keeping its colonies after World War II was
   (A) Germany
   (B) France
   (C) Great Britain
   (D) the United States
   (E) Portugal

4. Lenin's New Economic Policy
   (A) established collective farming
   (B) resulted in decreased agricultural production
   (C) forbade the ownership of private property
   (D) allowed some elements of capitalism
   (E) was continued by Joseph Stalin

5. The communist ruler whose economic policies were most like those of Lenin was
   (A) Mao Zedong
   (B) Deng Xiaoping
   (C) Joseph Stalin
   (D) Jiang Jieshi
   (E) Fidel Castro

6. Which of the following leaders would have agreed most with the policies of Benito Mussolini?
   (A) Fidel Castro
   (B) Nikita Khrushchev
   (C) Juan Perón
   (D) V. I. Lenin
   (E) Mohandas Gandhi

7. Which of the following communist-controlled countries was allowed private land ownership and freedom of worship?
   (A) Czechoslovakia
   (B) Poland
   (C) East Germany
   (D) Hungary
   (E) The Soviet Union

8. Mikhail Gorbachev allowed all of the following EXCEPT
   (A) the production of consumer goods
   (B) discussion of government policies
   (C) private land ownership
   (D) democratic government
   (E) foreign investments

› Answers and Explanations

1. **D**—Stalin was noted for his practice of exiling or executing millions of his opponents.

2. **A**—The Cuban Missile Crisis illustrated that the Cold War was fought through diplomacy that placed the superpowers always on the brink of war. Neither the Arab–Israeli War (B) nor the Iran–Iraq War (C) was a conflict between the superpowers. The Cultural Revolution was a repressive policy of Mao Zedong (D), and the Korean War (E) involved direct confrontation between the communist and free worlds.

3. **B**—France wanted to regain and maintain its colony in Indochina. Germany (A) lost its colonies during World War I, whereas Great Britain, the United States, and Portugal gradually granted independence to their colonies (C, D, E).

4. **D**—Lenin allowed some private ownership of land and small businesses (C) and some degree of free market economy. Collective farming was established under Stalin (A). The NEP increased agricultural production (B). The NEP ended with Lenin (E).

5. **B**—Deng Xiaoping allowed some elements of a market economy and some foreign investment. Mao and Stalin did not follow these policies (A, C). Castro allowed some foreign investment only in recent years after the breakup of Soviet communism (E). Jiang Jieshi was not a communist leader (D).

6. **C**—Perón's government followed fascist models; he was reputed to have had fascist sympathies. Castro (A), Khrushchev (B), and Lenin (D), all communists, were opposed to fascism. Mohandas Gandhi, the nonviolent leader of Indian independence, was not aligned with either philosophy (E).

7. **B**—Poland was the only satellite nation that was allowed to experience private land ownership and religious freedom. Neither the Soviet Union (E) nor the other satellite nations listed enjoyed such freedoms (A, C, D).

8. **D**—Although Gorbachev allowed a measure of free market economy, foreign investments, consumer goods, and free discussion of governmental policies, his government remained dedicated to the ultimate welfare of the state (D).

CHAPTER 27

End of the Cold War and Nationalist Movements

IN THIS CHAPTER

Summary: By the late 1980s, economic setbacks in the Soviet Union were producing social unrest. Worldwide nationalist movements were weakening the hold of communist regimes upon their people. The fall of the Berlin Wall in 1989 precipitated the end of other communist governments, culminating in the overthrow of communist governments in the Soviet Union. As former Soviet republics declared their independence, democratic movements continued throughout the world, especially in Latin America and Africa. The end of communism in the Soviet Union saw the emergence of a single superpower: the United States.

Key Terms

Al-Qaeda*   Persian Gulf War*

cartels*   World Bank*

International Monetary Fund*

The Breakup of the Soviet Union

While Gorbachev was instituting reforms to save the Soviet Empire, the small nations of Eastern Europe were steadily moving toward independence. In 1988, Poland inaugurated a noncommunist government. In 1989, the people of Berlin dismantled the Berlin Wall; by the end of 1990, the two Germanys were reunited. Czechoslovakia ended its communist government in 1989; it later peacefully separated into the Czech Republic and Slovakia.

The end of communism did not come without discord. A key example was Yugoslavia, where bitter conflict broke out in Bosnia among Muslims, Serbs, and Croats in the early 1990s. Fighting continued in 1998 to 1999 between Serbs and Albanians in the province of Kosovo. In 2004, Kosovo again became the scene of ethnic conflict in the newly founded Republics of Serbia and Montenegro. The province declared its independence in 2008.

The Final Days of the Soviet Union and Thereafter

In the summer of 1991, the Baltic republics declared their independence. Independence movements spread throughout the European border republics of Belarus, Ukraine, and Moldova, and also in the Muslim regions of central Asia. In December 1991, the Soviet Union was dissolved and replaced by the Commonwealth of Independent States. The Communist Party was terminated, and the elected president of the Russian Republic, Boris Yeltsin, became the leader of the Commonwealth of Independent States.

The new commonwealth was faced with conflicts between ethnic groups and also with economic difficulties resulting from its new status outside the Soviet economy. Yeltsin, who initiated policies that allowed for a move toward private enterprise, was faced with continuing opposition during his rule and resigned in 1999. In 2000, a new president, Vladimir Putin, was elected; he was reelected in 2004, and in 2008 was appointed prime minister by the newly elected Russian president. Russia continued to struggle with economic weakness and organized crime. Ethnic clashes, especially within the Muslim-dominated province of Chechnya, plagued the commonwealth.

In 2008, violence broke out as Russian forces entered the Democratic Republic of Georgia in retaliation for Georgia's attempt to put down a separatist revolt in the province of South Ossetia. Because Georgia had a security relationship with the United States, the Georgia–Russia conflict renewed concerns of increasing tensions between the Putin government and the United States.

Latin America

At the end of the Cold War, more Latin American nations were moving toward democracy. Still, resistance to democratic rule was seen in groups such as the leftist Sendero Luminoso in Peru, which attempted to disrupt free elections in 1990. El Salvador remained under the control of its military, and the government of Nicaragua, no longer under the control of the Sandinistas, had to chart a new course under the direction of its elected president, Violeta Chamorro. The end of the twentieth century and the beginning of the twenty-first century also saw new challenges to democracy in Colombia and Venezuela. In Colombia, violence caused by drug traffickers and armed rebels resulted in the flight of some Colombian citizens to neighboring countries. In Venezuela, the left-leaning Hugo Chávez was elected president in 1999. Concerned over fluctuating oil prices, Chávez nationalized a number of Venezuelan industries, including petroleum. In 2007, Venezuelans voted down proposed constitutional changes that would have given Chávez additional powers.

Additional issues plagued Latin American nations. Some of them owed large foreign debts; and in some, huge international drug **cartels** threatened government stability. The end of the twentieth century, however, saw renewed hope for enduring democracies and popular participation in Latin America. In Mexico in 2000, for example, the PRI lost its dominant status with the election of Vicente Fox of the PAN party as president. The new administration continued to struggle with poverty and illegal immigration to the United States.

New Challenges

As communism dissolved in the Soviet Union, new challenges arose in the noncommunist nations. In 1990, Iraqi leader Saddam Hussein annexed oil-rich Kuwait, precipitating the **Persian Gulf War** between Iraq and a U.S.-led coalition of United Nations forces. Saddam Hussein's defeat and the liberation of Kuwait led to only a short truce. In 2003, the Iraqis were again at war with a U.S.-led coalition over Saddam Hussein's repressive regime and his potential for unleashing weapons of mass destruction. A new democratically elected Iraqi government executed Saddam Hussein in December 2006.

In 1998, India and Pakistan, long in conflict with each other over the territory of Kashmir, announced their development of nuclear weapons. A 2008 terrorist attack in the city of Mumbai, India, attributed by some to Pakistani terrorist organizations, increased global concern over the unstable relationship between the two countries. The nuclear capacity of North Korea also remained a troublesome issue.

In Africa and Asia, new nations often did not have the resources to further their development and had to look to developed nations or international organizations such as the **World Bank** and the **International Monetary Fund** for assistance. Violent ethnic conflicts plagued both regions. Repeated negotiations failed to bring lasting peace in the Middle East or to settle the problem of Palestinian refugees. Warfare continued between the United States and Iraq and the **Al-Qaeda** terrorist organization of Afghanistan.

The end of the twentieth century saw a series of economic problems throughout parts of Asia and Southeast Asia, especially Japan. By 1999, some recovery was apparent. Hong Kong was returned to the People's Republic of China in 1997.

In spite of challenges in Africa and Asia, the future appeared hopeful. India remained the world's largest democracy. In the 1990s, South Africa ended apartheid and held elections in which all adult South Africans had the right to vote. New governments based on increased civil rights were emerging in both Afghanistan and Iraq.

❯ Rapid Review

The breakup of the Soviet Empire in 1991 resulted in the formation of a loose organization of former Soviet republics. Ethnic rivalries continued in the former Soviet republics and in Yugoslavia. Newly founded republics battled with economic problems. In Latin America, repressive governments gradually gave way to more widespread democracy. South Africa saw the end of apartheid and the beginnings of universal suffrage. Challenges remained, especially in the Middle East and South Asia, where Arab–Israeli conflicts continued and U.S.-backed coalitions had been engaged in Afghanistan and Iraq.

› Review Questions

1. Ethnic strife occurred in the Balkan province of
   (A) Czechoslovakia
   (B) Kosovo
   (C) Hungary
   (D) Belarus
   (E) Ukraine

2. The end of the twentieth century saw
   (A) increased economic prosperity for Japan
   (B) a general decline in democracy throughout Latin America
   (C) ethnic conflict in Russia and in Africa
   (D) the resolution of the problems of Palestinian refugees
   (E) economic prosperity for Africa

3. Which of the following nations did NOT acquire a new government in the latter years of the twentieth century?
   (A) Nicaragua
   (B) Czechoslovakia
   (C) Germany
   (D) The Soviet Union
   (E) Japan

4. The world's most populous democracy is
   (A) the United States
   (B) Great Britain
   (C) Canada
   (D) India
   (E) France

5. Which of the following has been a common problem of both Japan and Russia in the latter years of the twentieth century to the present?
   (A) Ethnic conflicts
   (B) Political instability
   (C) Economic downturns
   (D) Huge foreign debts
   (E) Drug cartels

› Answers and Explanations

1. **B**—Kosovo experienced a renewal of its ethnic conflicts in 2004. The remaining areas mentioned are not located in the Balkans.

2. **C**—Russia attempted to suppress independence movements from its ethnic groups, whereas Africa experienced conflicts between ethnic groups concerning political and economic dominance. Japan's economy crashed in the 1990s (A). Democracy made considerable inroads into Latin America (B). Hundreds of thousands of Palestinians remained refugees (D). Africa continued to experience weak economies (E).

3. **E**—Japan maintained the same government since the time of its occupation after World War II. Nicaragua saw political unrest and a new government (A), whereas Czechoslovakia split between the Czech Republic and Slovakia (B). Germany reunited (C), and the Soviet Union saw the downfall of communism (D).

4. **D**—India, with a population of one billion people, is the world's largest democracy.

5. **C**—Japan's economy weakened sharply in the early 1990s, while Russia continued to struggle with the establishment of a market economy. Only Russia experienced ethnic conflicts (A). Neither has seen political instability, huge foreign debts, or a problem with drug cartels (B, D, E).

CHAPTER 28

Global Trade

IN THIS CHAPTER

Summary: The twentieth century witnessed active commercial and trade interactions in virtually every region of the globe. The Great Depression illustrated the impact of a decline in trade in one region over trade throughout the world; an example was the manner in which the imposition of national tariffs in Western Europe and the United States weakened global trade in general. Price and supply manipulations by oil-producing nations in 1973 and 1979 affected the globe. Multinational corporations, often using cheap labor in developing nations, increased their influence. Especially after the decline of communism, more nations implemented free-market economies. Regional trade associations were organized to facilitate trade, and mass consumerism created a truly global marketplace. The following sections summarize key events in global trade between 1914 and the present.

KEY IDEA

Key Terms

euro*
European Economic Community
European Union*
import substitution
  industrialization*
McDonaldization

North American Free Trade
  Agreement (NAFTA)*
Organization of Petroleum
  Exporting Countries (OPEC)*
World Trade Organization (WTO)*

The Middle East (Southwest Asia)

- In 1960, the **Organization of Petroleum Exporting Countries (OPEC)** was founded to regulate oil prices and control oil distribution.
- Southwest Asia participated in the international drug trade.

Asia

- By the 1920s, Japanese exports of silk were reduced after the West began production of synthetic fabrics.
- Between the world wars, China prospered in the global drug trade.
- Southeast Asian economies based on rubber exports were damaged by the decline of the U.S. and European automobile industry during the Great Depression.
- By the 1930s, Japanese industrial manufacturers were entering international trade markets.
- By the 1930s, Vietnam had become one of the world's leading exporters of rice. Like other plantation economies, the production of an export crop left the Vietnamese people without sufficient crops for their families.
- Before World War II, Japan's regional empire supplied it with food and raw materials. Korean peasants were forced to produce rice for export to Japan and other countries.
- In the 1960s and 1970s, the production of automobiles and electronics in Japan cut into U.S. and Western European manufacture of those products.
- By the 1970s, South Korea was producing inexpensive consumer goods, textiles, steel, and automobiles for worldwide markets.
- By the 1970s, Taiwan competed successfully in global textile trade, including supplying a variety of products to Japan.
- By the 1980s, Hong Kong was noted for its exports of clothing and heavy industry.
- The "**McDonaldization**" of world trade extended to the Soviet Union, which opened a McDonald's in Moscow during the Gorbachev regime.
- Singapore became the world's fourth largest port. Its factories produced textiles, electronics, and refined oil.
- Indonesia exported exotic woods.
- Korea's Hyundai Corporation exported automobiles, supertankers, and electronics.
- In 2001, China joined the **World Trade Organization (WTO)**.
- Because of significant industrial growth, India and China have markedly increased their demand for oil.
- China, India, the Philippines, and other Asian nations benefitted from employment that was outsourced by U.S. companies. By 2008, India, for years the foremost location for outsourcing, lost some of its outsourcing contracts to other nations such as China and the Philippines.
- The global economic crisis of 2008–2009 negatively affected the volume of world trade.

Africa

- After World War I, most African nations did not have the economic resources to purchase industrial goods from other regions.
- European and South African miners prospered in the 1930s from exports of gold and copper from South African mines.

- Since World War II, African nations have had to rely on the sale of minerals and cash crops to finance their fledgling industries. Constant fluctuation in the prices of these goods hampered economic growth.
- Nigeria was an oil-producing country and a member of OPEC.
- Africa exported native art.

Europe

- During World War I, European nations, and Great Britain in particular, failed to recover their dominant export position, losing out to the United States and Japan.
- In the first half of the twentieth century, most Eastern European nations were primarily agricultural, relying on sales of their products to Western Europe.
- The **European Economic Community** (Common Market) was organized in 1958 by West Germany, France, Italy, Belgium, Luxembourg, and the Netherlands. It reduced tariffs among member nations and created a common tariff policy for other world nations.
- In 1992, Great Britain joined the European Economic Community, and was later joined by Ireland, Denmark, Greece, Spain, and Portugal.
- In the mid-1990s, Finland, Sweden, and Austria joined the economic community, now called the **European Union**.
- In 2002, a common currency, the **euro**, was accepted by most member nations of the European Union, with Great Britain serving as a notable exception.

Latin America

- World War I and European trade brought prosperity to Latin America. Latin American nations also had to produce for themselves the products they could no longer import from Europe during the war, a concept known as **import substitution industrialization**.
- The Great Depression caused a decline in the purchase of Latin American products.
- The United States was Cuba's leading trade partner prior to 1959. Fluctuation in world demands for sugar made Cuban prosperity uncertain.
- After the Cuban Revolution, Cuba's economy was tied into that of the Soviet Union. Cuba's economy deteriorated rapidly after the fall of the Soviet Union.
- Colombia was a major participant in the international drug trade.
- Brazil exported exotic woods.
- Venezuela, an OPEC member, and Mexico were oil-producing countries.
- At the beginning of the twenty-first century, Latin American nations were more heavily industrialized than before.

North America

- During World War I, U.S. exports rose so rapidly that, for the first time in its history, the United States became a creditor nation.
- After World War I, the United States exported motion picture films. The United States also distributed food such as wheat and corn to war-torn European nations after both world wars. By the 1960s and 1970s, U.S. fast foods had reached locations around the

globe, including the Soviet Union and the People's Republic of China. Industrial supplies continued as a major U.S. export throughout the twentieth century.

- In 1994, the **North American Free Trade Agreement (NAFTA)** went into effect. NAFTA abolished tariffs between Canada, the United States, and Mexico. Opposition to NAFTA broke out among Indians in the Mexican state of Chiapas.
- In Seattle in 1999, demonstrators protested against the World Trade Organization (WTO). The WTO was established in 1995 in order to organize world trade.
- U.S. trade created a worldwide diffusion of its products and culture. Advertising led to familiar logos and global recognition of U.S. products.

› Rapid Review

Twentieth- and twenty-first-century global economies were so interconnected that a crisis in one sector affected nearly all regions of the globe. Former colonial economies often had difficulty recovering from the production of a plantation cash crop to a diversified economy. East Asian nations proved fierce competitors in the export of automobiles, textiles, and electronics. OPEC oil prices became a major focus of world attention. Mass consumerism characterized the latter years of the twentieth century and the beginning of the twenty-first century as U.S. values and products diffused throughout most of the world.

› Review Questions

1. OPEC
   (A) is an organization of Middle Eastern nations
   (B) originated after the establishment of the European Union
   (C) was founded after NAFTA
   (D) has members in Latin America and Africa
   (E) embraced all oil-exporting nations

2. East Asian nations are noted for the export of all of the following products EXCEPT
   (A) textiles
   (B) films
   (C) automobiles
   (D) heavy industry
   (E) electronics

3. The impact of regional trade on global trade in the twentieth century was especially noticeable
   (A) on plantations during the imperialist age
   (B) before and during the Great Depression
   (C) after the establishment of NAFTA
   (D) during the revolution in Chiapas, Mexico
   (E) during the Seattle protest against the WTO

4. The European Union
   (A) established a currency used by all its members
   (B) originated with Great Britain
   (C) has the same basic purpose as NAFTA
   (D) does not adjust tariffs outside the European community
   (E) is a union of northern European nations

5. Which of the following cultures has diffused most widely during the period 1914 to the present?
   (A) Japanese
   (B) Russian
   (C) French
   (D) British
   (E) U.S.

› Answers and Explanations

1. **D**—Both Venezuela and Nigeria are OPEC members, making response (A) incorrect. OPEC originated about 30 years before the European Union (B) and NAFTA (C). Mexico, which is not a member of OPEC, is an oil-exporting nation (E).

2. **B**—The United States is a key exporter of films, whereas the other items listed are exports of Taiwan, Japan, and Korea.

3. **B**—The imposition of protective tariffs in Europe and the United States during the Great Depression slowed down trade throughout the world. The plantation economies were a better example of the impact of global upon regional trade (A), as was the protest against the WTO (E). The impact of NAFTA is most noticeable in North America (C), as was the anti-NAFTA protest in Chiapas (D).

4. **C**—Both NAFTA and the EU are regional trade organizations. Some European nations, such as Britain, do not use the euro (A). Britain was not among the first members of the EU (B). The EU adjusted tariffs for other world nations (D) and includes northern and southern European nations (E).

5. **E**—The current global culture is most heavily influenced by the United States.

CHAPTER 29

Technological Developments

IN THIS CHAPTER

Summary: The period since 1900 was one of rapid technological developments. From new medical discoveries to more sophisticated military technology to improvements in transportation, technology dominated the twentieth and twenty-first centuries. Labor-saving devices in the household increased leisure time, and new forms of mass entertainment filled that leisure time. The space race increased Cold War tensions as the development of nuclear weapons raised new uncertainties.

KEY IDEA

Key Terms

deoxyribonucleic acid (DNA)* International Space Station*
Helsinki Accords* service industries*
Hubble Space Telescope Sputnik

World War Firsts

World War I was the first conflict in which several new types of technology were used for the first time. Airplanes were used in combat. Dirigibles, tanks, more sophisticated weaponry, and poison gas also made their debut during the first world war. Radio technology was used during World War I for communication purposes. After the war, radio was extended to commercial and private use. In 1920, the first commercial radio broadcast was aired in Philadelphia. By 1930, millions of U.S. citizens owned radios, which they used to listen to news, sportscasts, and serials (soap operas). Government control of the airwaves in Europe made radio ownership less common on that continent.

World War II and the dropping of the atomic bomb ushered in a new scientific age. The second world war also added jet engines, tape recordings, and radar to its list of firsts.

The Postwar Period

Technology assisted Europe in its recovery from the world wars. New equipment and improved seeds increased agricultural yields, while modern industrial equipment increased production of textiles and metal goods, including automobiles and appliances.

In the 1950s, scientific technology led British and U.S. scientists to discover the composition of **deoxyribonucleic acid (DNA)**. Scientific farming based on genetics led to further improvements in seeds and pesticides. Genetic research produced the first incident of animal cloning (a cloned sheep) in Scotland in 1997.

Medical treatments and sanitation improved. New drugs, such as penicillin (discovered in 1928), as well as immunizations against diphtheria and poliomyelitis lowered the death rate. X-rays, ultrasound, and imaging assisted medical diagnoses. Indoor plumbing improved sanitation.

In 1949, the Soviet Union developed its own atomic bomb. From that time until the 1980s, both the United States (1952) and the Soviet Union (1953) built hydrogen bombs and developed ever more sophisticated weapons of war and defense. In 1972, as a result of the nuclear arms race, European countries convened a conference on security issues in Helsinki, Finland. In 1975, the **Helsinki Accords** called for contacts between nations on both sides of the Iron Curtain and also addressed the issue of human rights.

The Space Age

The twentieth century saw the exploration of new horizons in space. In 1957, the Soviet Union launched **Sputnik**, the first satellite, and in 1961 sent the first manned flight into space. The United States soon followed in the space race, succeeding in landing astronauts on the moon in 1969. In the 1970s, the United States and the Soviet Union cooperated in docking spacecraft and later cooperated in work on the **International Space Station**. Cooperation between the United States and European nations led to the development in 1990 of the **Hubble Space Telescope**, which is capable of observing objects in remote areas of the universe. U.S. orbiter landings on Mars have provided opportunities for investigation of potential landing sites on the Red Planet.

Entertainment Technology

The film industry created new opportunities for entertainment, especially after the addition of sound in the late 1920s. By the early 1950s, television had begun to enter many homes in the West. In the 1970s the entertainment industry born in Hollywood was surpassed by Bollywood, the name given to the film industry based in Mumbai, India. Since the 1970s India has ranked as the world's largest film producer.

Technology in the Information Age

As the world's societies entered the twenty-first century, more and more of the world's citizens were linked by computer technology, cellular phones, video games, and electronic readers. Robots, first used in Japan and adopted in Europe for use in mines and the automobile industry, increased industrial productivity. More people in the postindustrial world worked in **service industries** because of increased mechanization of agriculture and industry.

› Rapid Review

World Wars I and II saw a number of technological firsts, from improved transportation and communications to more elaborate weaponry. The atomic bomb ushered in a nuclear age that was among the focal points of the Cold War era. Technology created new leisure time activities, improved sanitation, and helped in the discoveries of new breakthroughs in medical science. The use of technology to transmit information characterizes the twenty-first century.

› Review Questions

1. Postindustrial economies are characterized by a large number of people involved in
   (A) manufacturing
   (B) mining
   (C) agriculture
   (D) service industries
   (E) nuclear weaponry

2. Which of the following was NOT used first during World War I?
   (A) Tanks
   (B) Airplanes
   (C) Radar
   (D) Dirigibles
   (E) Poison gas

3. The Helsinki Accords
   (A) were a reaction against the insecurities of the nuclear age
   (B) were a nuclear disarmament plan
   (C) increased Cold War rivalries
   (D) called for a reduction in manned space flights
   (E) intended to increase communications among nations of the free world

4. Technology in the twentieth century accomplished all of the following EXCEPT
   (A) unmanned space flights
   (B) genetic engineering
   (C) the use of robotics
   (D) manned space flights
   (E) the invention of railroads

5. Twentieth-century inventions and accomplishments
   (A) did nothing to improve household chores
   (B) popularized radio, especially in Europe
   (C) saw continued U.S.–Soviet competition throughout the twentieth century
   (D) were sometimes detrimental to the quality of life
   (E) did not enhance leisure time activities

› Answers and Explanations

1. **D**—Postindustrial economies, in which agriculture, mining, and industry are highly productive, feature relatively large numbers of employment opportunities in service industries.

2. **C**—Radar was first used in World War II. The other answer choices were initially used in World War I.

3. **A**—The Helsinki Accords called for communication between communist and noncommunist nations, making (C) and (E) incorrect responses. They did not address nuclear disarmament (B) or space flights (D).

4. **E**—Railroads were a nineteenth-century invention, whereas the remaining response choices were developed in the twentieth century.

5. **D**—Twentieth-century developments included nuclear weaponry. They also included household appliances (A) and advances in entertainment (E). At the end of the twentieth century, the United States and the Soviet Union cooperated in space dockings and an international space station (C). Radio was more popular in the United States than in Europe (B).

Social Changes

IN THIS CHAPTER

Summary: The twentieth-century world wars produced two basic responses: the first, a feeling of skepticism concerning the future and, the second, the desire to possess the many new products on the market after both wars. In an attempt to secure a comfortable future for their citizens, Western and Japanese governments established social welfare systems, particularly for the aged. Women's rights increased at the same time that traditional female roles persisted. A new global culture saw the dominance of Western influence.

Key Terms

cubism*	mass consumerism*
evangelical*	National Organization for Women (NOW)*
fundamentalism*	New Deal*
Kabuki theater*	No theater*
Liberation Theology*	welfare state*

Society After World War I

During the 1920s, Western society, most noticeably the United States, saw a rise in **mass consumerism**, especially in household appliances and in automobiles. The automobile decreased isolation and also allowed new freedoms for some adolescents in the United States. Some women turned to fashions that called for shorter skirts and hairstyles and behavior that allowed freer self-expression.

The movie industry was not only an outlet for artistic expression but also a new source of family entertainment. Modern painters such as Pablo Picasso combined geometric figures with non-Western art styles, particularly African, to create a new style called **cubism**. Modern architecture featured the use of concrete and broad expanses of glass.

At the same time, postwar Western society was characterized by a general feeling of skepticism. The devastation brought by the century's first global war was heightened by the despair of the Great Depression. Working classes and middle classes faced the prospect of unemployment or reduced salaries. In Japan, the depression increased suspicions of the Western way of life. Western states provided old age and medical insurance that eventually led to the institution of the **welfare state**. In the United States, the **New Deal** took government spending to new heights in an attempt to resolve the economic stagnation of the depression and provide for social security programs. Western European governments began to provide assistance to families with several children.

Post–World War II Western Society

After World War II, more women entered the workforce. Divorce was made more accessible, and effective birth control more conveniently available with the introduction of the birth control pill. Many European countries provided day care centers for working mothers. In the United States, the **National Organization for Women (NOW)**, founded in 1966, campaigned for women's rights. The role of the church in family life declined as church attendance fell, especially in Europe.

In the 1950s and 1960s, the United States experienced a civil rights movement that ended segregation of African Americans and increased voting rights. Student protests against U.S. involvement in the Vietnam War swept university campuses in the 1960s and early 1970s.

In the 1970s and 1980s, some Westerners began to question the concept of the welfare state. Both Great Britain and the United States elected leaders who adopted a more conservative approach toward government spending. Welfare programs were decreased under the leadership of Britain's Prime Minister Margaret Thatcher and U.S. President Ronald Reagan. Western European economic growth soared during the 1980s, producing a marked increase in consumer goods. Educational opportunities broadened throughout the world.

Society in the Soviet Union

Soviet leaders also built a system of welfare services, including protection for the sick and the aged. Soviet schools taught that religion was a myth. Western styles of art were denounced as decadent.

By the 1950s, the Soviet Union and most Eastern European nations were industrialized. Unlike the Western world, the factories in the communist bloc favored the production of heavy goods over consumer goods. As industrialism spread through Eastern Europe, more families engaged in sports activities and movie and television viewing. By the 1960s, cultural exchanges with the West gave Soviet citizens some contact with Western media and ways of life. An emphasis on sports programs made Soviet athletes intense competitors in the Olympic games.

Japan

In the 1920s, Japan also experienced a rise in mass consumerism. The film industry became popular, and secondary education reached greater numbers of students. After World War II, the new U.S.-influenced government in Japan provided for woman suffrage and abolished Shintoism as the state religion. The Japanese preserved their traditional respect for their elders by creating a social security system for the elderly. After the end of the U.S. occupation, the Japanese government began asserting more control over the lives of its citizens, including controlling the content of student textbooks. Traditions such as the tea ceremony and **Kabuki** and **No theater** continued.

Japanese work schedules allowed for less leisure time than in Western societies. One leisure activity that became extremely popular was baseball, introduced to Japan during the U.S. occupation. Women continued to occupy traditional homemaking and childrearing roles.

China

China's May Fourth Movement (1919) honored the role that women had played in the Chinese revolution by increasing women's rights. Footbinding was outlawed, and women were given wider educational and career opportunities. Although the Guomindang attempted to return Chinese women to their more traditional roles, Chinese communists gave them a number of roles in their revolution. Women were allowed to bear arms in the military. Since the institution of Mao's government in 1949, Chinese women have been expected to work outside the home while maintaining their traditional responsibilities in the home as well.

Latin America

After the Mexican Revolution, Mexican artists such as Diego Rivera painted murals on public buildings. The murals depicted scenes from the revolutions and hopes for social progress in the future. Latin American folk culture includes strong elements of the native Indian and African cultures. Although the region remains largely Roman Catholic, the latter decades of the twentieth century and the beginnings of the twenty-first century saw significant increases in the popularity of **evangelical** Protestant denominations throughout Latin America. Also popular in Latin America as well as in sub-Saharan Africa is **Liberation Theology**, a belief that emphasizes social justice for victims of poverty and oppression.

Throughout the twentieth century, Latin American women tended to retain their traditional roles. Women were not allowed to vote until 1929, when Ecuador became the first Latin American nation to allow woman suffrage. By the latter part of the twentieth century, Latin American women controlled small businesses and were sometimes active in politics, including membership in legislatures.

Africa

Woman suffrage was written into the constitutions of new nations. The participation of women in African independence movements was rewarded, resulting in some opportunities for women to hold political office. Many of the new nations also granted women increased opportunities for education and employment. Early marriage, however, often continued to confine women to traditional roles. Government imposition of *shariah* law in regions of Nigeria and other Muslim-dominated African nations threatened not only the independence but also the security of women.

A Global Culture

In today's world, the global culture has been dominated by Western trends and styles, a situation that has especially produced disapproval in East Asian and Islamic cultures. English is the language of commerce and of the Internet. The Western appreciation for science has been a hallmark of the global age.

Sometimes reactions to globalization created changes in religious beliefs and practices. Beginning in the 1960s, New Age Religions, dependent upon astrology, emerged. **Fundamentalism**, or the return to traditional beliefs and practices, became the goal of many practitioners of major religions, especially Christianity and Islam.

The new global culture placed more emphasis on monetary wealth, education, and professional position rather than on land ownership or inherited position. At the same time, traditions continued. In India, for example, remnants of the caste system caused some Indians to cling to caste restrictions even though they had been outlawed. Laws of almost all nations allowed woman suffrage. The global culture continued to display regional traditions and characteristics, while national pride surfaced in international athletic competitions such as the Olympic Games and World Cup Soccer, or FIFA.

› Rapid Review

In the interim between the world wars and after World War II, labor-saving devices transformed leisure time in Europe and the United States. Movies and television provided family entertainment, whereas the automobile created a new lifestyle for Western teenagers. Governments instituted welfare programs, and women's political rights were broadened worldwide. Religion declined in popularity, especially in Europe, and the Soviet Union denounced the importance of religion. Although women's rights were increased, women were expected to continue to carry out traditional roles. The new global culture emphasized the importance of professional status and knowledge over family social position. The dominance of Western culture and the English language met with disapproval in some Eastern and Islamic cultures.

› Review Questions

1. By the twenty-first century, almost all women across the globe
   (A) were freed from traditional homemaking roles
   (B) were allowed to serve in combat in the armed forces
   (C) were granted educational opportunities equal to men
   (D) were given career opportunities equal to men
   (E) had been granted the right to vote

2. In the twentieth century, a blend of African and Western cultures could be found most readily in
   (A) architecture
   (B) literature
   (C) painting
   (D) sculpture
   (E) film

3. What did the Soviet Union, Japan, the United States, and Western Europe have in common in the twentieth century?
   (A) A program of social security for the aged
   (B) Free elections
   (C) An emphasis on the production of consumer goods
   (D) An appreciation for Western styles in art
   (E) The adoption of U.S. sports

4. Which of the following is true concerning the status of religion in the twentieth century?
   (A) European church membership declined significantly.
   (B) Catholicism gained a stronger hold in Latin America.
   (C) The United States encouraged the Japanese to maintain the traditional status of Shintoism.
   (D) Hindu traditions were abolished in India.
   (E) The Soviet Union presented religion as truth.

5. Which of the following is true regarding the role of women in Communist China?
   (A) Military service was limited to support roles.
   (B) They were discouraged from working outside the home.
   (C) Restrictive Confucian tradition was outlawed.
   (D) They had fewer rights than under the Guomindang.
   (E) Women who worked outside the home were exempt from traditional household roles.

› Answers and Explanations

1. **E**—The twentieth century ended with woman suffrage granted in almost all nations. Most societies still expected women to maintain their traditional roles (A). Although educational and career opportunities for women increased (C, D), they were generally not as broad as those for men. Most nations did not allow women in combat, with China and the Soviet Union notable exceptions (B).

2. **C**—Picasso's cubist paintings often featured African themes combined with the geometric designs of the modern cubist style.

3. **A**—All have social security programs for the elderly, whereas the Soviet Union did not have free elections (B), an emphasis on consumer goods (C), an appreciation for Western art styles (D), or a desire to adopt U.S. sports (E).

4. **A**—After World War II, European church membership declined significantly. Protestantism made substantial inroads into Latin American religion (B), whereas the U.S. occupation ended the status of Shintoism as a state religion (C). Although the Hindu caste system was legally ended, many Indians continue its traditions (D). The Soviet Union presented religion as a myth (E).

5. **C**—Footbinding, a Confucian tradition, was outlawed. Chinese women were allowed to serve in combat (A). Women were encouraged to work outside the home, but were still expected to fulfill their traditional home obligations (B, E). Women had more rights under communism than under the Guomindang (D).

CHAPTER 31

Demographic and Environmental Developments

IN THIS CHAPTER

Summary: Although the Industrial Revolution generated overall improvements in living standards, it also caused atmospheric pollution in industrialized cities. Environmental challenges of the twentieth and twenty-first centuries included efforts to resolve poor environmental quality from industrial and automobile emissions. Potential threats to the environment also resulted from oil spills, the devastation of warfare, and the danger of meltdowns from nuclear plants.

Since 1914, warfare, famine, disease, and migration have affected global population distribution. Most migrants moved from developing to developed nations in search of improved economic opportunities.

KEY IDEA

Key Terms

Green Revolution*   ozone depletion*

guest workers*   xenophobia*

The War Years

World War I resulted in the deaths of 10 million Europeans and eliminated nearly a generation of young European men. The lack of potential husbands forced many European women to remain unmarried. The drastic decline in marriages lowered the European birth rate and population growth in future generations. Bombs and troop movements destroyed cities, factories, and agricultural land. Another 35 million people lost their lives in World War II. Because of postwar boundary changes, hundreds of thousands of displaced persons were forced to relocate.

Population Changes

Rapid population growth, especially in developing nations, became a persistent concern of the twentieth and twenty-first centuries. Sometimes religious and cultural beliefs prohibited efforts at population control. In the early twentieth century, efforts to eradicate disease and improve sanitation led to marked population increases in developing nations in Asia. In Africa, which began the century with low population levels, high birth rates and lower mortality rates resulted in significant population increases. These population trends continued in spite of the high incidence of AIDS in Africa.

Despite advances in health care, those living in poverty continued to struggle with diseases such as cholera, tuberculosis, and malaria. New epidemics emerged, such as the influenza pandemic of 1918 to 1919, Ebola, and AIDS. The incidence of diseases such as Alzheimer's disease, heart disease, and diabetes increased because of increases in life expectancy and lifestyle changes.

In Europe, the population decline and labor shortages of the 1950s and 1960s caused Western European governments to seek workers from southern Europe and the non-Western world. Many of these **guest workers** migrated to Western Europe from the West Indies, North Africa, Turkey, and Pakistan. Guest workers received very low wages and were often subjected to discrimination and violence from Western Europeans. This discrimination heightened in the 1980s because of a slowdown in European economies and the growing size of the guest worker population. Not all immigrants were welcomed. **Xenophobia**, an intense fear of foreigners, often was shown in protests, race riots, and government policies restricting citizenship.

In contrast to European demographic patterns, East Asian countries experienced high population growth. By the 1980s, for example, South Korea had the highest population density in the world. As a result, many South Koreans migrated to other countries. The government of South Korea encouraged its people to limit the size of their families, while the Japanese government addressed its ever-increasing population by promoting birth control and abortion.

The People's Republic of China attempted to control its huge population by instituting policies designed to limit family size. In the 1960s, rural couples were limited to one child and urban couples to two. By the 1980s, only one child per family was allowed. These programs greatly reduced the Chinese birth rate at the expense of forced abortions and sterilizations. Female infanticide increased. Other infants were hidden among family members in rural areas where recordkeeping was not as accurate as in urban areas. By 2007, the one-child policy had relaxed in some regions of China to permit urban couples who themselves were only children to give birth to two children.

In Central Asia, the Soviet Union experienced ethnic divisions as a result of population changes. By the 1970s, the Muslim population in the southern Soviet republics had grown rapidly and presented a threat to the dominance of the Russian culture.

Efforts to Improve Agricultural Production

One of the solutions to growing population concerns was to improve agricultural productivity in developing nations. The **Green Revolution** was a program that increased crop yields through the use of high-yield, disease-resistant crops; as well as fertilizers, pesticides, and efficient irrigation methods. Especially effective in India and other parts of Asia, it also experienced some success in Latin America. The Green Revolution was criticized for its use of pesticides and fertilizers that caused pollution and cancer. Also, chemicals were expensive, making the program more accessible to large landowners and agricultural businesses.

In Egypt, President Nasser attempted to improve agricultural productivity through the construction of the Aswan Dam. Although the project provided additional farmland, its interference in the normal flood patterns of the Nile River deprived the land of the fertile silt deposited by the Nile's flooding. Also, parasites that caused blindness appeared in greater numbers, and increased deposits of salt were found in the soil.

Migration Patterns

After World War I, the population of Latin America swelled as immigrants continued to pour into Argentina and Brazil as well as into other Latin American countries. Urban areas grew rapidly. Latin America experienced sizable migration within the continent as the inhabitants of rural areas migrated to urban regions in search of employment. Newcomers often were forced to live in shantytowns on the outskirts of urban areas. Sometimes these settlements were incorporated into urban areas, resulting in somewhat improved living conditions within the former shantytowns.

In the 1920s, workers from Mexico crossed into the United States at the same time that Central Americans were crossing into Mexico in search of employment. During the 1940s, the United States set up programs with Mexico to provide workers. Hundreds of thousands of migrants, both legal and illegal, continued to cross the border into the United States. Throughout Latin America, migration in search of employment occurred across national borders. Other migrants reached, or attempted to reach, the United States to escape political oppression and warfare. This last group included immigrants from Cuba, Haiti, Nicaragua, and El Salvador.

Population flight from countries undergoing ethnic or religious strife or alterations in political boundaries remained an issue in the period since 1914. The largest displacement of people in history occurred in South Asia in 1947 and 1948, when the partition of India and Pakistan produced a major migration of Muslims to Pakistan and Hindus to India. The first Arab–Israeli War in 1948 created hundreds of thousands of Palestinian Arab refugees. In 1998, in the Balkan region of Kosovo, thousands of ethnic Albanians of the Muslim faith fled the region in the face of Serbian massacres. From 2000 to 2004, religious conflict in Nigeria caused Christians and Muslims to flee to areas where their religion was the majority faith. In the Sudan, inhabitants of the southern region of the country, most of them Christians or practitioners of native religions, were displaced from their homes when Sunni Arabs from the northern regions of Sudan attempted to impose Islamic law upon the southern regions. By 2004, the Sudanese conflict focused on the region of Darfur and involved a conflict between Arab and non-Arab Muslims.

Another pattern of migration involved the movement of South Asians and Arabs toward the oil-producing regions of the Middle East. Also, workers from developed nations including the United States sought employment with their own nation's companies in the oil fields of the Middle East.

Environmental Concerns

The world faced a number of environmental issues: damage to marine life from oil spills, the danger of meltdowns from nuclear plants, and the devastation of warfare. During the Vietnam War, for example, the United States employed chemical defoliants in South Vietnam. During the Persian Gulf War, Iraq's Saddam Hussein spilled huge amounts of oil into the Persian Gulf and set fire to Kuwaiti oil fields. Industrial pollution and human waste continued to plague many of the world's waterways. In Eastern Europe industrialization severely polluted half the area's rivers and endangered farmland. Pollution was responsible for respiratory diseases and higher rates of infant mortality. Population growth in rural areas of Africa and Asia often led to overgrazing and deforestation; depletion of the rain forest was a factor in global warming.

Some progress in protecting the environment was made. Governments of industrialized nations identified the chemicals that cause **ozone depletion** in the upper atmosphere and limited their use. Antipollution devices were installed on automobiles, planes, and industrial smokestacks.

› Rapid Review

Population issues in the period since 1914 have revolved around migration and control of population growth. Migration in the period has most frequently been from developing to developed nations and, second, from rural to urban areas. The latter often has resulted in the establishment of shantytowns along the perimeters of major urban areas. Guest workers often became the victims of discrimination, especially in Europe. Although some governmental programs limited population growth, many rural areas in Africa and Asia suffered from depleted farmland insufficient to handle their population. Issues of poor air and water quality, global warming, and the devastation wrought by warfare remained.

› Review Questions

1. Which of the following is the LEAST common migration pattern from the 1960s to the present?
   (A) From Asia to Europe
   (B) From Europe to the United States
   (C) From Mexico to the United States
   (D) From the Middle East to Europe
   (E) From Africa to Europe

2. The largest displacement of people in the twentieth century was
   (A) Albanian refugees leaving Kosovo
   (B) the exchange between Muslim and Hindu areas after the partition of India
   (C) illegal Mexican immigrants to the United States
   (D) displaced persons after World War II
   (E) refugees from Vietnam in 1975

3. Which of the following is true of population growth since 1914?
   (A) The AIDS crisis has produced a marked decline in African population.
   (B) Religious opposition has caused China to abandon its one-child policy.
   (C) Population growth is not detrimental to rural environments.
   (D) Cultural traditions and religious beliefs often promote population growth.
   (E) Non-Western governments have not interfered in population control.

4. The key pattern of migration in the twentieth and twenty-first centuries has been
   (A) from wartorn areas to those at peace
   (B) from rural to urban areas
   (C) from urban to rural areas
   (D) from developing to developed nations
   (E) from developed to developing nations

5. Which of the following was NOT true concerning the Green Revolution?
   (A) It was highly ineffective in increasing agricultural yields.
   (B) It reinforced class distinctions.
   (C) It disseminated pollutants.
   (D) It was an expensive solution to crop improvements.
   (E) It involved improved irrigation practices.

› Answers and Explanation

1. **B**—Since the most common pattern of migration in the twentieth century has been from developing to developed nations, migration from Europe to the United States would be the least common of the patterns listed. The remaining answer choices describe migrations from developing to developed countries.

2. **B**—The migration of Hindus to India and Muslims to Pakistan after the creation of those independent states in 1947 was the largest exchange of peoples in the twentieth century.

3. **D**—Cultural and religious traditions often oppose efforts to curb population growth. African population continues to grow in spite of AIDS (A). China continues with its one-child policy (B). Population growth has caused improper land usage, including overgrazing (C). China, Japan, and India, for example, have implemented population control policies (E).

4. **D**—The main migration pattern has been from developing to developed nations in search of better economic opportunities.

5. **A**—The Green Revolution was successful in its goals, especially in India. The expense of the program often led to more benefits for elite than for lower classes (B). Pesticides used in the program caused pollution (C), and the program was expensive (D). Irrigation was part of the program (E).

PERIOD 6 Summary: Accelerating Global Change and Realignments (c. 1900 to the present)

Timeline

1904–1905	Russo-Japanese War
1905	Revolution of 1905 (Russia)
	Einstein's theory of relativity
1908–1918	Young Turk era
1910–1920	Mexican Revolution
1911–1912	Chinese Revolution; end of Chinese dynastic rule
1914	Opening of the Panama Canal
1914–1918	World War I
1917	Bolshevik Revolution
1918	Treaty of Brest-Litovsk
1918–1919	Influenza pandemic
1918–1920	Russian civil war
1919	Treaty of Versailles
	May Fourth Movement in China
1921–1928	Lenin's New Economic Policy
1923	End of the Ottoman Empire
	Establishment of the Republic of Turkey
1928–1932	First of Stalin's Five Year Plans
1929	Beginning of the Great Depression
1931	Japanese invasion of Manchuria
1933	Hitler's rise to power in Germany
1935	Government of India Act
1937	Japanese invasion of China
1939	German invasion of Poland
1945	Atomic bombs dropped on Hiroshima and Nagasaki
	End of World War II
1947	Truman Doctrine
	Partition of India
1948	Marshall Plan
	Creation of Israel
	Establishment of apartheid in South Africa
	Universal Declaration of Human Rights
1949	Division of Germany
	Establishment of NATO
	Establishment of the People's Republic of China

1950–1953	Korean War
1954	Division of Vietnam
1955	Establishment of the Warsaw Pact
1956	Suez Crisis
	Soviet invasion of Hungary
1957	Independence in Ghana
1958–1961	Great Leap Forward in China
1959	Cuban Revolution
1960	Establishment of OPEC
1961	Construction of the Berlin Wall
1962	Cuban Missile Crisis
1964	Sino-Soviet Rift
1967	Establishment of the European Community
1968	Prague Spring
1972	Beginning of détente
1973	Arab–Israeli War
	Beginning of Arab oil embargo
1975	Fall of Vietnam
1979	Iranian Revolution
1980–1988	Iran–Iraq War
1989	Fall of the Berlin Wall
1990	Reunification of Germany
1990–1991	Gulf War
1991	Fall of the Soviet Union
	End of the Cold War
1993	Establishment of NAFTA
1995	Establishment of the World Trade Organization
1997	Transfer of Hong Kong to China
2001	Terrorist attacks on the United States
2003	U.S. Coalition–Iraq War
2008–2010	Global economic crisis

Key Comparisons

1. Postwar governments of Western nations versus the Soviet bloc
2. Decolonization in Africa versus India
3. The effects of World War I versus the effects of World War II
4. The Russian Revolution versus the Chinese Revolution
5. Reactions of Western versus non-Western nations to U.S. consumer society
6. Female roles in China and the West
7. Patterns of immigration in the Eastern versus the Western hemispheres
8. Patterns of economic development in Africa versus Latin America
9. Global trade in the Pacific Rim versus the West
10. Political and economic conditions in Russia before and after communism

Change/Continuity Chart

KEY IDEA

REGION	POLITICAL	ECONOMIC	SOCIAL	CHANGES	CONTINUITIES
East Asia	End of the Qing dynasty World wars Japanese occupation Chinese communism Korean War	Great Leap Forward Electronics Automobiles Textiles	Chinese one-child policy Women working outside home (China) Baseball	Depression Footbinding outlawed High-tech industries	Shintoism Buddhism Confucianism U.S. recognition of China
Southeast Asia	Vietnam War Communism	Rice	Buddhism	Decolonization Communism Tourism Immigration from Asia	Buddhism
Oceania	Participation in world wars British Commonwealth	Tourism Farming Sheep-raising Industry	Greater rights for aborigines	Introduction of capitalism in Russia	Herding Grazing
Central Asia	Russian Revolution World wars Cold War *Glasnost* End of communism	NEP Five-Year Plans Collective farming Perestroika	Allowance of some Western influences	Decolonization Partition Nuclear power	Economic difficulties Ethnic conflict
South Asia	World wars Independence movements	Green Revolution	Laws against caste system	Mandates Creation of Israel Arab-Israeli wars	Hinduism Islam Buddhism

Region					
Southwest Asia (Middle East)	Iranian Revolution, Iran–Iraq War Persian Gulf War War in Afghanistan Terrorism U.S. Coalition–Iraq War	OPEC Oil	Guest workers	Decolonization Guest workers	Islam Arab-Israeli conflicts
North Africa	Independence movements Suez Crisis	Oil OPEC Aswan Dam	Shantytowns (Cairo)	Decolonization End of apartheid	Islam
Sub-Saharan Africa	Independence movements Ethnic conflicts	Oil Native art Famine	AIDS Population increase Apartheid	Depression Loss of world dominance Economic prosperity, guest workers	Poverty Unstable governments
Western Europe	World wars Fascism Berlin Wall Terrorism	European Union Euro Auto industry	Population decrease Drop in religious observance	Industrialization Emancipation of slaves Increased suffrage	Racism
Eastern Europe	End of empire World wars Communism	Solidarity Industry	Religious freedom (Poland)	Depression End of communism	Ethnic conflict
North America	World wars Cold War U.S. as superpower Civil rights movement	Depression NAFTA	Transmission of U.S. culture Feminism	Fight against terrorism Transmission of U.S. culture	Dominance of the United States
Latin America	Mexican Revolution Coups PRI Cuban Revolution Sandinistas Democracy	Depression Industry Oil Panama Canal	Immigration from Europe Shantytowns	Industry Increased trade Popularity of Protestantism	Agriculture Roman Catholicism

STEP **5**

Build Your
Test-Taking Confidence

Practice Test One
Practice Test Two

PRACTICE TEST ONE

Answer Sheet

1 (A) (B) (C) (D)	26 (A) (B) (C) (D)	51 (A) (B) (C) (D)
2 (A) (B) (C) (D)	27 (A) (B) (C) (D)	52 (A) (B) (C) (D)
3 (A) (B) (C) (D)	28 (A) (B) (C) (D)	53 (A) (B) (C) (D)
4 (A) (B) (C) (D)	29 (A) (B) (C) (D)	54 (A) (B) (C) (D)
5 (A) (B) (C) (D)	30 (A) (B) (C) (D)	55 (A) (B) (C) (D)
6 (A) (B) (C) (D)	31 (A) (B) (C) (D)	56 (A) (B) (C) (D)
7 (A) (B) (C) (D)	32 (A) (B) (C) (D)	57 (A) (B) (C) (D)
8 (A) (B) (C) (D)	33 (A) (B) (C) (D)	58 (A) (B) (C) (D)
9 (A) (B) (C) (D)	34 (A) (B) (C) (D)	59 (A) (B) (C) (D)
10 (A) (B) (C) (D)	35 (A) (B) (C) (D)	60 (A) (B) (C) (D)
11 (A) (B) (C) (D)	36 (A) (B) (C) (D)	61 (A) (B) (C) (D)
12 (A) (B) (C) (D)	37 (A) (B) (C) (D)	62 (A) (B) (C) (D)
13 (A) (B) (C) (D)	38 (A) (B) (C) (D)	63 (A) (B) (C) (D)
14 (A) (B) (C) (D)	39 (A) (B) (C) (D)	64 (A) (B) (C) (D)
15 (A) (B) (C) (D)	40 (A) (B) (C) (D)	65 (A) (B) (C) (D)
16 (A) (B) (C) (D)	41 (A) (B) (C) (D)	66 (A) (B) (C) (D)
17 (A) (B) (C) (D)	42 (A) (B) (C) (D)	67 (A) (B) (C) (D)
18 (A) (B) (C) (D)	43 (A) (B) (C) (D)	68 (A) (B) (C) (D)
19 (A) (B) (C) (D)	44 (A) (B) (C) (D)	69 (A) (B) (C) (D)
20 (A) (B) (C) (D)	45 (A) (B) (C) (D)	70 (A) (B) (C) (D)
21 (A) (B) (C) (D)	46 (A) (B) (C) (D)	
22 (A) (B) (C) (D)	47 (A) (B) (C) (D)	
23 (A) (B) (C) (D)	48 (A) (B) (C) (D)	
24 (A) (B) (C) (D)	49 (A) (B) (C) (D)	
25 (A) (B) (C) (D)	50 (A) (B) (C) (D)	

PRACTICE TEST ONE

Section I

Time—55 minutes
70 Questions

Directions: Each of the incomplete statements or questions below is followed by four answer choices. Choose the answer that is best and write the letter of your choice on the answer sheet supplied.

1. Which of the following belief systems owned monasteries, spread across trade routes, and appealed to a variety of social classes?
   (A) Christianity and Buddhism
   (B) Buddhism and Islam
   (C) Islam and Hinduism
   (D) Judaism and Christianity

2. Which of the following is true of both the Han Empire and the Roman Empire?
   (A) Both developed advanced navigational technology.
   (B) Both paid tribute to nomadic tribes on their frontier.
   (C) Both built societies without the use of slave labor.
   (D) Both had long-established central governments followed by a period of ineffective rulers.

3. The Hindu social order included
   (A) matrilineal descent
   (B) social structures based on Harappan traditions
   (C) divisions based upon ethnicity
   (D) social mobility

4. Which of the following was introduced after the other three?
   (A) The *Quran*
   (B) The Gospels of the New Testament
   (C) The *Analects* of Confucius
   (D) The Eightfold Path

5. Which of the following reflects a similarity between the expansion of the Arabs in the seventh century and the expansion of the Vikings in the ninth century?
   (A) Both carried with them the seeds of a major religion.
   (B) Both took advantage of their contacts with principal trade routes.
   (C) Both were conscious efforts to extend their respective cultures.
   (D) Both expanded throughout the Mediterranean world.

6. Which of the following is correct concerning Indian Ocean trade from 1000 to 1450?
   (A) Active Silk Roads overland trade diminished Indian Ocean trade.
   (B) Europeans did not participate.
   (C) East Africa was left out of its trade network.
   (D) It was dominated by South Asian merchants.

7. During the period from 600 to 1450, long-distance travel
   (A) was hindered by a lack of safe trade routes between Europe and Asia
   (B) included African slavery in the Mediterranean basin and India
   (C) was confined to overland routes
   (D) bypassed Western Europe

8. Which of the following was the most industrialized during the period 1000 to 1450?
   (A) Russia
   (B) England
   (C) China
   (D) India

9. The term *shogun* describes a role in feudal Japan most like what role in feudal Europe?
   - (A) Serf
   - (B) Lord
   - (C) Free peasant
   - (D) Guild member

10. Which of the following groups of women saw their roles change most profoundly in the period between 600 and 1450?
    - (A) European women
    - (B) Islamic women
    - (C) Hindu women of India
    - (D) African women

11. Buddhism spread from China to present-day
    - (A) Indonesia
    - (B) Korea
    - (C) India
    - (D) Sri Lanka

12. In the period between 1000 and 1300
    - (A) regional states arose in both Africa and Europe
    - (B) Islam reached North Africa, while Christianity became dominant in East Africa
    - (C) trans-Saharan trade decreased as Mediterranean trade increased
    - (D) early Bantu kingdoms broke up into kinship-based societies

13. The Mongols
    - (A) brought foreign administrators into China
    - (B) expanded their rule into Japan in the thirteenth century
    - (C) persecuted Christians within their empire
    - (D) encouraged intermarriage between themselves and the Chinese

14. Which of the following is true concerning the Chinese and European presence in the Indian Ocean in the fifteenth century?
    - (A) Europeans were concerned with demonstrating their military might.
    - (B) The Chinese intended to establish harmony in the Indian Ocean.
    - (C) European trade decreased in the latter part of the century.
    - (D) The Chinese intended to impose their control over foreign trade.

15. In 1450, the Indians of the present-day countries of Mexico and the United States
    - (A) shared a common written language
    - (B) were isolated from one another
    - (C) began to establish trans-Atlantic trade connections
    - (D) were isolated from the rest of the world

16. The least common destination for slaves crossing the Atlantic Ocean was
    - (A) Mexico
    - (B) Spanish America
    - (C) the Caribbean
    - (D) British North America

17. Between 1500 and 1750, Europeans were interested in colonies in the Americas for all the following reasons EXCEPT
    - (A) they wanted to Christianize the indigenous peoples
    - (B) they wanted to empower Spain to reconquer its territories under Muslim control
    - (C) they wanted to enrich the treasuries of Europe
    - (D) they wanted to bring honor to their respective nations

18. The pattern illustrated on the facade shown on the facing page would most commonly be found in
    - (A) Mughal India
    - (B) Ming China
    - (C) Renaissance Italy
    - (D) East Africa

19. The design illustrated above reflects an era in which
    - (A) European women rose in status
    - (B) European serfdom was on the rise
    - (C) Japan opened up to trade with the West
    - (D) Mesoamericans demonstrated advanced architectural and engineering skills

20. Which of the following is true of the African slave trade between 1450 and 1750?
- (A) East Africa was not involved in the slave trade.
- (B) African monarchs united in an effort to abolish the slave trade.
- (C) Within African societies, male slaves were valued more highly than female slaves.
- (D) Europeans tapped into African slave trade routes already in existence.

21. During the period of the Tokugawa Shogunate
- (A) Buddhist and Confucian scholars practiced tolerance toward Christians
- (B) the Portuguese gained unique trading privileges with Japan
- (C) dependence on Chinese traditions prevented the development of Japanese art forms
- (D) Japan continued to be influenced by neo-Confucian thought from China

22. The Protestant Reformation
- (A) produced sweeping reforms in the teachings of the Roman Catholic Church
- (B) strengthened the rise of nation-states in Europe
- (C) resulted in a decline in European education
- (D) discouraged capitalist ventures among members of the Christian faith

23. Prior to its conquest by the Ottoman Turks, Byzantium was weakened by
- (A) inadequate military technology
- (B) its policy of continued expansion
- (C) the decline of regional trade routes
- (D) the political ambitions of neighboring peoples

24. When the Mexican liberal Ponciano Arriaga referred to the Indians of Mexico as "proletarians," he was echoing
- (A) the proclamation of the Young Turks
- (B) Marx and Engels
- (C) the Declaration of the Rights of Man
- (D) the Monroe Doctrine

25. In calling the Mexican Indians "proletariat," Arriaga was referring to their role as
- (A) workers
- (B) indentured servants
- (C) slaves
- (D) revolutionaries

26. African influences on American culture included all of the following EXCEPT
- (A) language
- (B) agricultural knowledge
- (C) commerce
- (D) religious practices

27. Which of the following facilitated European advances into Asia in the nineteenth century?
- (A) Communication cables that linked Asia with Europe
- (B) Intense rivalries among major Asian nations
- (C) The popularity of Christianity in East Asia
- (D) Weakening Asian economies that welcomed European trade

28. Japan's response to the opening of trade with the United States and Europe was
    (A) to protect the territorial integrity of Korea
    (B) to assist China in resolving unequal treaties with European powers and the United States
    (C) to engage in conflict with Russia
    (D) to end the power of its traditional ruling dynasty

29. The reasons for India's history of fragmented government have included all of the following EXCEPT
    (A) its religious diversity
    (B) its diverse economic activity
    (C) its varied landscape
    (D) its cycle of monsoons

30. The concept of extraterritoriality is associated with
    (A) Japan and India
    (B) Korea and the Russian Empire
    (C) Indonesia and Vietnam
    (D) China and the Ottoman Empire

31. The Indian National Congress
    (A) remained separate from the Muslim League
    (B) was against Indian self-rule
    (C) felt that India's future lay in cooperating with Great Britain
    (D) agreed with the Ottoman Empire's Young Turks that reform was necessary to withstand European imperialism

West Asia Road Map

32. Which of the following best describes the message of the cartoon above?
    (A) The United States is skeptical of peace efforts in the Middle East.
    (B) The road to Middle Eastern peace has only a few minor rough spots.
    (C) A middle-of-the-road path to peace is easier in theory than in practice.
    (D) Palestine has the upper hand in current Middle Eastern relations.

33. The road map illustrated in the cartoon represents
    (A) the military presence of the Israelis
    (B) the plight of dispossessed Palestinians
    (C) a plan for resolving Israeli–Palestinian conflicts
    (D) camps of terrorist organizations

34. African decolonization
    (A) influenced U.S. social issues in the 1960s
    (B) was not influenced by the Cold War
    (C) healed ethnic divisions throughout the continent
    (D) witnessed a peaceful transition in France's North African possessions

35. Which of the following is true regarding the role of women in World War II?
    (A) American women became a permanent part of the work force as a result of their wartime factory jobs.
    (B) Japanese women entered the work force in large numbers.
    (C) Soviet and Chinese women served in combat.
    (D) German women were encouraged to serve in combat.

36. All of the following are true of environmental concerns of the twentieth century EXCEPT that
    (A) air pollution produces global warming
    (B) the extension of agricultural activity aids biodiversity
    (C) global warming poses the risk of a rise in sea levels
    (D) urbanization reduces biodiversity

37. Compared to Egypt, Sumer
    (A) had a monotheistic religion
    (B) was more isolated
    (C) engaged in more extensive long-distance trade
    (D) constructed fewer large urban areas

38. The map below illustrates Africa
    (A) in 1800
    (B) in 1850
    (C) in 1910
    (D) in 2000

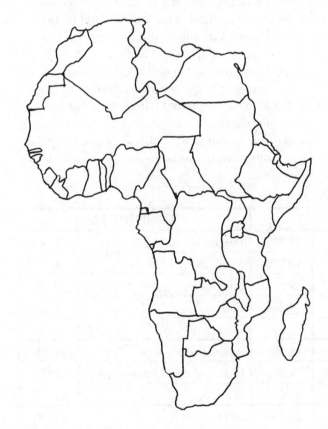

39. Which of the following religions uses the symbols above?
    (A) Judaism
    (B) Buddhism
    (C) Christianity
    (D) Hinduism

40. Which of the following statements regarding the tenets of Buddhism is most accurate?
    (A) Buddhism teaches that followers can attain a state of perfect peace.
    (B) Buddhism supported the Indian caste system.
    (C) Buddhism is polytheistic.
    (D) Buddhism does not accept reincarnation.

41. Which of the following is NOT true of Confucianism?
    (A) It instituted the Chinese civil service examination.
    (B) One of its tenets is filial piety.
    (C) It has fostered a patriarchal society.
    (D) It involves the worship of Confucius.

42. In the chart below, Country #2 is found in which region?
    (A) Europe
    (B) Sub-Saharan Africa
    (C) Latin America
    (D) East Asia

43. Country #2's relationship with its top trade partner is the result of
    (A) globalization
    (B) multinational corporations
    (C) trans-Saharan trade
    (D) colonialism

44. Country #1 is
    (A) China
    (B) Bangladesh
    (C) India
    (E) Canada

45. Before 1000, the most common governmental structure in sub-Saharan Africa was the
    (A) stateless society
    (B) kingdom
    (C) city-state
    (D) empire

46. In the period 1000 to 1450
    (A) Europeans learned of sugarcane cultivation from the Crusades
    (B) Europe ceased expansion
    (C) Australians developed agriculture
    (D) pastoral nomadism declined markedly

47. Which language was a blend of the language of migratory farmers and that of traders of Southwest Asia?
    (A) Urdu
    (B) Proto-Bantu
    (C) Arabic
    (D) Swahili

48. The Mongols
    (A) mastered Asian territories by blocking trade routes
    (B) added Vietnam to their territorial possessions
    (C) promoted commercial ties between Russia and the West
    (D) created the largest land empire

49. Trade was a key method of exchange between which of the following pairs?
    (A) The Mongol Empire and the Gupta Empire
    (B) Qing China and Mexico
    (C) Korea and the Byzantine Empire
    (D) Songhay and the Mongol Empire

50. Which of the following is true regarding missionary campaigns in the period 1000 to 1450?
    (A) Roman Catholic Christianity gained little support in Spain and Sicily
    (B) In the fourteenth century, Christianity became popular with East Asians
    (C) Mongols embraced Christianity in large numbers
    (D) The spread of the bubonic plague temporarily halted Christian missionary efforts to East Asia

	COUNTRY #1		COUNTRY #2	
Import Partners	Japan	18.1%	Belgium	14.6%
	Taiwan	10.5%	South Africa	14.2%
	South Korea	9.7%	Nigeria	10.3%
	United States	9.2%	France	9.5%
	Germany	5.6%	Germany	7.3%
GDP by Sector	Agriculture	15.2%	Agriculture	55.0%
	Industry and Construction	51.2%	Industry and Construction	11.0%
	Services	33.6%	Services	34.0%
Age Structure	0–14 years	23.1%	0–14 years	48.3%
	15–64 years	69.5%	15–64 years	49.2%
	65 and over	7.4%	65 and over	2.5%
Population Growth Rate		0.6%		2.9%

Source: CIA World Factbook, *2003*

51. All of the following are true concerning the African slave trade EXCEPT
    (A) Portuguese slavers carried slaves to Atlantic islands
    (B) in sub-Saharan Africa, wealth was determined by control of human labor rather than by private property
    (C) most slaves exported from Africa came from central Africa
    (D) some slaves were transported across the Sahara to the Mediterranean basin

52. Which is true concerning Indian Ocean trade in the period 1450 to 1750?
    (A) Portuguese dominance increased after 1600.
    (B) Indian Ocean mariners sailing from China to East Africa relied on the monsoons.
    (C) English merchants concentrated on Indonesian trade.
    (D) The emergence of the joint-stock company increased commercial risks.

53. Which of the following is NOT true regarding the Seven Years' War?
    (A) It was the first global war.
    (B) It occurred during the period of Portuguese dominance in the Indian Ocean.
    (C) It laid the basis for British imperial dominance.
    (D) It involved the Indian Ocean and the Caribbean.

54. All of the following are true of political institutions in the seventeenth and eighteenth centuries EXCEPT
    (A) Europe experienced the rule of absolute monarchs
    (B) Enlightenment theories altered Russian political thought
    (C) Japan's government became more centralized
    (D) Ottoman power was in decline

55. In the early nineteenth century, the most urbanized nation was
    (A) China
    (B) Russia
    (C) the United States
    (D) Great Britain

56. Which is NOT true of Russian expansion in the period 1500–1800?
    (A) It was stopped by the Ottoman Empire.
    (B) It included expansion into Siberia.
    (C) It added territory by participating in the partition of Poland.
    (D) It forged a cultural alliance with Slavic peoples in the Balkans.

57. What was the response of China to foreign influence in the period 1450 to 1750?
    (A) The Chinese were unimpressed by European technology.
    (B) The Qing closely supervised foreign merchants in China.
    (C) Under Qing rule, most Chinese ports were open to foreigners.
    (D) Chinese authorities established trading companies patterned after those of the Europeans.

58. The growth of rubber and palm oil production in Africa produced all of the following effects EXCEPT
    (A) greater technology transfer to Africans
    (B) production concentrated around European needs and desires
    (C) disruption of village life
    (D) malnutrition

59. In the period between 1750 and 1914, the Chinese empire was weakened by all of the following EXCEPT
    (A) the Boxer Rebellion
    (B) defense treaties with Great Britain and Japan
    (C) the opium trade
    (D) loss of tribute

60. Which of the following is true of the Russians and Japanese from 1750 to 1914?
    (A) They both built increasingly powerful empires.
    (B) Their governments encouraged rapid industrialization.
    (C) They both had a well-educated populace.
    (D) Both had decentralized governments.

61. Which of the following is true concerning imperialism in the period 1750 to 1914?
    (A) Europeans set up a number of settler colonies in Southeast Asia.
    (B) Imperialism prevented the integration of local economies into global trade networks.
    (C) Western Europe, the United States, and Japan were all imperialist powers.
    (D) Colonies became ready markets for Western manufactured goods.

62. All of the following are true of the Balkans in the nineteenth century EXCEPT
    (A) Russia wanted to extend the Pan-Slavic movement to the Balkans
    (B) Balkan states were controlled by Austria-Hungary and the Ottomans
    (C) it was the focus of Europe's imperialist powers
    (D) it was a region of potentially volatile nationalist sentiment

63. Which of the following is NOT true of industrialization in the nineteenth century?
    (A) The Second Industrial Revolution was based on mechanization in the textile industry.
    (B) After the 1850s, industrial machines were often run by electricity.
    (C) Railroads were a key element of industrialization.
    (D) Belgium became the first industrialized state of continental Europe.

64. Which of the following was a problem encountered by both the United States and Latin America in the period 1750 to 1914?
    (A) Dependence on primary levels of production
    (B) Conflicts with indigenous peoples
    (C) Well-defined social classes
    (D) Assertion of power by military leaders

65. In which order did the following events occur?
    (A) Suez crisis, creation of Israel, Iranian revolution, Iran–Iraq War
    (B) Iranian revolution, Suez crisis, creation of Israel, Iran–Iraq War
    (C) Creation of Israel, Suez crisis, Iranian revolution, Iran–Iraq War
    (D) Creation of Israel, Iranian revolution, Iran–Iraq War, Suez crisis

66. The country with the largest Muslim population is located in
    (A) the Middle East
    (B) Southeast Asia
    (C) East Asia
    (D) North Africa

67. In the twentieth century, external migration patterns were usually
    (A) from rural to urban areas
    (B) from urban to rural areas
    (C) from developed to developing nations
    (D) from developing to developed nations

68. The world region below that has experienced the most rapid recent industrial growth is
    (A) North America
    (B) Latin America
    (C) North Africa
    (D) Western Europe

69. All of the following were true of the Iranian Revolution EXCEPT that
    (A) it led to more restrictive policies for Iranian women
    (B) it resulted in a war with Iraq
    (C) it involved traditional Islamic sectarian divisions
    (D) it reflected pro-foreign sentiment

70. Which of the following is NOT true concerning globalization?
    (A) Regional trade organizations have risen in response to the World Trade Organization.
    (B) Guest workers have been frequent victims of violence.
    (C) The AIDS crisis is especially prevalent in Southeast Asia.
    (D) Woman suffrage is almost universal.

End of Section I

› Answers and Explanations

1. A Both Christianity and Buddhism share these three characteristics. Islam (B) did not establish monasteries. Hinduism (C) did not have monasteries and had a rigorous caste system. Judaism did not have monasteries and did not generally spread along trade routes (D).

2. D Both had weak rulers at the end of their rule, leading to government by generals. Only Han China developed advanced navigational technology (A). Han China paid tribute to the Xiongnu along its borders (B). Both had slaves (C).

3. C The Hindu caste system was based on skin color. Descent was patrilineal (A), and social structures were based on Aryan traditions (B). Social mobility was almost nonexistent because of the strict caste system (D).

4. A The correct order of introduction is: the Eightfold Path, the *Analects,* the Gospels, and the *Quran.*

5. B Arabs connected with trade routes in the Arabian peninsula, while the Vikings connected with northern European trade routes. The Vikings later adopted Christianity after settling in Europe (A). The Vikings were concerned more with exploration and conquest than with the diffusion of their culture (C). Only the Arabs expanded in the Mediterranean world (D).

6. B Europeans were not involved in Indian Ocean trade until the fifteenth century. Silk Roads trade was active in this period and included Indian Ocean trade routes (A). East African Swahili states were an active part of Indian Ocean trade (C), which was dominated by Muslim merchants in this period (D).

7. B African slaves were carried to the Mediterranean basin and also to India. Silk Roads trade routes were protected by the Mongols (A). Trade routes involved both overland trade and sea lanes (C) and were connected to Western Europe, most notably Islamic Spain (D).

8. C Although it was not mechanized, the Chinese iron industry was active. India (D) had a prosperous cotton domestic industry, whereas the other areas mentioned did not have any sort of industrial structure within the time period.

9. B Like the feudal lord in Western Europe, the *shogun* granted land and other benefits to the *samurai* warrior class.

10. B Islamic women initially could engage in local trade and run small businesses; during this time period, however, the custom of seclusion and the wearing of the veil was instituted. European women gained a degree of status during the medieval period, but regressed somewhat during the Renaissance (A). Hinduism retained its traditional patriarchal society in India (C). African women continued to have a voice in village and tribal decisions (D).

11. B Buddhism spread to Korea from China during the Han dynasty. Islam spread to Indonesia (A). India was the homeland of Buddhism (C). Buddhism spread from India to Sri Lanka, or Ceylon (D).

12. A Regional states had arisen in Europe at this time, while local African kingdoms began merging into regional states, with Kongo as an example. Trans-Saharan gold–salt trade was very active (C). Christianity had reached East Africa, but it was not dominant in the region; Islam was prominent in East Africa (B). Bantu societies became regional kingdoms (D).

13. A The Mongols, not known for their administrative efficiency, brought foreign administrators into China. *Kamikaze* winds prevented the Mongol invasions of Japan in the thirteenth century (B). Christians were tolerated (C). Mongols forbade intermarriage between Mongols and Chinese (D).

14. D The Chinese hoped the magnificence of their expedition would open up new trade opportunities in the Indian Ocean. Europeans were interested in trade (A). The Chinese were motivated by displaying their military power and trade dominance (B). European trade increased in the late fifteenth century (C).

15. D The Americas were outside the global network until after the arrival of Columbus. In 1450, the American Indians north of Mexico did not have written languages (A). There is evidence of trade routes between present-day Mexico and the Southwest United States before 1450 (B). Trans-Atlantic trade connections began with the Columbian Exchange (C).

16. D Only about 5 percent of Africans who crossed the Atlantic were destined for British North America, and most of them arrived in the West Indies before being sent to British North America. Slaves were used extensively on the sugar plantations of Spanish America (B), the Caribbean (C), and Brazil, as well as in the mines of Mexico (A).

17. B The Spanish had already completed the reconquest of Christian territories from the Muslims in 1492. The remaining responses describe European motives for colonization.

18. C The panel is from the façade of the Cathedral of Florence and was designed during the Italian Renaissance.

19. D During the same time period as the Italian Renaissance, Mesoamerican societies constructed massive pyramids and temples in addition to the Aztec capital of Tenochtitlán with its system of causeways. European women experienced a decline in their status during the same time period (A). European serfs were beginning to escape to towns and to Eastern European lands to work for pay (B). Japan was isolated during its feudal era (C).

20. D Portuguese and other Europeans simply magnified African trade routes already in existence. All parts of Africa were involved (A). While some African monarchs opposed the slave trade, many supported it as a source of wealth and technology (B). Within Africa, women were more highly valued as domestic slaves (C).

21. D Neo-Confucianism's emphasis on respect for authority made the Chinese philosophy popular throughout the Tokugawa Shogunate. Christians were persecuted (A). The Dutch gained trading privileges (B). Japan developed its own art forms, such as Kabuki theater (C).

22. B The decline of the power of the papacy as a result of the Protestant Reformation strengthened the power of monarchs and nation-states. The Roman Catholic Church preserved its traditional teachings (A). Both the new Protestant churches and the Roman Catholic Church emphasized education as a result of the Reformation (C). Protestants allowed, and even encouraged, capitalist ventures (D).

23. D Byzantium was weakened by both the Seljuk and Ottoman Turks, as well as by states established by Germanic invaders of the Western empire. Byzantium had adequate military technology, including "Greek fire" (A). Byzantium was losing, not expanding, its territory (B). Trade routes continued to flourish, even after the fall of Byzantium (C).

24. B "Proletariat" is a term used in *The Communist Manifesto* to describe the working class. The other documents listed do not speak of the "proletariat."

25. A The proletariat refers to the working class.

26. C African commercial institutions did not transfer to American culture. Elements of African language have influenced the Gullah language of the southeastern United States as well as dialects used by some African Americans (A). Agricultural knowledge of African slaves was prized, especially on the sugar plantations of the Caribbean and Brazil, and the rice paddies of the southern United States (B). African religious practices often blended with Catholicism, especially in Latin America (D).

27. A Submarine cables, invented in the 1850s, made possible the transmission of messages between Europe and Asia in a few hours. There were no intense rivalries among major Asian nations until the very end of the nineteenth century, long after imperialism was well established (B). Christianity was unpopular in Asia in the nineteenth century (C). Asian economies were prosperous from regional and long-distance trade (D).

28. C In 1904–1905, Japan engaged in war with Russia over domination of Korea. Japan forced Korea to accept an unequal treaty with Japan (A) and negotiated an unequal treaty between itself and China (B). Japan restored its traditional imperial family (D).

29. D The Indian people learned to use the monsoons to their advantage in trade and agriculture. India's religious diversity (Hindu, Buddhist, Muslim) has prevented social and political unity (A). Its landscape (mountains, plateaus, fertile farmlands, and seacoasts) and its economic variety (farming, fishing, trading, and textile manufacturing) created a number of distinct societies within one sub-continent (B, C).

30. **D** Within the Chinese spheres of influence, foreigners were granted the right of extraterritoriality. Although the Ottoman Empire declined, especially after 1750, it became dependent on Western technology and, in turn, granted Western powers extraterritoriality. The other nations listed were not involved in extending this privilege.

31. **D** Both the Indian National Congress and the Young Turks of the Ottoman Empire supported reform as the best method to combat imperialism. In 1906, the Indian National Congress joined with the Muslim League (A) to support Indian self-rule (B). The Indian National Congress articulated grievances against British imperialism (C).

32. **C** The road map shows an unobstructed path when following the middle of the road, while the actual road is filled with huge potholes. The figure of Uncle Sam is giving a sign of approval to the journey (A). The problem areas are many and deep (B). Both Palestine and Israel are steering through the course (D).

33. **B** The camp scene represents one of the key issues complicating peace efforts in the Middle East: the issue of a homeland for Palestinian refugees forced to live in refugee camps.

34. **A** African independence movements provided a spark for the U.S. Civil Rights Movement. The Cold War caused some African states to depend on U.S. aid, and others on assistance from the Soviet Union (B). Ethnic divisions continued (C). The French colony of Algeria won its independence only after a long, violent struggle (D).

35. **C** Soviet and Chinese women bore arms in World War II. American women worked in factories in a temporary capacity only (A). Japanese and German women were expected to remain at home and raise children (B, D).

36. **B** Biodiversity, or the maintenance of a variety of species of animals and plants, is diminished by increased agricultural activity. Urbanization also reduces biodiversity (D). Air pollution releases excessive carbon dioxide, which produces global warming (A), which, in turn, poses the risk of a rise in sea levels and resultant flooding (C).

37. **C** Sumer traded with Indian peoples, while Egypt concentrated more on regional trade. Egypt was more isolated by its desert and sea barriers, allowing it to develop its culture more independently (B). Both civilizations had polytheistic religions (A). Sumer established more and larger urban areas than did Egypt, which remained a village-based civilization (D).

38. **C** The map is one of colonial possessions in Africa prior to World War I. Only a few regions of Africa had been divided into colonies by 1850 (B), and none were colonized by 1800 (A). All of Africa was decolonized by 1990, making response (D) incorrect. Clues to the identification of the political boundaries on the map as European colonies are the shape of Egypt and the large expanse of territory in western and northern Africa that was colonized by France.

39. **C** The three concentric circles represent the Trinity; the fish represents Jesus Christ; and the shell, Christian Baptism.

40. **A** According to Buddhist belief, nirvana, a state of perfect peace, can be reached by going through a number of reincarnations (D). Buddhism rejected the caste system (B). Buddhism is not polytheistic; some Buddhists regard Buddha as a god, an idea that Buddha himself rejected (C).

41. **D** Confucius is not considered a god. Confucianism is responsible for the civil service exam (A). Confucianism stressed filial piety, or obedience and respect to parents and elders (B) and has been associated with patriarchal society (C).

42. **B** The population statistics and import patterns suggest a developing country that trades widely with African countries. The country represented is the Democratic Republic of Congo.

43. **D** King Leopold II of Belgium originally colonized the Congo as his personal possession. Later, his violation of human rights caused the transfer of the Congo to Belgium. The trade relationship between the Democratic Republic of Congo and Belgium, therefore, is a result of colonization rather than merely one produced by globalization (A) or multinational corporations (B). The Congo did not participate in trans-Saharan trade (C).

44. **A** The slow population growth is a result of China's one-child policy, while the age distribution and large GDP indicate a country in transition from a developing to an industrialized nation. The top two import partners also are logical trade partners for China. Bangladesh is not a major exporter and has a small adult population (B). Canada has a much larger older population (D). India has a much higher rate of population growth (C).

45. **A** The stateless society, based on tribal or clan relationships, was the most common political form. After 1000, kingdoms (B), and empires (D) arose. Africans did not form city-states (C).

46. **A** Europeans encountered Middle Eastern peoples who taught them about sugarcane cultivation. Europe expanded into the North Atlantic and Baltic territories (B). Australians did not develop agriculture until their encounter with Europeans in the eighteenth century (C). Mongols and Turks continued their nomadic lives (D).

47. **D** Swahili emerged from an encounter between the migrating Bantu and Arabs on the east coast of Africa. Urdu is a language of Pakistan (A). Proto-Bantu is the language family from which the Bantu languages developed (B). Arabic came from the Arabian peninsula (C).

48. **D** The vast Mongol Empire stretched from Persia to China to Russia. While warfare temporarily interfered with trade on occasion, the Mongols were noted for their facilitation of trade along established Eurasian routes (A). They occupied Vietnam temporarily, but were unable to adapt to its climate and did not annex its territory (B). The Mongols controlled Russia by discouraging Russian trade with the West (C).

49. **B** The Manila galleons carried trade between China and Mexico from the sixteenth to the nineteenth centuries. The other choices were societies that had no trade contacts.

50. **D** Christian missionary journeys were disrupted during the time of the bubonic plague. Roman Catholicism was popular in Sicily and Spain (A) but unpopular among East Asians (B) and Mongols (C).

51. **C** Whereas many slaves came from central Africa, the majority came from western Africa.

The Portuguese carried slaves to islands such as the Madeira and Canary Islands (A). Africans did not recognize private property; slaves were a sign of wealth (B). Muslims tapped into African slave routes to carry slaves to the Mediterranean (D).

52. **B** The monsoons could be used to facilitate navigation from China, throughout the Indian Ocean, and on to East Africa. Portuguese dominance decreased after 1600 (A). English merchants concentrated on Indian trade (C). Joint-stock companies limited commercial risks (D).

53. **B** The time frame of the war (1756–1763) was during a period of Dutch and English dominance in the Indian Ocean. Because it involved Europe, the Americas, and India (D), it was the first global war (A). It laid the basis for 150 years of British imperial dominance (C).

54. **B** Catherine the Great prevented Enlightenment thought from having too large a sway over Russian politics. Under the Tokugawa Shogunate, Japan became more centralized (C). Choices (A) and (D) are also correct.

55. **D** By 1800, the most urbanized nation was Great Britain, with about 75 percent of its population living in cities. Britain was followed by Continental Europe, the United States, and Japan.

56. **A** The Russians expanded into the territories of the Ottoman Empire, which was too weak to stop them. Siberia was opened up in the sixteenth century (B). In the late eighteenth century, Russia participated with Austria and Prussia in the partition of Poland (C). Russia's pro-Slavic movement created an alliance with the Balkan Slavic states based on a common Slavic culture (D).

57. **B** Although foreign merchants were allowed to trade in a few ports in China (C), the activities of foreign merchants were closely monitored. The Chinese were especially impressed by European clocks (A). Chinese authorities denied their subjects opportunities to create trading companies (D).

58. **A** Although Europeans brought their technology to Africa, they failed to adequately train indigenous peoples in its use and maintenance. Plantation products created a single cash crop

designed to meet European needs (B). Plantation schedules and demands disrupted daily African life (C). African families had fewer men to work their village lands, resulting in the cultivation of fewer crops and subsequent malnutrition (D).

59. B Unequal treaties were signed with Britain and Japan. The Boxer Rebellion against foreign intervention (A) and the opium trade with Britain (C) weakened the Qing Empire. The Chinese lost authority over the tributary states of Burma, Korea, and Vietnam (D).

60. B Both Japanese and Russian governments sponsored rapid industrialization in the late nineteenth century. Although the power of Japan was rising, that of Russia was in gradual decline (A). Although the Japanese were well educated, the masses of Russian peasants were not (C). Both had centralized governments during the time period (D).

61. C Western European nations concentrated on colonies in Africa, Asia, and Oceania; the United States on Pacific islands and economic imperialism in Latin America; and Japan on Korea and Asian Russian territories. Europeans did not settle in large numbers in Southeast Asia (A). Raw materials from colonies became an integral part of world trade (B). Colonies did not purchase large quantities of Western manufactured goods (D).

62. C Except for Russia, which wanted to include Serbia in its Pan-Slavic movement (A), Europe's imperialist powers were forced on non-Western nations. The Balkans were composed of a number of countries, some under the Austro-Hungarian Empire, others under the Ottomans (B). Intense nationalist sentiment made the Balkans potentially volatile (D), especially in the general global framework of nationalism in the nineteenth century.

63. A The Second Industrial Revolution was based on electricity and steel. Railroads were key to industrialization, with both a major railway for Canada and a transcontinental railway constructed in the United States. Japan also built a network of railways (D). Responses (B), and (C) also are correct.

64. B The United States engaged in conflicts with Native Americans while Latin Americans, especially those in Argentina and Chile, also pushed aside native peoples. While the United States industrialized, Latin America continued to provide primarily raw materials (A). Latin American society was more stratified than that of the United States (C). *Caudillos,* or military leaders, often came to power in Latin America (D).

65. C is the correct sequence.

66. B Indonesia, the country with the largest Muslim population, is located in Southeast Asia.

67. D Most people who migrated during the twentieth century migrated from developing to developed nations to acquire a better economic future. Choices (A) and (B) are both cases of internal migration. Although the twentieth century saw a pattern like (C), it was not the most common.

68. B Latin America has seen the most rapid industrial growth, especially in Brazil.

69. D The Iranian Revolution was especially hostile to the United States, which had supported the regime of Shah Pahlavi, who was overthrown by the revolt. The revolt imposed greater restrictions on Islamic women, including the wearing of the veil in public (A). Hussein of Iraq took advantage of Iran's revolt to attempt an invasion of Iran (B). The revolution brought into power a group of very traditional Shi'ites (C).

70. C The AIDS crisis is especially widespread in sub-Saharan Africa. Regional trade organizations such as ASEAN, NAFTA, and the European Union have risen in response to the WTO (A). Guest workers from Africa and Asia have experienced violence from antiforeign protestors in Europe (B). Most women have the right to vote but many fewer opportunities to hold office than men (D).

Section II

DOCUMENT-BASED QUESTION (DBQ)

Suggested reading time—10 minutes
Suggested writing time—40 minutes

1. Using the documents and your knowledge of world history, analyze imperialism as a positive and negative force in the nineteenth-century world.

Document 1

Source: William Bentinck, head of the British East India Company, from a speech, 1829.

Whether the question be to continue or to discontinue the practice of *sati*, the decision is equally surrounded by an awful responsibility. To consent to the consignment year after year of hundreds of innocent victims to a cruel and untimely end, when the power exists of preventing it, is a predicament which no conscience can contemplate without horror. But, on the other hand, if heretofore received opinions are to be considered of any value, to put to hazard by a contrary course the very safety of the British Empire in India, and to extinguish at once all hopes of those great improvements . . . is an alternative which even in the light of humanity itself may be considered as a still greater evil.

Document 2

Source: Thomas Babington Macaulay, resident of Calcutta and member of the British "Supreme Council for India," "Minutes of 2 February 1835 on Indian Education."

All parties seem to be agreed on one point, that the dialects commonly spoken among the natives of this part of India, contain neither literary nor scientific information, and are, moreover, so poor and rude that, until they are enriched from some other quarter, it will not be easy to translate any valuable work into them. . . . What then shall that language be? One-half of the Committee maintain that it should be the English. The other half strongly recommend the Arabic and Sanskrit. The whole question seems to me to be, which language is the best worth knowing?

The intrinsic superiority of the Western literature is, indeed, fully admitted by those members of the Committee who support the Oriental plan of education.

Document 3

Source: Kaiser Wilhelm II, German leader, "Speech to the North German Regatta Association," 1901.

It will now be my task to see to it that this place in the sun shall remain our undisputed possession, in order that the sun's rays may fall fruitfully upon our activity and trade in foreign parts, that our industry and agriculture may develop within the state and our sailing sports upon the water, for our future lies upon the water. The more Germans go out upon the waters, whether it be in races or regattas, whether it be in journeys across the ocean, or in the service of the battle flag, so much the better it will be for us.

Document 4

Source: Dadabhai Naoroji, the first South Asian member of Parliament, from The Benefits of British Rule, 1871.

The Benefits of British Rule for India:

Peace and order. Freedom of speech and liberty of the press. Higher political knowledge and aspirations. Improvement of government in the native states. Security of life and property. Freedom from oppression caused by the caprice or greed of despotic rulers, and from devastation by war. Equal justice between man and man (sometimes vitiated by partiality to Europeans). Services of highly educated administrators, who have achieved the above-mentioned results . . .

Loans for railways and irrigation. Development of a few valuable products, such as indigo, tea, coffee, silk, etc. Increase of exports. Telegraphs . . .

The Detriments of British Rule:

In the Cause of Humanity: Nothing. Everything, therefore, is in your favor under this heading . . .

Repeated breach of pledges to give the natives a fair and reasonable share in the higher administration of their own country, which has much shaken confidence in the good faith of the British word. Political aspirations and the legitimate claim to have a reasonable voice in the legislation and the imposition and disbursement of taxes, met to a very slight degree, thus treating the natives of India not as British subjects, in whom representation is a birthright . . .

The natives call the British system . . . the "knife of sugar."

Document 5

Source: Moshweshewe, Chief of the Basuto people, from a letter to Sir George Grey, 1858.

Boers asked permission to live upon our borders. I was led to believe they would live with me as my own people lived, that is, looking to me as to a father and a friend . . .

But instead of this, I now heard that the Boers consider all those farms as their own, and were buying and selling them one to the other, and driving out by one means or another my own people.

Document 6

Source: Jules Ferry, premier of France, from "Speech before the French National Assembly," 1883.

Yes, what is needed for our great industry . . . is export markets. Why? Because our neighbor Germany is surrounded by barriers, and across the ocean, the United States of America has become protectionist . . . shrinking its great markets and making access more difficult for our industrial products. Also, these great states are beginning to pour products never before seen into our own markets . . .

It must be stated publicly that, in effect, superior races have rights over inferior races . . .

[France] cannot be merely a free country; she must also be a mighty country, exercising all of her rightful influence over the destiny of Europe, that she ought to spread this influence throughout the world and carry everywhere possible her language, her customs, her flag, her weapons, and her genius.

Document 7

Source: Fifty-fifth Congress of the United States of America, from a joint resolution for annexing the Hawaiian Islands to the United States, December 6, 1898.

The existing laws of the United States relative to public lands shall not apply to such lands in the Hawaiian Islands; but the Congress of the United States shall enact special laws for their management and disposition; Provided, That all revenue from or proceeds of the same, except as regards such part thereof as may be used or occupied for the civil, military, or naval purposes of the United States, or may be assigned for the use of the local government, shall be used solely for the benefit of the inhabitants of the Hawaiian Islands for educational and other public purposes.

Document 8

Source: Queen Liliuokalani of Hawaii, from a letter to the House of Representatives of the United States, December 19, 1898.

I, Liliuokalani of Hawaii, named heir apparent on the 10th day of April, 1877, and proclaimed queen of the Hawaiian Islands on the 29th day of January, 1801, do hereby protest against the assertion of ownership by the United States of America of the so-called Hawaiian Crown Lands amounting to about one million acres and which are my property, and I especially protest against such assertion of ownership as a taking of property without the process of law and without just or other compensation.

CONTINUITY AND CHANGE OVER TIME ESSAY

Suggested writing time—40 minutes

Directions: *Write an essay on the following topic:*

2. Analyze the political, social, and economic changes that occurred between 1750 and the present in ONE of the following regions. Be sure to discuss the status of the region in 1750.

sub-Saharan Africa   Southwest Asia (Middle East)

COMPARATIVE ESSAY

Suggested writing time—40 minutes

Directions: *Write an essay on the following topic:*

3. Compare external migration in TWO of the following regions during the period 1914 to the present.

Western Europe   Southwest Asia (Middle East)   North America

Comments on Possible Solutions to the Free Response Questions

Document-Based Question

A good answer may begin by dividing the documents into those written by citizens of imperialist nations and those written by subject peoples. Among the opinions of inhabitants of imperialist nations included in the documents are that imperialism and the improvements it can bring are the duty of industrialized nations (Documents 1, 6). The changes brought by imperialism are beneficial to subject peoples (Documents 1, 4, 7). The force of nationalism is present in some arguments favoring imperialism (Documents 3, 6). Trade between colonizing powers and colonies is a benefit necessary and appropriate to the welfare of colonizing nations (Documents 3, 6). The notion that Western nations are superior and should spread their superior cultures through colonization is another issue (Documents 2, 6).

The opinions of subject peoples may be further divided into those reflecting advantages and others speaking of disadvantages. Document 4 addresses both benefits and disadvantages of British rule. Document 5 speaks of the willingness of the Basuto people to cooperate with imperialists and how this cooperation was used against the Basuto. Document 8 echoes the sentiment of Document 5 in protesting the loss of private property to imperialists.

Point of view is found in all eight documents. For example, representatives of imperialist nations and trading companies have a vested interest in those institutions. Native leaders of subject peoples are expected to protest loss of property to imperialist nations. Additional documents that would broaden the interpretation of the subject include documents of comments from the nonruling classes from both imperialist nations and subject peoples. Government statistics might also substantiate or refute claims that imperialism is beneficial.

Continuity and Change over Time Essay

A good response concerning sub-Saharan Africa may begin with a discussion of the depopulation and demoralization brought to Africa by the Atlantic and Indian Ocean slave trades. Some West African coastal states acquired great wealth through the slave trade. The mid-nineteenth century saw the beginnings of European imperialism in sub-Saharan Africa. With imperialists came Christian missionaries. Political boundaries were imposed on the Africans, village life was destroyed as ethnic groups were broken up, and plantation economies destroyed local agriculture. Africans served as support personnel and in combat on behalf of their colonizing nations during World Wars I and II, hoping to gain independence in return. Independence was gradually achieved after World War II. After independence, colonial boundaries were largely maintained and economic prosperity was elusive. Control of Africa's resources often produced bitter disputes, and ethnic rivalries and violence increased. In the twentieth century, trade declined, AIDS spread throughout sub-Saharan Africa, and famine and civil war added to the devastation. By the end of the twentieth century, the exportation of African art was capturing worldwide attention.

In 1750, the Middle East saw the steady decline of the Ottoman Empire. The empire's emphasis on the production of raw materials resulted in reliance on Western technology and grants of extraterritoriality to westerners. Tanzimet reforms and the programs of the Young Turks came too late to effect permanent change. Nationalist sentiment among the empire's various ethnic groups further weakened it politically. After World War II, the empire was broken up and its territories organized as mandates.

After World War II, the Middle East also saw the formation of the state of Israel and the displacement of Palestinians from their homeland. Tension between Arabs and Israelis have erupted in frequent warfare since 1948 and continues to the present. The discovery of oil in the Middle East in the early twentieth century added to the strategic significance of the region.

In the late twentieth and early twenty-first centuries, Islamic dictatorships and terrorists have been the focus of Middle Eastern relations with the West. Islamic fundamentalism has continued to impede progress for women in some Middle Eastern countries. Much of the Middle East suffers economically because of corrupt and irresponsible governments. Terrorist attacks on the United States and U.S. possessions have produced intermittent warfare against Islamic extremism in the region.

Comparative Essay

A good response regarding migration to Western Europe may begin with the Soviet expulsion of ethnic Germans back to Germany after World War II. Beginning in the 1960s, large movements of guest workers from Turkey and North Africa into Europe began. Many of these workers became permanent residents of Europe, often prompting violent racial tensions by neo-Nazis and skinheads. Western Europe also has seen temporary migration in the form of mass tourism.

Migration to North America in the twentieth century included Europeans seeking better economic conditions after World War I, and European Jews fleeing the oncoming threat of Nazism before World War II. Emigration from Europe to the United States and Canada continued after World War II. Central Americans have migrated into Mexico, with the United States as their ultimate destination. After the Vietnam War in the 1970s, boat people from South Vietnam migrated to the west coast of the United States. Like Europe, the United States has seen a considerable influx of tourists. In both the case of Europe and the United States, migration followed the more common pattern of movement from developing to developed regions.

Migration to Southwest Asia involved Jews from Europe and other locations to Israel, especially after 1948. Current migration into the Middle East often involves foreign workers from developed nations moving to Southwest Asia to work in the oil fields. Here the migration pattern is from developed to developing nations, the reverse of the pattern of migration to Europe and the United States.

Immigrants often faced discrimination from native inhabitants fearing job loss to immigrants. Migrants have often formed their own communities where they carried on their own traditions.

PRACTICE TEST TWO

Answer Sheet

1 Ⓐ Ⓑ Ⓒ Ⓓ
2 Ⓐ Ⓑ Ⓒ Ⓓ
3 Ⓐ Ⓑ Ⓒ Ⓓ
4 Ⓐ Ⓑ Ⓒ Ⓓ
5 Ⓐ Ⓑ Ⓒ Ⓓ
6 Ⓐ Ⓑ Ⓒ Ⓓ
7 Ⓐ Ⓑ Ⓒ Ⓓ
8 Ⓐ Ⓑ Ⓒ Ⓓ
9 Ⓐ Ⓑ Ⓒ Ⓓ
10 Ⓐ Ⓑ Ⓒ Ⓓ
11 Ⓐ Ⓑ Ⓒ Ⓓ
12 Ⓐ Ⓑ Ⓒ Ⓓ
13 Ⓐ Ⓑ Ⓒ Ⓓ
14 Ⓐ Ⓑ Ⓒ Ⓓ
15 Ⓐ Ⓑ Ⓒ Ⓓ
16 Ⓐ Ⓑ Ⓒ Ⓓ
17 Ⓐ Ⓑ Ⓒ Ⓓ
18 Ⓐ Ⓑ Ⓒ Ⓓ
19 Ⓐ Ⓑ Ⓒ Ⓓ
20 Ⓐ Ⓑ Ⓒ Ⓓ
21 Ⓐ Ⓑ Ⓒ Ⓓ
22 Ⓐ Ⓑ Ⓒ Ⓓ
23 Ⓐ Ⓑ Ⓒ Ⓓ
24 Ⓐ Ⓑ Ⓒ Ⓓ
25 Ⓐ Ⓑ Ⓒ Ⓓ

26 Ⓐ Ⓑ Ⓒ Ⓓ
27 Ⓐ Ⓑ Ⓒ Ⓓ
28 Ⓐ Ⓑ Ⓒ Ⓓ
29 Ⓐ Ⓑ Ⓒ Ⓓ
30 Ⓐ Ⓑ Ⓒ Ⓓ
31 Ⓐ Ⓑ Ⓒ Ⓓ
32 Ⓐ Ⓑ Ⓒ Ⓓ
33 Ⓐ Ⓑ Ⓒ Ⓓ
34 Ⓐ Ⓑ Ⓒ Ⓓ
35 Ⓐ Ⓑ Ⓒ Ⓓ
36 Ⓐ Ⓑ Ⓒ Ⓓ
37 Ⓐ Ⓑ Ⓒ Ⓓ
38 Ⓐ Ⓑ Ⓒ Ⓓ
39 Ⓐ Ⓑ Ⓒ Ⓓ
40 Ⓐ Ⓑ Ⓒ Ⓓ
41 Ⓐ Ⓑ Ⓒ Ⓓ
42 Ⓐ Ⓑ Ⓒ Ⓓ
43 Ⓐ Ⓑ Ⓒ Ⓓ
44 Ⓐ Ⓑ Ⓒ Ⓓ
45 Ⓐ Ⓑ Ⓒ Ⓓ
46 Ⓐ Ⓑ Ⓒ Ⓓ
47 Ⓐ Ⓑ Ⓒ Ⓓ
48 Ⓐ Ⓑ Ⓒ Ⓓ
49 Ⓐ Ⓑ Ⓒ Ⓓ
50 Ⓐ Ⓑ Ⓒ Ⓓ

51 Ⓐ Ⓑ Ⓒ Ⓓ
52 Ⓐ Ⓑ Ⓒ Ⓓ
53 Ⓐ Ⓑ Ⓒ Ⓓ
54 Ⓐ Ⓑ Ⓒ Ⓓ
55 Ⓐ Ⓑ Ⓒ Ⓓ
56 Ⓐ Ⓑ Ⓒ Ⓓ
57 Ⓐ Ⓑ Ⓒ Ⓓ
58 Ⓐ Ⓑ Ⓒ Ⓓ
59 Ⓐ Ⓑ Ⓒ Ⓓ
60 Ⓐ Ⓑ Ⓒ Ⓓ
61 Ⓐ Ⓑ Ⓒ Ⓓ
62 Ⓐ Ⓑ Ⓒ Ⓓ
63 Ⓐ Ⓑ Ⓒ Ⓓ
64 Ⓐ Ⓑ Ⓒ Ⓓ
65 Ⓐ Ⓑ Ⓒ Ⓓ
66 Ⓐ Ⓑ Ⓒ Ⓓ
67 Ⓐ Ⓑ Ⓒ Ⓓ
68 Ⓐ Ⓑ Ⓒ Ⓓ
69 Ⓐ Ⓑ Ⓒ Ⓓ
70 Ⓐ Ⓑ Ⓒ Ⓓ

PRACTICE TEST TWO

Section I

Time—55 minutes
70 Questions

Directions: Each of the incomplete statements or questions below is followed by four answer choices. Choose the answer that is best and write the letter of your choice on the answer sheet supplied.

1. Which of the following belief systems emerged from political disorder, did not worship a deity, and remained primarily regional beliefs?

   (A) Buddhism and Hinduism
   (B) Confucianism and Islam
   (C) Judaism and Islam
   (D) Confucianism and Daoism

2. Which of the following is true of both the Roman Empire and the Gupta Empire?

   (A) Both had centralized governments with established infrastructures.
   (B) Both depended on long-distance maritime trade.
   (C) Both relied heavily on forced labor.
   (D) Both were followed by centuries of global rule.

3. Which of the following statements draws an accurate similarity between early agricultural societies in the Americas and those in the Eastern Hemisphere?

   (A) American societies were matriarchal, while those in the Eastern Hemisphere were patriarchal.
   (B) Agricultural societies in both hemispheres were polytheistic.
   (C) Both groups of societies relied on human muscle rather than on technology to carry out manual labor.
   (D) Societies in the Western Hemisphere relied more on the flooding patterns of rivers than did those in the Eastern Hemisphere.

4. Which of the following concepts was introduced after the other four?

   (A) The Four Noble Truths
   (B) The covenant relationship
   (C) The Five Pillars
   (D) The forgiveness of sins

5. Which of the following reflects a similarity between Arabic settlements of the eighth century and Viking settlements of the ninth century?

   (A) Both established villages along the rivers of Russia.
   (B) Both reached areas of present-day northern France.
   (C) Both diminished intellectual activity in the regions they settled.
   (D) Both groups established settlements in Western Europe.

6. Which of the following is true of Pacific Ocean trade during the period 600 to 1450?

   (A) It was dominated by Malay sailors.
   (B) Pacific islanders concentrated on regional trade.
   (C) It included active trade between Mongol China and Japan.
   (D) Pacific islanders carried on trade with East Asia.

7. A comparison of the travel routes of Marco Polo and Ibn Battuta reveals that

   (A) both traveled throughout Southwest Asia
   (B) both traveled to North Africa
   (C) both traveled through Central Asia
   (D) both traveled to Islamic Europe

8. Which of the following was the most isolated from world trade during the period 600 to 1450?

   (A) Russia
   (B) Japan
   (C) China
   (D) East Africa

9. Japanese and European feudalism were similar in that

   (A) *bushido* and chivalry involved reciprocal relationships
   (B) both were based on group loyalties
   (C) both involved the receipt of contracts
   (D) both ended as their respective regions developed centralized governments

10. In the period between 600 and 1450, which of the following roles were pursued by many Indian and European women?

    (A) Workers in domestic industries and field workers
    (B) Political activists and public speakers
    (C) Long-distance merchants and guild leaders
    (D) Scholars and physicians

11. By 1450, Islam had spread to all of the following regions EXCEPT

    (A) Western Europe
    (B) East Asia
    (C) India
    (D) East Africa

12. In the period between 600 and 1450

    (A) agriculture increased the aboriginal population of Australia
    (B) North American nations north of Mexico were more settled than those of the natives of Mesoamerica
    (C) North American and Mesoamerican societies were connected by trade
    (D) metallurgy was more advanced in Polynesia than in Mesoamerica and South America

13. Which is true of the Mongol Empire?

    (A) It was responsible for spreading Buddhism to Japan.
    (B) It was based upon tribute.
    (C) The Mongols displayed their efficient administrative skills in Persia.
    (D) It imposed harsh rule over Russia.

14. Which of the following is true concerning trade in Eurasia and the Americas in the period 600 to 1450?

    (A) Both involved overland and oceanic trade.
    (B) Trade in Eurasia moved along an east–west axis, while that in the Americas moved along a north–south axis.
    (C) Both involved the interchange of major religions.
    (D) Both involved nomadic peoples as trade facilitators.

15. The journals of Captain James Cook describe one of the societies he encountered as people who placed a greater value on European tools and iron more than on anything else because the only weapons they had were stones. (*Source:* James Cook, *The Journals of Captain Cook.* Ed. by Philip Edwards. London: Penguin, 1999.)
    Which society is described in these journals?

    (A) The Hawaiians
    (B) The people of Madagascar
    (C) The Native Americans
    (D) The Chinese under the Qing dynasty

16. Most plantations in the Americas in the seventeenth and eighteenth centuries produced

    (A) sugar
    (B) cotton
    (C) rice
    (D) indigo

17. The Columbian Exchange

    (A) affected only Europe and the Americas
    (B) reversed America's disease-resistant environment
    (C) created Native American enthusiasm for food crops of the Eastern Hemisphere
    (D) created a permanent labor force of Native Americans for the Europeans

18. The statue above commemorates the founding of the city of

    (A) Calcutta
    (B) Cuzco
    (C) Capetown
    (D) Tenochtitlán

19. Between 1450 and 1750

    (A) Indian Ocean trade became dominated less by Europeans and more by Muslims
    (B) the Ottoman Empire increased production of factory goods for exports
    (C) China's treasury was drained of silver from unequal trade with Europe
    (D) Japan changed its position of initial interest in Western goods to resistance to Western influence

20. All of the following are true regarding the Native Americans of North America north of the Rio Grande River and the Indians of Latin America EXCEPT that

    (A) peoples north of the Rio Grande tended to be settled farmers more often than Indians of Mesoamerica
    (B) natives of the southwest United States traded with Mesoamerican civilizations
    (C) both built massive ceremonial structures
    (D) while most of the natives of Mesoamerica had a written language, those north of the Rio Grande did not

21. Slavery and Russian serfdom were similar in that

    (A) they were both forms of bondage
    (B) both denied personal freedoms
    (C) neither offered a way to escape conditions of servitude
    (D) they were both based on skin color

22. Which of the following did NOT contribute to the fall of the Aztec Empire to the Spaniards?

    (A) Military assistance of Mesoamerican peoples
    (B) Epidemic disease
    (C) Mesoamerican traditions
    (D) The economic weakness of the Aztecs

23. Which country's revolution was both an independence and an antislavery movement?

    (A) Mexico
    (B) Haiti
    (C) Brazil
    (D) Venezuela

24. Karl Marx's use of the term "bourgeoisie" to refer to factory management was also used to describe

    (A) the *ancien regime* in France
    (B) the Western-educated Chinese leaders opposed to the Qing dynasty
    (C) the free black society of Haiti
    (D) the initiators of the French Revolution

25. "Take up the White Man's burden—
    The savage wars of peace—
    Fill full the mouth of Famine
    And bid the sickness cease."
    (Source: Rudyard Kipling, "The White Man's Burden")

    Kipling's poem received its rationale from which of the following nineteenth-century philosophies?

    (A) Conservatism
    (B) Romanticism
    (C) Liberalism
    (D) Social Darwinism

26. Both the wearing of corsets in Europe in the nineteenth century and the custom of footbinding in China were designed

    (A) for use among lower-class women
    (B) to deny women status in their respective society
    (C) to restrict women to work in the fields
    (D) to restrict women's freedom of activity

27. The most useful tool used to trace patterns of migration is

    (A) agricultural methodology
    (B) a deposit of artifacts used in trade
    (C) language diffusion
    (D) disease transmission

28. Japan was more accepting of Western advances than China in the nineteenth century because

    (A) Japan feared the power of Great Britain in East Asia
    (B) Japan feared the power of Korea
    (C) Japanese leaders wanted a democracy patterned after the United States
    (D) Japan recognized the need to open up trade relations with the West in order to increase its national power

29. Which of the following societies did NOT share a similar knowledge of metallurgy?

    (A) Kushites
    (B) Incas
    (C) Bantu peoples
    (D) Aryans

30. The concept of extraterritoriality involves

    (A) unique economic privileges within a foreign country
    (B) the grant of citizenship to foreigners
    (C) the annexation of new territories
    (D) the privileged leagal treatment for foreigners

31. The cartoon above comments on the anti-AIDS efforts of the World Health Organization. Which of the following best summarizes the cartoon?

    (A) AIDS patients are opposed to World Health Organization treatment policies.
    (B) The World Health Organization is making moral judgments against AIDS patients.
    (C) The World Health Organization is winning the war on AIDS one person at a time.
    (D) The efforts of the World Health Organization to solve the AIDS problem are insufficient in light of the problem's severity.

32. Which of the following was NOT the result of colonialism in the period 1750 to 1914?

    (A) Global trade increased significantly.
    (B) National identities among subject peoples were eliminated.
    (C) Global migration increased because of imperialist recruitment of labor forces.
    (D) Sometimes imperialists built a plantation economy around a traditional crop of the colony.

33. The world region most profoundly affected by AIDS is

    (A) North America
    (B) Latin America
    (C) Africa
    (D) Southeast Asia

34. All of the following are true concerning the nationalist struggle in Vietnam EXCEPT

    (A) the French wanted to use Indochina to regain its world status
    (B) unlike other former colonies, the Vietnamese were untouched by the Cold War
    (C) it bore similarities to the American Revolution
    (D) the new South Vietnamese government was unpopular with the general public

35. All of the following are true of World War I EXCEPT

    (A) European colonists from Africa and Asia served as military and support personnel
    (B) the territories of the former Ottoman Empire became independent
    (C) the war's end saw the dissolution of most empires in Europe
    (D) European power declined

36. One of the major problems of the current age is the unequal distribution of income and resources. One explanation for this problem is

    (A) resistance to globalization by new Western nations
    (B) uneven distribution of resources in spite of a worldwide surplus of resources
    (C) the overall failure of the Green Revolution
    (D) the effects of colonialism

37. During classical times

    (A) Malay merchants sailed from Southeast Asia to East Africa
    (B) central Asians guarded trade routes but did not participate in trade themselves
    (C) there was a favorable balance of trade between Rome and China
    (D) North Africa was bypassed by Silk Roads trade

38. The map above illustrates

    (A) areas under Qing dynasty rule in the 1930s
    (B) spheres of influence
    (C) locations of the Taiping Rebellion
    (D) locations of European colonies

39. Which of the following religions is suggested by the symbols above?

    (A) Hinduism
    (B) Buddhism
    (C) Islam
    (D) Judaism

40. Hinduism

    (A) developed many of its ideas from the *Vedas*
    (B) developed the caste system about the time of the birth of Jesus
    (C) believed that reincarnation could move a person to only a higher caste
    (D) developed its caste system based on economic status

41. Which of the following best describes patriarchal relationships?

    (A) They involve abuse of female family members.
    (B) They prevent women from engaging in commercial activity in public.
    (C) Women are secluded behind veils.
    (D) Women's inferior status places them under the protection of male family members.

42. The altar pictured above is found in

    (A) India
    (B) Latin America
    (C) Southeast Asia
    (D) Russia

43. A historian describes China as a country in which the northern region had always surpassed the southern region in education, social structure, and political power. About 600, however, the southern region had begun to overtake northern China.

    All of the following were causes of this exchange EXCEPT
    (A) the introduction of Champa rice
    (B) the construction of the Grand Canal
    (C) provements in navigation
    (D) long-distance trade

44. Which territories were most actively a part of world trade patterns in the first five centuries C.E.?

    (A) Islamic empires
    (B) Australia
    (C) Japan
    (D) The Italian peninsula

45. The oldest permanent communities of African Christians are found in present-day

    (A) Nigeria
    (B) South Africa
    (C) Congo
    (D) Ethiopia

46. The Chinese halted exploration in the 1430s for all of the following reasons EXCEPT

    (A) the expense of the voyages
    (B) pressure from the scholar-gentry
    (C) disinterest in trade
    (D) fear of additional Mongol invasions

47. Which of the following Indo-European languages was spread to India through migration about 1500 B.C.E.?

    (A) Hindi
    (B) Sanskrit
    (C) Arabic
    (D) Mandarin

48. Which of the following is NOT true of the Mongols?

    (A) Their government was organized around kinship groups.
    (B) They improved Persian infrastructure by constructing *qanat* irrigation systems.
    (C) They tended to use local administrators to rule conquered lands.
    (D) They were driven back from Japan by *kamikaze* winds.

49. Conquest united all of the following cultures EXCEPT

    (A) Mongols and Ottoman Turks
    (B) nomadic Berbers from North Africa and the people of Spain
    (C) Ottoman Turks and Byzantines
    (D) Aryans and Indus valley peoples

50. Which of the following is NOT true regarding new crops in the period 1000 to 1450?

    (A) Muslims introduced rice to West Africa.
    (B) Europeans introduced Muslims to refined sugar.
    (C) Cotton became the main textile in sub-Saharan Africa.
    (D) Knowledge acquired during the Crusades affected the economy of the Western Hemisphere.

51. The diaspora of the African population

    (A) resulted in the complete loss of African languages
    (B) created compliant slave societies that did not resist their masters
    (C) sometimes resulted in self-governing communities of runaways
    (D) produced slave communities in Latin America that depended on natural slave increase more than in North America

52. In the sixteenth century, Mediterranean trade was dominated by

    (A) North Africa and Spain
    (B) Portugal and France
    (C) Spain and Portugal
    (D) Muslim Turks and Italian city-states

53. Which of the following is NOT true regarding the Manila galleons?

    (A) Chinese merchants supplied silk goods that were traded with Mexico.
    (B) Most Chinese luxury goods crossed the Atlantic to Spain.
    (C) Asian luxury goods from the galleons did not remain in Mexico.
    (D) European merchants exchanged silver for Chinese gold.

54. Which of the following rulers held the LEAST power over his subjects during the eighteenth century?

    (A) The Russian tsar
    (B) The Qing emperor
    (C) The Japanese emperor
    (D) The Ottoman sultan

55. In the period 1500 to 1800, global population increased with the introduction of new crops from

    (A) the Middle East
    (B) the Americas
    (C) Western Europe
    (D) China

56. By the fifteenth century, Russia had forged the closest cultural ties with

    (A) the Ottoman Turks
    (B) the Byzantine Empire
    (C) the Mongol Empire
    (D) Western Europe

57. How was India changed by foreign influence in the period 1450 to 1750?

    (A) Christian missionaries from Europe were banned.
    (B) The collapse of the Mughal Empire allowed Britain the opportunity to rule India.
    (C) Indian Muslims objected to Mughal rule.
    (D) Hindus accepted the unifying force of the Mughal rulers.

58. In which of the following regions were plantation economies NOT established?

    (A) Indian Ocean islands
    (B) Europe
    (C) Southeast Asia
    (D) Atlantic Ocean islands

59. Which of the following describes the relationship between the Ottoman Empire and European nations from 1750 to 1914?

    (A) The Ottomans lost their territory in Anatolia to European states.
    (B) Nationalist uprisings forced the Ottomans to recognize the independence of Greece and Serbia.
    (C) The Ottomans gained Egypt from France.
    (D) The Ottomans gained territory from the weakening Russian Empire.

60. Which of the following is true regarding Russia in 1914?

    (A) Continuing serfdom weakened its industrial development.
    (B) Its Russification policy promoted ethnic harmony.
    (C) It lost territory to the Ottomans.
    (D) Its economy was unable to manage the tsar's desire for expansion.

61. Which of the following is NOT true of imperialism in Southeast Asia in the period 1750 to 1914?

    (A) Much of central Asia was brought under Russian control.
    (B) By 1900, all of Southeast Asia was under colonial rule.
    (C) The Roman Catholic Church became prominent in Vietnam.
    (D) British-controlled Singapore became an active trade center.

62. In the nineteenth century, the Ottoman and Russian empires were examples of

    (A) nation-states
    (B) socialist empires
    (C) religious toleration
    (D) religious diversity

63. By the middle of the eighteenth century, both China and Great Britain

    (A) had a network of banks and financial institutions
    (B) had accessible deposits of coal
    (C) lacked accessible water transportation
    (D) possessed colonies to supply raw materials

64. Which of the following was true of Latin American society in the period 1750 to 1914?

    (A) Society was egalitarian.
    (B) Few migrants came to Latin America.
    (C) Intellectuals produced works based on Latin American values.
    (D) The Argentine gaucho enjoyed a type of admiration equal to that of the U.S. cowboy.

65. "I believe that it must be the policy of the United States to support free peoples who are resisting attempted subjugation by armed minorities or by outside pressures."

    The quotation above is taken from

    (A) the Monroe Doctrine
    (B) the Roosevelt Corollary
    (C) the Balfour Declaration
    (D) the Truman Doctrine

66. The statement in the quotation from Question 65 illustrates the policy of

    (A) nonalignment
    (B) containment
    (C) appeasement
    (D) nationalism

67. Which of the following is true concerning women in the twentieth century?

    (A) Women were not allowed to bear arms in World War II.
    (B) Soviet women were expected to serve the Communist state by staying home and bearing children.
    (C) Women in Africa and Asia fought in wars for independence, often gaining legal rights.
    (D) In contrast to those in industrial societies, women in developing nations work mainly in low-paying jobs.

68. By 2009, the global economy was characterized by all of the following EXCEPT

    (A) decreased energy consumption in India and China
    (B) conflict over Russia's energy sources
    (C) decreased outsourcing in India
    (D) economic recession

69. Mao Zedong's government

    (A) was unpopular with peasants
    (B) strengthened the Chinese economy through the Great Leap Forward
    (C) enacted policies that improved the status of women
    (D) created a Chinese Renaissance through the Cultural Revolution

70. "West European publics and leaders already perceive a reduced military threat from the Warsaw Pact and will expect continued attempts by the Soviet Union and its East European allies to focus on political and economic relationships with the West, reduce the size of their military forces, and shift resources from defense to civil production."

    In what year was the above document written?

    (A) 1949
    (B) 1962
    (C) 1989
    (D) 2004

End of Section I

› Answers and Explanations

1. **D**—Confucianism and Daoism both arose as a reaction to the turmoil in China at the end of the Zhou dynasty. Neither recognized a deity, and both remained primarily regional belief systems of East Asia. Buddhism emerged from the questions of Siddhartha Gautama concerning the suffering in the world; it spread throughout the Eastern world. Hinduism was an outgrowth of the Aryan culture (A). Islam (B) worships the god Allah, originated in the revelations of Muhammad, and spread throughout the world. Judaism (C) worships Yahweh and is a revealed religion that spread throughout the world via the Jewish diaspora.

2. **A**—Both Rome and Gupta India were centralized governments, although that of Rome was more centrally organized than that of the Gupta. Roman trade concentrated more on its connections to overland routes, while Gupta Indian embraced both overland and, particularly, maritime routes (B). The Gupta Empire relied on the caste system, while the Romans relied heavily on slave labor (C). The Roman Empire deteriorated into local rule after its fall, while the aftermath of Gupta rule was the emergence of regional kingdoms in India (D).

3. **B**—Both the peoples of the Americas and those of the river valley civilizations were polytheists. Both groups of societies were also patriarchal (A). While Sumerians contributed the wheel to the societies of the Eastern Hemisphere, early American peoples relied on human muscle to accomplish their tasks (C). The livelihood of only the river valley civilizations of the Eastern Hemisphere depended upon the flood patterns of rivers (D).

4. **C**—Observance of the Five Pillars is key to Islam, which is the youngest of the belief systems listed. The Four Noble Truths applies to Buddhism (A), the covenant relationship to Judaism (B), and the forgiveness of sins to Christianity (D). The correct sequence is: Judaism, Buddhism, Christianity, and Islam.

5. **D**—The Vikings settled in northern France, while the Arabs settled in Spain. The Vikings traded, and sometimes settled, along the rivers of Russia, while the Arabs did not (A). The Arab advance into northern France was turned back at the Battle of Tours in 732; the Vikings settled in Normandy in northern France about 1000 (B). Although the Vikings were not known for an interest in spreading learning, the Arabs preserved the Greco-Roman culture and contributed their own intellectual advances as well, especially in Spain (C).

6. **B**—During this time period, Pacific islanders concentrated on regional trade from island to island and, therefore, did not include trade with China and Japan (C), nor with other parts of East Asia (D). The Malay sailors concentrated on the Indian Ocean (A).

7. **A**—Both Marco Polo and Ibn Battuta traveled throughout Southwest Asia, or the Middle East. Only Ibn Battuta traveled through North Africa (B) and Islamic Europe (D). Only Marco Polo visited central Asia (C).

8. **B**—The island nation of Japan carried on primarily regional trade under the shogunate. Russia had traded with the Vikings prior to the Mongol period (A), while China and East Africa engaged in Indian Ocean trade (C, D).

9. **D**—Japanese feudalism ended with the rise of the Tokugawa Shogunate and, later, the Meiji Restoration; European feudalism ended with the rise of regional governments and nation-states. Only chivalry was a reciprocal (A) and a contractual (C) relationship. *Bushido* was based on group loyalties (B).

10. **A**—Both Indian and European women worked in producing textiles at home and in agricultural roles. In this time period, neither had opportunities for political activism or public speaking (B). European women could be guild members, but not guild leaders; Indian women had more opportunities in long-distance trade (C). Neither had opportunities to serve as scholars or physicians (D).

11. **B**—Islam did not spread to East Asia during this time period. It had reached the other regions, with Spain as its domain in Western Europe (A).

12. **C**—The societies and empires of Mexico traded as far north as the Anasazi societies of present-day southwestern United States. Agriculture was unknown to Australia during this period (A). The natives of Mesoamerica were more settled (B). Polynesians did not have metal resources (D).

13. **B**—The Mongol Empire was a tribute empire. Mongol influence did not reach Japan (A). Mongols, never gifted administrators, especially relied on local rulers in Persia (C). The Mongols set up a tribute empire in Russia and did not rule it directly (D).

14. **B**—Trade in Eurasia tended to move east and west along both overland and water routes, whereas that in the Americas followed a more north–south pattern. Trade in the Americas was overland (A). The Americas did not exchange major world religions (C). Eurasian trade involved the assistance of nomadic peoples such as the Mongols (D).

15. **A**—The passage describes Captain Cook's meeting the Hawaiians, who lived in Pacific islands noted for their lack of deposits of metals.

16. **A**—Although the other response choices were also produced in the Americas, sugar was the major crop of plantation agriculture.

17. **B**—Prior to the Columbian Exchange, the isolation of the Americas kept the Western Hemisphere largely free of the diseases of the rest of the world. Africa and Asia also benefited from the exchange of American crops (A). Native Americans tended to be unimpressed with foods of the Eastern Hemisphere (C). Native Americans did not serve as a permanent labor force because of their high mortality from European diseases (D).

18. **D**—The Aztecs were told to establish their capital city at the site where they saw an eagle perched on a cactus and holding a snake. According to legend, they found such a site in Lake Texcoco, where they built the capital of Tenochtitlán.

19. **D**—At the beginning of the Tokugawa Shogunate, Japan was open to Western technology, then later suspicious of foreigners and closed trade with the West. Europeans came to dominate Indian Ocean trade more and more as the period progressed (A). The Ottoman Empire continued to depend on the export of raw materials (B). European trade supplied the Chinese with silver (C).

20. **A**—Whereas some of North American tribes were farmers, many of them were nomadic; most Mesoamerican societies were settled agrarian communities. Mesoamericans and North Americans were sometimes trade partners (B). The Moundbuilders of North America and the Mesoamerican societies built large ceremonial pyramids and other structures (C). Only the Mesoamerican societies had a written language in the form of glyphs (D).

21. **A**—Russian serfs were bound to the land, while slaves were bound to their masters. Russian serfs enjoyed some personal freedoms (B). Slaves were sometimes allowed to purchase their freedom or were freed by their masters (C). Only slavery was based on skin color (D).

22. **D**—The Aztec Empire was rich in natural resources and enjoyed a complex infrastructure at the time of the conquest. The Spanish conquest was aided by Mesoamericans conquered by the Aztecs (A). Smallpox took the lives of thousands of Aztecs (B). Mesoamerican traditions included the legend of Quetzalcóatl; the Spanish expedition was received as the possible return of this god (C).

23. **B**—Haiti's revolution, led by black slaves, led to both its independence and abolition.

24. **D**—"Bourgeoisie" also refers to the members of the Third Estate who initiated the French Revolution. The *ancien regime* refers to the old government before the French Revolution (A). The term "bourgeoisie" did not apply to any group associated with the Chinese or Haitian revolutions (B, C).

25. **D**—Social Darwinism, the belief that the fittest in society were destined to prosper, was used to justify imperialism. Conservatism was a political

philosophy advocating strong central, and often monarchical, government (A), whereas liberalism advocated political rights and parliamentary government (C). Romanticism was a literary and artistic movement that valued emotion in its presentations (B).

26. **D**—Footbinding and corsets restricted female activity by making activity painful. Both were more common among women of elite classes (A) and gave women a privileged status (B). Women who participated in these customs were incapable of working in the fields (C).

27. **C**—Patterns of language diffusion are the most accurate tool to trace the paths of migratory peoples. The transmission of agricultural methods (A), trade artifacts (B), and disease (D) is less likely to occur as a result of migration.

28. **D**—The U.S. expedition to Japan and its powerful gunboats convinced Japan that long-distance trade was in its best economic and political interests. Rather than fearing Great Britain, Japan purchased modern warships from the British (A), which it then used to impose its power on Korea (B). Japanese leaders in the Meiji government restored its imperial rulers and set up a parliament (C).

29. **B**—The Incas were not skilled in ironworking. The Kushites of Meröe were among the first people to understand ironworking (A). Both the Bantu peoples (C) and the Aryans (D) spread the knowledge of iron metallurgy.

30. **D**—Extraterritoriality granted foreigners exemption from the laws of the land where they lived. The other choices do not define an element of extraterritoriality.

31. **D**—The size of the AIDS patient in relation to the WHO physician suggests the enormity of the disease in relation to the effectiveness of the treatment. The patient is accepting the treatment willingly (A). The cartoon does not suggest the existence of moral judgments (B). The size of the AIDS figure suggests that the WHO is not winning the AIDS war (C).

32. **B**—Colonialism increased nationalist sentiments among subject peoples. Global trade (A) and migration (C) increased tremendously. An example of choice (D) is British transformation of cotton production into a major cash crop.

33. **C**—Although Haiti in Latin America (B) has a high incidence of AIDS, sub-Saharan Africa is most widely affected by the disease. The other choices have a lower incidence of the disease (A, D).

34. **B**—The Vietnamese were immediately drawn into the Cold War, with the northern government backed by Communist China and the South by the United States. The French hoped to use its colony to regain the status it had lost through the German occupation of France during World War II (A). The Vietnamese under Ho Chi Minh issued a declaration of independence modeled after that of the United States (C). Diem's government, backed by the United States, was unpopular with the South Vietnamese (D).

35. **B**—The former Ottoman territories became mandates, largely under British control. Europe's colonists supported the war in hopes of gaining independence afterward (A). The following empires fell as a result of the war: Russia, Austria–Hungary, Ottoman, and Germany's Second Reich (C). Europe's economic decline led to a decline in world power (D).

36. **D**—Colonialism destroyed local economies. Globalization, not resistance to it, had generated incredible wealth for some nations (A). There has been a depletion of resources worldwide (B). The Green Revolution has increased agricultural productivity, especially in Asian nations (C).

37. **A**—Malay merchants journeyed across the Indian Ocean, transmitting their language and the cultivation of the banana in East Africa. Central Asians participated in Silk Roads trade (B), and sea routes connected Egypt with Silk Roads trade (D). There was a trade imbalance between Rome and China, with the Romans more interested in Chinese trade items than China was in Roman goods (C).

38. **B**—The map illustrates the location of spheres of influence in China in the nineteenth century. The Qing dynasty had been overthrown by the 1930s, making response (A) incorrect. The Taiping

Rebellion was fought only in southern China (C). The areas are not colonial locations (D).

39. **C**—Although authorities disagree on their origin, the crescent and the star have been used to represent Islam.

40. **A**—The *Vedas,* oral literature introduced by the Aryans, became the basis of Hindu belief. The caste system, which was based on skin color (D), developed shortly after the arrival of the Aryans about 1500 B.C.E. (B). Reincarnation could produce movement to a higher or lower caste, depending on one's *karma* (C).

41. **D**—Patriarchal systems have in common the belief in female inferiority. They do not necessarily endorse mistreatment of women (A) nor their seclusion behind veils (C). Some women in patriarchal societies are allowed to engage in business activities (B).

42. **B**—The inclusion of American Indian figures suggests that it is from Latin America. The altar portrayed is located in Balboa, Panama.

43. **B**—The Grand Canal, constructed to transport Champa rice (A) and other crops of southern China to the northern part of the country, was a result, rather than a cause, of the increasing prosperity of southern China. The Chinese improved the sail (C), and overseas trade created port cities in the south (D).

44. **D**—The Italian peninsula was connected to major trade routes throughout all but the last years of the period. Islam was not in existence (A). Australia and Japan were involved in regional trade only (B, C).

45. **D**—Ethiopia, influenced by the Christian Kingdom of Axum, provided the oldest continuous Christian communities in Africa. Christianity spread to Nigeria (A) and the Congo (C) during the period of the new imperialism. The Dutch brought Christianity to South Africa in the seventeenth century (B).

46. **C**—The Chinese continued to remain active in regional trade. The scholar-gentry (B) put pressure on the Ming government to save money (A) to repair the Great Wall in order to repel the threat of future Mongol invasions (D).

47. **B**—Sanskrit, the language of the Aryans, was transmitted through Aryan migration. Hindi developed later in Indian history (A). Arabic developed on the Arabian peninsula (C), whereas Mandarin is a Chinese tongue (D).

48. **B**—The Mongols destroyed the Persian underground irrigation system. Their nomadic society was governed by kinship groups (A). The Mongols preferred to use local administrators to run their conquered territories rather than establish strong central governments (C). Twice in the thirteenth century, Mongol attempts at invading Japan were thwarted by "divine" winds called *kamikaze* (D).

49. **A**—The Mongols and Ottoman Turks had no contacts with each other. In 1711, Berbers conquered Spain; their occupation of Spain contributed Islamic learning to Europe (B). The Ottoman Turks conquered Byzantium, contributing their culture (C). Aryans conquered Indus valley peoples, contributing the Sanskrit language and the *Vedas,* which became the basis for Hinduism (D).

50. **B**—During the Crusades, Muslims taught Christians to refine the sugar from sugarcane. Responses (A) and (C), and (D) are true. The knowledge of sugarcane and refined sugar produced the growth of sugar plantations in the Western Hemisphere (D).

51. **C**—Runaway slaves, or maroons, often founded their own self-governing communities. Many African languages survived in the form of creole tongues (A). Slaves often refused to do work or ran away rather than comply (B). Plantation communities in North America depended more on natural increase than did those in Latin America (D).

52. **D**—The Muslim Ottomans and the wealthy Italian city-states dominated Mediterranean trade in the sixteenth century. This dominance prompted Portugal and Spain to seek routes around Africa and across the Atlantic to reach Eastern trade routes (A, C). French explorers sought a northwest passage through North America to reach Eastern routes (B).

53. **C**—Some Asian goods remained in Mexico, while the majority made their way to Spain to be sold throughout Europe (D). Choices (A) and (B) are true of the Manila galleons.

54. **C**—Under the Tokugawa Shogunate, the Japanese emperor served as a figurehead. The Russian tsar (A), Qing emperor (B), and Ottoman sultan (D) exercised absolute rule over their subject peoples.

55. **B**—Throughout the period, American crops spread throughout most parts of the globe, producing population increases. Although the Ottomans in the Middle East (A), Western Europe (C), and China (D) were largely agricultural lands, the volume of new crops did not match that of the Americas.

56. **B**—Since the tenth century, Russia had traded extensively with the Byzantine Empire and had adopted the Eastern Orthodox religion. The conquest of Byzantium in 1453 did not diminish Russia's cultural ties with Byzantium, nor forge close ties between Russia and the Ottomans (A). Mongol conquests had been eliminated in the fourteenth century (C). Not until the last year of the seventeenth century did Russia begin to westernize to a degree (D).

57. **B**—In the eighteenth century, Mughal collapse allowed the British to extend their commercial interests to political influence in India. The Portuguese port of Goa became a center for Christian missionaries (A). Indian Muslims reacted positively to Mughal rule (C), while Hindus resented Mughal persecution of members of their faith (D).

58. **B**—Agriculture in Europe was based on small farms. Europeans established plantations in the Indian Ocean islands (A). Southeast Asia was a region of rubber plantations (C). Sugarcane plantations were established by the Portuguese and Spanish in the Atlantic islands off the northwest coast of Africa (D).

59. **B.**—Greece and Serbia, both former Ottoman territories, gained their independence in 1839 and 1861, respectively. The Ottomans kept Anatolia (A), but lost Egypt to Napoleon's France (C). The Ottomans lost territory to Russia in central Asia and the Caucasus (D).

60. **D**—The Russian economy was unable to support an enlarging empire. The serfs were emancipated in 1861 (A). Russification failed to unite the various Russian ethnic groups under one culture (B). Russia expanded into Ottoman territory (C).

61. **B**—Siam (present-day Thailand) was left independent to serve as a buffer state between French Indochina and British-controlled Burma. The other statements are true.

62. **D**—Both the Ottoman and Russian empires were ethnic mixtures, especially of Muslims, Christians, and Jews. The Ottoman Empire was one of numerous nations within its borders, and was not, therefore, a nation-state (A). Neither empire had a socialist government in the nineteenth century (B). Although the Ottomans generally tolerated religious diversity, the Russians persecuted Jews (C).

63. **A**—Both Britain and China had urban areas with financial institutions. Although both had abundant supplies of coal, those of Great Britain were much more easily accessible than those of China (B). Both possessed a number of navigable rivers and canal systems (C). Great Britain, but not China, controlled colonies that supplied raw materials (D).

64. **D**—The Argentine gaucho developed a culture and mystique similar to that of the U.S. cowboy. Latin American society was divided into classes based on color and ethnicity (A). Indentured servants from Asia and European migrants went to Latin America (B). Intellectuals produced works based on European and U.S. values (C).

65. **D**—The quotation is from the Truman Doctrine, issued in support of the anticommunist struggles of Greece and Turkey. The Monroe Doctrine was a "hands-off" policy against European colonization in the Americas issued by the United States (A). The Roosevelt Corollary broadened the Monroe Doctrine to assert the U.S. right to police Latin American nations having difficulties with foreign powers (B). The Balfour

Declaration was the initial step in granting a Jewish homeland (C).

66. **B**—Containment was the U.S. Cold War policy of preventing further expansion of Soviet Communism. Nonalignment was the practice of some developing nations of not seeking assistance from either the United States or the Soviet Union (A). Appeasement is the policy of giving in to the threat of aggression, such as at the Munich Conference (C). Nationalism is extreme pride in one's nation or culture (D).

67. **C**—African and Asian women received increased political rights as a result of their participation alongside men in colonial independence movements. Soviet and Chinese women bore arms (A). Soviet women also were given opportunities to work outside the home (B). Women in industrial societies also tended to work in low-paying jobs (D).

68. **A**—The early years of the twenty-first century witnessed a global energy crisis, created in part because of the increasing energy demands of the industries of India and China. The other responses are correct. In 2008, utilization of Russia's energy resources was challenged by Georgia and Ukraine (B). India, once the primary location of outsourced industry, lost some of its sites to China, the Philippines, and Panama (C). Financial problems in the United States, especially in the mortgage and banking industries, contributed to a global economic recession and a decrease in world trade (D).

69. **C**—Mao's policies ended arranged marriages and encouraged women to acquire an education and enter the professions. Mao Zedong's land redistribution policies were popular with peasants (A). The Great Leap Forward was actually a backward leap economically (B). The Cultural Revolution closed universities and killed opponents of Mao (D).

70. **C**—The document was written in 1989 during the course of the fall of European communism. Key phrases that indicated this time frame are those that point to a declining threat to Western Europe from the Warsaw Pact and to the Soviet Union and its allies shifting resources to civil production. Response (A) indicates a date prior to the creation of the Warsaw Pact, while (B) occurs during the height of the Cold War. Response (D) refers to a post-Soviet era.

Section II

DOCUMENT-BASED QUESTION (DBQ)

Suggested reading time—10 minutes
Suggested writing time—40 minutes

1. Using the documents and your knowledge of world history, compare the nature of the postwar world envisioned by the victorious nations after World War I and World War II.

Document 1

Source: The Treaty of Trianon, June 4, 1920.

The Serb-Croat Slovene State recognizes and confirms in relation to Hungary its obligation to accept the embodiment in a Treaty with the Principal Allied and Associated Powers such provisions as may be deemed necessary by these Powers to protect the interests of inhabitants of that State who differ from the majority of the population in race, language or religion, as well as to protect freedom of transit and equitable treatment of the commerce of other nations.

Document 2

Source: Report of the Commission to Determine War Guilt, May 6, 1919.

On the question of the responsibility of the authors of the war, the Commission, after having examined a number of official documents relating to the origin of the World War, and to the violations of neutrality and of frontiers which accompanied its inception, has determined that the responsibility for it lies wholly upon the Powers which declared war in pursuance of a policy of aggression, the concealment of which gives origin of this war the character of a dark conspiracy against the peace of Europe.

This responsibility rests first on Germany and Austria, secondly in Turkey and Bulgaria. The responsibility is made all the graver by reason of the violation by Germany and Austria of the neutrality of Belgium and Luxembourg, which they themselves had guaranteed. It is increased, with regard to both France and Serbia, by the violation of their frontiers before the declaration of war.

Document 3

Source: The Covenant of the League of Nations, The Versailles Treaty, 1919.

The high contracting parties, In order to promote international cooperation and to achieve international peace and security by the acceptance of obligations not to resort to war by the prescription of open, just and honorable relations between nations by the firm establishment of the understandings of international law as the actual rule of conduct among Governments, and by the maintenance of justice and a scrupulous respect for all treaty obligations in the dealings of organized peoples with one another Agree to this Covenant of the League of Nations.

Document 4

Source: The Versailles Treaty, 1919.

The best method of giving practical effect to this principle is that the tutelage of such peoples should be entrusted to advanced nations who by reason of their resources, their experience or their geographical position can best undertake this responsibility, and who are willing to accept it, and that this tutelage should be exercised by them as Mandatories on behalf of the League. . . . Certain communities formerly belonging to the Turkish Empire have reached a stage of development where their existence as independent nations can be provisionally recognized subject to the rendering of administrative advice and assistance by a Mandatory until such time as they are able to stand alone.

Document 5

Source: The Balfour Declaration, 1917.

His Majesty's Government view with favor the establishment in Palestine of a national home for the Jewish people, and will use their best endeavors to facilitate the achievement of this object, it being clearly understood that nothing shall be done which may prejudice the civil and religious rights of existing non-Jewish communities in Palestine, or the rights and political status enjoyed by Jews in any other country.

Document 6

Source: Franklin Delano Roosevelt and Winston Churchill, The Atlantic Charter, August, 1941.

. . . they desire to see no territorial changes that do not accord with the freely expressed wishes of the people concerned;

. . . they respect the right of all peoples to choose the form of government under which they will live; and they wish to see sovereign rights and self government restored to those who have been forcibly deprived of them . . .

Document 7

Source: The Potsdam Conference, August 1, 1945.

German education shall be so controlled as completely to eliminate Nazi and militaristic doctrines and to make possible the successful development of democratic ideas.

Document 8

Source: General George Marshall, from a speech at Harvard University, June 5, 1947.

It would be neither fitting nor efficacious for the Government to undertake to draw up unilaterally a program designed to place Europe on its feet economically. This is the business of the Europeans.

Document 9

Source: Kellogg-Briand Pact, 1928.

The High Contracting Parties solemnly declare in the names of their respective peoples that they condemn recourse to war for the solution of international controversies, and renounce it, as an instrument of national policy in their relations with one another . . .

This Treaty shall, when it has come into effect as prescribed in the preceding paragraph, remain open as long as may be necessary for adherence by all the other Powers of the world. Every instrument evidencing the adherence of a Power shall be deposited at Washington and the Treaty shall immediately upon such deposit become effective as between the Power thus adhering and the other Powers parties hereto.

Document 10

Source: Preamble to the Charter of the United Nations, 1945.

. . . to establish conditions under which justice and respect for the obligations arising from treaties and other sources of international law can be maintained, and

to promote social progress and better standards of life in larger freedom . . .

. . . to employ international machinery for the promotion of the economic and social advancement of all peoples . . .

Document 11

Source: Universal Declaration of Human Rights, 1948.

Everyone is entitled to all the rights and freedoms set forth in this Declaration, without distinction of any kind, such as race, color, sex, language, religion, political or other opinion, national or social origin, property, birth or other status. Furthermore, no distinction shall be made on the basis of the political, jurisdictional or international status of the country or territory to which a person belongs, whether it be independent, trust, non-self-governing or under any limitation of sovereignty . . .

. . . Everyone has the right to a nationality. No one shall be arbitrarily deprived of his nationality nor denied the right to change his nationality . . .

. . . Everyone has the right to take part in the government of his country, directly or through freely chosen representatives . . .

. . . The will of the people shall be the basis of the authority of government; this will shall be expressed in periodic and genuine elections which shall be by universal and equal suffrage and shall be held by secret vote or by equivalent free voting procedures . . .

CONTINUITY-AND-CHANGE-OVER-TIME ESSAY

Suggested writing time—40 minutes

Directions: *Write an essay on the following topic:*

2. Describe changes and cintinuities in trade patterns in TWO of the following regions in the period 1450 to 1914. Be sure to begin with a discussion of trade in 1450.

East Asia   South Asia   North America

COMPARATIVE ESSAY

Suggested writing time—40 minutes

Directions: Write an essay on the following topic:

3. Compare slave systems in TWO of the following regions between 1450 and 1750.

   Middle East   Africa   Latin America

Comments on Possible Solutions to Free Response Questions

Document-Based Question

A good response may examine the treatment of vanquished nations after both wars. Document 2 starts out as an attempt to assign war guilt, especially to the participants in the "dark conspiracy" that promoted the wars. The phrase "dark conspiracy" illustrates a degree of bias in the commission's findings. The Potsdam Conference (Document 7) details plans for changing Nazi Germany's policies and sentiments to align them with democratic sentiments. At the same time, General George Marshall (Document 8) institutes a plan by which the defeated European nations after World War II were given a second opportunity for economic recovery to ensure political recovery.

The treatment of subject peoples and respect for nationalist fervor entails some differences after the two world wars. Documents 1, 4, and 5 address the problem of treatment of the various nations within the boundaries of the former empires. The Versailles Treaty shows bias by drawing a clear line between the states of the former Ottoman Empire and the "advanced nations" that now oversee them as mandates. Students may point out that European territories created from dissolved empires were granted independence rather than being kept as mandates. The Atlantic Charter (Document 6), Charter of the United Nations (Document 10) and Universal Declaration of Human Rights (Document 11) display a different sentiment: one that respected the rights of Europeans and people everywhere to choose their destiny.

Students may mention the different nature of the two international organizations founded after the world wars, pointing out from their own background knowledge that the United States did not join the League of Nations, but became a key member of the United Nations. The covenant of the League of Nations (Document 3) does not mention a means of enforcing its ideals, while the Charter of the United Nations does (Document 10). A similarity between the two postwar periods is found in the idealism of the Kellogg-Briand Pact (Document 9) and the Universal Declaration of Human Rights (Document 11).

Documents that would broaden the interpretation of the topic include statements from officials representing the newly created mandates after World War I. Accounts from peoples of the various minority nations within new political units such as Yugoslavia and Czechoslovakia would also add perspective.

Continuity-and-Change-over-Time Essay

A good answer regarding trade in East Asia would begin with the withdrawal of China from active world trade by 1450. Regional trade with Southeast Asia and Japan continued, however. By the early sixteenth century, China also traded with Europe by means of the Manila galleons. In the nineteenth century, an active trade arose between Great Britain and China in Indian opium. China was divided into spheres of influence in the period prior to World War I.

In 1450, South Asia was part of the Indian Ocean network, trading with East Africa and Southeast Asia. In the sixteenth and seventeenth centuries, the Columbian Exchange introduced American food crops to South Asia. In the sixteenth century, the Portuguese established the treaty port of Goa in India. European influence continued as the French and English established trading posts with India in the seventeenth century. By the eighteenth century, the British had gained control of trade rights as well as political control over India. In the nineteenth century, Indian opium became the center of controversy in the commercial relations between China and Britain. The English also introduced their inexpensive cotton manufactures to India, destroying the local textile trade.

In 1450, North America was involved only in hemispheric trade, as peoples of Mesoamerica exchanged goods with those of present-day southwestern United States. After the voyages of Columbus, however, the Columbian Exchange saw an exchange of crops, livestock, and diseases across the Atlantic. The African slave trade changed forever the social composition of North America. In the seventeenth and eighteenth centuries, the slave trade was part of a greater system of triangular trade that joined Europe, Africa, and the Americas. In the nineteenth century, the United States was instrumental in opening up trade relations between Japan and the Western world as the United States increasingly extended its commercial contacts across the globe. Canada continued not only as a trade partner of the United States, but also as a member of the British Commonwealth with the economic as well as political ties with Britain that its status entailed.

Comparative Question

A good response regarding the Middle East may discuss the trans-Saharan slave trade that extended to the Middle East. Other slaves entered the Middle East through trade routes from sub-Saharan Africa through the Indian Ocean and the Red Sea. Many of these slaves were used as household servants; some of them were children, including boys intended for eunuchs used as harem guards. The Ottoman Empire also used the *devshirme,* which took Christian boys for use as Janissaries, or military slaves, in the Ottoman army.

By 1450, Africans were carrying on an active slave trade with Portugal in exchange for Portuguese gold and technology, including guns. African society deteriorated as guns increased the frequency of slave raids. The trans-Atlantic slave trade tapped into already existing slave routes. Both Atlantic and Indian Ocean slave trade depopulated some areas of Africa. Within Africa, as in the Middle East, women were prized as household servants, whereas the trans-Atlantic trade differed in preferring men for the heavy-duty plantation labor. African villages suffered as men were carried off, leaving a void of workers to carry out more rigorous tasks.

Latin American slavery in 1450 usually involved prisoners of war among the Aztecs and Incas. In the Aztec empire, some of these slaves were used for human sacrifices. In contrast to the Middle East and Africa, Latin American slavery involved plantation labor rather than household labor. As the Spanish and Portuguese arrived, Indians were used as slaves until they died in large numbers from European diseases. Africans were then imported as laborers in the sugar and coffee plantations and in the mines.

abacus An ancient Chinese counting device that used rods on which were mounted movable counters.

absolute monarchy Rule by a king or queen whose power is not limited by a constitution.

Afrikaners South Africans who were descended from the Dutch who settled in South Africa in the seventeenth century.

age grade An age group into which children were placed in Bantu societies of early sub-Saharan Africa; children within the age grade were given responsibilities and privileges suitable for their age and in this manner were prepared for adult responsibilities.

Agricultural Revolution The transition from foraging to the cultivation of food occurring about 8000–2000 B.C.E.; also known as the Neolithic Revolution.

Allah The god of the Muslims; Arabic word for "god."

Alliance for Progress A program of economic aid for Latin America in exchange for a pledge to establish democratic institutions; part of U.S. President Kennedy's international program.

Allied Powers In World War I, the nations of Great Britain, France, Russia, the United States, and others that fought against the Central Powers; in World War II, the group of nations including Great Britain, France, the Soviet Union, and the United States, that fought against the Axis Powers.

Al-Qaeda A terrorist group based in Afghanistan in the late twentieth and early twenty-first centuries.

animism The belief that spirits inhabit the features of nature.

Anschluss The German annexation of Austria prior to World War II.

apartheid The South African policy of separation of the races.

appeasement Policy of Great Britain and France of making concessions to Hitler in the 1930s.

aristocracy Rule by a privileged hereditary class or nobility.

artifact An object made by human hands.

artisan A craftsman.

astrolabe A navigational instrument used to determine latitude by measuring the position of the stars.

Austronesian A branch of languages originating in Oceania.

ayatollah A traditional Muslim religious ruler.

ayllus In Incan society, a clan or community that worked together on projects required by the ruler.

bakufu A military government established in Japan after the Gempei Wars; the emperor became a figurehead, while real power was concentrated in the military, including the *samurai*.

Bantu-speaking peoples Name given to a group of sub-Saharan African peoples whose migrations altered the society of sub-Saharan Africa.

Battle of Tours The 732 battle that halted the advance of Muslim armies into Europe at a point in northern France.

benefice In medieval Europe, a grant of land or other privilege to a vassal.

Berlin Conference (1884–1885) Meeting of European imperialist powers to divide Africa among them.

Black Death The European name for the outbreak of the bubonic plague that spread across Asia, Europe, and North Africa in the fourteenth century.

bodhisattvas Buddhist holy men who accumulated spiritual merits during their lifetime; Buddhists prayed to them in order to receive some of their holiness.

Boers South Africans of Dutch descent.

Boer War (1899–1902) War between the British and the Dutch over Dutch independence in South Africa; resulted in British victory.

bourgeoisie In France, the class of merchants and artisans who were members of the Third Estate and initiators of the French Revolution; in Marxist theory, a term referring to factory owners.

Boxer Rebellion (1898) Revolt against foreign residents of China.

boyars Russian nobility.

Brahmin A member of the social class of priests in Aryan society.

brinkmanship The Cold War policy of the Soviet Union and the United States of threatening to go to war at a sign of aggression on the part of either power.

British Commonwealth A political community consisting of the United Kingdom, its dependencies, and former colonies of Great Britain that are now sovereign nations; currently called the Commonwealth of Nations.

bushi Regional military leaders in Japan who ruled small kingdoms from fortresses.

bushido The code of honor of the *samurai* of Japan.

caliph The chief Muslim political and religious leader.

calpulli Aztec clans that supplied labor and warriors to leaders.

capital The money and equipment needed to engage in industrialization.

capitalism An economic system based on private ownership and opportunity for profit-making.

caravel A small, easily steerable ship used by the Portuguese and Spanish in their explorations.

cartels Unions of independent businesses in order to regulate production, prices, and the marketing of goods.

Catholic Reformation (Counter-Reformation) The religious reform movement within the Roman Catholic Church that occurred in response to the Protestant Reformation. It reaffirmed Catholic beliefs and promoted education.

Central Powers In World War I, Germany, Austria-Hungary, Bulgaria, the Ottoman Empire, and other nations who fought with them against the Allies.

chinampas Platforms of twisted vines and mud that served the Aztecs as floating gardens and extended their agricultural land.

chivalry A knight's code of honor in medieval Europe.

civilization A cultural group with advanced cities, complex institutions, skilled workers, advanced technology, and a system of recordkeeping.

climate The pattern of temperature and precipitation over a period of time.

coalition A government based on temporary alliances of several political parties.

Code Napoleon Collection of laws that standardized French law under the rule of Napoleon Bonaparte.

Cold War The tense diplomatic relationship between the United States and the Soviet Union after World War II.

collectivization The combination of several small farms into a large government-controlled farm.

Columbian Exchange The exchange of food crops, livestock, and disease between the Eastern and Western hemispheres after the voyages of Columbus.

commercial revolution The expansion of trade and commerce in Europe in the sixteenth and seventeenth centuries.

communism An economic system in which the state controls the means of production.

conscription Military draft.

conservatism In nineteenth-century Europe, a movement that supported monarchies, aristocracies, and state-established churches.

containment Cold War policy of the United States whose purpose was to prevent the spread of communism.

Cossacks Russians who conquered and settled Siberia in the sixteenth and seventeenth centuries.

covenant Agreement; in the Judeo-Christian heritage, an agreement between God and humankind.

criollos **(creoles)** A term used in colonial Spanish America to describe a person born in the Americas of European parents.

cubism A school of art in which persons and objects are represented by geometric forms.

cultural diffusion The transmission of ideas and products from one culture to another.

Cultural Revolution A Chinese movement from 1966 to 1976 intended to establish an egalitarian society of peasants and workers.

cuneiform A system of writing originating in Mesopotamia in which a wedge-shaped stylus was used to press symbols into clay.

daimyo A Japanese feudal lord in charge of an army of *samurai*.

Dar al-Islam The House of Islam; a term representing the political and religious unity of the various Islamic groups.

Declaration of the Rights of Man A statement of political rights adopted by the French National Assembly during the French Revolution.

Declaration of the Rights of Woman A statement of the rights of women written by Olympe de Gouges in response to the Declaration of the Rights of Man.

Deism The concept of God common to the scientific revolution; the deity was believed to have set the world in motion and then allowed it to operate by natural laws.

democracy A political system in which the people rule.

deoxyribonucleic acid (DNA) The blueprint of heredity.

devshirme A practice of the Ottoman Empire to take Christian boys from their home communities to serve as Janissaries.

dharma The position in the Hindu caste system that was determined by one's birth.

diaspora The exile of an ethnic or racial group from their homeland.

divine right The belief of absolute rulers that their right to govern is granted by God.

domestic system A manufacturing method in which the stages of the manufacturing process are carried out in private homes rather than a factory setting.

Duma The Russian parliament.

Dutch learning Western learning embraced by some Japanese in the eighteenth century.

dynasty A series of rulers from the same family.

economic imperialism Control of a country's economy by the businesses of another nation.

economic liberalism The economic philosophy that government intervention in and regulation of the economy should be minimal.

Edict of Milan A document that made Christianity one of the religions allowed in the Roman Empire.

empirical research Research based on the collection of data.

enclosure movement The fencing of pasture land in England beginning prior to the Industrial Revolution.

encomienda A practice in the Spanish colonies that granted land and the labor of Native Americans on that land to European colonists.

Enlightenment A philosophical movement in eighteenth-century Europe that was based on reason and the concept that education and training could improve humankind and society.

entrepreneurship The ability to combine the factors of land, labor, and capital to create factory production.

estates The divisions of society in prerevolutionary France.

Estates-General The traditional legislative body of France.

euro The standard currency introduced and adopted by the majority of members of the European Union in January 2002.

European Union An organization designed to reduce trade barriers and promote economic unity in Europe; it was formed in 1993 to replace the European Community.

evangelical Pertaining to preaching the Gospel (the good news) or pertaining to theologically conservative Christians.

excommunication The practice of the Roman Catholic and other Christian churches of prohibiting participation in the sacraments to those who do not comply with church teachings or practices.

extraterritoriality The right of foreigners to live under the laws of their home country rather than those of the host country.

factor An agent with trade privileges in early Russia.

fascism A political movement that is characterized by extreme nationalism, one-party rule, and the denial of individual rights.

feminism The movement to achieve women's rights.

feudalism A political, economic, and social system based on the relationship between lord and vassal in order to provide protection.

fief In medieval Europe, a grant of land given in exchange for military or other services.

filial piety In China, respect for one's parents and other elders.

Five Pillars Five practices required of Muslims: faith, prayer, almsgiving, fasting, and pilgrimage.

Five Year Plans Plans for industrial production first introduced to the Soviet Union in 1928 by Stalin; they succeeded in making the Soviet Union a major industrial power by the end of the 1930s.

footbinding In China, a method of breaking and binding women's feet; seen as a sign of beauty and social position, footbinding also confined women to the household.

foraging A term for hunting and gathering.

fundamentalism A return to traditional religious beliefs and practices.

Geneva Conference A 1954 conference that divided Vietnam at the seventeenth parallel.

genocide The systematic killing of an entire ethnic group.

geocentric theory The belief held by many before the Scientific Revolution that the earth is the center of the universe.

glasnost The 1985 policy of Mikhail Gorbachev that allowed openness of expression of ideas in the Soviet Union.

Glorious Revolution The bloodless overthrow of English King James I and the placement of William and Mary on the English throne.

gold standard A monetary system in which currency is backed up by a specific amount of gold.

Gothic architecture Architecture of twelfth-century Europe, featuring stained-glass windows, flying buttresses, tall spires, and pointed arches.

Gran Colombia The temporary union of the northern portion of South America after the independence movements led by Simón Bolívar; ended in 1830.

Great Depression The severe worldwide economic downturn that began in the late 1920s and continued into the 1930s throughout many regions of the world.

Great Leap Forward The disastrous economic policy introduced by Mao Zedong that proposed the implementation of small-scale industrial projects on individual peasant communes.

Green Revolution A program of improved irrigation methods and the introduction of high-yield seeds and fertilizers and pesticides to improve agricultural production; the Green Revolution was especially successful in Asia but also was used in Latin America.

griots Storytellers of sub-Saharan Africa who carried on oral traditions and histories.

guano Bird droppings used as fertilizer; a major trade item of Peru in the late nineteenth century.

guest workers Workers from North Africa and Asia who migrated to Europe during the late twentieth century in search of employment; some guest workers settled in Europe permanently.

Guomindang China's Nationalist political party founded by Sun Yat-sen in 1912 and based on democratic principles; in 1925, the party was taken over by Jiang Jieshi, who made it into a more authoritarian party.

Hadith A collection of the sayings and deeds of Muhammad.

hajj The pilgrimage to the Ka'aba in Mecca required once of every Muslim who was not limited by health or financial restrictions.

harem A household of wives and concubines in the Middle East, Africa, or Asia.

heliocentric theory The concept that the sun is the center of the universe.

Hellenistic Age The era (c. 323–30 B.C.E.) in which Greek culture blended with Persian and other Eastern influences spread throughout the former empire of Alexander the Great.

Helsinki Accords A 1975 political and human rights agreement signed in Helsinki, Finland, by Western European countries and the Soviet Union.

hieroglyphics A system of picture writing used in Egypt.

hijrah The flight of Muhammad from Mecca to Medina; the first year in the Muslim calendar.

Holocaust The Nazi program during World War II that killed 6 million Jews and other groups considered undesirable.

imperialism The establishment of colonial empires.

import substitution industrialization An economic system that attempts to strengthen a country's industrial power by restricting foreign imports.

Inca The ruler of the Quechua people of the west coast of South America; the term is also applied to the Quechua people as a whole.

indentured servitude The practice of contracting with a master to provide labor for a specified period of years in exchange for passage and living expenses.

Indian National Congress Political party that became the leader of the Indian nationalist movement.

Indo-Europeans A group of seminomadic peoples who, around 2000 B.C.E., began to migrate from central Asia to India, Europe, and the Middle East.

indulgence A document whose purchase was said to grant the bearer the forgiveness of sins.

Industrial Revolution The transition between the domestic system of manufacturing and the mechanization of production in a factory setting.

International Monetary Fund An international organization founded in 1944 to promote market economies and free trade.

International Space Station A vehicle sponsored by sixteen nations that circles the earth while carrying out experiments.

investiture The authority claimed by monarchs to appoint church officials.

Jacobins Extreme radicals during the French Revolution.

Janissaries Members of the Ottoman army, often slaves, who were taken from Christian lands.

jati One of many subcastes in the Hindu caste system.

Jesuits Members of the Society of Jesus, a Roman Catholic missionary and educational order founded by Ignatius of Loyola in 1534.

jihad Islamic holy war.

junks Large Chinese sailing ships especially designed for long-distance travel during the Tang and Song dynasties.

Ka'aba A black stone or meteorite that became the most revered shrine in Arabia before the introduction of Islam; situated in Mecca, it later was incorporated in the Islamic faith.

Kabuki theater A form of Japanese theater developed in the seventeenth century that features colorful scenery and costumes and an exaggerated style of acting.

kamikaze The "divine wind" credited by the Japanese with preventing the Mongol invasion of Japan during the thirteenth century.

karma In Hindu tradition, the good or evil deeds done by a person.

Khan A Mongol ruler.

kowtow A ritualistic bow practiced in the Chinese court.

kulaks Russian peasants who became wealthy under Lenin's New Economic Policy.

laissez-faire economics An economic concept that holds that the government should not interfere with or regulate businesses and industries.

lateen sail A triangular sail attached to a short mast.

latifundia Large landholdings in the Roman Empire.

League of Nations International organization founded after World War I to promote peace and cooperation among nations.

liberalism An Enlightenment philosophy that favored civil rights, the protection of private property, and representative government.

Liberation Theology A religious belief that emphasizes social justice for victims of poverty and oppression.

limited liability corporation (LLC) A business organization in which the owners have limited personal legal responsibility for debts and actions of the business.

Magna Carta A document written in England in 1215 that granted certain rights to nobles; later these rights came to be extended to all classes.

Malay sailors Southeast Asian sailors who traveled the Indian Ocean; by 500 C.E., they had colonized Madagascar, introducing the cultivation of the banana.

Mamluks Turkic military slaves who formed part of the army of the Abbasid Caliphate in the ninth and tenth centuries; they founded their own state in Egypt and Syria from the thirteenth to the early sixteenth centuries.

Manchus Peoples from northeastern Asia who founded China's Qing dynasty.

mandate A type of colony in which the government is overseen by another nation, as in the Middle Eastern mandates placed under European control after World War I.

mandate of heaven The concept developed by the Zhou dynasty that the deity granted a dynasty the right to rule and took away that right if the dynasty did not rule wisely.

manorialism The system of self-sufficient estates that arose in medieval Europe.

Maori A member of a Polynesian group that settled in New Zealand about 800 C.E.

maroon societies Runaway slaves in the Caribbean who established their own communities to resist slavery and colonial authorities.

Marshall Plan A U.S. plan to support the recovery and reconstruction of Western Europe after World War II.

mass consumerism Trade in products designed to appeal to a global market.

matrilineal Referring to a social system in which descent and inheritance are traced through the mother.

May Fourth Movement A 1919 protest in China against the Treaty of Versailles and foreign influence.

medieval Pertaining to the middle ages of European history.

Meiji Restoration The restoration of the Meiji emperor in Japan in 1868 that began a program of industrialization and centralization of Japan following the end of the Tokugawa Shogunate.

mercantilism A European economic policy of the sixteenth through the eighteenth centuries that held that there was a limited amount of wealth available, and that each country must adopt policies to obtain as much wealth as possible for itself; key to the attainment of wealth was the acquisition of colonies.

mestizos In the Spanish colonies, persons of mixed European and Indian descent.

metropolitan The head of the Eastern Orthodox Church.

Mexica The name given to themselves by the Aztec people.

Middle Ages The period of European history traditionally given as 500–1500.

Middle Kingdom Term applied to the rich agricultural lands of the Yangtze River valley under the Zhou dynasty.

Middle Passage The portion of trans-Atlantic trade that involved the passage of Africans from Africa to the Americas.

minaret A tower attached to a mosque from which Muslims are called to worship.

mita A labor system used by Andean societies in which community members shared work owed to rulers and the religious community.

moksha In Hindu belief, the spirit's liberation from the cycle of reincarnation.

Mongol Peace The period from about 1250 to 1350 in which the Mongols ensured the safety of Eurasian trade and travel.

monotheism The belief in one god.

Monroe Doctrine (1823) Policy issued by the United States in which it declared that the Western Hemisphere was off limits to colonization by other powers.

monsoon A seasonal wind.

mosque The house of worship of followers of Islam.

Mughal dynasty Rulers who controlled most of India in the sixteenth and seventeenth centuries.

mulato (mulatto) In the Spanish and Portuguese colonies, a person of mixed African and European descent.

Muslim "One who submits"; a follower of Islam.

mystery religion During the Hellenistic Age, religions that promised their faithful followers eternity in a state of bliss.

National Organization for Women (NOW) U.S. organization founded in 1969 to campaign for women's rights.

nation-state A sovereign state whose people share a common culture and national identity.

natural laws Principles that govern nature.

natural rights Rights that belong to every person and that no government may take away.

Neo-Confucianism A philosophy that blended Confucianism with Buddhism thought.

New Deal U.S. President Roosevelt's program to relieve the economic problems of the Great Depression; it increased government involvement in the society of the United States.

New Economic Policy (NEP) Lenin's policy that allowed some private ownership and limited foreign investment to revitalize the Soviet economy.

New Testament The portion of the Christian Bible that contains the Gospels that relate the account of the life of Jesus; letters from the followers of Jesus to the early Christian churches and the Book of Revelation, a prophetic text.

nirvana In Buddhism, a state of perfect peace that is the goal of reincarnation.

nonalignment The policy of some developing nations to refrain from aligning themselves with either the United States or the Soviet Union during the Cold War.

North American Free Trade Agreement (NAFTA) An organization that prohibits tariffs and other trade barriers between Mexico, the United States, and Canada.

North Atlantic Treaty Organization (NATO) A defense alliance between nations of Western Europe and North America formed in 1949.

Northern Renaissance An extension of the Italian Renaissance to the nations of northern Europe; the Northern Renaissance took on a more religious nature than the Italian Renaissance.

northwest passage A passage through the North American continent that was sought by early explorers to North America as a route to trade with the East.

No theater The classical Japanese drama with music and dances performed on a simple stage by elaborately dressed actors.

Opium War (1839–1842) War between Great Britain and China began with the Qing dynasty's refusal to allow continued opium importation into China; British victory resulted in the Treaty of Nanking.

oracle bones Animal bones or shells used by Chinese priests to receive messages from the gods.

Organization of Petroleum Exporting Countries (OPEC) Organization formed in 1960 by oil-producing countries to regulate oil supplies and prices.

ozone depletion The thinning of the layer of the gas ozone high in the earth's atmosphere; ozone serves as a protection against the sun's ultraviolet rays.

Pan-Slavic movement A Russian attempt to unite all Slavic nations into a commonwealth relationship under the influence of Russia.

parallel descent In Incan society, descent through both the father and mother.

parliament A representative assembly.

parliamentary monarchy A government with a king or queen whose power is limited by the power of a parliament.

pastoralism The practice of herding.

patriarchal Pertaining to a social system in which the father is the head of the family.

Pax Romana The Roman Peace; the period of prosperity and stability throughout the Roman Empire in the first two centuries C.E.

peninsulares In the Spanish colonies, those who were born in Europe.

People of the Book A term applied by Islamic governments to Muslims, Christians, and Jews in reference to the fact that all three religions had a holy book.

perestroika A restructuring of the Soviet economy to allow some local decision making.

Persian Gulf War The 1991 war between Iraq and a U.S.-led coalition to liberate Kuwait from an Iraqi invasion.

perspective An artistic technique commonly used in Renaissance painting that gave a three-dimensional appearance to works of art.

pharaoh An Egyptian monarch.

philosophes French Enlightenment social philosophers.

pogrom Violence against Jews in tsarist Russia.

polis A Greek city-state.

polytheism The belief in many gods.

Pope The head of the Roman Catholic Church.

Potsdam Conference A 1945 meeting of the leaders of Great Britain, the United States, and the Soviet Union in which it was agreed that the Soviet Union would be given control of eastern Europe and that Germany would be divided into zones of occupation.

Prague Spring A 1968 program of reform to soften socialism in Czechoslovakia; it resulted in the Soviet invasion of Czechoslovakia.

predestination The belief of Protestant reformer John Calvin that God had chosen some people for heaven and others for hell.

proletariat In Marxist theory, the class of workers in an industrial society.

Protestant Reformation A religious movement begun by Martin Luther in 1517 that attempted to reform the beliefs and practices of the Roman Catholic Church; it resulted in the formation of new Christian denominations.

purdah The Hindu custom of secluding women.

purges Joseph Stalin's policy of exiling or killing millions of his opponents in the Soviet Union.

Quechua Andean society also known as the Inca.

quipus A system of knotted cords of different sizes and colors used by the Incas for keeping records.

Quran The holy book of Islam.

radicalism Western European political philosophy during the nineteenth century; advocated democracy and reforms favoring lower classes.

Ramadan The holy month of Islam which commemorates the appearance of the angel Gabriel to Muhammad; fasting is required during this month.

Reconquista **(Reconquest)** The recapture of Muslim-held lands in Spain by Christian forces; it was completed in 1492.

Red Guard A militia of young Chinese people organized to carry out Mao Zedong's Cultural Revolution.

Reign of Terror (1793–1794) The period of most extreme violence during the French Revolution.

reincarnation Rebirth; a belief of both Buddhism and Hinduism.

Renaissance The revival of learning in Europe beginning about 1300 and continuing to about 1600.

reparations The payment of war debts by the losing side.

repartamiento In the Spanish colonies, a replacement for the *encomienda* system that limited the number of working hours for laborers and provided for fair wages.

Revolution of 1905 Strikes by urban workers and peasants in Russia; prompted by shortages of food and by Russia's loss to Japan in 1905.

Revolutions of 1848 Democratic and nationalistic revolutions, most of them unsuccessful, that swept through Europe.

romanticism A literary and artistic movement in nineteenth-century Europe; emphasized emotion over reason.

Russification A tsarist program that required non-Russians to speak only Russian and provided education only for those groups loyal to Russia.

Russo-Japanese War (1904–1905) War between Japan and Russia over Manchurian territory; resulted in the defeat of Russia by the Japanese navy.

samurai The military class of feudal Japan.

Sandinistas A left-wing group that overthrew the dictatorship of Nicaraguan Anastacio Somoza in 1979.

sati The custom among the higher castes of Hinduism of a widow throwing herself on the burning funeral pyre of her husband.

scholar-gentry The Chinese class of well-educated men from whom many of the bureaucrats were chosen.

Scientific Revolution A European intellectual movement in the seventeenth century that established the basis for modern science.

Second Industrial Revolution The phase of the Industrial Revolution beginning about 1850 that applied the use of electricity and steel to the manufacturing process.

self-strengthening movement A late nineteenth-century movement in which the Chinese modernized their army and encouraged Western investment in factories and railways.

separation of powers The division of powers among the legislative, executive, and judicial branches of government.

Sepoy Rebellion (1857) Revolt of Indian soldiers against the British; caused by a military practice in violation of the Muslim and Hindu faiths.

sepoys South Asian soldiers who served in the British army in India.

serf A peasant who is bound to the land he or she works.

service industries Occupations that provided a service rather than a manufactured or agricultural product.

Seven Years' War (1756–1763) Conflict fought in Europe and its overseas colonies; in North America, known as the French and Indian War.

shamanism A belief in powerful natural spirits that are influenced by shamans, or priests.

shariah The body of law that governs Muslim society.

Shi'ite The branch of Islam that holds that the leader of Islam must be a descendant of Muhammad's family.

Shinto The traditional Japanese religion based on veneration of ancestors and spirits of nature.

shogun Military leaders under the *bakufu*.

shogunate The rule of the shoguns.

Silk Roads Caravan routes and sea lanes between China and the Middle East.

Six-Day War A brief war between Israel and a number of Arab states in 1967; during this conflict, Israel took over Jerusalem, the Golan Heights, the Sinai Peninsula, and the West Bank.

slash-and-burn cultivation An agricultural method in which farmers clear fields by cutting and burning trees, then use the ashes as fertilizer.

social contract Enlightenment concept of the agreement made by the people living in a state of nature to give up some of their rights in order for governments to be established.

Social Darwinism The application of Darwin's philosophy of natural selection to human society.

socialism Political movement originating in nineteenth-century Europe; emphasized state control of the major means of production.

Solidarity A Polish trade union that began the nation's protest against communist rule.

sovereignty Self-rule.

Spanish-American War (1898) Conflict between the United States and Spain that began the rise of the United States as a world power.

Spanish Civil War A conflict from 1936 to 1939 that resulted in the installation of fascist dictator Francisco Franco as ruler of Spain; Franco's forces were backed by Germany and Italy, whereas the Soviet Union supported the opposing republican forces.

specialization of labor The division of labor that aids the development of skills in a particular type of work.

spheres of influence Divisions of a country in which a particular foreign nation enjoys economic privileges.

stateless society A society that is based on the authority of kinship groups rather than on a central government.

steppe A dry grassland.

steppe diplomacy The skill of political survival and dominance in the world of steppe nomads; it involved the knowledge of tribal and clan structure and often used assassinations to accomplish its goals.

stock market A market where shares are bought and sold.

Stoicism The most popular Hellenistic philosophy; it involved strict discipline and an emphasis on helping others.

Suez Canal Canal constructed by Egypt across the Isthmus of Suez in 1869.

Sufis Muslims who attempt to reach Allah through mysticism.

sultan An Islamic ruler.

Sunni The branch of Islam that believes that the Muslim community should select its leaders; the Sunnis are the largest branch of Islam.

syncretism A blend of two or more cultures or cultural traditions.

system of checks and balances Constitutional system in which each branch of government places limits on the power of the other branches.

Taiping Rebellion (1853–1864) Revolt in southern China against the Qing Empire.

Tanzimet reforms Nineteenth-century reforms by Ottoman rulers designed to make the government and military more efficient.

tea ceremony An ancient Shinto ritual still performed in the traditional Japanese capital of Kyoto.

Tehran Conference A 1943 meeting of leaders of the United States, Great Britain, and the Soviet Union; it agreed on the opening of a second front in France.

Ten Commandments The moral law of the Hebrews.

theocracy A government ruled by God or by church leaders.

Tiananmen Square Beijing site of a 1989 student protest in favor of democracy; the Chinese military killed large numbers of protestors.

Torah The first five books of the Jewish scripture.

Treaty of Brest-Litovsk The 1918 treaty ending World War I between Germany and the Soviet Union.

Treaty of Nanking (1842) Treaty ending the Opium War that ceded Hong Kong to the British.

Treaty of Tordesillas The 1494 treaty in which the pope divided unexplored territories between Spain and Portugal.

Treaty of Versailles The 1919 peace treaty between Germany and the Allied nations; it blamed the war on Germany and assessed heavy reparations and large territorial losses on the part of Germany.

triangular trade The eighteenth-century trade network between Europe, Africa, and the Americas.

tribute The payment of a tax in the form of goods and labor by subject peoples.

Truman Doctrine A 1947 statement by U.S. President Truman that pledged aid to any nation resisting communism.

Twelve Tables The codification of Roman law during the republic.

umma The community of all Muslim believers.

United Nations The international organization founded in 1945 to establish peace and cooperation among nations.

universal male suffrage The right of all males within a given society to vote.

untouchables The social division in Hindu society that fell in rank below the caste system; it was occupied by those who carried out undesirable occupations such as undertaking, butchering, and waste collection.

varna A caste in the Hindu caste system.

vassal In medieval Europe, a person who pledged military or other service to a lord in exchange for a gift of land or other privilege.

Vedas The oral hymns to the Aryan deities, later written down, that formed the basis of the Hindu beliefs during the Vedic Age (1500–500 B.C.E.).

viceroyalty A political unit ruled by a viceroy that was the basis of organization of the Spanish colonies.

Wahhabi rebellion An early nineteenth-century attempt to restore Ottoman power through a return to traditional Islam and strict *shariah* law.

Warsaw Pact The 1955 agreement between the Soviet Union and the countries of eastern Europe in response to NATO.

welfare state A nation in which the government plays an active role in providing services such as social security to its citizens.

World Bank An agency of the United Nations that offers loans to countries to promote trade and economic development.

World Trade Organization (WTO) An international organization begun in 1995 to promote and organize world trade.

xenophobia An intense fear of foreigners. Yahweh Jehovah, the god of the Jews.

Yalta Conference A meeting of the leaders of the Soviet Union, Great Britain, and the United States in 1945; the Soviet Union agreed to enter the war against Japan in exchange for influence in the Eastern European states. The Yalta Conference also made plans for the establishment of a new international organization.

yin and *yang* In ancient Chinese belief, the opposing forces that bring balance to nature and life.

Young Turks Society founded in 1889 in the Ottoman Empire; its goal was to restore the constitution of 1876 and to reform the empire.

zaibatsu A large industrial organization created in Japan during the industrialization of the late nineteenth century.

ziggurat A multitiered pyramid constructed by Mesopotamians.

Zoroastrianism An ancient Persian religion that emphasized a struggle between good and evil and rewards in the afterlife for those who chose to follow a good life.

BIBLIOGRAPHY

In addition to this manual and your textbook, the following titles may help you in your preparation for the AP World History examination:

Adams, Paul V. et al. *Experiencing World History.* New York: New York University Press, 2000. ISBN: 0-8147-0691-6.

Diamond, Jared. *Guns, Germs, and Steel: The Fates of Human Societies.* New York: W. W. Norton & Company, 1999. ISBN: 0-393-31755-2.

McNeill, J. R., and William H. McNeill. *The Human Web: A Bird's-Eye View of World History.* New York: W. W. Norton & Company, 2003. ISBN: 0-393-05179-X.

Stearns, Peter N. *Cultures in Motion: Mapping Key Contacts and Their Imprints in World History.* New Haven, CT: Yale University Press, 2001. ISBN: 0-300-08229-0.

The following are websites that may help you in your test preparation:

http://www.worldhistorynetwork.org

http://www.collegeboard.com

http://www.fordham.edu/halsall/mod/modsbook.html

NOTES